KANT

AN INTRODUCTION

C. D. Broad was Knightbridge Professor of
Moral Philosophy at Cambridge from 1933
to 1953, and this book is based on his
undergraduate lectures on Kant. Broad died
in 1971 and Dr Lewy has since edited the
book for publication.

BROAD, Charlie Dunbar. Kant: an introduction, ed. by C. Lewy.
   Cambridge, 1978. 319p index   77-80829.   31.00   ISBN
   0-521-21755-5; 8.95 pa ISBN 0-521-29265-4. C.I.P.
This volume contains C.D. Broad's Cambridge lectures on Immanuel Kant,
delivered in the academic year 1950–51 and again in 1951–52. The lectures
concentrate almost exclusively on Kant's *Critique of pure reason,* ignoring
for the most part his works on practical reason and aesthetics. Broad's
presentations of Kant's views are quite lucid and intelligible, and his
commentary and criticisms often further the understanding of Kant's basic
intentions. Several of Broad's interpretations of certain passages in the
Critique may now be outdated by more recent Kant scholarship, but the
extraordinary clarity and readability of this work nonetheless recommends
it as an invaluable addition to the Kant literature. This reviewer considers it
one of the strongest introductory works on Kant. Recommended for
advanced undergraduate and graduate students.

CHOICE   *JAN. '79*

Philosophy

KANT
An Introduction

C. D. BROAD

Edited by C. Lewy

Cambridge University Press

CAMBRIDGE
LONDON · NEW YORK · MELBOURNE

Published by the Syndics of the Cambridge University Press
The Pitt Building, Trumpington Street, Cambridge CB2 1RP
Bentley House, 200 Euston Road, London NW1 2DB
32 East 57th Street, New York, NY 10022, USA
296 Beaconsfield Parade, Middle Park, Melbourne 3206, Australia

First published 1978

Phototypeset by Western Printing Services Ltd, Bristol
Printed in Great Britain at the University Press, Cambridge

Library of Congress Cataloguing in Publication Data
Broad, Charlie Dunbar, 1887–1971

Kant: an introduction

Includes index

1. Kant, Immanuel, 1724–1804.
I. Title.
B2798. B74   193   77–80829

ISBN 0 521 21755 5 hard covers
ISBN 0 521 29265 4 paperback

CONTENTS

EDITOR'S PREFACE

This volume contains C. D. Broad's Cambridge lectures on the philosophy of Kant. Broad had lectured on Kant before, but the course in its present form was first given in the academic year 1950–51 and repeated, with some revisions, in 1951–52. As I mentioned in my preface to Broad's lectures on Leibniz,[1] he always wrote out his lectures fully beforehand, and the MS. on Kant is in a very good state. But his handwriting is small and close and in places difficult to decipher. I fear that in spite of all my efforts some words may have been misread.

I have tried to reproduce the text so far as possible as it is in the MS. But I have expanded Broad's abbreviations, and have introduced greater uniformity in punctuation, spelling, and the use of capital letters, italics and quotation marks. I have also supplemented Broad's references, especially to works other than the *Critique of Pure Reason*. My own references are in footnotes enclosed in square brackets.

So far as the *Critique of Pure Reason* is concerned, Broad's page references are always to the translation by Norman Kemp Smith. But it seems that the actual translations may have been Broad's own: at any rate, they often differ, at least slightly, from those of Kemp Smith.

I am grateful to the Editor of the Aristotelian Society for permission to include material which Broad published in the *Proceedings* of the Society, vol. 55 (1954–55).[2] For the greater part the relevant portion of the MS. is the same as the *Proceedings* article; but at certain points the article contains additions which I have incorporated in the text.

I am also grateful to the Editor of the Society for permission to make use

---

[1] C. D. Broad, *Leibniz: An Introduction*, ed. by C. Lewy (Cambridge, 1975).
[2] 'Kant's Mathematical Antinomies'. Copyright: The Aristotelian Society, 1955.

of the material which Broad published, in an earlier version, in the *Proceedings*, vol. 26 (1925–26),[1] and vol. 42 (1941–42).[2]

I should point out however that the bulk of the present book has not been published before.

C. LEWY

Trinity College, Cambridge
June 1977

[1] 'Kant's First and Second Analogies of Experience'. Copyright: The Aristotelian Society, 1926.
[2] 'Kant's Theory of Mathematical and Philosophical Reasoning'. Copyright: The Aristotelian Society, 1942.

1

GENERAL INTRODUCTION

I shall begin by trying to state in general terms what Kant wanted to do in the *Critique of Pure Reason*, and to explain certain notions which he constantly uses.[1]

1 The main problem

Kant's main problem was the nature, limits, and validity of *a priori* knowledge. He thought that he could point to two sciences which profess to be *a priori* and to prove propositions which are not merely analytic. These were mathematics and metaphysics. Intermediate between them came physics, which Kant personally believed to involve certain synthetic *a priori* principles, such as the permanence of substance and the law of causation. If we consider the attitude of Kant's predecessors about these alleged sciences we see that they were as follows. (1) Leibniz believed both mathematics and metaphysics to be *a priori*, but he also believed that all *a priori* propositions are analytic. Kant was convinced, on the other hand, that the propositions of arithmetic, like '7 + 5 = 12', and of geometry, like 'Two straight lines cannot enclose a space', are synthetic. (2) Hume seems to have regarded arithmetical propositions as *a priori* but analytic, and geometrical propositions as synthetic but empirical. And, of course, Hume regarded our beliefs in the law of causation and the permanence of substance as non-rational products of custom and association, and took an entirely sceptical view about metaphysics. We shall see that Kant very largely agreed with Hume about metaphysics. But about propositions like the law of causation and the permanence of substance he reached a conclusion which, as far as I know, is quite original. He held that these propositions require and are capable of proof and that they are in a certain sense *a priori*. But the proof is of a very peculiar kind, viz. what Kant calls a 'transcendental argument'. And the *a priority* is also of a peculiar kind, which is specially connected with this notion of a transcendental proof.

Now Kant noticed that of the two alleged *a priori* sciences of mathematics and metaphysics the former had made steady progress whilst the latter had hardly progressed at all. And he asked himself: 'What is the cause of

[1] All references to the *Critique of Pure Reason* are to the pages of N. Kemp Smith's translation (London, 1933). I have added the references to A and B which Kemp Smith gives in the margin of his translation.

this difference, and could metaphysics ever be made into a genuine science like mathematics?' He says that it was Hume's attack on the law of causation which 'aroused him from his dogmatic slumbers', and that he soon came to see that Hume had touched only one particular case of a fundamental general problem. Kant puts the general problem in the form 'How is synthetic *a priori* knowledge possible?'

His answer is that there is such knowledge, but its range is severely limited. Synthetic *a priori* knowledge is possible only so far as it is about objects of possible sense-perception. The moment you try to apply these *a priori* propositions to objects like God and the soul, which could not possibly be perceived by the senses, they lose all intelligible meaning. And they show this by leading to contradictions, which he calls 'paralogisms' and 'antinomies'. Here we have two propositions which are or seem to be contradictory, and just as good reasons for accepting one as for accepting the other. He calls the application of *a priori* principles to objects of possible sense-perception 'immanent', and their attempted application beyond this range he calls 'transcendent'. ('Transcend*ent*' must not be confused with 'transcenden*tal*'. The former is a term of reproach in Kant's usage; the latter refers to a particular mode of argument, which we shall consider later. But Kant does often use one where he obviously means the other. In general he is very fond of drawing clear distinctions and ever afterwards neglecting them.) His work, then, falls into two main parts:

(1) To justify the use *within* experience of certain universal propositions which are not derived by induction *from* experience.

(2) To show that these same propositions, though not derived from experience, have no legitimate application beyond the range of possible sense-perception.

These two parts are connected in the following way. In justifying the immanent use of these propositions we have to consider their nature very carefully. Now they turn out to be principles of organisation or connexion which convert a chaotic mass of sensations into the perception of what is ostensibly a world of permanent extended law-abiding objects. And it follows that they have no application outside the range of possible sense-perception, because beyond that range there are no sensations for them to connect and organise.

I shall now try to explain three closely connected notions which are very important in Kant's philosophy; viz. (1) his notion of the *a priori*, (2) the Copernican revolution in philosophy, and (3) transcendental arguments.

2 Kant's notion of the a priori

Kant meant several different things by the adjective *a priori*, and never stated very clearly what they were. We must begin by noting one fundamental distinction, viz. that between *a priori* judgments or propositions and *a priori* concepts. Kant would say that the principle that every event is caused is an *a priori* proposition and that *cause* is an *a priori* concept. Let us begin with the term *a priori* as applied to propositions or judgments.

2.1 'A priori' as applied to judgments

In discussing this question I think it is convenient to distinguish two pairs of opposites, viz. *necessary* and *contingent* and *a priori* and *empirical*. These are closely connected with each other, but they are different. The terms 'necessary' and 'contingent' are logical or ontological. They apply to propositions or to facts. It is a necessary proposition or fact that $2 \times 2 = 4$ or that the square root of 2 is irrational. It is a contingent proposition or fact that all animals which have cloven hoofs chew the cud. The terms '*a priori*' and 'empirical' are epistemological. They apply to knowledge of facts or to belief in propositions. Let us use the word 'judgment' to cover knowing facts and believing propositions. Now the ordinary use of *a priori* as applied to judgments is this. One's knowledge of *p* is *a priori* if and only if one can see that *p* is necessary. One may come to recognise that *p* is necessary either *directly* through inspecting its terms and reflecting on them or *indirectly* by showing that *p* follows, in accordance with the principles of formal logic, from other propositions each of which one can see by direct inspection to be necessary. We may distinguish the two cases by saying that *a priori* knowledge may be either *intuitive* or *demonstrative*. It follows from these definitions that any fact or proposition which is or could be known *a priori* is necessary. Conversely, any fact or proposition which is necessary, and only such facts or propositions, might conceivably be known *a priori*. But there may be many necessary facts or propositions which are not known *a priori* by a particular person at a particular time. And there may be many necessary facts or propositions which never have been and never will be known *a priori* by any human being. There are many propositions, e.g. about the properties of numbers, with regard to which we can know that they are *either* necessarily true *or* necessarily false. But with regard to many of these no human being has so far been able to see either by direct inspection or by demonstration that they are necessarily true or to see that they are necessarily false. Here *a priori* knowledge is theoretically possible but does not actually exist. If a person in fact believes one of these propositions with more or less confidence, his belief is empirical. Again, suppose that I accept on authority a mathematical proposition which has been proved by an expert. Then the expert's knowledge of that necessary proposition is *a priori*, but my belief in that same proposition is empirical.

If a fact or a proposition is contingent, then knowledge of that fact or belief in that proposition must be empirical and cannot be *a priori*. There is genuine knowledge of *singular* contingent facts. E.g. I *know* that I am now having certain experiences, e.g. certain visual and auditory sensations. But it is doubtful whether there is genuine knowledge, as distinct from rationally justifiable *strong belief*, in any *universal* contingent proposition, e.g. that all cloven-footed animals chew the cud.

I think that the above is a fair account of the ordinary use of '*a priori*' and 'empirical' as applied to knowledge and belief. This is certainly what Kant's predecessors, such as Leibniz and Locke and Hume, meant by it, and it is what Kant begins by meaning. But I think it is quite certain that he introduced another sense of '*a priori*' as applied to judgments. In order to see what this is we must first consider the distinction between *analytic* and *synthetic* judgments, which plays an important part in Kant's philosophy. We may confine our attention here to universal judgments, such as 'All negroes are black' and 'All crows are black'. Kant would say that the judgment 'All S is P' is analytic if and only if the concept of the class S contains explicitly or implicitly the concept of the characteristic P, so that by merely analysing the concept of S one could see that it would be *self-contradictory* to suppose that there might be an instance of S which did not have the characteristic P. Thus, e.g., it would be self-contradictory to suppose that there might be a negro who was not black, and we can see this by reflecting on the meaning of the word 'negro'; but it would not be self-contradictory to suppose that there might be a crow which was not black. Kant regarded the principles of formal logic, e.g. the principle of the syllogism, as analytic. The judgment 'All S is P' is synthetic if it is not analytic, i.e. if the concept of S does not contain explicitly or implicitly the notion of P, so that it is *not self-contradictory* to suppose that there might be an instance of S which did not have the property P.

I think that there are considerable difficulties and obscurities in the notion of an analytic judgment. In the first place, to talk of *the* concept of S begs questions. Is there anything that can be called *the* concept of a negro or a crow or an ellipse? May not different men have different concepts of the same term at the same time, and may not the same man have different concepts of the same term at different times? And may not some of these concepts of S contain the notion of P, and others of them not contain the notion of P? Again, the phrase 'contain the notion of P' is plainly metaphorical, and the literal meaning of the metaphor is highly obscure. Does the concept of the circle 'contain' every property which could be shown to belong to all circles and only to circles? If so, what does 'contain' mean? If not, on what principle do you subdivide these properties into those which *are* contained in the concept of the circle and those which are *not*?

If we consent to waive these difficulties, it is evident that any judgment which was analytic would be *a priori* in the traditional sense. The proposition judged would be seen to be necessary, because the opposite of it would be seen to be self-contradictory and therefore impossible. But it does not follow from our definitions that every judgment which was *a priori* in the traditional sense would be analytic. For it is at least conceivable that I might be able to see that 'All *S* is *P*' is necessary, either by direct inspection or by deductive inference, without its being the case that the opposite of it would be *self-contradictory*. Many people, e.g., claim to be able to see on inspection that every event must be causally determined. Yet most people would admit that the notion of being causally determined is not part of the concept of an event, and that there is nothing *self-contradictory* in the supposition that there might be an event which was not causally determined.

Thus we cannot rule out by definition the possibility that there might be judgments which are both synthetic and *a priori* in the traditional sense. There are plenty of judgments, e.g. those of ordinary geometry, which seem *prima facie* to combine both these properties. And many of Kant's predecessors, e.g. Locke, held that there are in fact plenty of judgments which are both *a priori* in the traditional sense and synthetic. Others, e.g. Leibniz, held that this is a mistake, and that all judgments which are *a priori* in the traditional sense must be analytic.

Now Kant begins by talking as if he accepted the view that there are judgments which are synthetic and yet are *a priori* in the traditional sense. He talks of the propositions of arithmetic and geometry, and of the principle of universal causation, as synthetic *a priori* judgments. And he professes to be concerned with the question 'Granted, as we must do, that there is synthetic *a priori* knowledge, how is it possible?' But, when we look at his attempts to answer this question, we find that he does not really admit these judgments to be *a priori* in the traditional sense. He holds them to be *a priori* in a new sense, which he never explicitly defines, but which can be understood by reflecting on his arguments.

This point comes out quite plainly in Kant's dealings with the law of universal causation and the principle of the permanence of substance. He describes these as synthetic principles which are or can be known *a priori*. Now he certainly did not admit that they are self-evident, i.e. that we can see their necessity by reflecting on their terms. For he devotes an immense amount of trouble to proving them. And when we look at the proofs we find that they do not start from premises which are self-evident. The ultimate premises of these arguments are found to be certain very general but quite contingent facts about the nature of human experience. E.g. one premiss is that our knowledge of physical objects and events is based on sensations which arise in us successively. Another premiss is that we can and do distinguish between the temporal order in which we get our sensations and an objective temporal order of the things or events which we perceive by means of our sensations. A third important premiss is that each of us recognises his own persistence and self-identity throughout his changing experiences, although he is not acquainted introspectively with a persistent unchanging ego. Now all these premisses, though very general and pervasive, are quite contingent. It is therefore clear that, when Kant describes our knowledge of the law of causation or of the permanence of material substance as '*a priori*', he cannot be using '*a priori*' in the traditional sense. For, in that sense, any proposition which could be known *a priori* would be necessary. But these propositions, according to Kant, are inferable only from premisses which are contingent; and the consequences of contingent premisses are themselves contingent.

I will distinguish the traditional sense of *a priori* by the name '*absolutely a priori*' and Kant's peculiar sense of it by the name '*transcendentally a priori*'. We must now try to state what Kant meant by '*transcendentally a priori*'.

If we look at the judgments which Kant regards as transcendentally *a priori*, we notice that they are all hypothetical and that there is a common feature in the antecedents of all of them. E.g. Kant does not claim to have proved that *every* event has a cause or that *no* substance can begin or cease to exist. He distinctly says that it is impossible for us to know whether this is so or not. What he claims to prove about causation is that any event which could possibly be an object of human sense-perception must be caused by some such earlier event. What he claims to prove about substance is that all *perceptible* change is change in the states of perceptible substances and not the coming into existence or the cessation of such substances. This characteristic of being 'perceptible by a human mind' which qualifies the subjects of all Kant's transcendentally *a priori* propositions needs a little further explanation. 'Perceptible' must be taken in a very wide sense. A thing or event would not cease to be 'perceptible by a human mind', in Kant's sense, merely because no human being happens to have acute enough sense-organs or to have been in the right place at the right time to perceive it. E.g. an event happening in the sun before there were any human beings would count as 'perceptible' for Kant's purpose. Kant only requires that the event shall be such that it *would* have been perceived by any mind which worked on the same general principles as ours, provided that it was in the right place at the right time and had suitable sense-organs. (I think that Kant would have difficulty, in view of his own doctrine about the subjectivity of space and time, in putting a satisfactory interpretation on the phrase 'in the right *place* at the right *time*'. But that is a difficulty which he shares with many other philosophers, e.g. with phenomenalists.)

If we look at Kant's proofs of the judgments which he counts as synthetic and *a priori*, we find that they all start with certain very general premisses, positive and negative, about the way in which human minds work. He then claims to deduce from these premisses that any object of possible human sense-perception must have such-and-such a property. We can now define a 'transcendentally *a priori* judgment'. It is a judgment which asserts, with regard to all objects of possible human sense-perception, that they must have certain characteristics, because the latter are entailed by certain very general facts about the way in which human minds work. Kant's transcendentally *a priori* judgments are not judgments of *intrinsically* necessary propositions. If Kant is right, they are judgments of propositions which are *necessary consequences* of certain facts about the human mind; but these facts are contingent and so are their consequences.

If my interpretation is correct, Kant answered his original question only by altering its meaning. The original question was: 'How are synthetic *a priori* judgments possible?' This meant originally: 'How can we come to see that a proposition of the form "All S is P" is necessarily true, in cases where the notion of P is *not* contained either explicitly or implicitly in the concept of S, and therefore the supposition that there might be an instance of S which is not P is *not* self-contradictory?' To this question Kant's answer is that, in this sense of '*a priori*', synthetic *a priori* judgments are not possible. So far as I can see, Kant is in complete agreement with Leibniz and with Hume, and in disagreement with Locke, on this point. According to him, the only judgments which are or can be *a priori* in the absolute sense are analytic. What he then proceeds to do is to introduce a new sense of '*a priori*', viz. the transcendental sense, and to try to show that many important judgments, which are synthetic, and were thought to be *a priori* in the absolute sense, are *a priori* in the transcendental sense. Now, this has at least the merit of originality. Before Kant's time there were three alternative views about such judgments as 'Every event has a cause'. (1) The orthodox rationalist view that they are knowings of facts which are intrinsically necessary and can be seen to be so by reflecting upon the terms involved in them. Kant agreed that Hume had upset this view. (2) The orthodox empiricist view, which we find in Mill, that they are proved or rendered probable by induction. This Kant also rejected on the grounds that induction could not account for the fact that we make these judgments with complete confidence about *every* member of an *unlimited* class of possible subjects. Moreover some of them seem to be presupposed in all inductive arguments. (3) The sceptical view of Hume that such judgments have no rational ground at all, but are simply irrational expectations caused by constant experience of regularity. Hume took this view because he rejected the first and second theories and could think of no other alternative. Now Kant held that our geometrical and arithmetical judgments raise precisely the same kind of problem as our belief in the law of universal causation. And he thought that, if Hume had realised this, he would have hesitated to adopt his sceptical view.

However that may be, Kant's great originality was to think of a fourth alternative. Stated very roughly, it may be put as follows. Each of us, when awake and sane, ostensibly perceives a world consisting of many independent extended movable things, of various recognisable kinds, occupying positions in a single spatial system and interacting with each other. He ostensibly perceives each of these things as persisting, as having a history consisting of various successive states, and as simultaneously possessing many different properties. He is able to identify a particular thing on various occasions, in spite of profound changes in its appearances, its states, and its relationships. He ostensibly perceives himself as the persistent owner of a whole set of very various experiences, simultaneous and successive. And he regards his own experiences and the events in all other things as dated in a single temporal system. This is one of Kant's premisses, and it must be accepted as substantially true.

Kant's other premiss is that the only empirical data on which all this is based are sensations, images, feelings and emotions of various kinds, which are passively received and are fleeting and come and go in a most chaotic way. Now it seemed to Kant that the only way in which one could explain how the characteristic experience of a sane waking man can arise from such empirical data is this. One must suppose that each of us unconsciously combines, separates, modifies, and supplements the crude passively received data in accordance with certain very general innate principles. Propositions like the law of universal causation are explicit formulations of the innate principles in accordance with which we unconsciously operate on the crude data in generating normal waking sense-perception and self-consciousness.

Such a view carries certain consequences with it. (1) Principles like the law of universal causation must be stated in a more restricted form. They must not be applied to events as such and without restriction, but only to events which are capable of being objects of human sense-perception. (2) It follows at once that both the orthodox rationalist view and the orthodox empiricist view of our knowledge of such principles must be rejected. But Hume's sceptical view would also be undermined. For, according to Kant, the regular experience, which Hume postulates in order to explain the formation of our habitual expectations, could not have existed unless these principles, in their restricted form, had been true. For no coherent perceptual experience at all, e.g. no experience in which persistent things are distinguished and identified on various occasions, would have been possible unless these principles had been true.

2.2 'A priori' as applied to concepts and percepts

We will now consider what Kant means by '*a priori*' as applied to concepts and to percepts. I will begin with concepts, and I will first treat the matter in my own way and then try to relate Kant's view to what I have said.

2.2.1 Concepts

We derive our concepts of certain characteristics by abstraction from particulars met with in sense-perception or introspection, which present themselves to us as having those characteristics. Thus we derive the concept of 'red' by abstraction from things which we have seen and which looked red and of the concept of 'painfulness' by abstraction from experiences which we have had which were painful. Then, again, we have the power of conceiving complex characteristics which have never been presented to us in sense-perception or introspection, provided that instances of their component characteristics have been presented to us. We can form the concept of a mermaid, although we have never seen one, because we have seen women and fish, and can then combine the notion of having a woman's body with that of having a fish's tail. Now I would define an 'empirical concept' as one which has been formed in one or other of these two ways. And I would define an *a priori* concept as one which is not empirical in this sense. This is of course a definition in purely negative terms.

Now it seems plausible to hold that we have some concepts which are *a priori*, in the sense that they are not derived in either of these two ways. The most plausible instances would be the concepts of cause and of substance. Again, if ethical words like 'morally right', 'ought', etc. stand for characteristics, then it seems plausible to hold that our concepts of these characteristics are *a priori*, in the sense of being non-empirical. Kant did in fact describe the concepts of cause and of substance and of moral obligation as '*a priori*'. So at any rate the phrase '*a priori* concept', as I have defined it and as Kant used it, has much the same range of application.

Now, even if such concepts as cause and substance are not *abstracted from* instances presented to us by sense-perception or by introspection, no doubt special kinds of experiences are necessary before we can explicitly formulate them. Probably we should never have explicitly formulated the notions of cause or of substance unless certain kinds of sensation had occurred frequently in conjunction or immediate sequence. What is asserted by those who call these concepts '*a priori*' is that such features in our experience are only the *occasions* and the *necessary conditions* for us to formulate explicitly the concept of cause and of substance. These peculiar experiences do not *present us with instances* of causation or substantiality, from which these concepts could literally be abstracted, as the experience of seeing a pillar-box presents us with an instance of redness from which the concept of redness could be abstracted. At most they present us with instances of conjunction or of sequence. You cannot literally *see* with your eyes a moving stone *causing* a window to break. All that you can literally see is the stone coming in contact with the window and immediately afterwards the continuous pane of glass being replaced by falling fragments. I think that all this would be admitted and asserted by Kant about the concepts which he describes as '*a priori*'.

Now persons who hold that there are concepts which are *a priori*, in the negative sense of non-empirical, are naturally inclined to supplement this with some positive view as to the nature of such concepts. Two types of positive view have been held, which might be called *objectivist* and *subjectivist*. According to the objectivist view, the causal relation and the relation of an event to a substance in which it occurs, e.g., are objective features of the world, quite independent of the processes in human or other minds. We just become aware of these independent features, on the occasion of certain appropriate kinds of sense-experience, by a peculiar kind of rational insight. So far as I can understand, Hegel held a form of the objectivist view. According to the subjectivist view, the notions of cause and substance, e.g., are innate ideas peculiar to human minds; and we, so to speak, 'project' these ideas into the world on the occasion of certain appropriate kinds of sense-experience. Now there is no doubt that Kant held a form of the subjectivist view as to the nature of *a priori* concepts. The form in which he held it is peculiar to himself, and difficult to state briefly and fairly at this stage. But it may be put very roughly as follows. In passing from merely having sensations to the experience of ostensibly perceiving a world of independent persistent identifiable extended interacting things we must have unconsciously performed various elaborate processes of synthesis upon the crude data of sense. These various processes must in fact take place in accordance with certain very general rules or principles which are the same for all men at all times. For the perceptual experiences of all men are on the same general plan and fit more or less satisfactorily together. Now, when we come to reflect upon our ordinary waking perceptual experience, we make judgments which involve such notions as 'cause and effect', 'substance and states', and so on. According to Kant these notions, which become explicit in such judgments, correspond to the various fundamental types of synthesis which have been taking place unconsciously and have generated the perceptual experience to whose objects these judgments refer. So Kant's view seems very roughly to be as follows. Each different *a priori* concept is correlated with and corresponds to a different fundamental type of innate unconscious synthetic process, whereby the human mind generates out of crude sensations the experience of ostensibly perceiving a world of independent persistent extended indentifiable interacting things.

2.2.2 Percepts

Kant, unlike almost all other philosophers, held that there are *a priori* percepts as well as *a priori* concepts. He asserts that space and time are *a priori* and that they are perceptual and not conceptual. We shall have to discuss this view, and Kant's reasons for it, in detail later. At present all that can usefully be said is this. Kant took it to be a fact that our geometrical and arithmetical knowledge is synthetic and non-empirical, and at the same time categorical and not merely conditional. He thought that the only way to account for this was to suppose that the human mind imposes, in accordance with innate principles, spatial and temporal characteristics upon data which are in themselves neither spatial nor temporal. He thought that all the other kinds of synthesis involve and are involved by this imposition of spatial and temporal characteristics. It is therefore easy to see why he calls space and time '*a priori*' in the same sense in which he calls the concepts of cause and substance '*a priori*'.

The sort of reasons which he had for calling space and time percepts, and not concepts, may be stated very roughly as follows. We do literally *see* things as extended and shaped and as forming a single extended pattern in which the various things occupy various positions. We do not literally *see* one event causing another. Then, again, we conceive of the totality of actual and possible extended things as forming a single spatial whole, which might conceivably be perceived as such in one glance, though no human being is ever in fact in a position to do this. Rather similar remarks apply to time. In a single specious present one is directly acquainted with certain events as simultaneous, and with others as successive. And we conceive of the totality of actual and possible events as forming a single temporal whole, which might conceivably be the contents of a single indefinitely long specious present. These are genuine and important differences between space and time, on the one hand, and what Kant calls 'categories' of *a priori* concepts, e.g. the notion of cause or of substance, on the other.

2.3 Implications of Kant's notion of the a priori

Kant's view of *a priori*, as applied to judgments and to concepts, has certain implications and leads to certain questions which he is concerned to answer. They may be stated roughly as follows.

(1) When the notion of a certain characteristic has been reached by abstraction from actual perceived instances of it we cannot doubt that the

notion has application. But about any notion, such as cause or substance, which has not been reached in that way, the following question arises. What reason is there to think that it applies to anything? How do we know that it is not a mere fiction? We know that many empirical notions which we construct, e.g. that of a mermaid or a dragon, are fictitious. How can we be sure that all *a priori* notions, such as cause and substance, are not, so to speak, innate fictions or 'idols of the tribe' as Bacon might have said? This is one of the questions which greatly troubled Kant.

(2) There is also another question. There are certain universal judgments which involve these notions and are not merely analytic; e.g. 'Every event has a cause', 'All changes are merely changes in the states of permanent substance', 'No substance can come into or go out of existence', and so on. Men claim to *know* these propositions. What right have we to feel so certain of such very sweeping statements?

(3) Now Kant's answer to both these questions involves the second sense of *a priori*, viz. that which make an *a priori* notion be the notion of a characteristic imposed by the mind in a process of synthesis. For it is roughly as follows. We can be sure that *a priori* notions are not mere fictions if and only if they be notions of characteristics which our minds impose on all objects that they perceive. This view at once guarantees that these notions have application and limits the range of their application. It ensures that they shall apply to all perceptible objects, and at the same time it shows that we have no reason to believe that they will apply beyond the range of possible sense-perception. I am not going to criticise this theory or to go into further details about it at present. It suffices to say here that it is a characteristic doctrine of Kant's, and that it explains the connexion between the various senses in which he uses the term '*a priori*'.

3 The Copernican revolution

We can now understand what Kant means when he claims to have made a revolution in philosophy like that which Copernicus made in astronomy. The analogy is as follows. The apparent movements of the planets in the sky are extraordinarily complex; each planet appears not to move in any simple curve, and certain planets seem to move sometimes in one direction, sometimes to stand still, and sometimes to move in the opposite direction. Up to Copernicus's time it was commonly assumed that the earth did not itself move; and, so long as this was assumed, no simplification or unification could be made in the movements of the planets. But Copernicus suggested that the earth is also moving, and that the apparent movements of the planets are compounded out of their own proper movements and the movements of the observer who is carried with the earth. It was then found that all the appearances could be explained by supposing that the earth and the planets move in ellipses round the sun as focus. Now Kant says that the older pre-critical metaphysics is like the pre-Copernican astronomy. It regards our minds as mere mirrors which passively reflect things-in-themselves, just as the old astronomers thought that the earth was at rest and that the apparent movements of the planets were identical with their own proper motions. His own view is that the objects of our knowledge are not things-in-themselves, but are manufactured products in making which our minds play a part. Some of the properties which we ascribe to external objects are really due to the mental processes by which we have unconsciously constructed such objects out of crude sense-data. So there is a real analogy between Kant's step in metaphysics and Copernicus's step in astronomy. There is also, however, an equally important *contrast*, which Kant does not mention. The pre-Copernican made man the centre of nature, whilst Copernicus regarded the earth as just one moving planet among others. But the pre-Kantians regarded man as a mere observer of nature, whilst Kant makes man a constructor, though not a creator of nature. We do not indeed *create* nature on his view; for our materials are crude sense-data and these are due to things-in-themselves. But we certainly do *construct* it on Kant's view; for the sensa as they come to us are a mere chaotic mass, and every definite object of human knowledge – such as chairs, tables, atoms, etc. – has been made by selecting and combining sensa according to rules which are innate in our minds.

4 Transcendental arguments

Kant makes great use of transcendental arguments, and considers that he introduced this kind of argument into philosophy. But so far as I am aware he nowhere explicitly discusses the notion of transcendental arguments. So far as I can see, the following are the characteristics of a transcendental argument. (1) One premiss always is, not merely that a certain proposition *is* true, but also that it is *known* to be true. E.g. in his transcendental arguments about geometry Kant's premiss is not simply that two straight lines *cannot* enclose a space, but that we *know* that they cannot. Of course the latter propostion entails the former, but the former does not entail the latter. This suffices to distinguish a transcendental argument about geometry from an ordinary geometrical argument. Even if geometers do in fact know that two straight lines cannot enclose a space, they never use the fact that they know this as a premiss in their arguments. Their premiss is the fact about two straight lines and not the fact that they know this fact. (2) The next step is to ask: How can we know such propositions? What conditions must be fulfilled if such knowledge is to be possible? (3) The third stage is to argue forward from the conditions that have been discovered at the second stage. And here it seems to me that two different cases arise, one of which is illustrated by Kant's arguments about geometry and the other of which is illustrated by his proofs of the law of causation and of the permanence of substance.

(a) Sometimes the premiss takes the following form: 'I know that so-and-so is true in *some* sense and within a *certain* range of application; but I don't know precisely in *what* sense or within *what* range of application it is true.' In that case the object of the transcendental argument is simply to determine the sense and the limits in which the original propositions can be known to be true. This is the case that arises over geometry. Kant took it for granted that we know that the propositions of Euclidean geometry are true, in some sense, always and everywhere. He then argued that we could know this if and only if the spatial characteristics of perceived objects are supplied by the mind which perceives them. And then he argued from this that we can know such propositions *only* if we interpret 'always and everywhere' to mean 'in the case of all objects of possible human sense-perception'.

(b) The second form of transcendental argument is used where the proposition to be proved is one which not everyone would admit to be known to be true in *any* sense or within *any* range of application. E.g. in arguing with Hume about causation, it is useless to take as one's premiss that the law of causation is known to be true in some sense and within some range of application. For, even if this be so in fact, Hume would not have admitted it. Here Kant takes some other proposition which is admittedly known to be true. E.g. a man who would not admit that we know that every event has a cause might yet admit that we know that every event can be dated in a single temporal series. This is in fact one of the premisses which Kant takes in his proof of the law of causation. The transcendental argument then runs as follows. We first try to prove that unless certain conditions were fulfilled we could not know that every event can be dated in a single temporal order. And then we try to prove that if these conditions be fulfilled the law of causation must be true with a certain definite interpretation of it and within a certain assigned range of application.

We can now sum up the general features of all transcendental arguments. They all start with the premiss that a certain proposition is known to be true in some sense or other and within some range of application. They then try to determine what conditions must be fulfilled if such knowledge is to be possible. They then use these conditions as the basis of an argument, either to determine the precise meaning and limitations of the original proposition, or to prove that a certain other proposition must be true and to determine its precise meaning and range of application. It will be noticed that the first step of a transcendental argument is regressive; it argues from a fact to its conditions. Now such an argument can hardly be completely conclusive. We cannot be sure that the conditions which we have thought of are the only ones that could possibly explain the facts. So the conclusion of a transcendental argument cannot be more than very highly probable. A fallacy to which all such arguments are liable is the following. When we think that a certain bit of knowledge would be possible only under certain conditions this may be because we are making some tacit assumption about the way in which the mind works. This assumption might not be plausible if we explicitly recognised it. And, even if it be plausible, it may not be true. If we gave up this assumption, we might find that the facts could be explained in several alternative ways. Now Kant does apparently make two general assumptions, one explicit and the other implicit, about the mind; and both are open to question. The explicit assumption is that the ultimate data of sense must be simple isolated atoms. The mind cannot *know* any complex whole unless it has *synthesised* or *built up* this complex whole out of originally simple and isolated elements. This is a very large assumption, and it should not be accepted without discussion. The second and tacit assumption is that the ultimate data of sense are mind-dependent, and indeed are states of the mind which senses them. For Kant there is no distinction between sensations and sensa. This again is open to question. There is one other criticism to be made. What Kant claims to prove by his transcendental arguments is that certain propositions, such as the law of causation and the persistence of substance, are *true* with the interpretation and within the range of application which he gives them. But it is doubtful whether his arguments could prove more than that all human beings must *believe* them to be true, or must *act as if* they believed them to be true. And, if this is all that he has really proved, he has not answered Hume, though he has no doubt gone a good deal beyond Hume. For Hume admitted and asserted that in practice we cannot help acting as if we believed the law of causation to be true. What Kant would have added to Hume would be that no experience in the least like ours would be possible unless we did act in this way. This, if true, is important; but it is a supplement to Hume and not an answer to him.

The sum up. I do not think that there is any logical objection to transcendental arguments as such, provided we recognise that their conclusions are only probable. But we are liable to think that their conclusions are more probable than they really are, because we have made tacit assumptions about the mind and its ways of acting. And we are liable to think that they prove that '*x* must be true' when they really prove only that '*x* must be believed in practice by all human beings to be true'. I do not think that any of Kant's own transcendental arguments escapes these two criticisms; though it remains quite possible that transcendental arguments could be discovered which were not open to either of them.

2

SPACE, TIME, AND MATHEMATICS

1 Introductory remarks

For Kant the existence and the brilliant success and continual steady progress of mathematics was a fact of fundamental philosophical importance. It seemed to him plain that geometry and arithmetic provide innumerable instances of propositions which are at once necessary and synthetic, which are not merely conditional but categorical, and which we know *a priori*. Since he took this to be an indubitable fact, and also found it paradoxical and puzzling, it became for him a fundamental problem of philosophy to explain how we can know *a priori* the synthetic propositions of geometry and arithmetic, and can know moreover that they apply to everything in the actual world. His struggle with this problem was the starting-point of his system of critical philosophy; and the solution which he had reached in the *Inaugural Dissertation* of 1770 was the basis and the clue for all the further developments of his philosophy which first appeared in the *Critique of Pure Reason* in 1781.

The first book of the *Critique of Pure Reason*, called *Transcendental Aesthetic*, is wholly devoted to this subject. It covers very much the same ground as the *Inaugural Dissertation*. Throughout the whole of the *Critique of Pure Reason* and all his later writings Kant maintained the following three propositions about space and time. (1) That they are in some sense *subjective*, i.e. that spatial and temporal characteristics are in some sense imposed by human percipients on the objects which they perceive. (2) That our cognition of space and time is not merely conceptual or discursive, but is *intuitive*, i.e. is in some way analogous to perception, though it is not based upon sensation. (3) That the fact that we know the propositions of geometry and arithmetic *a priori*, although they are synthetic and categorical, can be explained on these two assumptions and on no others. But the *Transcendental Aesthetic*, though it looks complete in itself, certainly does not contain the whole of Kant's doctrine of space, and still less his whole doctrine of time or of mathematics. In the later parts of the *Critique of Pure Reason* Kant lays great stress on the notion of synthesis; and seems to hold that space can be cognised only as a result of a process of synthesis in time, analogous to mentally drawing a line or tracing a contour. Then, again, he seems to hold that time itself is cognised only as a result of a process of synthesis. Moreover, time plays a most important part in what Kant calls the *schematism of the categories*, i.e. roughly in concretising such abstract logical concepts as *ground and consequent* or *subject and predicate* into concepts such as *cause and effect* or *substance and state*, which are applicable to actual things and events and processes. Lastly, Kant devotes a whole important section quite near the end of the *Critique of Pure Reason*, viz. the first section of the *Discipline of Pure Reason*, to a discussion of the nature and peculiarities of mathematical reasoning. Now there is practically no hint of all this in the *Transcendental Aesthetic*. The most charitable explanation is that Kant could not say everything at once, and that he regarded the statements in the *Transcendental Aesthetic* as being a true account of the finished product of the processes of synthesis which he is going to describe later. I suspect that this is far too charitable. I think that he ought either to have completely rewritten this part of his old lecture notes in the light of his later doctrines, or at least to have provided it with copious footnotes referring the reader to what would be coming later.

2 The Transcendental Aesthetic

With this warning I shall now proceed to give an account of the doctrine of space, time, and mathematics which occurs in the *Transcendental Aesthetic*. Kant uses the word 'aesthetic' in its original literal Greek sense, viz. 'theory of perception'. He is not concerned here with 'aesthetics' in the modern sense, i.e. the theory of beauty. What he has to say about that is to be found in the first part of his *Critique of Judgment*.

2.1 General introduction

Kant begins by defining certain terms which he is going to use, and we will begin by considering his statements.

2.1.1 Intuition

He says that the mind has a faculty of intuition (*Anschauung*) which must be carefully distinguished from its other faculty of thinking. Intuition is not confused thinking, as Leibniz had supposed; and thinking is not just a faint copy of sensation, as Hume had supposed. The two kinds of mental activity are radically different; but both are essential to knowledge. In illustration of this view he remarks that our conception of right and wrong is confused, but it is not a sensation (p. 83, B61/A44). So far we may wholly agree with Kant. There is a faculty which makes us acquainted with particular existents, and there is a discursive faculty which is concerned with universals, facts, propositions, etc. And neither can be reduced to the other or dispensed with. But when Kant comes to tell us what he means by 'intuition' there are certain obscurities. I will first put together what he says, and then point out the difficulties. (1) When one intuits an object, he says, knowledge reaches its object *directly*. (2) This is possible only when the object is *given* to the knower (p. 65, A19). (3) In the case of human beings an object can be given to the mind only through the mind being 'affected' in a certain way. (4) These affections of the mind which are produced by objects are called 'sensations' (*Empfindungen*) (p. 65, A19). (5) When we intuit an object by means of a sensation the intuition is said to be 'empirical' (p. 65, B34/A20). (6) A phenomenon (*Erscheinung*) is 'the undetermined object of an empirical intuition' (p. 65, B34/A20). (7) The *matter* of a phenomenon is 'that in it which *corresponds* to the sensation'. The *form* of a phenomenon is that which enables the manifold matter of the phenomenon to be ordered in certain relations (p. 66, B34/A20).

Now, if we put all this together, we get a fairly clear doctrine. Objects act upon us and produce various mental modifications. These Kant calls 'sensations'. He does not distinguish within a sensation between an act of sensing and a sensum; he regards a sensation as a mental modification having a certain sensible quality. These sensations are arranged in various ways into certain complex wholes of characteristic kinds. Such a complex whole composed of interrelated sensations is a 'presentation' (*Vorstellung*). When I have a presentation I ostensibly perceive a certain object by means of it. This object is not to be confused with the presentation itself; it is simply what I take myself to be seeing or feeling or hearing or touching when I have the presentation. The object which the presentation ostensibly presents to me is called a *phenomenon*. In this phenomenon I distinguish matter and form. I regard the sensations of which the presentation is composed as corresponding to the matter of the phenomenon, and I regard the arrangement of the sensations within the presentation as corresponding to the form of the phenomenon. Empirical intuition is practically identical with what I should call sense-perception; the presentation is practically identical with a complex whole composed of interrelated sensations; and a sensation is practically identical with an isolated sense-impression regarded as a mental modification. The phenomenon is practically identical with what I should call the epistemological object of a perceptual situation. Kant certainly does not manage to stick to this view. He often confuses the phenomenon, which is presented by means of the presentation, with the presentation itself; and thus regards the presentation as itself being ostensibly perceived and the phenomenon as being itself composed of sensations. This is a serious mistake. The phenomenon might be a mere fiction, whilst the presentation was a perfectly genuine existent. E.g. the delirious patient who ostensibly sees pink rats is being presented with a certain phenomenon by means of a certain complex presentation composed of interrelated sense-impressions. But here, although the sense-impressions and the presentation composed of them exist, the presented phenomenon (viz. something answering to the description of a pink rat sitting on the bed) does not exist. The experience has an epistemological object, but there is no ontological object even remotely corresponding to it.

Now Kant held that, although all human perception of phenomena depends upon sensations, there might be another kind of intuition, which he calls 'intellectual'. This point is brought out in some remarks on pp. 89–90, B71–2. Apparently we should have intellectual intuition if we created objects by imagining them, instead of their manifesting themselves to us by causing sensations in us. Thus God may have intellectual intuition, but it is quite certain that we have not.

We must next notice that Kant constantly makes a verbal confusion, which is very common with all philosophical writers. He often uses the same word to denote (1) a certain kind of cognition, and (2) an object which is cognised by that kind of cognition. E.g. by a 'perception' people sometimes mean an act of perceiving and sometimes mean a perceived object. Kant certainly makes this confusion over the word 'intuition'. By an 'intuition' he sometimes means an act of intuiting and sometimes an intuited object. There is a further ambiguity which must be noticed. When people say that 'x is an intuition', and do not mean by this that 'x is an act of intuiting', they may still mean two different things. (1) They may mean that x is *in fact* being intuited by someone. Or (2) they may mean only that x is the kind of thing which *could be* intuited by someone. In connexion with all cognitive verbs like 'perceive', 'intuit', 'conceive', etc. we ought really to have three correlative terms, like 'perceiv*ing*', 'perce*ptum*', and 'percipi*bile*'. Thus a chair is a percipibile. If someone is actually perceiving the chair, it becomes a perceptum; and the act is an act of perceiving.

2.1.1.1 Pure and empirical intuition

We must now consider Kant's distinction between pure and empirical intuition. He says (p. 66, B34/A20): 'I call all representations in which there is nothing that belongs to sensation, *pure* in a transcendental sense. The pure form of sensuous intuitions in general, in which all the manifold which is intuited is intuited in certain relations, must be found in the mind *a priori*. And this pure form of sensibility may also itself be called the *pure intuition*.' Later on the same page he explains himself further. In the notion of a body we can distinguish three different factors: (1) those which can only be grasped by the understanding, e.g. substance, force, durability, etc.; (2) those which are manifested to us by sensation, e.g. colour, hardness, temperature, etc.; and (3) extension and shape. The last of these, he says, belong to pure intuition. Kant's doctrine may, I think, be summed up as follows. In every object of sense-perception we are immediately aware of certain qualities, such as colour, temperature, etc., pervading a certain area or volume which has a certain location. The former may be called 'the matter of the phenomenon' and the latter may be called 'the form of the phenomenon'. The matter of the phenomenon corresponds to the special sensations which compose the presentation; and the form of the phenomenon corresponds to the particular arrangement of these sensations in the presentation. Since the matter and the form of the phenomenon (i.e. its sensible qualities and its spatial characteristics) are both objects of intuition, we may talk of the form as a 'pure intuitum'; and we may talk of the matter as a 'sensuous intuitum'. And we may distinguish a corresponding pair of factors in the act of perceiving the phenomenon. We can say that every act of sense-perception involves a sensuous intuiting and a pure intuiting. The sensuous intuiting presents the matter of the phenomenon, i.e. the sensible qualities, and the pure intuiting presents the form of the phenomenon, i.e. the spatio-temporal characteristics. It does not of course follow that either pure or sensuous intuiting could occur in isolation from the other. They might be distinguishable, but inseparable, factors in every act of perceiving.

So far there is not much to criticise. But Kant proceeds to argue as follows (p. 66, B34/A20). 'That in which alone sensations can be posited and ordered in a certain way cannot itself be sensation . . . Therefore, while the matter of all phenomena is given to us *a posteriori* only, its form must lie ready *a priori* in the mind for the sensation. This form must therefore be capable of being considered apart from all sensation.' Again, on the same page, he says: 'Extension and shape belong to pure intuition, which, even without a real object of the senses or of sensation, exists in the mind *a priori* as a mere form of sensibility.'

What are we to say about this? Since a 'sensation' was defined by Kant as an affection produced in the mind by a perceived object, what he is asserting amounts to this. When one perceives an object as yellow or as hot, etc., this is because of certain effects which that object is producing in one's mind. But when one perceives its colour as covering a certain area, e.g. a spherical surface located at a certain position in one's visual field, and when one perceives the heat or the smell as coming from that position, this cannot be because of any effects which the object is producing in one's mind. These spatial features in what one perceives must be supplied by one's mind entirely from its own resources. Kant offers no reason here for this assertion. But surely it is by no means obvious.

2.1.1.1.1 Facts at the back of Kant's theory

Let us now consider the following question. What facts might have led Kant to draw this sharp distinction between our awareness of the spatio-temporal characteristics of perceived objects and our awareness of their colours, temperatures, etc.? And do they justify this sharp distinction? The following facts seem to be relevant.

(1) To be bounded by a closed surface of some definite size and shape, and to occupy some definite position at each moment, seem to be *part of the notion* of a perceptible object. It cannot be said to be part of the notion of a perceptible object to be coloured, or part of its notion to have temperature, and so on. It is true, I think, that it is part of the notion of a perceptible object to have *some* quality or *other* which covers an area or provides a volume, and thus marks it out from its surroundings. But the particular sensible qualities with which our sensations have made us familiar, such as colour, temperature, etc., are neither severally nor collectively essential to the notion of a perceptible object. Thus spatial characteristics seem to occupy a unique position in reference to perceptible objects in comparison with sensible qualities. I suspect that this was one of the facts which Kant had in mind.

(2) Sensations of colour, sensations of temperature, sensations of sound, and so on, seem to be logically quite independent of each other. There is no difficulty in supposing that any one of them might have existed in the absence of all the rest. But it certainly cannot be said that there are sensations of extension and position, which just exist alongside these other sensations and are logically independent of them as they are of each other. It is impossible to conceive of a sensation of colour which was not a sensation of an *expanse* pervaded by some colour and either filling the whole visual field or located within some limited area of it. Conversely it is impossible to conceive of being acquainted with an area of definite size, shape, and position unless it were marked out by *some* sensible quality, such as colour or temperature. Thus colour may be said to presuppose extension and position; whilst extension and position do not presuppose colour, though, in order to become perceptible, they do presuppose *some* extensible sense-quality or *other*. When Kant says in effect that space cannot be a sense-datum, one reason may well be this fact that extension, shape, and position stand to sensible qualities in a unique relation in which no one sense-quality stands to any other.

(3) The most notable instance of spatial perception is provided by the visual field. To simplify the situation as much as possible suppose that one is lying on one's back looking up at the sky on a cloudless day. One is aware of a vast expanse, with no sharp boundaries, pervaded by a uniform blue. In spite of there being no variations in the pervading colour, one has no difficulty in recognising that this expanse comprises an infinite variety of sub-regions of various shapes and sizes occupying various positions. Suppose now that a few small clouds appear. Then certain of these sub-regions become separately perceptible through being pervaded by a dif-

ferent colour (whiteness) which marks them out from the rest. We can perceive one and the same sub-region being pervaded and marked out at different times by the same or by different colours. And we can perceive different regions at the same time being pervaded and marked out by the same or by different colours. Any object that one sees appears to one visually as a certain sub-region of the total visual field, pervaded by certain colours, and thus marked out from the background and from other objects seen at the same time. If one is looking in a given direction at any moment, the particular pattern of colours which then occupies the visual field is quite independent of one's thoughts and volitions. If one continues to look in the same direction for a period, the variations in that pattern of colours from moment to moment are quite independent of one's thoughts and volitions.

Now it is plausible to interpret these facts as follows. It is plausible to think of oneself, in so far as one is a visual percipient, as the persistent centre of a constant system of spatial reference, of which one is always immediately aware. And it is plausible to think of the pattern of colours with which this spatial system is pervaded at any moment, and of the variations in that pattern from one moment to another, as due to objects independent of oneself and to independent changes among those objects.

I strongly suspect that such facts as I have been describing about the visual field are an important factor in Kant's doctrine of space and of pure intuition in the *Aesthetic*. I suspect that he thinks of each person as the centre of an innate system of spatial reference, of which he is perpetually and immediately aware. This awareness is pure intuit*ing*, and the spatial system which is its object is a pure intuit*um*. The concrete filling of this innate spatial system is the variegated and perpetually varying pattern of sensible qualities which pervade it. This is due to the action of foreign objects upon oneself, and one's awareness of it is *sensible* or *empirical* intuiting. To perceive an empirical object involves *at least* being aware of a certain region of one's innate spatial system as being pervaded by certain sensible qualities which mark it out from the rest. (According to Kant it involves also a great deal more than this. But this additional factor involves *thought*, as distinct from intuition, and is considered at length in the division of the *Critique* called *Transcendental Analytic*.) So to perceive an empirical object always involves both pure and sensuous intuition.

(4) There is one other fact which may be relevant. Anyone who is good at visual imagery can close his eyes and call up images at will of various figures in various positions. And he may be able at will to create these images in various colours, though the colours would generally be much less vivid than those of actually seen objects. Now Kant certainly held that the construction of figures in imagination plays an important part in geometry. I suspect that he may have thought that one is intuiting the same

innate spatial system both when one has one's eyes open and is actually seeing things and when one has one's eyes shut and is merely calling up images. In actual seeing the action of a foreign object upon one causes a certain region of this innate spatial system to be pervaded by certain colours and thus marked out. In visual imagining the action of one's own thoughts and volitions upon oneself causes a certain region of the same innate spatial system to be prevaded by certain colours and thus marked out. Here, Kant might say, you have an instance of pure intuition occurring in the absence of sensation. But I think that he would add that, unless one had at some time in the past had the stimulus of actual sensation, the faculty of pure intuition would probably never have come into action.

2.1.1.1.2 Kant's view of the difference between spatial characteristics and sensible qualities

I think there can be no doubt that these facts do show that there are very important differences between spatial characteristics, on the one hand, and sensible qualities, such as colour and temperature, on the other. But do they justify the particular distinction which Kant draws between them?

In the first place, it is not very easy to state clearly what precisely that distinction is. It is not enough to say that Kant held that spatial characteristics are subjective and are in some sense dependent upon or supplied by the mind of the percipient. For practically everyone had held the same view about sensible qualities, such as colour and temperature, ever since the time of Galileo and Descartes and Locke. And Kant certainly agreed that colours, temperatures, etc. are in some sense dependent upon or supplied by the mind of the percipient. One might therefore be tempted to say that all that Kant is doing is what Berkeley had already done, viz. to apply to spatial characteristics the same arguments which Locke had applied to secondary qualities and to conclude that all are alike subjective.

But Kant explicitly and indignantly repudiates this. The passage occurs on pp. 72–4 (B44–6/A28–30). He made some changes between the first and the second editions; but, if one takes the two together, the main points seem to be the following. (1) Our intuition of space gives rise to innumerable synthetic propositions which can be known a priori. We have no such synthetic a priori knowledge about colour, temperature, or any other sensible quality. (2) We cannot conceive or imagine any determinate colour which we have not seen, any determinate taste which we have not tasted, and so on. But we can and do conceive and construct, either on paper or in imagination, figures of which we have never perceived any instances. (3) To have some shape, size, and position is an essential part of what is meant by being a perceptible object. But it is no part of what is meant by being a perceptible object that it shall have colour, or that it shall have temperature, or that it shall have any particular sensible quality which you may choose to mention. (4) Colours and other sensible qualities cannot properly be regarded as properties of the bodies which we perceive as coloured, as hot, and so on. They must be regarded only as changes or modifications in the mind of the percipient. Moreover these changes may be different in different men.

Now, as regards the first three points, they are genuine and important differences, some of which we have already noted. The third needs, however, to be qualified by the addition that it *is* part of the meaning of a perceptible object to have *some* sensible quality or *other* which covers an area or pervades a volume, although there is *no one particular* sensible quality which it is essential that a perceptible object should have. As regards the fourth point, we must suppose that Kant intends us to supplement his statement about colours, etc. by an opposed statement about spatial characteristics. For otherwise there is no contrast. The opposed statement would run as follows: Shape, size, and position *can* properly be regarded as properties of the objects which we perceive as having them. They *cannot* be regarded only as changes or modifications in the mind of the percipient. Moreover they are *not* different for different men.

It seems to me that it is this statement on which we must concentrate our attention if we are to understand Kant's view. For it at once raises the following questions. (1) On Kant's view of space how can shape, size, and position be properly regarded as properties of perceived objects? Will they not have to be regarded as modifications in the mind of the percipient, just as much as colours and temperatures? (2) Are they not in fact very often different for different men? Does not the same object appear to have different shapes and sizes to different men, just as it may appear to have different colours or temperatures?

The second of these questions is the less fundamental, and I will clear it out of the way before dealing with the first. I suspect that Kant would have dealt with it as follows. Certainly the same thing, e.g. a penny, appears to have different shapes and sizes and even positions, to different men, *provided* that they are in different positions in relation to it or if one sees it through a homogeneous medium and the other through a heterogeneous medium, and so on. But these different conditions are themselves statable only in *spatial* terms. Two men looking at the same unchanged object from the same position relative to it and through the same medium will see it as having the same shape, size, and position. But all such external conditions might be the same and yet the colour or the taste or the temperature of the same object on the same occasion might be different for different men. E.g. one might be colour-blind and the other not. I think that the above statement would have to be qualified to some extent, e.g. a man who is drunk may see two similar objects in different positions when a sober man would see one. But I would admit it in the main, and I would admit that it constitutes another important difference between spatial and sensible characteristics. If *both* are subjective, then there is a sense in which the former are *less* subjective than the latter.

We come now to the fundamental question. On Kant's view of space must not shape, size, and position be regarded as modifications in the mind of the percipient, just as much as colours and temperatures? In order to discuss this question we must raise the following preliminary question. Suppose I perceive A as round and as occupying a position p_1 in my visual field, and that I perceive B as square and as occupying a position p_2 in my visual field. Does Kant wish to assert that my mind supplies to A the appearance of roundness and of occupying p_1, and supplies to B the appearance of squareness and of occupying p_2, *entirely on its own initiative* and without there being *any* corresponding difference between the sensation S_A which presents A to it and the sensation S_B which presents B to it? Or would he allow that there is always a relevant difference between S_A and S_B, and that it is this which makes me perceive A as round and occupying p_1 and B as square and occupying p_2? Would he wish only to make the following negative statements? (1) That these differences between the sensation S_A and S_B are not *themselves* differences in spatial characteristics. (2) That the differences in the foreign things-in-themselves a and β, which are responsible for these differences in the sensations S_A and S_B which they respectively evoke in my mind, are also not differences in spatial characteristics.

It is an extraordinary thing that Kant never raises the question of what it is that determines the particular shape, size, and position which a particular object is perceived to have on a particular occasion. It seems to me that there are great difficulties on either alternative. (1) Suppose we say that the mind of the percipient determines this entirely on its own initiative. On that alternative we can, no doubt, draw a clear and fundamental distinction between the spatial characteristics and the colour and other sensible qualities which one perceives an object as having. The particular shape, size, and position will be determined *entirely* by the percipient's mind. They will not be conditioned *directly* by some characteristic of the sensation, and therefore will not be conditioned *indirectly* by some characteristic in the foreign thing-in-itself which evokes the sensation. The particular colour, on the other hand, will be determined *directly* by the quality of the sensation, and therefore *indirectly* by some characteristic of the foreign thing-in-itself which evokes the sensation. But this alternative seems absolutely incredible. Surely there must be *some* condition, independent of my mind, which is necessary if not sufficient to determine whether I perceive a certain object on a certain occasion as round or as square, as in the middle of my visual field or as towards the edge of it, and so on?

(2) Let us then try the other alternative. We will now suppose that an *immediate* necessary condition of my perceiving an object as square and as located at a certain place in my visual field is a certain determinate non-spatial characteristic of the sensation. And we will suppose that a *remote* necessary condition is a certain determinate non-spatial characteristic in the foreign thing which evokes the sensation. This alternative is at least intelligible. But, if we take it, spatial characteristics and sensible qualities, such as colour, seem to be almost exactly on a level as regards subjectivity and objectivity, Still, I think that there would be one important difference on Kant's view. I think he would hold that the sensation which I have when I perceive an object as red *actually has* the quality of redness, and similarly for hotness, squeakiness, etc. But I think he would deny that the sensation which I have when I perceive an object as square or as round has the quality of squareness or of roundness, as the case may be. And I think he would deny that, when I perceive one object as in a certain spatial relation to another, the sensations by which I perceive the two objects respectively stand in any kind of spatial relation to each other. I think he would say that sensible qualities belong to *sense-impressions*, though not to things-in-themselves, whilst spatial qualities and relations belong neither to things-in-themselves nor to sense-impressions. They might be described as *perceptual*, but not sensible, characteristics.

In view of all this it seems to me that the least unsatisfactory view for Kant to hold would be the following. Suppose I am perceiving a certain object as red and as round and as located in the middle of my visual field. Then (1) A necessary immediate condition of my perceiving it as *red* is a certain determinate quality of the sensation by which it presents itself to me. And a necessary condition of my perceiving it as *round* and as located at the *middle* of my visual field is a certain other determinate quality of that sensation. (2) The sensation *actually is* red, and it is its redness which makes me perceive the object as red. (3) But the sensation is *not* itself round or located at a certain position, for sensations cannot literally have spatial characteristics. Therefore the quality of the sensation which makes me perceive the object as round and as located in the middle of my visual field must be a determinate form of a certain *non-spatial* determinable. We have no name for this in ordinary speech. Let us call it the 'space-locating' property. (4) Neither colour nor spatiality nor the space-locating property belongs to the foreign things-in-themselves which evoke our sensations. But presumably there is in a foreign thing-in-itself *some* characteristic which corresponds, as a remote necessary condition, to the determinate colour of the sensation which it evokes. And presumably there is also in it some *other* characteristic which corresponds, as a remote necessary condition, to the determinate form of the space-locating property of the sensation which it evokes. (5) The innate constitution of my mind is such that, whenever I have a sensation of a certain determinate colour and with a certain determinate form of the space-locating property, I ostensibly perceive an object which presents itself to me as having that colour and as having a certain determinate shape and size and position in space outside me.

2.2 Theory of space

We can now consider Kant's detailed arguments about space. He begins by saying that there are three possible views about space, and also about time. (1) The Newtonian view that they are existents of a substantival kind which could and would exist even if there were no things or events to occupy them and no persons to intuit them. (2) The Leibnizian view that they are a system of actual and possible relations between actual and possible things or events, and that these relations would hold whether the things and events were perceived or not. (3) Kant's own view, which he here describes by saying that 'they belong only to the form of intuition, and therefore to the subjective constitution of our minds, apart from which they could not be ascribed to anything whatever' (p. 68, A 23/B 38).

Coming to detail we find that Kant tries to prove the following two things about space. (1) That our knowledge of space is in some sense *a priori* and not empirical. (2) That this knowledge is in some sense intuitive and not merely discursive. He has two arguments specially directed to prove the first point, and two specially directed to prove the second. In addition to these he has two other arguments, each of which is supposed to prove both points. The first is called the *argument from incongruent counterparts*, i.e. from the existence of such pairs of objects as left and right hands, objects and their mirror-images, etc. The second is from the nature of our knowledge of geometry. I shall now take these arguments in turn, and consider in each case what, if anything, the argument proves.

2.2.1 Special arguments to prove that our knowledge of space is non-empirical

(1) *First argument.* 'Space is not an empirical concept which has been derived from outer experiences. For in order that certain sensations be referred to something . . . in another region of space from that in which I find myself . . . the representation of space must be presupposed . . . [It must also be presupposed] in order that I may be able to represent [certain sensations] as being not only different but as in different places. Therefore the representation of space cannot be empirically obtained from the relations of outer appearances. On the contrary, this outer experience is itself possible at all only through that representation' (p. 68, B 38/A 23).

I suppose that Kant means by 'outer experiences' experiences in which one ostensibly perceives objects as outside one's own body and in various positions relative to each other. The most typical example would be ordinary waking visual perception, though it is worth while to remark that the visual experiences which we have in dreaming have the same characteristic. Typical examples of experiences which are not 'outer' in this sense would be sensations of headache or stomach-ache, emotions, volitions, and so on. It is plain, however, that there is an important distinction to be drawn between some experiences which are not outer and others. Take, e.g., a feeling of toothache or headache. Though it is not 'referred to' a place outside one's body it is referred to a place within one's body. And, if one had a headache and a stomach-ache at the same time, they would be referred to different places, though neither of these places is outside one's body. Thus some experiences which are not 'outer', in Kant's sense, involve spatial reference just as much as those which are 'outer' in his sense. But other experiences which are not 'outer' seem to involve no spatial references at all. If I feel angry, e.g., I do not localise the anger either outside my body or inside it.

It is evident that that argument turns on the notion of 'referring' a sensation to a place, and it is difficult to see that it is relevant to the argument whether that place is outside one's body, as in visual perception, or inside one's body, as in feelings of toothache or stomach-ache. Let us, however, take the case of what Kant would call outer experiences. What exactly is meant by saying that in such experiences I 'refer' a sensation to a place outside my body? In the first place, it seems to me that we must distinguish between experiences of sight on the one hand, and experiences of hearing and smelling on the other. There is a fairly literal sense in which one refers a sensation of sound to a clock or a sensation of smell to an orange. One says that the sound 'comes *from*' the clock and the smell 'comes *from*' the orange. And one thinks of the sensation of sound or of smell as an effect produced in oneself by something which travels from the external object to the place where one is. Let us call this 'causal reference to an external source'. But this is certainly not the sense in which one 'refers' a sensation of colour to an external object. When I see a green leaf it would never occur to me to say that the greenness 'comes *from*' the leaf. I see it out there on the surface of the leaf and do not think of it as an effect produced in me by something coming from the leaf. Even if I look at a self-luminous object, such as the sun, I do not say the yellow colour 'comes *from*' the sun. I may say that *light* comes to me from the sun, and that this causes me to see the yellow colour, but I see the yellow colour on the surface of a shining round object in the sky. Now I think it is obvious that causal reference to an external source, such as occurs in hearing and smelling, presupposes the other kind of external reference which is characteristic of seeing and touching. Unless one had *seen* or *felt* remote objects such as bells and oranges, one would never have referred certain sensations of sound to the former and certain sensations of smell to the latter as their external sources. So in the end the question comes to this: What is meant by saying that in seeing an object I refer a sensation of colour to a place outside me? (A similar question could be raised about touch, but we can ignore this for the present purpose.)

Now I can think of only two answers to this. One is that it is merely a rather misleading way of stating the *fact* that in visual perception I am immediately aware of colours as spread out over surfaces at various places outside me. On that interpretation it is true, but it has no tendency to support Kant's conclusion that I cannot have derived the idea of space from reflecting upon outer experiences and their spatial qualities and relations. The other interpretation is that Kant must be assuming that this fact cannot be accepted as ultimate but presupposes a certain process performed by the mind upon its visual sensations. Let us consider this second alternative.

I suggest that Kant might have argued as follows. Sensations of colour are in themselves simply mental events produced in one's mind by the action of foreign objects. In this respect they are exactly on a par with sensations of sound, smell, etc. It would therefore be absurd to suggest that in themselves they have any spatial characteristics whatever. But in point of fact whenever one has a colour-sensation one does perceive a colour as spread out on a surface of some shape and size at some position outside one's body. Therefore we must suppose that one's mind behaves in a certain characteristic way on the occurrence of a colour-sensation in it. It reacts by producing a perceptual experience in which one is immediately presented with a colour as pervading a certain region at a certain external position. All the regions which a colour can ever be presented to one as occupying are so interrelated as to constitute a single three-dimensional spatial system.

Suppose that Kant meant something like this. Then, if you had said to him that we get our ideas of space by abstraction from our perceptual experiences of coloured objects of various shapes, sizes, and relative positions, he could have answered as follows. All these perceptual experiences, which are your empirical data, are, in their spatial aspect, products of the innate spatialising activities of your mind, which it exercises automatically on the occasion of your having sensations which are, in themselves, non-spatial. What you get out by explicit reflection, comparison, and abstraction, is simply the ground-plan of what you unconsciously put in when you converted bare colour-sensation into perception of coloured surfaces. At this point some of the ambiguities in the term *a priori*, as applied to concepts and percepts, become obvious. In one sense our notion

of space would be empirical and not *a priori*. For it would be derived from
our perceptual experiences of the coloured surfaces which we see, and their
shapes, and positions, and mutual relations, by abstracting in thought
from the variegated coloured contents of our visual field and thinking of
the homogeneous empty extended system of positions which would then
remain. But, if Kant is right, what we arrive at by this process is, in another
sense, *a priori* and not empirical. For it is the innate plan in accordance with
which the mind works in basing upon intrinsically non-spatial colour-
sensations perceptions of colours as spread out and located in the visual
field. This is the best that I can make of Kant's first argument.

(II) *Second argument*. This runs as follows. 'We can never represent to
ourselves the absence of space, though we can quite well think of it as
empty of objects. It must therefore be regarded as the condition of the
possibility of appearances, and not as a determination dependent upon
them. It is an *a priori* representation, which necessarily underlies outer
appearances' (p. 68, A24/B38–9).

What does Kant mean by his premiss 'We can never represent to
ourselves the absence of space, though we can quite well think of it as
empty of objects'? Does 'represent' just mean 'conceive'? In that case the
most plausible interpretation to put on his premiss would be the following. The mere *possibility* of there being extended objects involves, not
merely the possibility, but the *actuality* of space. It is conceivable that there
might never be and never have been any extended objects; but, if it is
intelligible to suppose that there *might be* extended objects, then it is
necessary to suppose that there *actually is* space. To put it in another way:
There might have been no space, but in that case there not merely *would not
have been* but *could not conceivably have been* any extended objects.

Now supposing that this were Kant's premiss, what would follow? It
seems to me that the premiss entails something like Newton's theory of
absolute space, i.e. the doctrine that space is a kind of pre-existing container, which might or might not have contained extended objects. Now
this is no doubt a step towards what Kant wants, for he is arguing here
against the Leibnizian view that space is just a system of actual and possible
relations between bodies. But the conclusion which he actually draws is
that 'space is an *a priori* representation, which necessarily underlies outer
appearances'. Now in the context this presumably means that space is
something which the percipient supplies from his own mind when he
automatically bases perceptions of externally located extended objects
upon the intrinsically non-spatial colour-sensations which foreign things
produce in him. I do not see that this conclusion follows from this premiss
alone.

It is therefore worth while to consider whether a different interpretation
could be given to the premiss 'We can never represent to ourselves the

absence of space . . .' Is it possible that at least part of what Kant means is that we can never divest ourselves of the intuition of space, though we can conceive that there might be no sensations to provide us with concrete perceptions of colours and other extensible qualities located in it? This is more like what Kant needs in order to prove his conclusion. Indeed it is little more than a rather more detailed statement of the conclusion. I rather suspect that Kant may have started with the proposition that we cannot conceive the *possibility* of extended objects without admitting the *actuality* of space. He may then have thought that it is equivalent to or entails the proposition that we can never divest ourselves of the intuition of space.

There is no doubt that he was convinced on various grounds of the following two propositions. (1) As between Leibniz's theory of space being nothing but a system of actual and possible relations between extended objects, and Newton's theory of space being logically prior to extended objects and their *de facto* relations, Newton was right and Leibniz wrong. (2) On the other hand, Newton's theory of space as a kind of infinite self-subsistent container is too absurd to be seriously maintained in philosophy, however convenient a fiction it may be in mathematical physics. Kant's own theory, which makes space in a sense logically prior to phenomenal objects and yet makes it dependent on the minds of human observers, would seem to him for that very reason to have all the advantages and none of the defects of the Newtonian theory. I suspect that such considerations as these are at the back of this second argument.

2.2.2 Special arguments to prove that our knowledge of space is intuitive

The proposition which Kant professes to be proving here is that 'Space is not a discursive or, as we say, general concept of relations of things in general, but a pure intuition.'[1] We must begin by considering what this means. (1) In the first place I take it that we can substitute for 'pure *intuition*' either 'pure intui*tum*' or 'pure intui*table*'. Kant means either that space is an individual whole with which a person *is* from time to time directly acquainted, or that it is at any rate the kind of thing with which a person *might conceivably* be directly acquainted. (2) The negative part of Kant's statement must be interpreted in reference to Leibniz's account of space. Leibniz's theory might be expressed as follows. We are familiar with sentences such as 'Space has three dimensions', 'Space is infinite', 'Space is endlessly divisible', and so on. These suggest that there is an individual something of which the word 'space' is a kind of proper name, as the words 'London' and 'Cambridge' are. But, according to Leibniz, this suggestion is quite misleading. All statements in which the word 'space'

[1] [P. 69, A25/B39.]

occurs as grammatical subject can be replaced by statements in which it does not occur but which are entirely about bodies and their spatial qualities and relations. Thus, e.g., we can replace 'Space is infinite' by 'Whatever the distance between two bodies A and B there would be a body further from A than B is'. Now I take it that Kant intends to deny this. He intends to assert that there are statements, in which the word 'space' occurs as grammatical subject, which cannot be replaced by statements about bodies, actual or possible, and their actual or possible spatial relations. He intends to assert that there *is* an individual something of which the word 'space' is a kind of proper name, and which therefore might conceivably be an object of acquaintance. Obviously the most conclusive way of showing this would be to show that it actually is an object with which some person is at some time acquainted. But it might be possible to show that space is an *intuitable* even if it is never as a whole an *intuitum*. No human being ever perceives the earth as a whole at any one moment, but the earth is the kind of object which might conceivably be so perceived.

(1) *First argument*. The argument runs as follows. 'In the first place, we can represent to ourselves only one space. If we speak of diverse spaces, we mean . . . only parts of one and the same unique space. Secondly, these parts cannot precede the one all-embracing space as . . . constituents out of which it can be composed; on the contrary, they can be thought of only as *in* it. Space is essentially one . . . the general concept of spaces depends solely on the introduction of limitations . . .' From this last statement Kant draws the further conclusion that 'an *a priori*, and not an empirical intuition, underlies all concepts of space' (p. 69, B39/A25). Let us first consider the premisses of the argument.

(1) We can agree with Kant that, when we talk of Space with a capital 'S', we think of it as something unique, which is the system of spatial reference in which all actual and conceivable physical things and events are located. And, when we talk of this, that, and the other 'space' with a small 's', we think of them as sub-regions within the one Space with a big 'S', and not as species under a genus as when we talk of this, that, and the other colour. It is true that, since Kant's time, geometers have talked about various spaces, e.g. Euclidean, elliptic, hyperbolic, and so on. But this is irrelevant. What is meant is that we can conceive that the one total space of nature might have had various alternative types of geometrical structure which can be formulated in alternative sets of axioms. If it had one structure, we should call it a 'Euclidean space'; if it had a certain other structure, we should call it an 'elliptic space', and so on. Kant could have admitted all this, and it would have made no difference to his premiss.

Now it seems to me that this premiss could quite well be formulated on such a view of space at Leibniz's. How would Leibniz interpret the statement 'Space is unique and there could not possibly be several Spaces with a capital "S" '? He would have to interpret it on somewhat the following lines. There would not be two simultaneously existing sets of material objects, A and A', such that all the members of A stood in spatial relations to each other, and all the members of A' stood in spatial relations to each other, but no member of A stood in any spatial relation to any member of A'. No doubt many refinements would be needed, but I see no reason to doubt that they could be supplied.

Perhaps Kant would answer as follows. He might say that, when the statement 'Space is unique' is interpreted in this way, we can see no kind of necessity in it, whilst we do in fact find it self-evidently necessary. But does Kant's own alternative explain this fact, if it be a fact, any better? Suppose that each of us does actually intuit a peculiar kind of individual whole to which the name 'space' can be applied as a proper name. Would this make it self-evident that there could not possibly be more than one such whole? Is it not in fact obvious that, on Kant's own subjective theory, there would be as many different 'Spaces' with a capital 'S' as there are different human percipients?

(2) The second premiss is that the various regions which are contained in the one space are not logically prior to it, as the bricks are to a house which is built of them. On the contrary, space as a whole is logically prior to its various sub-regions. Space is not really divisible into sub-regions, in the sense in which a bit of paper is divisible into smaller bits. For this would imply that sub-regions which are adjoined might conceivably be separated. This is intelligible in regard to the extended parts of a continuous extended material object; but it is quite meaningless as regards sub-regions of pure space. All that we can do in the way of 'dividing' space is to perceive or imagine a certain region as marked *out* from the rest by some peculiarity of its *content*, e.g. by its containing something which resists entry from all directions or by its having a special colour spread over its surface.

It seems to me that Kant is here pointing out some very important facts about our notion of space. I think it is also true that these facts about 'voluminosity', as it might be called, are neglected by such a theory as Leibniz's. That is concerned almost wholly with *position, distance,* and *direction.* These facts do suggest that we conceive space as a kind of individual voluminous whole logically prior to, and existentially independent of, any filling by matter or by colours. Whether they positively necessitate that view, or whether they could be translated wholly into facts about actual or possible bodies and their spatial qualities and relations, I do not know.

(II) *Second argument.* This argument occurs in a somewhat different form in the first and the second editions of the *Critique.* I will take the two forms in turn.

First edition (A) The two arguments begin alike with the statement 'Space is represented as an infinite given magnitude'. The argument in A then proceeds as follows: 'A general concept of space, which is found alike in a foot and in an ell, cannot determine anything in regard to magnitude. If there were not limitlessness in the progression of intuition, no concept of relations could yield a principle of their infinitude' (p. 69, A25).

(1) The first statement in this argument is merely trivial. It simply asserts that the notion of space cannot be identified with the notion of the abstract quality of being spatially extended. That quality is of course present, though in different determinate forms, 'alike in a foot and in an ell'. But surely no one ever did identify the notion of space with the notion of the quality of being spatially extended.

(2) The important point is the question raised in the latter part of the argument: 'Why do we ascribe infinite extension to space?' Now Kant seems here to imply at one place that we *do* and at another that we *do not* actually intuit space as a whole of infinite extent. This view seems to be implied in the assertion, common to both forms of the argument, that space is represented as an infinite *given* magnitude. The opposite seems to be implied in the statement that it is the unendingness of the progression of intuition, i.e. the fact that we can intuit larger and larger volumes like an unending series of Chinese boxes, which is at the basis of the notion of the infinity of space. I think that the solution is probably as follows. Kant does not wish to assert that anyone at any moment *actually does* intuit space as an individual whole. Nor does he wish to assert that at any moment a person has actually intuited *in succession* a set of adjoined regions which together make up space as an individual whole. I suspect that, by the statement that we represent space as an infinite *given* magnitude, Kant means that we conceive all the sub-regions which we intuit only successively as actually coexisting. We therefore think of them as together constituting a whole which might conceivably be taken in at one glance, though no finite mind could do this.

(3) The argument, then, comes to this. We intuit larger and larger regions in succession, each containing all and more than all that we intuited before. We come to no limit in this process. And, on the basis of this, we ascribe infinite extension to space. We cannot help regarding space as a whole containing *simultaneously* all the parts which we can intuit *only successively*, and therefore as something which might conceivably be taken in at one glance, although its infinity makes this impossible for any finite being. Moreover, our conviction that any region which we have intuited is contained in a larger region which we might go on to intuit is not merely empirical and inductive. It is self-evident and we know it *a priori*.

By some such argument as this I think that it could be made probable that the notion of space as an infinite collective whole involves the following two factors. (1) Notions such as volume, and the adjunction of one region with another along a common edge or face to form a larger region, and so on, which are exemplified in actual perception and are not merely conceived. (2) An intellectual construction which uses these notions, but passes beyond the limits of what could possibly be perceived. This passage beyond the limits of what is perceptible depends on the *a priori* conviction that there can be no maximum and no minimum regions of space.

It is worth while to add that we are quite certain that the actual spatial relations which we have perceived among bodies are only a tiny selection from the spatial relations which are possible. Taking a single body, e.g., I am quite certain that other bodies could exist at an infinite number of different distances from it and in a triply infinite number of different directions relatively to it. Yet it is plain that I have perceived only a few bodies at a few different distances from and in a few different directions relative to any other body that I have perceived. It is difficult to believe that inductive generalisation could account for my conviction that perceived spatial relations are a tiny selection out of an infinite number of systematically interconnected possible spatial relations. Yet this is part of the notion of space as a collective whole, and therefore that notion seems to involve non-empirical factors.

Second edition (B) The corresponding argument in B proceeds as follows after the common premiss that space is represented as an infinite given magnitude. 'Every concept must be thought of as a representation which is contained – as their common character – in an infinite number of different possible representations, and which therefore contains the latter *under* itself. But no concept, as such, can be thought of as containing an infinite number of representations *within* itself. It is in this latter way, however, that space is thought of; for all the parts of space coexist *ad infinitum*. Consequently the original representation of space is an *a priori* intuition, not a concept' (pp. 69–70, B 40).

The point which Kant is making in all this verbiage is quite simple. He is trying to point out that there is a fundamental difference between the sense in which a *universal*, e.g. redness, may be said to 'contain *under* it' an infinite number of possible *instances*, viz. every actual and possible red object, and the sense in which space may said to 'contain *in* it' an infinite number of sub-regions. Spatiality or extendedness *is* a universal, and, just like redness, it has instances but not parts. But space is *not* a universal; it has parts, viz. its sub-regions, but no instances. All this is quite obvious, but I think that it is trivial, for no one ever supposed that the word 'space' is the name of a universal in the sense in which the name 'red' is. That was not Leibniz's view and therefore the argument is irrelevant to him. His view would be expressed in modern terminology by saying that space is a logical construction out of bodies and their spatial qualities and relations.

All that follows from Kant's premiss is that it is not palpable nonsense to suggest that space might be an intuitable individual existent, as it would be to suggest that redness or extendedness might be. It does not suffice to prove that there *is* an actual individual existent, of which 'space' is a proper name, as 'Cambridge' is the proper name of a certain town. Still less does it suffice to prove that anyone ever actually intuits space as an individual whole. We must remember that, although any individual existent is in principle capable of being an object of intuition, whilst no universal is so, there are plenty of individual existents which no one is *in fact* capable of intuiting and which *in fact* can be cognised only conceptually. E.g. no one now alive can possibly perceive either Julius Caesar or the matter at the centre of the earth, although both are individual existents and not universals, and therefore in principle capable of being objects of intuitive cognition.

2.2.2.1 What did Kant think that he had proved?

Before leaving this section I would like to raise the following question. Does Kant profess to have proved that space as an individual whole *actually is* intuited by us, or only that we necessarily conceive it as something whose nature is such that it *might conceivably* be intuited as an individual whole, e.g. by God? (1) It should be noted that in other parts of the *Critique* Kant says quite definitely that we cannot *perceive* empty space or empty time. But this is not conclusive. For, in the first place, although perception is a form of intuition, i.e. acquaintance with particular existents, not all intuition is perception according to Kant. Perception involves sensation, whilst Kant holds that our spatial and temporal intuiting is a kind of non-sensuous acquaintance. So, if by 'perception' we mean acquaintance based upon sensation, it is obvious that we could not *perceive* empty space or time. But it would not follow that Kant wished to deny that we have *non-sensuous* aquaintance with space as an individual whole. Again, even if he intended to deny this in the later parts of the *Critique*, it does not follow that he may not be asserting it in the *Transcendental Aesthetic*. For this certainly belongs to a very early stage in the development of the critical philosophy. (2) Very far on in the *Critique* Kant makes the positive assertion that the notion of infinite space is, in his technical sense, an *idea of reason*. This would quite definitely make the notion *conceptual*, and would quite definitely rule out the possibility that any human being should be acquainted (even non-sensuously) with space as an individual whole. (3) Whatever Kant may be intending to assert on this point in the *Aesthetic*, it seems quite clear that we *are not* in fact acquainted with space as an individual whole, and that none of Kant's arguments have any tendency to show that we are. At most they have a tendency to show the following two things. (a) That we inevitably conceive space as an individual whole, i.e. as something which might conceivably be an object of intuition. And (b) that there are *a priori* factors in the transition from intuiting successively larger and larger regions to the concept of space as an infinite whole in which they all coexist. This would fit in very well with his later statement that the concept of infinite space is an idea of reason.

2.2.3 The arguments from incongruent counterparts

What Kant calls 'incongruous counterparts' are pairs of figures which have a peculiar kind of symmetry with each other and yet have also a characteristic unlikeness which we can all recognise. Examples are the left and right hands of the same person, an object and its image in a plane mirror, a right-handed and a left-handed screw of the same pitch and radius, and a pair of spherical triangles with a common base and otherwise exactly alike but in opposite hemispheres. Kant points out that such differences sometimes characterise different natural species, e.g. he says that all *hops* twine from left to right and all *beans* from right to left in their growth. Since his time we have learned that the occurrence of such counterparts among molecules determines the unlikenesses in the properties of certain organic compounds of exactly similar chemical composition and structure.

The history of Kant's dealings with this fact is as follows. The first published writing in which he uses it as the premiss for a philosophical argument is a short article, entitled *Von dem ersten Grunde des Unterschieds der Gengenden in Raume,* which appeared in 1768 in a Königsberg weekly journal.[1] The conclusion drawn here is that the facts are incompatible with the relational theory of space and compel us to accept the absolute theory. In 1770 Kant again made use of the same facts in his *Inaugural Dissertation.*[2] He now professes to infer from them that our knowledge of space is intuitive and not purely discursive. Kant made no use of these facts in his treatment of space either in the first edition of the *Critique of Pure Reason* (1781) or in the second edition (1787). But he had not ceased to think them important philosophically. They reappear in the *Prolegomena* (1783)[3] and in the *Metaphysical Foundations of Natural Science* (1786).[4] In both these works they are taken to show that spatial characteristics do not belong to things as they are in themselves, but are only ways in which such things appear when perceived by observers whose minds are provided with a certain

[1] [Eng. trans. in *Kant: Selected Pre-Critical Writings and Correspondence with Beck*, trans. by G. B. Kerferd and D. E. Walford (Manchester, 1968).]
[2] [*De mundi sensibilis atque intelligibilis forma et principiis*. Eng. trans. ibid.]
[3] [Eng. trans. *Prolegomena to Any Future Metaphysics That Will Be Able to Present Itself as a Science*, trans. by P. G. Lucas (Manchester, 1953).]
[4] [Eng. trans. by J. Ellington (Indianapolis and New York, 1970).]

innate form of sensibility. I will now consider each of these arguments in turn.

(1) *Von dem ersten Grunde* (1768). The argument here runs as follows. There is the following difference between two incongruent counterparts, viz. that anything, e.g. a glove, which exactly fits the surface of the one cannot possibly fit the surface of the other. Now this implies that there is a fundamental unlikeness between the *surfaces* of two incongruous counterparts. But, says Kant, the surface of a body is the limit of its extension, and is therefore something *intrinsic* to it. So he concludes that the unlikeness between two incongruous counterparts depends upon a difference in their *intrinsic spatial properties* and not on a difference in their *spatial relations to some third body*. But, on the other hand, this difference in the intrinsic spatial properties of two incongruous counterparts cannot consist in the parts of the one being *interrelated* in a different way from the parts of the other. For no such difference can be discovered.

This is certainly Kant's premiss here. As so often happens, he fails to state with complete clearness either the steps of his argument or the conclusion which he claims to establish. But I think there is no doubt that he held that the facts refute the Leibnizian doctrine of the relativity of space and compel one to accept the Newtonian doctrine of absolute position. I will now try to state in my own way what I think Kant may have had in mind.

I suggest that the conclusion which he draws here is this. The geometrical properties of a body are not ultimate but derivative. They do not consist in or depend upon direct unanalysable relations between the material particles which compose it, or between them and other material particles. On the contrary, they are derivative from a conjunction of two facts of entirely different kinds, one temporal and contingent, and the other timeless or sempiternal. The temporal contingent fact is that at a given moment each particle of the body is occupying a certain point of absolute space, a different point for each different particle. The timeless or sempiternal fact is that each of these points has timelessly or sempiternally its own determinate quality of absolute position, and that any two or more of them are interrelated timelessly or sempiternally by spatial relations which are founded upon and are necessary consequences of their several qualities of absolute position. Thus the geometrical properties of a body are consequences of the geometrical properties of the collection of points of absolute space which its particles happen to occupy, and the geometrical properties of any such collection of points of absolute space are founded upon the qualities of absolute position of the individual points.

If this is a correct account of the conclusion which Kant claimed to draw, how is it connected with the premisses from which he professed to derive it? The only explicit arguments which I can find are these.

(1) Kant says that it is logically possible that the first material thing to be created should have been a single human hand. Now, on a purely relational view of space, such a hand would have been neither a right nor a left hand. For, on that view, spatial relations hold directly between material particles and between nothing else. Now the mutual relations between the particles of a right hand are exactly similar to those between the corresponding particles of a left hand, and in the case supposed there are no other material particles except those. But it seems obvious to Kant that, if God had created a hand at all, it must have been either a right hand or a left hand from the very beginning. And it certainly seems plain that, if God should decide to create a second hand, he would have the choice of making one which was congruent to or was a mirror-image of the first, and that this would be a real pair of alternatives even if he were to annihilate the first hand before creating the second.

(2) Kant's second remark is difficult to state clearly, but I suggest that what he wishes to say may be this. Suppose that the geometrical properties of bodies *are* derivative from the qualities and relations of the points of absolute space occupied by their constituent particles. Then the set of points occupied by the particles of a body B might have certain geometrical properties to which nothing corresponds in the derivative mutual relations between those particles. So there might be two bodies, B and B', such that the derivative mutual relations between the particles of B correspond exactly to the derivative mutual relations between those of B', and yet the set of points occupied by the particles of B and the set of points occupied by those of B' might differ in some geometrical property which is not manifested in the mutual relations of the occupying particles.

Now admittedly only *bodies* and the spatial relations between their parts or between one *body* and another can be perceived by the senses. Therefore in the case supposed one would not be able to say anything about B alone which one could not equally say about B' alone, and vice versa. But it might be that the difference in geometrical property between the set of points occupied by the particles of B and the set of points occupied by the particles of B' would reveal themselves in certain observable differences in the derivative relations of B and B' to some third material object C, e.g. a glove.

So, if my attempts to interpret the argument and its conclusion are correct, the point which Kant wished to make is this. The difference between two incongruent counterparts is a difference in some *internal* property of them. But this cannot consist in a difference in the mutual relations of their corresponding parts, for there is none. Yet this is the only kind of internal difference which the relational theory of space could admit. So we can account for the facts only by distinguishing between the set of particles which constitute a body and the set of points which they occupy; by assuming that the geometrical relations between the former are derived from the geometrical relations between the latter; and by supposing that not all the geometrical properties of a set of points need be manifested in the derived mutual relations of the particles which occupy them.

This argument, whether valid or not, seems to me to be of great interest. For it is an argument for the absolute theory of space which confines itself to *geometrical* considerations and does not introduce kinematical or dynamical premises.

(II) The *Inaugural Dissertation* (1770). The facts are here used to show that space is something which has to be intuited and not merely conceived. The argument is as follows. Everyone can see that there is *some* difference between a right hand and a left hand, or a solid and its image in a plane mirror. But we find it impossible to *state* what this difference is. We can only *describe* it by taking some standard pair of incongruent counterparts, e.g. our hands, and saying of anything else that it resembles or is specially related to one or the other of the members of this standard pair. Kant says that the distinction *dari non intelligi*.

The difficulty seems to me to be to understand *how much* Kant thinks he has proved by this. I should be inclined to agree that we should not have got the idea of incongruent spatial counterparts unless we had perceived instances of such pairs of objects. But, when we have done this, we surely can and do form a general concept of incongruous counterpartness, and generalise it, and apply it to possible instances which we have never perceived. Even if the concept should be unanalysable, that would not prevent its being a concept; for presumably there must be some unanalysable concepts if there are any which are analysable. Moreover, we can certainly treat the whole theory of incongruent counterparts analytically, i.e. in terms of algebraical transformations and equations, though the interpretation of our algebraical formulae in spatial terms no doubt requires specifically spatial intuitions.

There is no doubt that what Kant generally wants to hold, in his doctrine that our cognition of space is intuitive and not conceptual, is that all spatial cognition presupposes the quasi-perceptual awareness of space as a single individual whole, in which particular figures are particular regions delimited by perceptible boundaries. I cannot see that the present argument has any tendency to prove that conclusion.

(III) *Prolegomena* (1783) and *Metaphysical Foundations of Natural Science* (1786). Here the same facts are taken to prove that space is something dependent on the mind of the observer.

The argument is very obscure, but I am inclined to interpret it as follows. I believe that he is really harking back to the old argument for absolute space in the *Von dem ersten Grunde* of 1768. Then there is a new premiss to the effect that absolute space would have certain properties which could not belong to a thing-in-itself but which might belong to a mind-dependent object of intuition. And so the conclusion is that space is a mind-dependent intuitum.

The argument starts in the old way by pointing out that the differences between incongruent counterparts must be intrinsic, although there is no intrinsic difference which we can describe in conceptual terms. Here, I think, should come a step which is explicit in the tract *Von dem ersten Grunde* but is not explicitly stated in the *Prolegomena*, viz. the conclusion that the facts require us to postulate absolute space which is logically prior to bodies and their geometrical properties. Then comes the new premiss, which I will state in Kant's own words. 'In absolute space the existence and nature of every part would be dependent on the existence and nature of the whole.' This I take to be simply the proposition that, although we can conceive of any bit of *matter* being annihilated and leaving an empty hole in the surrounding *matter*, it is nonsensical to talk of any region of *space* being annihilated and leaving an empty hole in *space*. The next step is this. Kant asserts that a thing-in-itself, i.e. something which is neither existentially nor qualitatively dependent on the mind of a percipient, could not have this peculiar property which is characteristic of absolute space. The only reason which he offers for this is that a thing-in-itself must be capable of being conceived by the intellect without help from intuition. He evidently assumes that the intellect is not capable of conceiving from its own resources a whole which is logically prior to its parts. So absolute space cannot be a thing-in-itself. On the other hand, Kant thinks that an intuited object which exists only in so far as it is actually intuited by someone might be a whole having this peculiar property. The fact is, I believe, that Kant thinks of space as a kind of mind-dependent undifferentiated visual field, which becomes differentiated into regions marked out in various special ways when we have special sensations.

Thus the conclusion of the argument is this. There is absolute space, for the reasons given in *Von dem ersten Grunde*. But it can no longer be regarded as an independent container in which things-in-themselves live and move and have their being, for it has a property which is incompatible with any such independent status. On the other hand, that property is compatible with its being a private mind-dependent *intuitum* in which various phenomena are so many sub-regions temporarily marked out by sensible qualities such as colours. So we must conclude that space is such a private mind-dependent intuitum. There is no incompatibility between the early tract and the later *Prolegomena*; the latter merely develops the conclusion of the former in a new direction by the use of new premisses.

2.2.3.1 Independent comments on the arguments

It would take me too far afield to discuss adequately the facts and the arguments. I will confine myself to the following remarks.

(1) There is one very important point which Kant does not explicitly notice, viz. that the facts in question are bound up with the number of dimensions which we assign to space. It is easy to show this as follows.

(a) We ascribe three and only three dimensions to the space of nature. Now all Kant's examples of incongruent counterparts are either *solids*, like the two hands, or *non-planar* curves, like the left-handed and right-handed spirals, or *non-planar* bounded surfaces, like the two spherical triangles.

(b) Kant remarks that *plane* bounded surfaces, e.g. a pair of *plane* triangles, are always congruent if they are exact counterparts. What he did not notice is that such figures *are* incongruent if we suppose them to be confined to a plane, i.e. a space of two dimensions. Consider, e.g., the two

scalene right-angled triangles 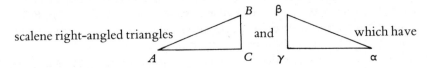 and which have

their corresponding sides equal. It is impossible to make either of them occupy a place previously occupied by the other by any process of sliding them about and turning them around, so long as they are confined to the plane in which they lie. It is impossible, subject to the same conditions, to set them so that each side of one is parallel to the corresponding side of the other. All these things can be done if and only if one is allowed to keep one side of one of them, e.g. *AB*, fixed in the plane and then turn the triangle *ABC* over about that side as an axis until it comes back into the plane with its opposite side upwards. But such an operation presupposes a third dimension, and so too does the notion of opposite faces. Thus we see that two-dimensional figures in a two-dimensional space may be incongruent counterparts. But, if two-dimensional figures in a three-dimensional space are exact counterparts, then they are necessarily congruent. Kant's example of incongruent counterpart spherical triangles falls under the heading of two-dimensional figures confined to a two-dimensional space. The space in question here is the surface of the sphere, to which the triangles are supposed to be confined.

These examples can be generalised into the following rule. In a space of *n*-dimensions any pair of figures of *less than n* dimensions will necessarily be congruent if they are counterparts. But there can be figures of *n* dimensions in such a space which are counterparts but are incongruent. If, however, this *n*-dimensional space be regarded as simply a section of an

$(n + 1)$-dimensional space, then the incongruent n-dimensional figures could be rendered congruent by a process in the $(n + 1)$-th dimension, analogous to turning the triangle ABC over about one of its sides as a fixed axis.

(2) If these are the facts, what precisely is their philosophical significance? I think that it may be put as follows. Consider any three figures, X, Y, and Z, in the same space, which are counterparts of each other. We may find that X *is* congruent with Y and that Z is *not* congruent with Y. Now, since X and Z are exact counterparts, they are two wholes, such that to each part of either there corresponds one and only one precisely similar part of the other, and such that corresponding parts in each are interrelated by precisely the same relations. Take, e.g., the two counterpart plane triangles ABC and $\alpha\beta\gamma$, which are incongruent when confined to a single plane. AB is exactly like $\alpha\beta$, BC is exactly like $\beta\gamma$, and CA is exactly like $\gamma\alpha$. And the corresponding angles are equal, so that all the mutual relations of corresponding parts are precisely the same in both triangles. Yet the two differ in a certain geometrical property. For one of them is, and the other is not, congruent with a certain third figure in the plane, e.g. with the triangle

$A'B'C'$.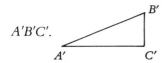

Now, no one would be surprised to find that two geometrically similar bodies differed in some of their *physical* properties, e.g. that one was soluble in nitric acid and the other was not. For we know that they might be composed of different materials, e.g. silver and gold. But in the case of incongruent counterparts the property in which they differ is a *purely geometrical* one. Now we do regard the *geometrical* relations of figures to each other as completely determined by the geometrical natures of these figures. Hence it seems impossible to believe that two figures which had no intrinsic geometrical dissimilarity to each other could yet have different geometrical relations to a third figure. Yet that is exactly what we do seem to find in the case of incongruent counterparts. I think that it is this apparent paradox which makes the case of incongruent counterparts of interest to philosophy.

(3) *Prima facie* two and only two types of solution seem to be possible.

(a) It might be suggested that the intrinsic nature of a figure is not completely exhausted by describing each of its geometrical parts and stating their geometrical relations to each other. If such a description leaves out some factor, then two counterparts may differ in respect of this factor in spite of the exact correspondence between their respective parts and the exact similarity of the relations between any two parts of the one and the corresponding two parts of the other. In that case we could understand how they may have different geometrical relations to a third figure. This appears to be the type of solution proposed by Couturat in the essay on Kant's theory of mathematics which is appended to his book *Les principes des mathématiques*.[1] He points out that, when two terms are related, we have to consider, not only the nature of the terms and the nature of the relations, but also the 'sense' or 'direction' in which the relation relates the terms. Let us take a non-geometrical example. There might be two events A and B, and two other events A', which is exactly like A, and B', which is exactly like B. And the only relation under consideration might be that of before-and-after in time. Obviously A might be *before* B and A' might be *after* B', or vice versa. Here we should have a case of *corresponding* terms related by the *same* relation but related by that relation in *opposite* senses. Couturat tries to argue that we have a similar instance of a more complicated kind in the case of a pair of incongruent counterpart figures. Corresponding sides are related by the same relation but in the opposite sense. It seems to me that there are difficulties and obscurities when one tries to work out this suggestion in detail, but I cannot go into them here and now.

(b) The other type of solution is to say that there is no *intrinsic* difference between two incongruent counterparts. Their difference consists simply in their having different relations to something other than themselves. But this other something is not another material thing; it is something of a radically different kind, viz. the space in which they exist. On this view the possibility or impossibility of superposing a certain figure X on a certain other Y, which is its counterpart, would in one sense be an adventitious property of X. For it depends on the actual relations of X to space, and it could have been altered even by us if there had been a fourth dimension and if we had had the power to do something analogous to turning the figure over in it. On the other hand, this property of X would *seem to us* to be intrinsic to it. For it would be an absolutely inseparable accident of X. The possibility or impossibility of superposing X upon Y would be wholly independent of the *materials* of which they were made, of the relations of X and Y to other bodies, and so on. Nothing that we could possibly do could alter this property of X. For the fact that we cannot perceive or operate in a fourth dimension, though quite contingent, would be a general condition governing every mechanical and physical change in nature as we know it.

This is obviously akin to Kant's solution in *Von dem ersten Grunde*. I think that there are strong objections to it also, but I cannot go into them here.

[1] [L. Couturat, *Les principes des mathématiques avec un appendice sur la philosopie des mathématiques de Kant* (Paris, 1905). See esp. pp. 292–7.]

2.2.4 The argument from our knowledge of geometry

Kant claims to prove from certain characteristics of our geometrical knowledge that space must be *a priori*, in the sense of being supplied by the mind of the human observer from its own innate resources. He also claims that it must be an object of *intuition* and not merely of discursive conceptual thinking. The argument appears in a very brief form in the first edition of the *Critique* (p. 68n, A24). It is stated much more fully in the second edition (pp. 70–1, B41–2). Much the same argument is in the *Prolegomena* in §2, §4, and the whole of the division called *How Is Pure Mathematics Possible?* The argument in the *Prolegomena* is rather more detailed, but there is no difference in principle.

The argument may be put as follows. All mathematical judgments have the following two characteristics. (1) They are *synthetic*, i.e. they do not state of a subject something whose notion is contained explicitly or implicitly in the notion of the subject. (2) They are assertions of facts which are and are seen to be *necessary*. I can say, not merely that the sum of the angles of any plane triangle is very likely to be equal to two right angles, but that it is necessary that it should be equal to two right angles. Now Kant's argument is that the synthetic nature of mathematical judgments proves that they rest on intuition and not on mere conception; and that the necessity of them proves that the intuition is not empirical perception but is, in a certain sense, *a priori*.

We will first consider Kant's premises and then his arguments. (1) We may agree that the propositions of pure mathematics are necessary. And Kant says that all that he requires is that this shall be admitted for *pure* mathematics. (p. 52, B15, and *Prolegomena*, §13, remark 1). For he thinks that the only way in which he can account for the necessary and synthetic character of pure mathematics will also guarantee its applicability to the existent world (*Prolegomena*, §13, remark 1). (2) The statement that all mathematical propositions are synthetic is perhaps less plausible. For the present purpose we can neglect arithmetical propositions and consider geometrical ones. Kant begins by pointing out three invalid reasons which have made people doubt that all geometrical propositions are synthetic. (a) When a complicated geometrical proposition is proved by logical deduction from other geometrical propositions it is true that the connexions between one proposition and the next in the chain of argument are analytic. But the axioms from which we start are themselves synthetic, and each proposition in the chain is synthetic. People confuse the fact that the hypothetical propositions 'If p then q', 'If q then r', 'If r then s' are analytic, with the proposition that p, q, r, and s are analytic (p. 52, B14, and *Prolegomena*, §2). I do not think that Kant consistently holds to this view. If he did he would have to hold that mathematical *reasoning* has nothing to do with intuition, and that it is only mathematical *axioms* which require intuition. But it is quite certain from what he says repeatedly elsewhere that he thinks that mathematical, and particularly geometrical, *reasoning* depend on intuition, and that he considers that this is proved by the fact that we draw figures and make constructions in proving geometrical propositions. What is certain is that Kant held that any connexion between propositions which is guaranteed by *formal logic*, e.g. the connexion between the premisses and the conclusion of a valid syllogism, rests ultimately upon the laws of identity, contradiction, and excluded middle; and therefore that the knowledge of such a connexion is analytic, even if the propositions thus connected be synthetic. (b) When people see that a proposition is necessary they are inclined to say that it must be analytic. For they say: 'Since *S must* be *P* the thought of *S ought* to contain the thought of *P*.' To this Kant makes the prefectly correct answer that what *ought* to be thought is not relevant, but only what *is* thought. If in fact a person can clearly understand what is meant by *S* without thinking of *P*, then the proposition '*S* is *P*' is not analytic no matter whether the connexion between *S* and *P* is necessary or contingent. Now, Kant remarks, a person can clearly understand what is meant by straightness (a purely *qualitative* conception) without thinking about distance (which is a *quantitative* conception). Hence the proposition that a *straight* line is the shortest *distance* between two points is synthetic, however necessary may be the connexion between the two concepts of straightness and shortest distance. (c) Kant admits that some propositions which are generally counted among the axioms of geometry are really analytic, e.g. that the whole is greater than its part. But geometry cannot get on with only axioms of this kind. And even such propositions need to be supplemented by intuition before we can see how they are to be interpreted in the special subject-matter of geometry. E.g. I suppose that Kant means that the notion of spatial whole and part is quite different from the notion of a whole class and a sub-class of it. And this seems to be true.

I shall have to discuss later on the question whether Kant was correct in holding that the propositions of pure mathematics, and in particular of Euclidean geometry, are necessary and synthetic. At present we will accept these two premises provisionally for the sake of argument, and consider the conclusions which Kant draws from them. The argument is as follows. If a judgment asserts of a subject *S* a predicate *P* which is not contained in the definition of *S* it must be because on actually inspecting instances of *S* we observe that they have the characteristic *P*. This is obvious in the case of singular empirical judgments. It is no part of the meaning of paper to be white. If I now say 'This paper is white' my only ground for the synthetic judgment is that I have looked at this paper and actually seen its whiteness. So Kant lays down the general principle that if

'S is P' be a synthetic judgment it must be based on the fact that we are directly acquainted with an S and that on observing it we have found that it manifests the characteristic P to us. This direct acquaintance with particulars, and with certain qualities which they manifest, is what Kant means by 'intuition' as opposed to thought or conception. So the synthetic character of geometrical judgments shows that they must be founded on intuition of some kind, i.e. on an immediate acquaintance with particulars, which reveals certain of their characteristics. But now we have to consider the other feature of geometrical judgments, viz. their universality and necessity. Ordinary empirical judgments, based on that kind of intuition which we call sense-perception, are of two kinds. Some are singular, like 'This paper is white'. Some are universal, like 'All lions roar'. Now neither is exactly like a geometrical judgment. *Singular* empirical judgments may be quite certain; but geometrical judgments are not merely singular. They are not about *this* figure that I happen to be looking at; they claim to be true of *all* figures of a certain kind. On the other hand, *universal* empirical judgments have no trace of necessity. They are simply inductive generalisations from observed to unobserved cases. And, as such, they are merely probable. Therefore, although geometrical judgments must be based on intuition of *some* kind, they cannot be based on the kind of intuition which we call 'sense-perception', and they cannot be of the nature of inductive generalisations. We want a kind of intuition which will reveal to us with complete certainty properties of things which we never have perceived and perhaps never will perceive. How can this requirement be fulfilled? (*Prolegomena*, §7.)

As Kant says in §8 of the *Prolegomena*, this requirement seems at first sight to be incapable of fulfilment. Intuition is acquaintance with particulars, and how can I be acquainted with particulars which do not yet exist, such as future triangles? Kant's answer in §9 of the *Prolegomena* is as follows. 'There is only one possible way in which my intuition can precede the reality of the objects and take place as knowledge *a priori* . . . It must contain nothing but that form of sensibility which precedes in my subject all real impressions by which I am affected by objects.' He then adds that I can *know a priori* that all objects of sense must be intuited in accordance with this form of sensibility, so that propositions concerning this pure form of sensible intuition will be valid for all possible objects of sense. But I can also be sure that I can have no *a priori* knowledge about the spatial characteristics of things-in-themselves; for there is no reason why they should accord with the conditions of the forms of my sensibility.

Kant's argument, then, comes to this. Space is an innate object of intuition which is mind-dependent and which can be intuited apart from all special sense-impressions. By intuiting it I learn its properties. But any extended phenomenon which I can ever be aware of will just consist of sensible qualities arranged in this innate container. Hence any geometrical properties which belong to the latter will also belong to the former. I can therefore be sure *a priori* that the laws of geometry will apply to all possible objects of sense perception. And, since there is no other theory of space which will explain my certainty of this, Kant's theory of space must be accepted.

This theory is open to several objections. (1) Kant evidently supposes that if space be *a priori*, in the sense of being a mind-dependent intuitum, my knowledge of its properties and therefore my knowledge of pure geometry must be *a priori*, in the sense of intuitively or demonstratively certain. This of course does not follow at all. Even if space were mind-dependent I should still have to learn about its properties by inspection. There would be no guarantee that its properties would be the same in all its parts, or the same on Tuesdays as on Fridays. It is a pure superstition that the mere fact that something depends on our minds is a guarantee that we can have adequate and accurate knowledge of it. This is obviously false in many cases. E.g. we have much more adequate and accurate knowledge of the constitution of the atom than of our own motives in many of our actions. So the mind-dependence of space would be no guarantee of the *a priority* of our knowledge of pure geometry. (2) When we come to applied geometry we have to distinguish two questions which Kant did not clearly distinguish. (a) Is the theory supposed to *account* for the fact that we believe very strongly that all objects of possible sense-perception will obey the laws of Euclidean geometry? Or (b) is it supposed to *justify* this belief without attempting to account for its origin? (a) It seems to me quite certain that the theory fails to account for the existence of the belief. No doubt, *if* a person believed that space was an innate container and that every perceived object is a region of this container pervaded by certain sensible qualities, he might be expected to believe that all the objects that he would ever perceive would have the spatial properties which characterise this container. But it is perfectly certain that, whether Kant's theory of space be true or false, it is not held by most people, and had never been thought of before his time. Hence the belief of most people that all objects that they will ever perceive will obey the laws of Euclidean geometry cannot be accounted for in this way. This belief is held quite as strongly by people who have never heard of Kant's theory, or who have rejected it, as by people who have accepted it. (b) The other alternative is that we must just accept the *existence* of the belief as an ultimate fact which Kant's theory leaves unexplained, but that Kant's theory and no other *justifies* this belief. Even this does not seem to me to be true. All that is really justified is the following proposition: 'In so far as my knowledge of the properties of my innate intuitum is accurate, and so long as these properties remain constant, I can be sure that any object that I shall perceive will obey the same laws of geometry.' But we could assert this much even if space were not mind-dependent. Suppose space were an independent container in which all the events of nature are arranged, as Newton held. Then I could equally say that so long as its properties keep constant all extended objects will obey the same laws of geometry. And I have no better guarantee that a container which depends on my mind will remain constant than that a container which is independent of my mind will do so. Indeed, I have rather less, since my mind is notoriously transitory and changeable, whilst an independent container might, e.g., be an attribute of God who is eternal, as Newton and Clarke were inclined to believe. (3) Kant has not proved even that space is *transcendentally a priori*. He would have proved this about cause and substance if we were to accept his arguments about the Transcendental Deduction of the Categories. For he does try to prove there that, if sensations should arise which could not be synthesised with our previous sensations on the same general plan as that on which these have been synthesised with our past sensations, they could not be *our* sensations. We should cease to exist as beings who can recognise our own identity through our changing experiences. So, if Kant is right, the categories would be essential factors in any possible organised experience of a self-conscious being. But he never even professes to prove this about space. He makes it quite clear from scattered remarks in the *Aesthetic* that he thinks that there could be intelligent beings with different forms of sensibility from ours. He does perhaps hold in certain late passages of the *Analytic* (e.g. *Refutation of Idealism*) that *some* form of spatial intuition is necessary if it is to be possible to recognise permanence through change. But he never suggests that this form of spatial intuition might not change in course of time for the same person, or that it must be the same in its determinate details for everyone. (4) The last criticism which I will make applies not only to this particular argument but also to Kant's theory of space as a whole. The belief which Kant has to account for and to justify is not merely each person's belief that all the objects that *he* will ever perceive will obey the same geometrical laws. What each of us believes is that all the objects which *any* human being will ever perceive will obey the same geometrical laws as the objects which he perceives have obeyed. This belief is neither accounted for nor justified by Kant's theory. Now it seems to me that this is just one aspect of a fundamental defect in Kant's theory of space. If space be an innate mind-dependent intuitum, then there are, strictly speaking, as many 'Spaces' (with capital 'S's) as there are different persons. But what each of us in fact believes is that there is one *common neutral* space, in which all bodies and all physical events and processes throughout all time have been, are, and will be located. I suppose that what Kant needed to do might be stated in modern terminology as follows. He needed to show, at least in outline, that our notion of a common neutral space is a legitimate 'logical construction' out of the innumerable subjective spaces each of which is private to a different individual percipient. This he never attempted; and he does not seem to have seen that it is required in order to reconcile his theory with beliefs which we all hold and which Kant himself regarded as in some sense justifiable.

2.2.5 Summary of Kant's theory of space

Before passing on to Kant's theory of time it will be useful to give a brief summary of the essential points in his doctrine of space in the *Transendental Aesthetic*.

My impression, for what it is worth, of what Kant taught about space in the *Aesthetic* is as follows. (1) He started from two already familiar alternative views about space. One was that of Leibniz, and the other that of Newton. We should nowadays express Leibniz's view by saying that the word 'space' is not a proper name for an existent substantive of a very peculiar kind. Space is a logical construction out of bodies and their spatial qualities and relations. This doctrine Kant definitely rejected, as failing to do justice to what we know about space. The other was that of Newton. This asserts that space *is* an existent substantive of a very peculiar kind; that it is logically possible that it should have existed without there being any bodies or other extended things; that the spatial qualities and relations of bodies are derivative from those of the regions of space which their particles occupy. Kant felt himself obliged for various reasons to accept something very like this alternative. (2) But he could not possibly swallow it in the form in which Newton had stated it. It seemed impossible to admit that infinite empty space was a kind of individual thing that could exist in its own right. As a matter of fact Newton had said vaguely that it is a kind of attribute of God; but Kant does not seriously consider whether anything can be made of this suggestion. (3) What Kant proposed might, I think, be formulated as follows. He proposes to assign to each percipient his own absolute space, and to make it subjective and innate to each individual human mind. He thus gets rid of the metaphysical difficulties in Newton's theory. But he is able to hold that each person's innate absolute space is a kind of individual whole with which that person actually is or conceivably might be directly acquainted. This kind of acquaintance he calls *pure* or *a priori* intuition, in contrast to acquaintance with particular things in space, which involves sensation. (4) When a person has an experience which we should describe as seeing an external object of a certain size and shape, localised at a certain place, what is happening is the following. (We are here confining our attention to the *intuitive* factors in the process, and ignoring the factors that belong to *thought*, which Kant regards as equally essential.) An independent foreign existent is producing an effect in the observer's mind, which may be called a 'sense-impression'.

This has a certain determinate sensible quality, e.g. a certain shade of red, but it has no spatial characteristics. Presumably, however, it has a certain determinate form of a certain determinable *non-spatial* characteristic which I have called the 'space-locating property'. The occurrence of such a sense-impression furnishes the occasion on which the observer's mind automatically presents to itself a certain region of its innate intuited absolute space as pervaded by a certain sensible quality and thus marked out from the rest. That which determines the precise shape, size, and location of the region thus marked out is the determinate form of the *space-locating property* possessed by the sense-impression. That which determines the sensible quality pervading that region is the sensible quality of the impression. (5) Since each of us is directly acquainted, through pure intuition, with his own private absolute space, and since it is innate to and wholly dependent on his mind, Kant thinks that each of us can have genuine *knowledge* of its properties. This knowledge is our knowledge of *pure* geometry. (6) Any extended external objects which a person could ever perceive would be simply a region of his own innate absolute space, which his mind presents to itself as marked out by certain sensible qualities on the occasion of having certain sensations. Therefore every proposition of pure geometry will certainly apply to every extended object that one could ever perceive. But there is no reason whatever to suppose that the independent foreign things, which produce the sensations on which our minds build up perceptions of extended, localised, coloured objects, are themselves extended or localised, any more than there is to suppose that they are coloured. (7) Suppose it were alleged that we derive our ideas of determinate shapes, sizes, and spatial relations by abstraction from per-ceived extended objects, and then proceed to generalise and amplify and idealise until we reach the refined concepts of pure geometry. Then I think that Kant would make two answers. (a) The empirical data would *not* lead to the concept of a single all-embracing infinite and infinitely divisible three-dimensional space, unless the processes of abstracting and general-ising and idealising were conducted in accordance with certain notions and principles which are innate in the mind. (b) In any case what you arrive at by all these processes is something which is logically prior to every particular extended localised perceptible object, viz. the innate absolute space in which any such object is simply a particular region marked out by certain sensible qualities. (8) We shall have to note, when we come to the *Transcendental Analytic,* that Kant's complete doctrine of space involves *a priori* factors of a *conceptual* kind which are expressed in the *Aesthetic.*

2.3 Theory of time

Kant says (p. 77, B49/A43): 'Time is nothing but the form of inner sense,

i.e. of the intuition of ourselves and our inner states.' In order to understand Kant's theory of time in the *Transcendental Aesthetic* we must face the
fact that Kant regards a person's introspective cognition of himself and his
own experiences as strictly analogous psychologically to sense-
perception. (I suppose that he would not deny that there are important
differences on the physiological side. Seeing and hearing involve special
organs, viz. the eyes and the ears. But there appears to be no analogy to this
in the case of introspecting.) Since Kant regards introspection as psychologically quite analogous to sense-perception, he will naturally apply
to the former the same kind of analysis which he has applied to the latter.
Now, according to Kant, what happens in ordinary sense-perception, e.g.
seeing, is this. A *foreign* thing affects a person's mind and produces a
modification in it, having certain non-spatial properties. Thereupon that
mind reacts by presenting to itself a certain region of its innate absolute
space as pervaded and marked out by certain sensible qualities. There is
absolutely no reason to believe that the foreign thing which produces the
modification in the person's mind has any spatial characteristics whatever.
Now apply this to the sort of experience which we should describe as a
person becoming introspectively aware of a feeling of anger. We shall have
to suppose either that a foreign thing affects that person's mind or that a
certain part of his mind affects a certain other part of it, and that in either
case a modification is thus produced in his mind. But *this* is a kind of
modification to which the mind reacts in a characteristically different way.
It does not now react by presenting to itself a certain region of its innate
absolute space as pervaded and marked out by a certain *sensible* quality, e.g.
a certain colour. Instead it reacts by presenting to itself a certain stretch of
its innate absolute *time* as pervaded and marked out by a certain *psychological* quality, viz. the emotional quality of anger. There is absolutely
no reason to believe that that which produces this modification, or the
modification itself, or one's own mind in which it is produced, has date or
duration or any kind of temporal quality or relation. But presumably the
modification must have some *non-temporal* quality or relation which
determines the particular date and the particular duration of the stretch of
time which the mind presents to itself as pervaded by the emotional
quality of anger.

Kant realises that this is a very queer theory about the nature of introspective awareness. He has found that many people who are willing to
accept his account of space and sense-perception refuse to swallow the
corresponding theory of time and introspection. He discusses this matter
on pp. 79–80 (B 53–5/A 36–8). The essential point which he makes may be
put as follows. People are inclined to say that, whether or not there be
change in the external world, there quite certainly is change in their own
minds. Their experiences do certainly succeed each other and last for

longer or shorter periods, and their minds do certainly persist through their various successive experiences.

To this Kant answers as follows. When I am introspecting I appear to myself to have successive experiences of various kinds, which last for various periods. When I am seeing I appear to myself to be in the presence of external objects of various shapes, sizes, and positions and colours. The realities which correspond immediately to these *physical* appearances are modifications of my mind which are intrinsically *non-spatial*. But they have certain determinate non-spatial characteristics which determine the shape, size, and position which the apparent physical things and events present themselves to me in sense-perception as having. Similarly, the realities which correspond immediately to these *psychological* appearances are modifications of my mind which are intrinsically *non-temporal*. But they have certain determinate non-temporal characteristics which determine the date and duration which the apparent psychological events and processes present themselves to me in introspection as having. He sums up by saying: 'Both are in the same position; in neither case can their reality as representatives be questioned, and in both cases they belong only to appearance . . .' (p. 80, B55/A38).

In spite of this, it does seem to me much harder to accept, or indeed to conceive clearly, the doctrine that particular existents only appear to have temporal characteristics, than the doctrine that they only appear to have spatial characteristics. The former view implies that nothing *either* changes *or* persists unchanged, that no two terms are *either* simultaneous *or* immediately successive *or* separated by an interval. If we take this seriously, what are we to make of Kant's statements that in sensation a foreign thing produces a modification in one's mind, and that in introspection the immediate basis of the psychological phenomenon which presents itself to one's mind is a modification produced in one's mind by certain of its own activities? Can we attach any meaning to such statements about modification and causation and activities except in terms of events and processes and the immediate sequence of an event in one thing on an event in another thing according to a rule?

Even if Kant's doctrine about the subjectivity of time be intelligible and consistent with his statements about sensations being modifications produced in the mind, it seems to me to be much less plausible than his doctrine about the subjectivity of space. When talking of spatial characteristics Kant does assume that sense-impressions are mental events and that mental events cannot literally have *spatial* qualities or relations. Both these assumptions are highly plausible and have been very generally accepted. Now it is certain that the objects which are presented to a person in sense-perception, on the occasion of his having certain visual sensations, are presented as extended, shaped, and localised. Hence it is more or less plausible to hold that the property of appearing to be spatial is imposed on perceived objects by the mind of the percipient. But, when we come to *temporal* characteristics, the case is different. It is not in the least plausible to hold that mental modification cannot literally have *temporal* qualities and relations, i.e. that it is literally false to talk of them as 'events' or to ascribe to them dates, durations, and simultaneity or sequence. On the contrary, any such view is widely paradoxical and most difficult even to conceive. But, if mental modifications can literally have temporal qualities and relations, then there seems no reason to suppose that the property of appearing to be temporal is imposed by the mind upon non-temporal objects in the process of introspecting. It is much more plausible to hold that introspecting consists in being directly acquainted with certain of one's own mental states, and that the temporal qualities and relations which they then appear to have really do belong to them.

2.3.1 Special arguments

Kant's special arguments about time in the *Transcendental Aesthetic* run parallel to his arguments about space, with the following exceptions. (1) There is, from the nature of the case, nothing comparable to the argument from incongruent counterparts. (2) It is by no means clear what science Kant supposes to stand to time in the relation in which geometry stands to space. Sometimes it seems to be a few propositions about the number of dimensions of time, and so on, sometimes the science of pure kinematics. Sometimes it seems to be suggested that the science is arithmetic, though I do not think that this is really borne out by Kant's statements. There is only one passage, viz. *Prolegomena*, §10, which suggests a parallelism between arithmetic and time, on the one hand, and geometry and space, on the other. It runs as follows: 'The pure intuition of space constitutes the basis of geometry. Arithmetic itself creates its concepts of numbers by successive addition of units in time. But above all pure mechanics can create its concepts of motion only by means of the presentation of time.' The natural interpretation of this is that the concept of number involves addition or counting, which involves succession; that arithmetic is thus closely connected with time; but that on the whole the connexion between pure mechanics and time is much more intimate, since time is *essentially* involved in the concept of motion and only adventitiously in that of number.

Arguments I and II on pp. 74–5 (B 46/A 30–1) correspond respectively to the first and second arguments to prove that our knowledge of space is *not empirical*. Arguments IV and V on p. 75 (B 47–8/A 31–2) correspond respectively to the first and second arguments to prove that our knowledge of space is *intuitive*. Sandwiched between comes argument III (p. 75,

B 47/A 31). This corresponds to the argument from the synthetic and *a priori* character of geometrical knowledge to the conclusion that space is a mind-dependent object of non-sensuous intuition. The science which is here taken to be specially connected with time might be called 'pure chronometry'. But Kant reverts to this type of argument on p. 76 in a new section which he added in B (B48–9). Here he takes as his basis the science of pure kinematics.

2.3.1.1 Arguments for the non-empirical and intuitive character of our knowledge of time

I shall not go into detail about arguments I and II or arguments IV and V. As in the case of the similar arguments about space I am inclined to think that the essential points in Kant's view of time are the following. For various reasons he found it impossible to accept Leibniz's relational theory of time. This may be stated in the form that the word 'time' is not a proper name for a peculiar kind of existent substantive. Time is a logical construction out of events and their temporal qualities and relations. This doctrine Kant rejected, as failing to do justice to what we know about time. Kant felt obliged for various reasons to accept something like Newton's view that time is an existent substantive of a peculiar kind; that it is logically possible that it should have existed without there being any events or processes occurring simultaneously or in succession; and that the duration and temporal relations of events and processes are derivative from those of the stretches of time which they occupy. But Kant rejected Newton's view that infinite empty time is a kind of individual thing that could exist in its own right. Kant proposes to get rid of such metaphysical difficulties by providing each self-conscious person with his own innate subjective absolute time, with which he actually is or conceivably might be directly acquainted through pure intuition. I think that this is the essence of what Kant had in mind when he asserted that our knowledge of time is non-empirical and that it is of the nature of acquaintance and not merely conceptual. It is open to much the same comments in these respects as his doctrine of space. I am inclined to think that the Leibnizian doctrine of the relativity of time is more obviously inadequate to the facts than the corresponding doctrine about space. To that extent I think that Kant is on somewhat stronger ground here. But in all other respects, as I have pointed out, his doctrine of time is much more paradoxical and less plausible than his doctrine of space. And it is difficult to reconcile it with his account of sensations as effects produced in the mind.

2.3.2 Argument from our knowledge of certain propositions about time

I will say a little about the argument by which Kant tries to prove both the *a priori* and the intuitive character of our knowledge of time by appealing to our alleged knowledge of certain synthetic and necessary propositions about it. In the first edition he takes as his propositions that time has only one dimension, and that different moments are successive and not simultaneous. This is what I called 'pure chronometry'. Now I should agree that the proposition that the *space* of human sense-perception is three-dimensional is synthetic. But I see no trace of necessity about it. In the case of the corresponding proposition that time is one-dimensional, I should be inclined to say that it is *either* synthetic but contingent *or* necessary but analytic. It seems to me that anyone who asserts that it is *impossible* for time to have more than one dimension is really basing his assertion on the fact that he would think it inappropriate to give the name 'time' or 'temporal' to any series which had more than one dimension. As regards Kant's second proposition, I should have thought that it is plainly analytic. If time has only one dimension, there can be only one kind of temporal distinction between a pair of moments or a pair of instantaneous events. Now a *moment*, as distinct from an instantaneous event, is by definition an instantaneous particular considered solely in respect of its determinate temporal position. Hence two moments must differ in their determinate temporal position, if they are to differ at all. And, since only one kind of difference of temporal position is possible, if time has only one dimension, to say that two moments differ in temporal position is equivalent to saying that they are successive. So it seems to me that neither of the propositions about time to which Kant appeals in argument III (p. 75) fulfils the condition of being both synthetic and necessary.

In the second edition (p. 76, B 48–9) Kant appeals to quite different propositions. Here his argument is as follows. The concept of change in general and of motion in particular is possible only through and in the representation of time. Unless we had an intuitive *a priori* representation of time, we could not conceive the possibility of change of any kind. The reason given by Kant for this assertion is that alteration implies 'the combination of contradictorily opposed predicates in one and the same object, e.g. the being and not being of one and the same thing in one and the same place'. This, he says, is possible only successively, i.e. in time. He goes on to add: 'Thus our concept of time explains the possibility of that body of *a priori* synthetic knowledge which is exhibited in the general doctrine of motion . . .'

What are we to say about this argument? (1) Certainly the notion of change involves the notion of succession and therefore of time. But this is true on any view of time and change. It has no tendency to support Kant's special theory that time is something which the mind contributes out of its own innate resources to the object which it presents to itself when it introspects. (2) Perhaps Kant wishes to argue that change in general, and motion in particular, could not be conceived unless we not only had the concept of time but actually intuited time. If so, I think that there is an important fact at the back of the argument. It seems to me that we should not understand what is meant by change and by motion unless we had actually been acquainted with changes and movements; e.g. unless we had *seen* flickering flames and moving clouds or had been *aware introspectively* of toothaches beginning, changing in character, and stopping. But, if that is what Kant had in mind, the fact would be better expressed as follows. The mere analytical concept of change as the possession by the same term of incompatible predicates at different moments is inadequate. There is a further change-quality or motion-quality, which can be revealed only by observing actual instances of it and contrasting them with instances of the quality of unvarying persistence or rest. But, if this is what Kant meant, it refers to change rather than to time as such. (3) I cannot see any logical connexion between the latter part of the argument, viz. the statement about pure kinematics, and the earlier part. Kant must be thinking here about the propositions on the composition of velocity and acceleration which appear at the beginning of treatises on dynamics. Now on p. 82 (A 41/B 58) Kant says definitely that the concept of motion presupposes something *empirical*, viz. the notion of something movable, which can be supplied only by sense-perception. And he says that even the concept of alteration, as distinct from motion, involves the empirically derived notion of something which exists in time. If that is so, it is difficult to see how the propositions of kinematics can be alleged to be something which we know *a priori* through our *a priori* intuition of time as an innate object independent of its empirical filling.

3 The nature of mathematics

The most complete account which Kant gives of his view of the nature of mathematics is to be found near the end of the *Critique,* in the first section of the part called the *Discipline of Pure Reason* (pp. 576–93, B 740–66/A 712–38). He is here concerned to show the differences between the methods of mathematics and philosophy, and to show that from the nature of the case the methods of mathematics cannot be employed in philosophy. It is plain that what Kant had primarily in mind was Euclidean geometry. He was struck with the part played by construction in the proofs in it, and he came to the conclusion that in all mathematical reasoning there must be construction of some kind. I should suspect that his theory was made up primarily to deal with geometry, and was then extended rather forcibly to arithmetic and algebra, where it is much less plausible. We will consider geometry, arithmetic, and algebra in turn.

3.1 Geometry

Kant says that it is characteristic of mathematics to start from *definitions* which are clearly adequate and from *axioms* which are self-evident and to reach conclusions which are rendered intuitively certain by *constructions and demonstrations*. He tries to show that there is nothing analogous to this in philosophy or empirical science. His illustrations are nearly all taken from geometry, and his remarks apply primarily to it.

(1) *Definitions*. Outside mathematics there is nothing strictly analogous to the definition of a figure, e.g. a circle, in geometry. In the first place, we may contrast it with an empirical concept of a natural kind or species, such as gold or horse. Strictly speaking, such concepts cannot be defined. We can, of course, take a certain set of perceptible qualities as marking out 'gold' or 'horse'. But in doing so we assume that this small set of perceptible qualities is a reliable sign of all the other innumerable characteristic properties of the species in question. E.g., the so-called definition of a man as an animal with two legs and no feathers is useful only in so far as we have reason to expect from past experience that anything that has these two properties will have all the other properties of what we commonly call a man. We have no guarantee that this expectation will always be fulfilled. And if in any case it should break down, we should hesitate to call a creature a man even if it had two legs and no feathers.

Secondly, one can never be sure that any attempted definition is adequate in the case of concepts which Kant regards as *a priori*, e.g. the concepts of cause, substance, etc. For these concepts are given to us in a confused form in the judgments which we make which involve them. Attempted definitions represent attempts to make the concepts clear and explicit, and one can never be sure that the analysis is adequate, even if it be accurate so far as it goes.

There is one and only one case where we can be certain that our definitions are both correct and adequate. This is when we arbitrarily make up a concept for ourselves and assign a name to it. As Kant says: 'Since it is such as I have deliberately made it to be, I must know what I have intended to think in using it' (p. 587, B757/A729). But the question then arises: 'What guarantee have you that there is anything answering to the concept which you have made up?' To this Kant replies that there is one and only one case where this question can be answered satisfactorily. 'There remain therefore no concepts which allow of definition except only those which contain an arbitrary synthesis that admits of *a priori* construction. Consequently mathematics is the only science that admits of definitions' (p. 587, B757/A729).

What Kant means is this. Suppose I define a circle as a plane curve all of whose points are equidistant from a fixed point. Then (a) I am not attempting to analyse a concept which I have derived by abstraction from perceived objects, e.g. pennies or biscuits. Nor am I trying to analyse a concept which is given to me in a confused form *a priori*. All that I am doing is to put on record that I propose to think of a plane curve all of whose points are equidistant from a fixed point, and to call it a 'circle' for short. (b) I can actually construct a figure answering to this definition, either on paper or in my mind's eye. I could do the latter even if I had never seen a physical object answering to the definition and had no compasses and paper for drawing one. For I am provided with a private innate absolute space with which I am acquainted by pure intuition. In this I can construct imaginatively, without help from sensation, any figure which I choose to define, whose nature is compatible with its properties. (c) Kant seldom distinguishes sharply between pure and applied mathematics. But I think that his argument could be continued as follows. For *pure* geometry all that is needed is this imaginative construction of something intuitable which answers to the arbitrary concept. But this imaginative construction takes place in pure space and time. Now any empirical object which can ever be presented to me will be presented as a region of my innate space marked out, for a certain stretch of my innate time, by certain sensible qualities. Thus I can be sure that any geometrical proposition which holds for a figure which I have constructed imaginatively will also hold for any empirical object which may happen to have that shape.

(2) *Axioms*. Outside mathematics, according to Kant, there are no propositions which are both self-evident and synthetic, and therefore no axioms in the mathematical sense. Kant's view is that one can never discover any necessary connexion between two concepts *a* and *b* by merely reflecting on them and comparing them, except in the trivial case where *a* is a conjunctive concept and *b* is a conjunct contained in it. He says: 'One concept cannot be combined with another synthetically and also at the same time immediately, since, to be able to pass beyond either concept, a third something is required to mediate our knowledge' (p. 589, B760/A732). Now in the one case of mathematical concepts we can construct imaginatively in our private absolute space and time an instance of the concepts. And we can inspect this by pure intuition. We may then be able to see (in the sense of knowing by acquaintance) the connexion between the two concepts. According to Kant, e.g., no amount of reflection on the mere concepts of *straightness* (which is purely qualitative) and *distance* (which is quantitative) would enable you to know for certain that the shortest distance between two points is the straight line joining them.

But you have only to imagine two points and then to join them in your mind's eye by a straight line and by other curves, and you will see directly that the two characteristics of straightness and shortest distance are necessarily connected.

Kant draws the conclusion that no synthetic *philosophical* proposition, e.g. 'Every event has a cause', can be directly seen to be necessary. 'The synthetic propositions of pure transcendental reason are . . . infinitely removed from being as evident . . . as the proposition that $2 \times 2 = 4$' (p. 589, B761/A733). On Kant's view all such propositions need proof, and the proof consists always in showing that without them such an experience as ours would be impossible. The mediating factor in all such cases is that human experience exists and that it has certain very general characteristics. 'Through concepts of understanding pure reason does, indeed, establish secure principles . . . [but it does this] not . . . directly from concepts alone, but always only indirectly through relation of these concepts to something altogether contingent, viz. possible experience' (p. 592, B705/A737).

(3) *Demonstrations*. Outside mathematics, according to Kant, there are no genuine demonstrations. The reasons are similar to those given in the case of axioms. Kant uses the word 'demonstration' here in a restricted sense, and not in the wider sense in which it is equivalent to any kind of conclusive proof. By a 'demonstration' Kant means literally 'pointing out in an actual instance, so that it can be distinctly seen'. His view is that in a geometrical proof each stage simply consists in placing the reader in a position to see (literally or with his mind's eye) the truth and necessity of some proposition which he was not in a position to see before. He takes as an example (pp. 578–9, B744/A716) the proof in Euclid of the proposition that the sum of the angles of a plane triangle is equal to two right angles. Take, e.g. the triangle ABC. The first step is to produce a side, e.g. BC, to D. This enables one to see directly that the angle ACB and ACD are together equal to two right angles. The next step is to draw a line CE within the angle ACD and parallel to the side AB. This enables one to see directly the following three facts. (a) That the angle $ACD = ACE + ECD$. (b) That ACE = the alternate angle CAB. (c) That ECD = the interior and opposite angle ABC. When one has seen these facts all is over except the shouting. The rest of the proof is merely analytical. We must agree with Kant that nothing in the least like this procedure is possible in philosophy, where we are concerned with concepts which cannot be exemplified in concrete intuitable instances.

3.1.1 Comments on Kant's account of geometry

(1) Kant's theory of geometry was of course based upon the conception of

geometry which was universally accepted in his time. One and only one system of pure geometry was known, viz. Euclid's, and it was not suspected that alternative systems of pure geometry can be worked out and shown to be self-consistent. Nowadays any system of *pure* geometry, including Euclid's, would be held to consist entirely of *conditional* propositions, viz. propositions of the form 'If such-and-such primitive propositions be supposed, then any figure answering to such-and-such a definition will have such-and-such properties.' The primitive propositions between them constitute the defining features of a particular system of pure geometry. Thus, e.g., if the primitive propositions of Euclidean geometry be supposed, then the circumference of any figure answering to the definition of a circle will be proportional to its radius. But, if the primitive propositions of hyperbolic or of elliptic geometry be supposed (and these are equally self-consistent), then the circumference of such a figure will *not* be proportional to its radius. Now in Kant's day everyone assumed that the primitive propositions of Euclidean geometry are not just *postulates*, i.e. propositions which are not asserted to be true but are simply supposed in order to work out their consequences. Everyone assumed that these primitive propositions are *axioms*, i.e. propositions which are, and can be seen to be, necessarily true. In that case of course anything that necessarily follows from them is also necessarily true. So the fundamental difference is this. According to modern geometers the only necessary propositions in a system of pure geometry are of the conditional form 'If P then Q', where P is a conjunction of the primitive propositions of the system. The antecedent propositions P are not alleged to be necessary or even to be true; they are merely supposed in order to work out their consequences. And the consequent propositions Q are not alleged to be necessary or even to be true; all that is alleged is that they *necessarily follow from* the antecedents. According to the geometers of Kant's day, the antecedent propositions P are, and can be seen directly to be, necessarily true. And therefore the consequent propositions Q are, and can be demonstrated to be, necessarily true. On this view, pure geometry contains necessarily true *categorical* propositions, viz. the axioms and their consequences, and not merely necessarily true conditional propositions stating that such-and-such consequences would follow from such-and-such suppositions. This was the view of geometry which Kant took as the basis for his philosophy of space. Since this view of geometry is no longer held by any competent mathematician, it can no longer be taken as an admitted basis for philosophical speculations and constructions.

(2) On the old view of geometry the philosophical questions raised by *pure* geometry would be these. (a) Granted that the axioms and their consequences are necessarily true categorical propositions, what are they true *of*? What is the *subject-matter* of pure geometry? Is it a peculiar kind of

existent substantive called 'space'? Or is it the spatial qualities and relations of *bodies*? As we have seen, Kant felt obliged to take the former alternative. (b) Granted that we can see directly that the axioms are necessarily true, and can demonstrate that the theorems follow from them and are therefore necessarily true also in their own right, how can we possibly know such things? Do we get our knowledge of the axioms merely by reflecting on concepts, such as straightness, distance, etc.? And is the process by which we derive our knowledge of the theorems from our knowledge of the axioms just ordinary logical inference, such as is treated, e.g., in the doctrine of the syllogism? As we have seen, Kant felt obliged to answer both these questions in the negative. He thought it incredible that a person could come to see a *synthetic* connexion between two concepts merely by reflecting upon them, and obvious that a person could not arrive at knowledge of a *necessary* connexion by inductive generalisation from observed instances of *de facto* conjunction. And he thought that the actual practice of geometers in proving theorems by the use of figures and constructions shows that geometrical demonstration is not just ordinary logical inference.

(3) On the modern view of pure geometry the question 'What sort of entity or entities are the propositions of a system of pure geometry about?' ceases to be significant. For the question presupposes that the primitive propositions of such a system describe the fundamental properties of certain existents of a peculiar kind, viz. points, lines, planes, etc., and that the theorems deduced from them describe the properties of more complex entities, viz. figures of various kinds, composed of points, lines, etc. But when a word like 'point', 'straight line', etc. occurs in a system of pure geometry, all that it comes to is this. A point, e.g., is *any* term a symbol for which can significantly occupy certain positions in the formulae expressing the primitive propositions of the system. A staight line, e.g., is *any* term a symbol for which can significantly occupy certain other positions in those formulae. And so on. Whether there are in nature or in our minds several or one or no kinds of existent entity answering to this description of a point or this description of a straight line, and so on, is a matter of complete indifference to the pure geometer. He does indeed need to satisfy himself on one matter, viz. whether a given set of primitive propositions is *self-consistent*. Now one way of doing this would be to point to things which we actually perceive and which obviously do answer to all the primitive propositions of the set. In such cases it might fairly be said that intuition is appealed to as a guarantor. But this does not help Kant's case. For, in the first place, the intuition which is appealed to is ordinary sense-perception. And, secondly, what it is required to guarantee is not the *truth* of the several primitive propositions of the system but their *consistency* with each other. Generally, however, we cannot show the consistency of a

set of primitive propositions in this way. The usual procedure of pure geometers is the following. They take it for granted that there is no contradiction in pure *arithmetic*. They then try to show that, if *numbers* be substituted, in accordance with certain rules, for the symbols for points, straight lines, etc. in the formulae for the primitive propositions, the latter become self-evidently true propositions of pure arithmetic. If they can think of rules for substituting numbers which will lead to this result, they conclude that the set of primitive propositions in question is self-consistent. Now in a very wide sense this might be called 'constructing the concepts of a system of pure geometry in the number-system'. But this, again, does not help Kant's case. For to exemplify geometrical concepts in terms of certain *numbers* and their arithmetical relations can hardly be called constructing them in *intuition*, and is obviously not what Kant had in mind. And, again, this construction is needed only to prove the *consistency* of the primitive propositions with each other, and not to prove the *truth* of them individually.

(4) As regards the nature of geometrical demonstration, it is now known that all the theorems of Euclid can be deduced by ordinary logical reasoning (though not by merely *syllogistic* reasoning), without the use of an actual or imaginary figure, from a comparatively small number of primitive propositions. The set of axioms proposed by Euclid is inadequate for the purpose, but that is a purely contingent defect which can be rectified. It is known, moreover, that sets of primitive propositions which differ in part from those which characterise Euclidean geometry and are inconsistent with the latter, are internally consistent and lead to equally complete alternative systems of pure geometry. In geometrical arguments, especially in Euclidean geometry, the use of a figure is often very helpful. But it is never essential, and it always introduces a danger of fallacies. If we want to know exactly what we are assuming and exactly what follows from it, it is safest to avoid all appeal to figures.

(5) A person might admit all that I have been saying and then argue as follows: 'Euclidean geometry *can* be regarded as just one system of pure geometry out of a large number of alternative systems, each of which is internally consistent, and all of which are inconsistent with each other. But we do not in fact regard it in that way. We are not content to say that Euclid's theorems are just a necessary consequence of Euclid's primitive propositions (or more accurately of these when suitably supplemented). We know that Euclid's theorems are *true*, because we know that his primitive propositions, from which the theorems follow, are true. These primitive propositions are not merely supposed for the sake of argument, they are facts which we know about the space of nature. And such facts can be known only by constructing and intuiting figures either in actual perception or in imagination.' What are we to say about this?

(6) The axioms of Euclid are no doubt ultimately derived by reflecting upon the spatial qualities and relations of bodies with fairly sharp outlines, on figures drawn with chalk or pencil, and on figures called up in imagination. And historically there is no doubt that the notion of alternative systems of geometry developed out of Euclidean geometry. The first alternative systems to be worked out differed in respect of only one primitive proposition from Euclid's. They differed only in rejecting his postulate that through any point outside a straight line there is *one and only one* straight line coplaner with it, which does not intersect the given straight line in either direction. Lastly, it must be admitted that most of us in fact find it impossible to imagine and very difficult to conceive an external world in which Euclid's axioms did not hold. This is what makes Kant's assertion that they are synthetic *a priori* propositions, founded on some kind of intuitive cognition of particular existents, so very plausible, even if we reject the details of his theory of space and of sense-perception.

(7) It seems to me that the axioms of Euclid are not all on a level and that we can distinguish them on the following principle. We can subdivide systems of geometry in the first place as follows. (a) Those which define a space in which it is geometrically possible for a body of given size and shape to be moved, without stretching or distortion, from any one place to any other. These are called *homaloidal*. The surface of a sphere is a two-dimensional example of a homaloidal space, so too is an ordinary Euclidean plane. (b) Those which define a space in which this is *not* geometrically possible. These are called *non-homaloidal*. The surface of an egg is a two-dimensional example of a non-homaloidal space. Now systems of geometry which define a homaloidal space may be subdivided as follows. (i) Those which define a space in which it is geometrically possible for there to be what are called 'similar figures', i.e. figures of precisely the same shape but of different size. These may be called *flat* homaloidal spaces. A two-dimensional example is an ordinary Euclidean plane. (ii) Those which define a space in which this is *not* geometrically possible. These may be called *curved* homaloidal spaces. A two-dimensional example is the surface of a sphere. Now the axioms of Euclid define a *flat homaloidal space of three dimensions*. We can therefore subdivide the axioms of Euclid as follows. (I) Those which distinguish a Euclidean space as *flat* from other kinds of homaloidal space. It is in fact the famous *parallel postulate* which does this. (II) Those which are common to Euclidean and other kinds of *homaloidal* space, and which distinguish them all from non-homaloidal spaces. These may be called the *axioms of free mobility*, to use a phrase of Russell's.[1] (III) Those which are common to all forms of metrical geometry, whether they define homaloidal or non-homaloidal spaces. An example would be the axiom that the shortest distance within a

[1] [B. Russell, *An Essay on the Foundations of Geometry* (Cambridge, 1897).]

given space between two points in that space is the straight line in that space which joins them. Let us now consider these three classes of axiom in turn.

(I) No intelligent person who studies non-Euclidean geometry has any difficulty in the end in conceiving the possibility that the Euclidean axiom of parallels may be false. One sees that two distinct notions, viz. the non-intersectance and the equidistance of two coplaner straight lines, have become extremely strongly associated in our minds. The difficulty is to overcome this association and to conceive the former in the absence of the latter. The fact is, I think, that the evidence for the axiom of parallels is empirical, but of rather a peculiar kind. The position is as follows. The laws of geometry and the laws of physics together form a single hypothesis to unify the observable facts of sight, touch, movement, etc. Suppose we assume that light in a homogeneous medium travels in straight lines, that a tightly stretched thin thread is practically rectilinear, and so on. Then it is certain that we can bring all ordinary observable facts about light, sound, electricity, motion, etc. under laws of a mathematically simple form, on the assumption that the space of nature is Euclidean. If we wanted to test that assumption further, we should have to make measurements on very large triangles, e.g. triangles whose corners are three distant stars, and see whether the sum of the angles differed appreciably from two right angles. Suppose we found that there was an appreciable divergence, and that it was found to be greater for larger triangles than for smaller ones. Then we should have to make *one or other* of the following two suppositions. Either(1) that light from distant stars *does* travel in straight lines, but that the space of nature is *not* Euclidean; or (2) that the space of nature *is* Euclidean, but that light from distant stars does *not* travel exactly in straight lines. We should probably choose the former if and only if the latter compelled us to reformulate most of the laws of physics in a much more complicated form. For the formulae of Euclidean geometry are considerably simpler than those of any alternative system.

(II) The axioms of free mobility, i.e. those which are common to *all* systems of geometry which make space *homaloidal*, are in a different position. They are involved in the distinction which we all draw between space and things in space. For they really amount to saying that *mere* change of position cannot *as such* make a difference to the shape or size of a body. Now this denial of causal influence to space itself is the only way in which space could be distinguished from a material medium continuously distributed throughout space. It seems to me therefore that these axioms are analytic, in the sense that they are part of what we mean by talking of space as distinct from materials which occupy space.

(III) Lastly I will consider an axiom common to all systems of metrical geometry, whether they define homaloidal or non-homaloidal spaces, viz.

the axiom that the shortest distance between two points is the straight line joining them. In the first place, this needs to be formulated more accurately as follows: 'If p and q be two points in the space defined by the geometry G, then the shortest of all the paths from p to q which are wholly confined to that space is the straight line joining p to q.' Now in the case of a *non-homaloidal* space I suspect that this axiom is a purely analytic proposition. For in such a space no meaning can be attached to the notion of 'straight line' except that of shortest possible path. The qualitative aspect of the concept of straightness ceases to apply, so far as I can see. But in a *homaloidal* space a straight line does have certain purely qualitative features. It is the one and only kind of line which has the following properties. (1) Each of such lines is completely determined by a *pair* of points. (2) *Every* pair of points determines one of these lines. (3) Any one of these lines is equally determined by any pair of points on it. So the proposition that the straight line joining two points in a homaloidal space is the shortest of all the alternative paths between them which are wholly confined to that space might seem to be synthetic. But I am not sure that it is. If distance is no part of the meaning of straightness, is not straightness part of the meaning of distance? How could one measure the distance between two points along a path which was *not* straight, except by imagining the curved path to be divided into an infinite number of infinitely short *straight* segments of varying direction adjoined end to end, and taking its length to be the limit of the sum of the lengths of these straight segments? If so, the basic axiom would seem to be that two sides of a triangle are together greater than a third side. This certainly seems self-evident. I should hesitate to say whether it is analytic or synthetic.

3.2 Arithmetic

The case of arithmetic is much less complex. It has never been suggested that there are several alternative systems of pure arithmetic, each internally consistent, and all inconsistent with each other. So there is no question which, if any, of them applies to the actual world. No one worth considering doubts that the propositions of arithmetic are necessary and that they are known *a priori*. The only question therefore is whether they are *synthetic*, and whether our *a priori* knowledge of them depends upon some kind of non-sensuous intuition.

Kant firmly maintained that arithmetical propositions are synthetic. He says that, however much you may reflect on the concepts of 7 and of 5 and of addition, you will never be able to see that $7 + 5 = 12$. For this purpose you must exemplify the numbers by dots or by your fingers, and must carry out the process of adding by counting the whole collection of dots which you have set down. You will then find that, when you have counted all the dots, you have got to the number 12. He says that this is still more obvious if you take larger numbers. No one would pretend that by merely reflecting on the concepts of 35728, 46391, and addition, you could see that the sum of these two numbers is 82119. These preliminary remarks occur in the Introduction to B, section v, §1 (p. 53, B 15–16). Kant develops his views of number and arithmetic more fully at later stages of the *Critique*. The following passage from the *Transcendental Analytic* (p. 112, B 104/A 78) is important: 'Our counting, as is easily seen in the case of the larger numbers, is a synthesis according to concepts, because it is executed according to a common ground of unity, as, e.g., the decade . . .' To this we may add the following passage from the *Schematism of the Categories* (p. 182, B 179/A 140). 'If five dots be set alongside one another, thus . . . . . , I have an *image* of the number 5. But if . . . I think only of a number in general, whether it be 5 or 100, this thought is rather the representation of a method whereby a multiplicity . . . may be represented in an image in conformity with a certain concept, than the image itself. For with such a number as 1000 the image can hardly be surveyed and compared with the concept. This representation of a universal procedure of imagination in providing an image for a concept, I entitle the *schema* of this concept.'

So far, I think, Kant's doctrine about arithmetic is fairly clear. With smaller numbers you can produce actual instances of each number by writing down dots or by some such means. As the first lot of dots remains on the paper when your write down the second lot, the aggregate of dots at the end of the process is an instance of the sum of the two numbers. If you now count this aggregate, the number that you reach is the number which is the sum of the two original numbers. But with larger numbers this method is not practicable, and is obviously not the method which we in fact use. What we do is to write down the symbols for the two numbers, in accordance with the Arabic notation on the scale of ten. (This is what Kant meant by the phrase about 'a common ground of unity, as, e.g., the decade'.) We then perform certain operations, in accordance with rules which we learned at our preparatory schools, and derive a new symbol. This represents, in accordance with the Arabic notation on the scale of ten, the number which is the sum of the two original numbers. Now Kant regards the Arabic notation as a rule for producing an instance of any given number, which makes it unnecessary actually to write down and count the dots which would constitute an instance. Take, e.g., the symbol 324. The rule for producing an instance of the number which this symbolises might be stated as follows: 'Write down ten rows each containing ten dots and do this *three* times; then write down one row of ten dots and do this *twice*; then write down *four* dots.' His view is that, in order to find the sum of two numbers, you must *either* produce actual instances of each and then count the instances, *or* have a system of symbols which you can write down and operate according to rules which enable you to dispense with actually instantiating the numbers of dots and actually counting the aggregate.

Now, if this is what Kant meant, it seems to me to be correct so far as it goes. But it calls for the following comments.

(1) What is the position about intuition in arithmetic? The sense in which we have to appeal to intuition seems to be different for small numbers and for larger ones. Probably it is only by operating with dots or fingers or something similar that we can originally discover the propositions about numbers which enable us to set up a single uniform method for symbolising *any* number in terms of a few fundamental symbols, e.g. the digits 0, 1. . . 9. But, after this notation has been set up and the rules for operating it have been deduced, there is no need to appeal to intuition in the original sense. We no longer need to construct and operate with actual collections of dots, etc. which instantiate the numbers in question. But in a wider sense we still have to appeal to intuition, viz. to the actual symbols on paper or in our mind's eye, which symbolise, in accordance with the rules of the notation, the numbers with which we are concerned.

(2) Where does the necessity of arithmetical propositions and the *a priority* of our knowledge come in? On Kant's view this ought to be somehow connected with the intuition being non-sensuous and being concerned with the innate intuita of space or of time or of both. But fingers and dots are objects of ordinary sense-perception, and so too are figures in the Arabic notation with which we do addition sums. Certainly *I* do not think that these facts have any tendency to show that arithmetical propositions are contingent or that our knowledge of them is merely empirical. But the question is how *Kant's* account of arithmetic fits in with his own view that it is necessary and that our knowledge of it is *a priori* and with his own view of the nature of *a priori* knowledge. All that I can say about this is that Kant certainly thought that there is some special connexion between arithmetic and the innate *intuitum* of time. But his statements are very obscure. In *Prolegomena*, §10, he says: 'The pure intuition of space constitutes the basis of geometry. Arithmetic creates its concepts of number by successive addition of units in time . . .' In the *Schematism of the Categories* (p. 184, B 182/A 143) he says: 'Number is . . . simply the unity of the synthesis of the manifold of a homogeneous intuition in general, a unity due to my generating time itself in the apprehension of the intuition.' I am far from clear as to the precise meaning of these statements, but it seems to me quite clear that they do not explain how the propositions of arithmetic are necessary and our knowledge of them *a priori*. Kant's theory of geometry does derive a certain plausibility from the fact that geometers draw figures and make constructions in proving their propositions and that nevertheless the argument evidently does not depend on whether the figures which

they draw answer exactly to the concept of exact straight lines, triangles, circles, etc. But there is nothing at all closely analogous to this in the procedure of arithmeticians, and certainly nothing to connect arithmetic with time as geometry is connected with space.

The problems which are solved by ordinary arithmetical processes may be illustrated as follows from simple addition: 'Given the symbols in the Arabic notation on the scale of ten for each of the numbers m and n, find the symbol for the number $m + n$.' Most of us at most times solve such problems by applying quite blindly rules which we learned by heart when we were children, and most of us never know the reasons for such rules. But of course there *are* reasons, and these are necessary propositions which can be proved by ordinary logical reasoning from self-evident premisses. Time, and our intuition of it, are in no way involved either in the concept of numbers in general, or in the concepts of particular numbers, or in the concepts of arithmetical operations such as addition and multiplication.

3.3 Algebra

Kant has very little to say about algebra. The only two passages which I can find are the following. Both come from the section called *Discipline of Pure Reason*. The first runs as follows: 'Even the method of algebra, with its equations from which the correct answer, together with its proof, is deduced by reduction,[1] is not indeed geometrical in nature, but is still constructive . . . The concepts attached to the symbols, especially concerning the relations of magnitudes, are presented in intuition. This method . . . secures all inferences against error by setting each one before our eyes . . .' (p. 590, §3, B762/A734). The other passage is as follows: 'In algebra by means of a *symbolic* construction, just as in geometry by means of an *ostensive* construction, i.e. the geometrical construction of the objects themselves, we succeed in arriving at results which discursive knowledge could never have reached by means of mere concepts' (p. 579, B745/A717).

It seems to me that Kant has now completely changed the sense in which he is using the phrase 'constructing a concept in intuition', and that in the new sense it bears no relation to the theory of mathematical reasoning with which he started when discussing geometry. In geometry 'constructing a concept' meant actually or imaginatively drawing a figure answering to the concept. In the arithmetic of small numbers it meant making a real or imaginary collection of dots which had the number in question. Such constructions are *ostensive* or *instantial* because they symbolise the concept by producing a concrete intuitable instance of it. At this stage Kant's theory appears to be roughly that geometry and arithmetic are *synthetic*

[1] I.e. solving an equation.

because we can and must make instantial constructions of our concepts in order to see their interconnexions; and that our knowledge of these interconnexions is *a priori* because we can make these constructions imaginatively at will in the innate absolute space or time which we intuit independently of sensation.

The simplicity of this view has already begun to fade when we deal with the arithmetic of large numbers. Here the intuited object by which we construct the concept is admittedly not instantial. It is not a collection of (say) seventy thousand two hundred and forty-seven dots. It is only the perceived or imagined *symbol* for this number in the Arabic scale of notation of the base of ten. Now in algebra we have a still further departure from the original sense of ostensive or instantial construction. We now introduce what Johnson[1] calls *illustrative* symbols, in addition to what he calls *shorthand* symbols. Our x's and y's stand, not for some definite number which they symbolise in accordance with a rule, as e.g. the symbol '479' does, but for *any* number chosen at random as an illustration.

As a matter of fact, our figures in geometry are really illustrative symbols of a peculiar kind. Suppose I am proving a general proposition about triangles, and that I draw a triangle. The figure drawn must be equilateral or isosceles or scalene, but, whichever it may be, it will be taken to illustrate triangles of all shapes and sizes. This is recognised by Kant in the numerous passages in which he insists that the intuitive construct of a geometrical concept is not really an image or a picture but a schema. The following passage is typical: 'No image could ever be adequate to the concept of a triangle in general. It would never attain that universality of the concept, which renders it valid of all triangles, whether right-angled, obtuse-angled, or acute-angled . . . The schema of a triangle can exist nowhere but in thought. It is a rule of synthesis of the imagination in respect to pure figures in space' (p. 182, B 180/A 141).

The substitution of schema for image or picture does not, however, remove the radical difference between the sense in which we construct concepts in geometry or in the arithmetic of small numbers and that in which we do so in the arithmetic of large numbers and in algebra. The schema of a triangle is not indeed an image or picture of a triangle, but it is a rule for imagining or drawing triangles. That is, it is a rule for making instantial construction, even though it is not itself an instantial construction. The schema of a number of several objects would seem to be a rule for writing down the symbol of the number in the Arabic notation on the scale of ten, rather than a rule for forming a collection of dots which has the number in question. And the schemata in algebra can only be rules for making *symbolic* construction, since no instantial constructions are here possible. Now Kant's original theory of mathematical reasoning, derived

[1] [W. E. Johnson, *Logic*, pt. 2 (Cambridge, 1922), ch. 3.]

from reflection on geometry, presupposed that the concepts are constructed *instantially* in our innate intuition of space and time. It loses all meaning when applied to the construction of non-instantial *symbols* for concepts, as distinct from accurate or approximately accurate *instances* of concepts.

It seems to me that Kant has provided no theory whatever of algebraical reasoning or of arithmetical operations with larger numbers. If we look at the remarks about algebra which I have quoted, we see that they might equally well have been made by Leibniz, whose theory of mathematical reasoning is utterly different from Kant's. All that his remarks come to is that a good system of symbolism, which makes all our assumptions explicit and can be operated mechanically according to rules, is very useful for enabling us to avoid fallacies and to solve complicated problems. But the question arises: Why should it be confined to mathematics? Why should it not be applied, e.g., to logic? On Kant's earlier theory, which makes mathematical reasoning depend on the *instantial* construction of concepts in the innate intuita of space and time, we can see why such reasoning must be confined to the properties of figures and numbers. For these are the only concepts which can be instantially constructed by us in imagination. But Kant is now extending the notion of construction in intuition to cover merely symbolic non-instantial construction of concepts. Of course these constructions will still be spatio-temporal, since the symbols will consist of perceived or imagined letters or marks of some kind. But there is no reason why concepts which have nothing to do with space or time should not be represented *symbolically* by spatio-temporal symbols. And of course this is in fact done when diagrams or symbols are used in logic.

3

THE TRANSCENDENTAL ANALYTIC

1 General remarks on the Analytic

This is the hardest, the most original, and the most important part of the *Critique*. It is here, if anywhere, that Kant answers Hume; and, whether he succeeds in this or not, he certainly says a great many things of extreme philosophic importance. The arrangement and subdivisions of this book rather obscure the argument, and I do not propose to follow them in the lectures. The actual arrangement is as follows. (1) Kant distinguishes between ordinary and transcendental logic. He tries to show that the analogy between the two is so great that we shall be able to make an exhaustive list of all the categories or pure conceptions of the understanding by following the ordinary divisions of the various kinds of judgment which are given in books on formal logic. (2) He produces a list of twelve categories, divided into four sets of three, and professes to show, from the intimate connexion between transcendental and ordinary formal logic, that these are all the categories that there can be. (3) Then comes an extremely important and difficult section entitled *Transcendental Deduction of the Categories*. This is an attempt to prove by a transcendental argument that such an experience as we actually have would be impossible unless we had and applied certain concepts which are not derived by abstraction from anything that is presented to us in sensation. He tries to prove in this way that these concepts must apply to all objects of possible sense-perception, but that they have no clear meaning and presumably no application when we try to extend them beyond the range of possible sense-perception. Now the title of this section makes one expect that it will contain a detailed proof that each of his twelve categories may and must be applied to all objects of possible sense-perception. But it contains nothing of the kind. In the *Transcendental Deduction* of the first edition nothing is said about the twelve categories or about the alleged analogies with formal logic which led to their discovery. And in the *Transcendental Deduction* of the second edition very little is said about it. It is almost true to say that in the whole of the section called *Transcendental Deduction of the Categories* nothing is said about any of the twelve categories except cause and substance. This defect, however, is remedied in a later section called *Analytic of Principles*. Here Kant really does try to prove in detail by transcendental arguments that his twelve categories may and must be applied to all objects of possible sense-perception, and that this leads to certain *a priori* principles which must be true of all such objects. (4) But he sandwiches between the end of the *Transcendental Deduction* and the beginning of the proofs of these *a priori* principles a large slice of further reflections on formal logic in general and transcendental logic in particular. This ends up with an important section entitled the *Schematism of the Categories*. He here distinguishes between the categories as such, and the 'schematised categories' which may roughly be described as 'the categories confined to existence in time'. All this ought to be taken along with the part that precedes the *Transcendental Deduction*. And the *Transcendental Deduction* ought to be followed immediately by the proofs of the *Principles of Pure Understanding*, which is a detailed development of the general results reached in the *Transcendental Deduction*.

So the order that I shall adopt is the following. (1) I shall take together (a) all that comes before the *Transcendental Deduction*, and (b) all that comes after it up to the beginning of Kant's proofs of the *Principles of Pure Understanding*. I.e. I take together pp. 92–119 (B 74–116/A 50–83) and then pp. 176–97 (B169–202/A130–61). This may be entitled *The Discovery of the Categories and Principles by help of Formal Logic*. (2) Then I take together the *Transcendental Deduction* and the proofs of the *Principles of Pure Understanding*. I.e. I take together pp. 120–75 (B116–69/A84–130) and then pp. 197–256 (B 202–94/A 162–235). I will entitle this *The Transcendental Deduction of the Categories and the Principles*. It is here, if anywhere, that Kant answers Hume.

2 Discovery of the categories and principles by help of formal logic

2.1 Discursive and intuitive cognition

Kant says that knowledge, properly so called, arises only from a combination of two different mental faculties. One is the capacity for being affected in various ways by foreign things and thus receiving sense-impressions. A sense-impression in itself is a mere modification in the state of one's mind. It is in fact due to a certain foreign thing and makes one aware of its presence, but it does not by itself constitute cognition about the nature of that thing. But, on the occasion of receiving an impression, the mind may judge that the object which is thus presented to it is of a certain kind and has certain characteristics, e.g. that it is a white horse. This Kant calls an act of *thought*, and in particular an act of the *understanding*. We may call the experience of having an individual object presented to one by sensation an *intuitive* cognition, and we may call the act of making a judgment about an object thus presented a *discursive* cognition.

Kant uses one word, *Vorstellung*, commonly translated by the word 'representation', to cover (1) the sense-impressions produced in us by an object by which we become aware of its presence, and (2) the thoughts of the qualities, relations, etc. which we ascribe to objects as predicates when we make judgments about them. The word *Vorstellung* is, I think, practically equivalent to the word 'idea' as used by Locke. But Kant uses 'idea' in a very special technical sense, and therefore it would be unsatisfactory to translate *Vorstellung* by 'idea'. On the other hand, I think that 'representation' has many misleading associations. I am going to use the artificial word *presentation*, which is an almost literal translation of *Vorstellung*. I shall then talk of sense-impressions as *'intuitive* presentations' and of thought as *'discursive* presentations'. Kant uses the word 'concept' for discursive presentations. As we have seen, Kant held that the spatial and temporal characteristics, which all perceptible objects are perceived as having, are supplied by the mind from its own resources. No doubt the determinate shape, size, position, etc. which one perceives a particular object as having on a particular occasion are determined by *something* in the sensations by which the foreign thing is presented to one. But this feature in the sensations is certainly not itself spatial or temporal, and there is no reason to believe that there is anything spatial or temporal in the foreign thing which is being presented to one by the sensations. So, according to Kant, there is a pure *a priori* element in all our perceptual cognition, notwithstanding the fact that such cognition in human beings always involves sensation. Kant is now going to raise the question whether the mind does not also supply from its own resources certain *conceptual* elements, i.e. certain *discursive* presentations. His answer is that it does. He argues that, unless it did, no coherent experience of a world of persistent things and persons, forming a single spatio-temporal and causal system, could arise. These pure or *a priori* concepts are what Kant calls 'categories'.

2.2 Transcendental logic

Taking this as a hypothesis, we can imagine a branch of philosophy which would deal with the *non-empirical conceptual* elements which the mind contributes to perceived objects, and only with this. Kant calls this *transcendental* (as opposed to *general*) *logic*. It might be defined as the science of the *a priori* conceptual elements in our cognition of objects, where *a priori* is understood to mean 'supplied by the mind from its own resources'. It would determine the scope and objective validity of such cognition. Kant distinguishes two parts of it, which he calls *analytic* and *dialectic*. We can ignore the latter for the present. The former is subdivided into two parts. One of these is concerned with the discovery of a complete list of the primary *a priori* concepts and with the question whether and within what limits they can justifiably be used. This is called *analytic of concepts*. Now

Kant thought that certain very important synthetic *a priori* propositions, involving these concepts, can be shown to hold necessarily of all objects which could possibly be perceived. An instance is the law of universal causation. These synthetic *a priori* propositions, involving the categories, are called by Kant *principles of pure understanding*. The second part of the *Transcendental Analytic* deals with them, and is entitled *Analytic of Principles*.

2.3 Nature of judgment

Kant's explicit account of judgment is in terms of subsumption under concepts. But he proceeds to make statements about judgment, and to make applications of the classification of judgments by logicians, which can hardly be reconciled with this view. It is unfortunate that he seriously discusses only one example, viz. the universal affirmative judgment 'All bodies are divisible'.

Kant's explicit theory, so far as I can understand it, is this. In sense-perception an object is cognised by what he calls an 'immediate' presentation of it, viz. the sense-datum by which it is presented to the percipient. Let us call this a *percept*. Suppose that on such an occasion I make the singular judgment which would be expressed by the sentence 'That is a house'. Then what I am doing primarily is to connect in thought *this* percept with certain other percepts, in virtue of certain common characteristics which make them all instances of *house*-percepts. These common characteristics were abstracted in the past by noting the outstanding resemblances between certain percepts, ignoring the unlikenesses, and thus forming the concept of house. Now in connecting in thought this percept with certain other percepts, I am also indirectly connecting in thought the *immediate object* of this percept with the immediate object of all other house-percepts. Kant definitely asserts that no *concept* is ever related immediately to an object. The only kind of presentation which is immediately related to an object is an *intuitive* presentation, i.e. what I have called a 'percept'. A discursive presentation, i.e. a concept, can relate to an object only mediately, and the last stage in the mediation must always be a percept.

Let us next consider an affirmative universal judgment, e.g. that which would be expressed by the sentence 'All houses have roofs'. Here the subject is no longer presented directly by perception; it is presented in thought by a concept, viz. that of house. Now, according to Kant, what we are primarily doing in making the judgment is to connect in thought the concept of house with certain other concepts, e.g. that of a stable, etc., in virtue of certain common characteristics which make them all subordinate to the concept of having a roof. In this judgment the predicate-concept 'having a roof' is referred immediately and explicitly to the subject-concept 'house'. But the subject–concept 'house' may itself be regarded as the predicate of a possible judgment of the form 'This is a house'. In that capacity it would refer immediately and explicitly to a certain percept, and mediately to a certain object. In this way the predicate-concept 'having a roof' refers indirectly, through a chain of intermediate links, to objects of sense-perception. Kant says explicitly that every concept may be regarded as the predicate of a possible judgment, and he seems to hold that every *empirical* concept, at any rate, refers ultimately, through a longer or shorter choice of intermediary presentations, to percepts and thence to perceived objects.

It is unfortunate that he does not tell us what he thinks is happening when we make particular judgments, such as 'Some houses are white', or negative judgments such as 'No houses are bomb-proof'. The only general summary which I would venture to make is this. Every judgment involves two presentations. At least one of these, viz. the predicate-presentation, *must* be a concept. The subject-presentation may be either a percept or a concept. To entertain a concept involves connecting in thought certain subordinate presentations, either concepts or percepts, in virtue of certain common features or resemblances. Therefore every judgment involves at least this kind of cognitive synthesis in the mere fact of entertaining the concept or concepts which occur in it. But every judgment involves a further act of cognitive synthesis in connecting in thought the subject-concept and the predicate-concept. Kant has given some account of his view of this in the one case of the universal affirmative judgment. But he has not stated his view of it in the cases of the other kinds of judgment which he recognises.

2.3.1 The table for classifying judgments

Immediately after this very imperfect account of the general nature of judgment Kant gives a table of headings under which judgments can be subdivided exclusively and exhaustively without reference to their content. If we look at this table, we note the following points in it. It is divided into four main heads, viz. *quantity, quality, relation*, and *modality*. Each head has three subdivisions under it; e.g. under *quantity* we have *universal, particular* and *singular*. Now, so far as I can see, *every* judgment is supposed to have *one and only one* of the three characteristics under *each* of the four main headings. Thus every judgment has some form of quantity, some form of quality, some form of relation, and some form of modality; whilst no judgment has *more than one* form of any of these. It would seem therefore that there must be 3^4, i.e. 81, different possible forms of judgment. An example of one of them would be a singular negative hypothetical assertoric judgment.

The table is in the main taken from the ordinary text-books on Aristotelian formal logic. But Kant made some changes, and he makes some remarks which should be noted. We will consider these before making criticisms.

(1) Kant quite rightly distinguished singular from universal judgments, although, for the purpose of working out the valid moods of the syllogism, logicians were accustomed to treat singular judgments as if they were universal. But obviously the judgment 'Socrates is mortal', which assigns an individual to a class, is fundamentally different from the judgment 'All men are mortal', which assigns a sub-class to a wider class.

(2) Under the head of quality the logicians distinguish only two possibilities, viz. affirmative and negative. They are concerned only with the nature of the copula and not with that of the predicate. They would therefore count 'S is P' as affirmative and 'S is not P' as negative, and would have no special name for 'S is not-P'. They would count the latter as affirmative. Kant holds that a judgment expressed by a sentence with an affirmative copula and a *negative* predicate involves a different kind of mental act from one expressed by either an affirmative or a negative copula and a *positive* predicate. He calls such judgments, e.g. 'The soul is not-mortal', *infinite*. I agree with Kant that 'S is not-P' is very different from any *affirmative* judgment with S as subject and a positive predicate. It is compatible with S having *any* positive predicate which is other than P and does not entail P. Kant no doubt uses the term 'infinite' because the collection of positive predicates which are left open to S by the judgment 'S is not-P' is unlimited. What is not so clear is that there is any fundamental difference between the judgment expressed by the sentence 'S is not-P' and that expressed by the sentence 'S is-not P'. If there is any difference, I think it comes to the following. If I were to say 'Hydrogen is-not green' I should commonly be understood to imply that this gas has some colour or other, but that its colour is other than green. Suppose I were to say 'Hydrogen is not-green'. This is a phrase which in fact hardly ever occurs outside books on logic or philosophy. But, if I did use it, I might be understood to be contemplating both the alternative that hydrogen gas has some colour other than green and the alternative that it has no colour at all. So Kant may perhaps be justified in distinguishing 'S is not-P' both from ordinary affirmative judgments with positive predicates and from the negative judgment 'S is-not P'. But, if so, ought he not to have considered also the case of a judgment with a negative copula and a negative predicate, viz. 'S is-not not-P'? In that case he would have had a four-fold subdivision under quality, and the symmetry of his table would have been lost.

(3) We now come to a remark which is highly significant. Kant admits that the fourth heading in his table, viz. *modality*, is in a wholly different

position from the other three. The first three headings exhaust all the possiblities about judgments considered in themselves. Modality, with its three subdivisions *problematic*, *assertoric*, and *apodeictic*, is concerned only with what Kant calls 'the value of the copula in relation to thought in general'. What he has in mind is the kind of differences expressed by the sentences '*S* may be *P*', '*S* is in fact *P*', and '*S* must be *P*'. It seems to me that the best way to look at modal sentences is to regard them as expressing judgments about judgments. Thus '*S* may be *P*' = '*S* is *P* is possible', and '*S* must be *P*' = '*S* is *P* is necessary'. '*S* is in fact *P*' = '*S* is *P* is true but not necessary'. However we may express it, Kant is certainly right in holding that there is a profound difference between his fourth main heading and the other three. But, if so, what guarantee have we of the completeness of a table of headings which is not made on any *one* general principle?

(4) Kant makes another highly significant remark about the third main heading *relation*. In the technical sense in which he here uses the phrase it covers the distinction between categorical, hypothetical, and disjunctive judgments. Now in this connexion Kant remarks that *all* relations of thought in judgment are either (a) of predicate to subject, or (b) of ground to consequent, or (c) of 'divided knowledge and of the members of the division taken together'. In the first kind we consider two *concepts*, in the second two *judgments*, and in the third *several judgments* which are mutually exclusive and collectively exhaustive in a certain field.

This calls for several comments. (1) In Kant's explicit theory of judgment he has dealt exclusively with the relation of subject and predicate between two concepts in a categorical judgment. Not a word has been said about the relations of categorical judgments as wholes to each other in hypothetical or disjunctive judgments. (2) The subdivisions under this heading are unsatisfactory. Obviously *categorical* is not on the same level as *hypothetical* and *disjunctive*, since each of the two latter presuppose the former. It seems to me that only two remedies are possible here. (a) One is to confine the main heading entirely to compound judgments formed by various kinds of logical synthesis out of simpler propositions which are all in the last resort categorical. We should then get the three subdivisions *conjunctive, hypothetical,* and *disjunctive,* i.e. '*p* and *q*', 'if *p* then *q*', and '*p* v *q*'. The subdivision *categorical* vanishes. (b) The other alternative would be to have two primary divisions, viz. *relation of concepts* and *relation of judgments*. The first of these would be undivided, and would be equivalent to *categorical*. Under the second there would be three, viz. *conjunctive, hypothetical, disjunctive*. On either alternative the symmetry of the table vanishes, and we have to introduce a certain relation between judgments, viz. the conjunctive relation, which Kant has omitted. (3) The notions of quantity and quality are concerned primarily with *categorical* judgments. It is not by any means obvious how they are to be applied to hypotheticals or disjunctives. What is the quantity and the quality of the hypothetical judgment 'If some *S* is *P* then no *S* is *Q*'?

There seems to be no doubt, in view of Kant's explicit statements and of the use which he proceeds to make of the table, that he held the following view about it. It is supposed to give an exhaustive list of all the fundamental modes of connecting terms in thought which a human mind employs in making judgments. In making any judgment on any topic a person will necessarily be connecting in his mind presentations (some of which must be, and all of which may be, conceptual) in one or another of the three ways under each of the four main headings in the table. The completeness of the table is supposed to be known with absolute necessity from reflecting on the nature of judgment. I think that the following things are clear from my comments on the table. (1) It is not founded on any one principle. The first three main headings are concerned with primary judgments, whilst the fourth, *modality*, is concerned with secondary judgments, i.e. judgments about judgments or propositions. The first two divisions, again, are concerned primarily with distinctions among *categorical* judgments, and have no obvious application to hypotheticals or disjunctives. (2) The third main heading *relation* and its subdivisions are incoherent. Categorical judgments cannot be put on a level with hypotheticals and disjunctives. To make this part coherent the notion of *conjunctive* judgments must be introduced, and the whole scheme of subdivisions rearranged. (3) The table has extremely little connexion with the explicit theory of judgment which immediately precedes it and is supposed to justify it. That theory is confined to categorical judgments, and even so, no categorical judgment is discussed in detail except the universal affirmative. For all these reasons I conclude that we have no guarantee whatever for the conclusion that in making a judgment a person will necessarily be connecting in his mind presentations in one or another of the three ways under each of the four main headings in the table.

2.4 Transition to the table of categories

From the table for classifying judgments Kant passes to his table of the categories. He thinks it certain that the systematic completeness of the former guarantees that of the latter. The transition occurs on pp. 111–13 (B 102–6/A 76–80). It is most obscure, and would certainly be quite unintelligible without reference to what comes later, in the *Transcendental Deduction of the Categories*. We have already met with synthesis of *presentations in a judgment*, which is ascribed to a faculty called *understanding*. Kant now suddenly throws at the reader the important and fundamentally new idea of synthesis of various *presentations in an intuition*. This is ascribed to a faculty called *imagination*, which has hardly appeared hitherto, but is destined to play an important part in the *Transcendental Deduction*.

2.4.1 Imaginative synthesis

Kant tells us almost nothing intelligible about this imaginative synthesis of various presentations in an intuition except in certain parts of the *Transcendental Deduction of the Categories* in the first edition. I think it is possible to guess the kind of thing which he had in mind, and to see that it is very important. But the details are extremely obscure and puzzling. I propose to discuss it under the following three headings: (1) What *is* imaginative synthesis? (2) What are the data to be synthesised? (3) What is the product of the synthesis?

2.4.1.1 What is imaginative synthesis?

We can start with a quotation from p. 111 (B 103/A 77). 'By *synthesis*, in its most general sense, I understand the act of putting various presentations together, and of grasping what is manifold in them in one cognitive act.' Now I think that the following would be a rough example of the kind of facts which Kant had in mind. A person, who is past infancy and has been familiar with the things which we call 'bells', now takes certain noises, certain visual sensa, and certain tactual sensa, as so many different appearances of a certain persistent physical object, e.g. a certain bell. But such sensa are not in the least alike in quality. The noises occurred along with many other simultaneous sounds in an auditory field, the visual sensa along with many other simultaneous colour-expanses in a visual field, and the tactual sensa with many other simultaneous tactual sensa. Gradually certain sensa have been discriminated from the rest of the auditory field and have been associated with certain sensa which have been discriminated from the rest of the visual field and with certain sensa which have been disciminated from the rest of the tactual field. When one is aware of a sensum of one of these kinds now (e.g. a certain characteristic auditory sensum) it calls up images of the associated sensa of the other kinds. And so on. This is a process of synthesis. As a result of it you have, on any given occasion, a single complex experience, consisting of a sensation of a certain kind (e.g. that of clanging repetitive noise) complicated by images of sensa of other associated kinds (e.g. an image of the visual appearance of a bell). There is a great deal more involved beside this, but it will serve to illustrate what Kant meant by synthesis. The product here is something which might be called *a percept* of a certain physical thing, viz. a certain bell.

Now I think that Kant would call what I have been describing so far an 'empirical synthesis'. This means that the details in the result depend upon the nature of the sensations which one is having now and the nature of the sensations which one has had in the past. If one were now having a *whistling* auditory sensation instead of a clanging one, and if one had had certain visual and tactual sensations in the past along with whistling auditory sensations, the result of the synthesis would be a percept of a *whistling locomotive* instead of a percept of a *striking bell*. But Kant would say that all the various empirical syntheses, which produce percepts of this or that particular thing of this or that particular kind, presuppose *pure* or *a priori* synthesis. Now I am pretty sure that one part of what he meant is that they all take place in accordance with certain very general rules, which constitute a kind of common ground-plan or theme. And I am practically certain that another part of what he meant is this. This fundamental ground-plan for synthesising a plurality of sensations of various kinds, had on various occasions, into the percept of a single physical object, is something innate to the human mind. We instinctively put upon the complex wholes formed by empirical synthesis of sense-data and images a certain kind of interpretation, which is not forced upon us by anything in our sensations but is imposed by us upon them. And we discriminate and join together certain sensa and ignore others because we have this inter-pretative scheme in mind.

In order to see what kind of grounds there are for such statements let us consider what we all take to be essential features in the notion of any physical thing, e.g. a stone or drop of water. (1) We will begin with temporal characteristics. (a) We think of it as having a continuous history through time, and existing and occupying space and interacting with other things during periods when we are not perceiving it. That is, we think of it as a *substance* or *continuant* which has various states or occurrents at successive times. (b) We think of it as combining at one and the same time many different qualities, of which some are capable of being manifested to one sense, e.g. sight, others to another sense, e.g. touch, and some perhaps to none of our senses. When we are only seeing it, we believe it to have still such qualities as temperature, hardness, etc. And, when we are only touching it, we believe it to have still such qualities as colour. That is, we think of it as a substance which has many *contemporary* attributes. (2) Next, take its spatial characteristics. We think of it as a solid three-dimensional object having an inside as well as an outside, a back as well as a front, and so on. We think of the back as *coexisting* with the front, although we never perceive both at the same time. And it may fairly be said that we never perceive the *inside* of anything, except in so far as something which *was* inside is opened out and becomes a part of the outside. (3) So far I have considered only the temporal and the spatial characteristics of each physical thing taken separately. Let us now take them collectively. (a) We take for granted that all events, and therefore the histories of all substances, can be dated in a single time-system. (b) We distinguish, moreover, between the temporal order in which we happen to perceive or to remember two events and the objective temporal order in which they occurred. E.g. I perceive first the flash of a distant gun and some time later the bang, but I believe that the physical events which manifest themselves to me by the auditory and the visual sensation are simultaneous. This distinction is certainly bound up with considerations about causation. (c) All physical objects and all physical events are held to be located in a single spatial system of three dimensions. This system is supposed to be independent of lapse of time, so that one can talk of a body occupying at a later moment *the same position* as was occupied by itself or by another body at an earlier moment. (4) Reverting to individual things, we think of each thing as having a number of causal or dispositional properties, what Locke called 'powers'. We think of it as acting upon and being acted upon by other things in various characteristic ways. And we think of its actual history as being one particular manifestation of the possibilities latent in it, which is called forth by the particular circumstances in which it has found itself. E.g. it was solid at a certain period because the surrounding temperature was below its melting-point, and liquid at a certain other period because the surrounding temperature was above its melting-point. A thing of a different kind would have had a different history in similar circumstances, and this thing would have had a different history if the circumstances had been different in certain respects.

Now contrast all this with our sensations and images as they come and go if we just sit passively and receive them without any interpretative presuppositions. If I shut my eyes, my whole visual field vanishes; if I turn my head, it changes altogether. My images come and go in a temporal order which bears no relation to the order of the events which gave rise to them. Regular sequences of sensations even of a crude kind are the exception rather than the rule. The more subtle sequences would certainly never have occurred unless we had deliberately arranged suitable conditions, under the guidance of our belief in persistent substances subject to causal laws, and with a view to testing some suggested particular causal law.

In view of these facts, positive and negative, the following conclusion seems not unreasonable. Suppose we had just passively received our sensations and images as they come and go. Suppose we had not approached them and selected them and connected them in accordance with a certain innate scheme of interpretation, involving concepts such as substance and cause, which cannot possibly be literally manifested in sensation. Then they, and their mere *de facto* sequences and coexistences, would never have sufficed to produce anything like the commonsense view of the external world. As Kant puts it in a famous sentence, our experiences would have been 'a mere play of presentations, less even than a dream'. (For, after all, in a dream we do take ourselves to be in the presence of persistent independent interacting things and persons, however mistaken we may be in detail.) Now we do all in fact hold this commonsense view of the external world, and it is implicit in the grammatical forms of our language with its nouns and adjectives and verbs – active and passive, transitive and intransitive – and so on. Therefore we must admit the existence and the fundamental importance of this innate interpretative scheme. That, at any rate, was Kant's view in outline; and these, I think, were some of the facts at the back of it.

Kant ascribes the process of synthesis to a department of the mind which he calls 'imagination'. He describes this as 'a blind but indispensable function of the soul, without which we should have no knowledge whatever, but of which we are scarcely ever conscious' (p. 112, B103/A78). By calling the imaginative process 'blind' I think that Kant means two things. First, that we are not as a rule conscious of it. And second that, although it takes place in accordance with certain innate principles, we are not conscious of these principles at the time and are not deliberately following them. The process might be compared with the development of an embryo or with talking in accordance with the rules of grammar. He says that we do not get knowledge, properly so called, until the synthesis has been 'brought to concepts' by the understanding. I think that this means until we make judgments about perceived objects. The logical forms of the judgments which we make about physical objects, e.g. the subject-predicate form, the conditional form, and so on, correspond to and make manifest the fundamental rules which we have unwittingly followed in synthesising sensa and images into percepts. Finally there comes the stage of philosophical reflection. We then form explicit concepts of the fundamental features in the innate plan of synthesis. These concepts are the categories. So each category is the concept of one fundamental factor in the innate plan which we unconsciously follow in synthesising sensa and images into percepts of physical objects.

In this connexion it is important to bear in mind a theory which Kant held about the nature of concepts in general. He was evidently much impressed by the importance of the process of *construction*, in the quite literal sense of drawing a figure, in geometry. He regarded it as an essential part of the concept of any geometrical figure that it is the concept of a rule by which we could construct instances of the figure on paper or in imagination. He seems to have extended this to empirical concepts and to categories. Thus, he seems to have held that the concept of a horse is, or involves as an essential factor, the concept of an empirical rule in accordance with which the percept of a horse is synthesised. The only meaning that I can attach to this is the following. If you see something and describe it as a horse, you are no doubt thinking in part of the kind of experiences which you *would* have, if you *were* to do certain things, e.g. to go up to it and touch it, and so on. To that extent, in ascribing the concept of horse as predicate to what you are now perceiving as subject, you are thinking of an empirical rule of sequence and coexistence of sensations under certain conditions. In the same way Kant held that a category, e.g. that of substance, is the concept of an innate rule of synthesis which is followed *whenever* sensa and images are synthesised to produce the percept of *any* physical object whatever.

2.4.1.2 What are the data to be synthesised?

In the above account of synthesis I have assumed that the data to be synthesised are sensa and images. But in Kant's own account of pure or *a priori* synthesis there are a number of quite explicit statements which involve a different view. This may be called the 'pure manifold theory'. According to this theory the two innate forms of intuition, described in the *Transcendental Aesthetic*, supply us respectively with a manifold of *purely spatial* elements and a manifold of *purely temporal* elements. The categories are concerned in the first instance only with these. They are concepts of the innate rules which we unwittingly follow in synthesising these purely spatial and purely temporal elements into purely spatial and purely temporal wholes, respectively. The categories get their hold on the empirical data, given to us by sensation, only at second hand. *All* these sense-given data are automatically provided by the mind with positions in its innate time-system. And all those which belong to what Kant calls the 'outer sense' are also automatically provided by the mind with positions in its innate space-system. So, in synthesising these two systems out of purely innate data, in accordance with the categories, we *ipso facto* synthesise their contingent sense-given contents on the same plan. I am well aware that this sounds fantastic, but I have little doubt that Kant held it or something like it.

I will quote some passages in support of this. (1) 'Space and time contain a manifold of pure *a priori* intuition. But they are also conditions . . . under which alone the mind can receive presentations of objects. They must therefore also always affect the concept of these objects. But, if this manifold is to be cognised . . . it must be gone through in a certain way, taken up, and connected. This act I call *synthesis* . . . Synthesis is *pure*, if the manifold is not empirical but is given *a priori*, as is the manifold in space and time . . . What must first be given, with a view to the *a priori* cognition of all objects, is the *manifold* of pure intuition' (pp. 111 and 112, B 102–4/A 77–9). (2) 'Time . . . contains an *a priori* manifold in pure intuition' (p. 181, B 177/A 138). (3) (This is a very interesting passage from a part which appears only in the second edition.) 'Space and time are presented *a priori*, not merely as *forms* of sensible intuition, but as themselves *intuited objects* which contain a manifold of their own . . . [*Note*] Space when presented as an *object* (as we need to do in geometry) contains more than mere form of intuition. It also contains *combination* of the manifold . . . in an intuitive presentation . . . In the *Aesthetic* I treated this unity merely as belonging to sensibility . . . But as a matter of fact it presupposes a synthesis which does not belong to the senses . . . By its means space and time are given as intuited objects' (p. 170, B 160).

I think that we can best understand how Kant was led to this theory if we suppose that he started from the view of space which I ascribed to him in the *Aesthetic*, viz. that each person is provided with his own absolute space, which is innate to him, and that it is an individual whole with which he actually is or conceivably might be directly acquainted. Then he applied to this doctrine his general principle that we cannot cognise a whole unless we have ourselves synthesised it out of elements. This principle is stated quite explicitly at the beginning of the new form of the *Transcendental Deduction of the Categories* which Kant substituted in the second edition for the original form of *Transcendental Deduction*. The following is an actual quotation: 'We cannot present to ourselves anything as combined in an object which we have not ourselves previously combined . . . Only as having been combined by the understanding can anything that allows of analysis be presented . . .' (pp. 151 and 152, B 130). With this general statement we may compare the following particular one, which occurs in the *Axioms of Intuition*. 'I cannot present to myself a line, however small, without drawing it in imagination, i.e. generating from a point all its parts one after another . . . Similarly with all times, however small' (p. 198, B 203/A 162–3). This seems to me to be palpably false as regards myself. I have no difficulty in calling up an image of a short line without imagining it gradually growing from a point. And surely everyone can *see* a line at one glance if it is not too long. However, Kant certainly held this principle.

His argument would then run as follows. 'I certainly do intuit a kind of innate absolute space, in which I locate the various images which I call up, and in which the objects which I perceive by my senses seem to be placed. This is certainly a complex whole, since I can distinguish in it adjoined regions which together make it up. Therefore I must have synthesised it out of intuited elements in order to be able to intuit it as an individual whole. For reasons given in the *Aesthetic* these elements cannot be impressions received through the stimulation of my senses. Therefore they must constitute a *purely* spatial manifold, which the sensitive, as opposed to the intellectual, part of my mind supplies out of it own resources.' I suspect that Kant regarded the synthesis, by which the elements of the pure spatial manifold are united to form a single intuited absolute space, as analogous to the process by which we voluntarily produce an image of a line of a given kind by imagining a point moving in a certain way and leaving a track behind. In the latter case we *start* with an *explicit* concept of a *particular* rule of construction, according to whether the image is to be that of a straight line or of a circle or of some other figure. In the former case the construction is performed blindly by the imagination in accordance with a certain innate general ground-plan. This plan becomes explicit, or to use Kant's phrase 'is brought to concepts', only when the geometer or the philosopher of geometry subsequently reflects on the finished products of the synthesis.

Having applied this argument to space, Kant probably proceeded to apply it almost automatically to time. I do not think that the theory, as it stands, could possibly be defended in either case. The best that can be said for it is this. (1) It is in some respects an improvement on the crude preliminary doctrine of the *Aesthetic* that space and time are 'infinite *given* wholes'. Plainly there are conceptual elements, as well as perceptual ones, involved in the notion of space as a single all-embracing three-dimensional continuous system of coexisting points, and of time as a single all-embracing one-dimensional continuous series of successive instants. (2) Certainly a special kind of synthesis, viz. adjunction of areas at their edges, of volumes at their faces, and of periods of time at their end points, is involved in developing these notions. (3) In order to account for the development of these highly unified and comprehensive notions out of the very scrappy and crude data supplied by sense-experience it seems quite likely that we must postulate certain innate tendencies in human thinking about space and time.

But when we come to the details, and in particular to the notion of pure manifolds, the theory becomes hopelessly vague. What is the nature of the elements of the pure spatial and the pure temporal manifold? Are they supposed to be little empty volumes and short unoccupied durations, each with its own positional quality, of the spatial or temporal kind, as the case may be? Or are they literally punctiform or instantaneous, as the case may be? On either view, is there any reason to believe that there really are such elements? Again, what precisely is the nature of the synthesis? How could *categories*, such as cause and substance, apply to mere empty volumes without any pervading qualities, or to mere durations without any concrete filling of events or processes? And, lastly, how is the synthesis of homogeneous purely spatial elements and of homogeneous purely temporal elements supposed to be related to the synthesis of the variegated and contingent *contents* of space and time?

2.4.1.3 What is the product of synthesis?

Whether we suppose the process of synthesis to be applied to sense-impressions or to purely spatial and purely temporal elements which the mind supplies from its own resources, there remains an ambiguity as to the nature of the product. Does it produce *objects* of various kinds, or does it produce what may be described as *percepts* of objects of various kinds? There is great obscurity about this, and I think that it springs from the following source. When Kant is at his best, and in particular when he is trying to escape the charge of being a mere Berkeleian, he quite clearly draws the following important *three-fold* distinction. He distinguishes (1) things-in-themselves, (2) *empirical or phenomenal* objects, (3) *presentations* of empirical objects. By 'empirical or phenomenal objects' he means such things as chairs, trees, clouds, etc., as we cognise them by sense-perception and by scientific theory based on sense-perception, induction, and mathematical reasoning. By 'things-in-themselves' he means here the ultimate causes of our sense-impressions. ('Things-in-themselves' include both these and also ourselves as we really are; but we can ignore the latter complication for the present.) On Kant's view, it would be a fundamental mistake to ascribe to things-in-themselves any of the qualities or relations which we perceive in phenomenal objects or which science ascribes to them. They are, e.g., certainly neither spatial nor temporal. By 'presentations of empirical objects' Kant means percepts composed of sense-impressions and associated images, etc., on the occurrence of which one takes oneself to be in presence of an empirical object of a certain kind. An example would be a visual experience of such a kind as would lead one to say: 'There's a cow over there!'

Now, although Kant drew this distinction, he more often than not ignored it and fell back on a two-fold distinction, in which the thing-in-itself remains but no distinction is made between presentation and phenomenal object. Now, according to whether we do or do not explicitly distinguish between presentation and phenomenal object, we get two different views of the results of synthesis, which I will now try to describe.

(1) On the view which does *not* distinguish between presentation and phenomenal object, the synthesis theory takes the following form. The result of synthesising elements is actually to produce extended enduring objects of various kinds. These are, however, mind-dependent, since they are made out of subjective mind-dependent materials, viz., either sense-impressions or elements of the pure manifolds of space or time. On this interpretation we actually *produce* spaces and times and extended and enduring objects by processes of imaginative synthesis, though they do not exist apart from our sensations and our syntheses. Undoubtedly many of Kant's statements imply this view, e.g. all analogies to construction of figures in geometry seem to do so. And some of his statements definitely assert particular applications of it. Cf., e.g., the following extraordinary remark on the top of p. 184 about '. . . my generating time itself . . .' (B 182/A 143). Such a view seems to be inconsistent with the statements at

the beginning of the *Aesthetic*, e.g. that we intuit objects 'by *means* of sensations', that the matter of a phenomenon is that in it which '*corresponds to* the sensation', and so on. Again, it is extremely difficult to make sense of the statement that I 'generate time' by a process of synthesis, which presumably takes place in time.

(2) Let us now take the alternative which clearly distinguishes between presentations of empirical objects and empirical objects themselves. Here we must make up a theory as best we can, for we shall find very little explicit in Kant.

I should be inclined to put the case as follows. The isolated sense-impression is a mere mental event produced somehow in a mind by a foreign thing-in-itself. It is neither a cognition of an object nor an object of cognition. But, when a number of sense-impressions and images have been synthesised by the imagination in accordance with the innate ground-plan which becomes explicit in the categories, we get a product which may be called a 'perception of a phenomenal object'. This has two properties which do not belong to isolated sense-impressions. (a) It can itself be inspected by the person in whom it occurs, and thus becomes an object of psychological and philosophical study. (b) More important, it has the property of being a presentation *of* such-and-such a phenomenal object *to* the person in whom it occurs. By this I mean simply the following. That person will, rightly or wrongly, take himself to be in presence of a certain foreign thing, which manifests to him certain determinate characteristics, e.g. a certain shape, size, colour, etc., and which he conceives as a persistent independent three-dimensional thing, located in the one objective spatio-temporal system and having characteristic active and passive powers. I should express this by saying that the synthesised perception has a certain determinate *epistemological* object, whether or not there be any *ontological* object corresponding to it. Another way of putting it would be to say that the synthesised perception *ostensibly presents* to the percipient an empirical object of a certain determinate kind, whether or not anything answering to the description of the object is *in fact* presenting itself to him. A dream-perception ostensibly presents a certain empirical object to the dreamer, just as much as an ordinary waking perception does to a waking percipient. But presumably in the case of the dream-perception there is no ontological object answering even remotely to the description of the epistemological object. If Kant's philosophy is correct, the ontological object in the case of waking perception, viz. the relevant thing-in-itself which supplies the sense-impressions out of which the perception is synthesised, answers in hardly any respect to the description of the epistemological object. The discrepancy is not just one of detail, as when a straight stick looks bent. It is radical and fundamental; for none of the determinables, such as colour, shape, position, date, duration, etc., in terms of which we describe the epistemological object, have any application to the ontological object.

We may summarise this alternative as follows. The result of the synthesis, according to it, is not to produce an actual, though mind-dependent, *perceived object*, but to produce a *perception* which *ostensibly presents* to the percipient a phenomenal or empirical object answering to a certain description.

I have stated this alternative view of the *products* of synthesis on the assumption that the *elements* to be synthesised are sense-impressions. But I suppose that it could be combined with the view that the elements are purely spatial and purely temporal data. We should then have to deny that the result of synthesising such pure elements is to produce an actual, though mind-dependent, *intuitable object* of a peculiar kind, e.g. a finite volume of pure space with a certain shape, size, and position. Instead we should have to say that the result is to produce a peculiar kind of *intuitive experience*, which ostensibly presents to the person who has it an object which he would describe as a finite volume of pure space of such-and-such a kind.

2.4.1.4 Sketch of a possible account of synthesis

In my opinion the least unplausible theory that could be made up on Kant's general lines would be the following. As regards the elements to be synthesised, I would drop the pure manifolds altogether, and assume that synthesis is always concerned with *sense-impressions*. As regards the product, I would assume that synthesis produces, not actual though mind-dependent presented objects, but experiences which ostensibly present objects answering to the description of bodies in a single three-dimensional space, etc. It is idle to pretend that Kant ever stated this theory himself, or to deny that many of his explicit statements are inconsistent with one or both parts of it. But I think it may be worthwhile to give a brief sketch of a theory on these lines which would fit in with Kant's view of space and time as something which the mind contributes from its own resources. The theory may be stated as follows, but we must remember that there is no reason to think that Kant would have accepted it.

(1) There is only one kind of manifold, viz. a mass of originally disconnected sense-impressions. These are due ultimately to the action of foreign things-in-themselves on that thing-in-itself which is one's mind *as it really is* and not merely as it appears to oneself when one introspects. (2) We must assign to each sense-impression two radically different kinds of characteristic. One kind is the basis of the determinate spatial position, shape, etc. which we perceive a particular empirical object as having, and for the determinate temporal position which we perceive it as having. We

will call these *locating* characteristics, and subdivide them into *space-locating* and *time-locating*. The other kind is the basis of the various determinate sensible qualities, e.g. colour and temperature, etc., which we perceive a particular empirical object as having. These may be called *quality-determining* characteristics. (3) Sense-impressions in themselves are neither spatial nor temporal. So the space-locating characteristic of a sense-impression is not itself a spatial characteristic, and its time-locating characteristic is not itself a temporal characteristic. But sense-impressions do themselves have sensible qualities; and it is the sensible quality, e.g. the redness or the coldness, of a sense-impression which makes one perceive an empirical object as having that sensible quality. (4) An isolated sense-impression does not suffice to constitute a percept of an empirical object. It is only when a number of sense-impressions and images have been synthesised in various complicated ways by the imagination according to an innate ground-plan that one has an experience which can be described as an ostensible perception of an empirical object answering to such-and-such a description. (5) The perception of an object as a solid of a certain shape and size located at a certain place in an objective three-dimensional space arises through the application of synthesis, in accordance with certain innate principles, to sense-impressions in respect of their space-locating characteristics. Similarly, the perception of it as existing throughout a certain stretch of objective time arises through the application of synthesis, in accordance with certain innate principles, to sense-impressions in respect of their time-locating characteristics. Lastly, the perception of it as having such-and-such sensible qualities spread over its surface or pervading its volume arises through the application of synthesis, in accordance with certain innate principles, to sense-impressions in respect of their sensible qualities. (6) These principles, which have been followed blindly by the imagination, become explicit in the logical forms of the judgments which we make about space and time and empirical objects, e.g. the subject-predicate form, the conditional form, and so on. By reflection on these a philosopher can form explicit concepts of the fundamental features in the innate general plan of synthesis. These concepts are the categories.

2.4.2 Transition from judgments to categories

After all these preliminary explanations Kant's transition from the table of judgments to the table of categories is rather an anti-climax. All that he explicitly says in justification of this vitally important step occurs in the following passage at the foot of p. 112 (B105/A79–80). 'The same function which gives unity to the various presentations in a *judgment* also gives unity to the . . . synthesis of various presentations in an *intuition* . . . The same understanding, through the same operations by which in concepts by means of analytical unity it produces the logical form of a judgment, also introduces a transcendental content into its presentations by means of the synthetic unity of the manifold in intuition in general.' What Kant is asserting is this. It is one and the same mental operation which is being performed when one's mind does either of the two following things: (1) When it unifies in thought one percept with others under a common concept, as in the judgment 'That is a horse', or unifies in thought one concept with others under a higher concept, as in the judgment 'All horses are mammals'. (2) When it unifies in accordance with an innate scheme a number of sense-impressions and images, of various kinds and had on various occasions, into a percept of an empirical object answering to the description of a horse or of a mammal. All that I can say is that this seems most unlikely, and that Kant has not produced the slightest reason for believing it. As this is his only ground for holding that the table of judgments is a satisfactory clue to discovering a complete table of categories, I regard the transition as quite baseless.

2.5 The table of categories

I have already said (1) that the table for classifying judgments is founded on no one principle, and therefore we have no guarantee of its completeness; and (2) that the only ground alleged by Kant to justify transition from it to the table of categories is most unplausible. All that I have to add is this. Even if Kant had shown conclusively that there must be *one* and can be *only* one category corresponding to each of the twelve final subdivisions in the table of judgments, the following question would arise: What guarantee have we that Kant has chosen the right category to correspond to each ultimate difference among judgments? We have only his own assertion. It is plain that Kant thinks that in every case but one the correspondence is obvious on inspection. The one exception is the correspondence between the category which Kant calls 'community', i.e. the notion of a whole of reciprocally determining parts, and the disjunctive judgment. He deals with this on p. 117 (B 112–13). But I do not think that anyone else would find the correspondence obvious on inspection in most of the other cases.

However that may be, the table of categories, like the table for classifying judgments, is divided into the four main headings of *quantity*, *quality*, *relation*, and *modality*. Under each of these headings there are three subdivisions which are supposed to correspond to the subdivisions under the corresponding heading in the judgments table. Thus, e.g., under *quantity* there come *unity*, *plurality*, and *totality*; and these are supposed to correspond respectively to the distinctions of *universal*, *particular*, and *singular* in the case of judgments. I think that it is only in the case of the first two categories under the heading *relation* that there is much plausibility in the correlation. There is no doubt an analogy between the logical notion of subject and predicate in a categorical judgment and the ontological notion of substance and attribute. And there is an analogy between the logical notion of antecedent and consequent in a conditional judgment and the ontological notion of ground and consequent.

2.5.1 Kant's comments on the table

Kant makes certain comments on his table of categories, and it will be worth while to mention some of these.

(1) He alleges that the third subdivision under each of his main headings is a kind of synthesis of the other two. Thus, e.g., the notion of totality is the notion of a plurality taken as a collective unity. *But* he claims that the third is always a *new* concept and not just definable in terms of the first two. This suggestion was taken up by Hegel and developed into the notion of a dialectical system of categories arranged in triads, of which the third member was a synthesis of the first (which he called the 'thesis') and the second (which he called the 'antithesis').

(2) Kant groups the categories of quantity and quality together under the name of 'mathematical'; and he groups those of relation and modality together under the name of 'dynamical'. His grounds for this distinction are rather obscure. Such as they are, they are to be found on p. 116 (B110) and pp. 196–7 (B199–202/A160–2).

(a) One alleged peculiarity of the categories of quantity and quality and the principles based upon them is that they are concerned with the gradual synthesis of *homogeneous* elements into a whole which is of the same kind as the elements themselves. The categories and principles of relation and modality are supposed to be concerned with the connexion between *heterogeneous* elements, e.g. substance and attribute, ground and consequent. In this connexion Kant remarks that each dynamical category involves a pair of correlative terms, e.g. ground and consequent, whilst no mathematical category does so. I do not think that much weight can be laid upon this. In the case of categories of modality Kant gets his correlatives only be taking a pair of *opposites*, e.g. possibility and impossibility, as a single category. It is obvious that there is no analogy between such pairs of opposites and pairs of genuine correlatives such as substance and attribute or ground and consequent. Moreover, it would have been quite easy to get pairs of opposites or of correlates under quantity. E.g. unity and plurality, which he counts as two categories, might just as well be counted as correlates or even as opposites.

(b) A second alleged difference is that in quantity and quality the connexion of the elements is contingent, whilst the dynamical categories are concerned with necessary connexions. I suppose that the kind of thing which Kant has in mind is that any of the parts of a spatial or temporal whole might have existed without the other parts and therefore without the whole having existed. On the other hand, an event which is a state of a substance could not have existed except as a state of that substance, and a completed condition could not exist without its consequences existing too. I do not think that there is much in this. In the first place I do not see that it applies to the categories of modality at all. Secondly, the contingency or necessity in each case seems to be one sided. It is true that the parts of a spatial whole could have existed without it; but, on the other hand, *it* could not have existed without them. Conversely it is true that an event which is a state of a certain substance could not have existed unless that substance had done so; but, on the other hand, the substance might have existed without ever being in that state.

(c) The third alleged distinction is stated very obscurely, but it may be of some importance. He says (pp. 196–7, B 119–202/A 160–3) that the categories of quantity and quality are concerned with 'the mere *intuition* of a phenomenon in general', whilst those of relation and modality are concerned with 'the *existence* of a phenomenon in general'. He concludes from this that the principles which involve the mathematical categories 'allow of *intuitive* certainty', whilst those which involve the dynamical categories 'are capable only of a merely *discursive* certainty'. He adds that the certainty is equally *complete* in both cases.

The interpretation which I am inclined to put on these statements is the following. The notions of extensive magnitude, intensive magnitude, and number apply directly to the sense-data or percepts by which we perceive empirical objects as well as to the empirical objects which we perceive by means of them. So the mathematical categories could be applied, and the mathematical principles would be valid, even in respect of dreams and hallucinations. But the dynamical categories, e.g. substance and cause, and the principles which involve them, e.g. the permanence of substance and the law of universal causation, apply only to the physical objects and events which we perceive by means of our sensations. Both sets of principles are equally certain, considered as conditional propositions, but the mathematical ones are certain subject to a less restricted hypothesis than the dynamical ones. All that the mathematical ones need to assume is that I shall go on having *sensations* of some kind. The dynamical ones presuppose that I shall go on having *perceptions*. Now the latter implies that I shall not only go on having sensations but that these will continue to come in certain groupings and that I shall continue to synthesise them on certain innate general principles.

If this is the kind of thing that Kant meant, then I think that his distinction is valid. I can say that the brown-looking rounded-looking sense-datum, which is the appearance of a penny to me, has extensive magnitude, and also that the penny, which I perceive by means of it, has extensive magnitude. I can say also that my sensation of temperature has a certain degree and that an external body has a certain degree of physical temperature. But I should never call a sense-datum a *substance*, or say that one sense-datum *causes* another. I describe as a substance only such things as stones, pennies, etc., which I perceive by means of my synthesised sensations. And I ascribe causal interaction only to such things and to events in them.

2.6 The doctrine of schematism

So far we have considered the pure categories and have ignored Kant's distinction between pure categories and schemata. But in point of fact the schemata are of more practical importance than the pure categories. For the synthetic *a priori* propositions which Kant claims to prove, and which he calls *principles of pure understanding*, involve the schemata and not the pure categories. We must now consider what Kant meant by this distinction and why he thought it necessary to draw it. What he says is most obscure, and I do not pretend to understand it in detail.

2.6.1 Kant's problem

I think that the problem which Kant has in mind here might be stated as follows. If I judge that an object which I perceive falls under a certain concept, I can always raise the question: 'What is my ground for making that judgment?'

(1) If the concept is that of a sensible quality, the answer is fairly simple. Suppose I am looking at something, and make the judgment 'That is red'. Then my ground is that it looks red to me, that I am viewing it in ordinary daylight, and that I believe my eyesight to be normal.

2.6.1.1 Schemata of geometrical and empirical class-concepts

(2) Next suppose that I am looking at something, and judge that it is *round*, meaning by this that its contour answers to the geometrical definition of a circle. According to Kant the geometrical definition of a circle *is*, or at any rate *involves*, a rule for constructing instances of circles in imagination, e.g. the rule 'Imagine a set of points in a plane all at the same distance, but all in various directions, from a fixed point'. Now Kant evidently holds that, by making an imaginative construction according to this rule, one would know what a circular contour would look like even if one had never seen one. (This seems to me most unplausible with regard to more complicated contours, e.g. ellipses.) However that may be, on Kant's view one's

ground for judging that the contour of a perceived object is an instance (or at any rate an approximate instance) of the concept of geometrical circularity is this. The contour of the object presents a certain characteristic visual appearance. This approximates closely to what I already know, from making imaginative constructions in accordance with the definition, that an instance of geometrical circularity would look like.

(3) Suppose next that I am looking at something and judge that it is a member of a certain natural kind or species, e.g. that it is a dog. Different kinds of dog *look* extremely different. Cf., e.g., a fox-terrier, a poodle, a dachshund, and a collie. For my own part I should be inclined to say that one's ground for calling a certain object, which one sees, 'a dog', is roughly the following. (a) Past experience has justified one in expecting that any object which presents any one of a number of different visual appearances, falling within certain very wide and rather ill-defined limits, will have the defining properties of a dog. E.g. it will bark, it will bite but not scratch, it will have a keen sense of smell, and so on. All these tests themselves come down to descriptions of the kind of sensation which one would have in connexion with such an object in certain kinds of perceptible situation. (b) *This* object, which I am now seeing, presents a visual appearance which falls well within the wide and ill-defined limits mentioned above.

Kant does not explicitly mention either of these points, but I do not think he should have objected to them. What he is specially concerned with seems to be this question. How does one recognise that the visual appearance of the object which one is seeing on any particular occasion falls within the required limits? He points out that no single dog-image would be adequate. It would inevitably be of a certain definite kind, e.g. an image of a fox-terrier. How would this help one to recognise as a dog an object which presented the appearance, not of a fox-terrier, but of a poodle?

His positive answer to the original question is very obscure. I suggest that his theory may be somewhat as follows. The concept of a dog, considered simply as a visible object, is, or involves, the concept of a rule for calling up images which fall within certain limits. That rule is of empirical origin. It must be contrasted in this respect with the rules for constructing in imagination various kinds of geometrical figures, of which one may never have seen an instance. The empirical rule becomes embodied somehow in an acquired disposition of the imagination to produce images that fall within the required limits. I think that Kant may have held that, when this disposition has been established, the mind throws up rapidly fluctuating images, e.g. of a fox-terrier which melts into a poodle which melts into a dachshund, and so on. He uses in this connexion the curious phrase 'an art concealed in the depths of the human soul' (p. 183, B 180–1/A 141). If the visual appearance of the seen object agrees reasonably well with any one of these dog-images which the mind throws up on the occasion, one classifies the object as a dog. If it is very unlike any of them, one hesitates or refuses to call it a dog.

It will be worth while to compare this with a slightly more complicated geometrical example than that of circularity. All circles look exactly alike in shape. But the ratio of the smaller to the greater axis of an ellipse may have any value between 1 and 0, and the contour presents a different appearance for each different value. I take it that Kant would say that the concept of an ellipse is, or involves, the concept of a rule for constructing any kind of ellipse in imagination. One such rule would be 'Imagine a set of points such that the sum of the distances of each from two fixed points is the same'. He would hold that it is possible to construct any ellipse in imagination by this rule, and to tell what it would look like. But in judging whether the contour of a perceived object was or was not elliptical, it would be of no use to have an image of any one kind of ellipse to compare it with. I think that Kant would hold that here too the mind has a disposition to throw up rapidly fluctuating images of all the various possible kinds of ellipse. The important differences between this case and that of the concept of a dog are these. (i) In the case of the ellipse all the possible varieties are *deducible* from the concept, whilst it is a mere empirical fact that the concept of a dog covers poodles, fox-terriers, collies, etc. (ii) In the case of the ellipse the imaginative disposition is one which the geometer *establishes in himself*, apart from any sense-perceptions which he may have had, merely by constructing elliptical images in accordance with the rule. In the case of the concept of a dog the imaginative disposition is gradually established in a person by experiences of seeing dogs of various kinds.

(4) So far we have considered only concepts which can more or less literally be instantiated in sense-perception and in imagination. In such cases Kant uses the word 'schema' in roughly the following sense. He distinguishes it (a) from the *concept* which it schematises, and (b) from any *particular image*, which would illustrate just one particular species under the concept. Again, he says quite definitely that a schema is always a product of *imagination*. So far there is no doubt about his meaning. What is doubtful is exactly what he takes the schema to be in such cases. I suggest that it might be a set of images, fluctuating within certain limits, which the imagination produces in rapid succession when the mind is considering a certain geometrical or empirical concept. This imaginative process is specially active when one is debating whether or not to apply a certain concept to a perceived object, and one's decision depends on whether the visual appearance of the object does or does not agree fairly closely with one of these fluctuating images.

If this is Kant's doctrine, I would make the following criticisms of it. (1)

I think that there is very little direct introspective evidence for the view that such images commonly occur or play an essential part in determining one's decision to apply or not to apply a concept. (2) In any case the theory could apply only to *visual* perception and to objects which are *seen*. (3) Does the theory really explain the facts? The question was: 'How do I know whether or not to apply a certain concept to an object which I am seeing?' The answer is: 'It depends on whether the visual appearance sufficiently resembles one or other of a number of rapidly fluctuating images which your imagination throws up when your mind reflects on the concept.' But this is no answer unless one can decide at once that these images provide illustrations of the concept. But, if one can decide this with regard to a visual *image*, why should one not be able to decide it *directly* with regard to a visual *percept*?

2.6.1.2 The notion of the transcendental schema of a category

We now come at last to the question of the schematisation of *categories*, as distinct from geometrical and empirical concepts. Let us take as examples the categories of ground and consequent and of substance and attribute. The question now is: What sort of ground could one ever have for saying of a perceived object 'That is a substance', or of a perceived event 'That is a state of a substance', or of two perceived events 'This is the cause of that'? You cannot literally see with your eyes that so-and-so is a substance, as you can literally see that it is red or is round and almost literally see that it is a dog. You cannot literally see with your eyes the causing of a breach of continuity in a pane of glass by the coming in contact with it of a moving stone. What you can literally see is merely the immediate following of the one event on the other. Kant would say that the same remarks apply to all the other categories. Now it is plain that a schema, in the sense in which we have so far considered it, will be of no help here. For a schema, in that sense, was supposed to work by supplying a set of fluctuating images, which answer to the various possible cases which the concept covers and which can be directly compared with the perceived object. But it is plain that no image can illustrate a highly abstract structural notion, such as the category of substance or of cause. It is, e.g., no more possible literally to have an image of this causing that than it is literally to see this causing that. So much at least is clear. So Kant says that something special is needed, in the case of the categories, to mediate between these highly abstract notions and the world of concrete perceptible objects. To this special kind of intermediary he gives the name of a 'transcendental schema'.

Beyond this point the only things that can be said with certainty about Kant's doctrine are the following. (1) He thinks that *time* is the basis of the mediation between pure categories and empirical objects. (2) His ground appears to be the following. Time resembles the pure categories in two fundamental respects. In the first place it is something which the mind supplies from its own resources. Secondly it is involved in every possible perceptible object. And here 'perceptible' must be taken in its widest possible sense. It covers both sense-perception of external bodies and physical events and also introspective awareness of oneself and one's own experiences. All these present themselves to us as having dates and durations in a single time-system. On the other hand, temporal characteristics are supplied to phenomenal objects by the passive non-intellectual department of our minds. In this respect temporal characteristics resemble sensible qualities, and differ from the categories, which are part of our active intellectual discursive equipment. (3) Each pure category is the concept of one of the fundamental features in the innate plan on which the imagination selects and combines and supplements the data provided by sensation and thus produces a coherent experience of a world of independent empirical objects. (4) The transcendental schema of a category is supposed to be something which is produced by imagination synthesising elements which are *purely temporal* and not sense-given, in accordance with that rule of which the category is the concept. (5) Kant does not actually use the phrase 'schematised category'. But presumably a schematised category would be the concept of a process of imaginative synthesis, carried out in accordance with a certain innate rule, and restricted in its application to purely temporal elements. Such a process would generate the transcendental schema of the category in question.

I think that this is a fair account of Kant's explicit statements. If this is what he means by the transcendental schema of a category, I must confess that I can form no clear idea of what a transcendental schema would be like. I think I can see what would be meant by selecting and combining *sense-impressions* according to a certain innate plan and thus producing percepts of *empirical objects*. But I simply do not know what would be meant, e.g., by combining *purely temporal* elements according to the rule of synthesis of which the category of ground and consequent is the concept. And I have not the faintest idea what the product of such a process would be, if there were such elements and if it could be performed upon them. So the best thing to do is to pass on to Kant's own list of the transcendental schemata and the principles of pure understanding which he associates with them. We shall then get some idea of what in fact he had in mind.

2.6.2 Kant's list of transcendental schemata and principles

Kant's list of schemata, with his comments on it, occurs on pp. 183–7 (B 181–7/A 142–7). His list of the corresponding principles of pure understanding, with his comments on it, occurs on pp. 196–7 (B200–2/A161–2). The following points should be noticed.

(1) There is only one schema, viz. *number*, corresponding to the three categories under the head of *quantity*, and only one schema, viz. *intensive magnitude*, corresponding to the three categories under *quality*. Similarly there is only one principle in each case, viz. the principle that all perceptible objects have extensive magnitude and the principle that the qualities of perceptible objects all have intensive magnitude. But there are three schemata and three principles corresponding to the three categories under *relation*, and the same is true of the three categories under modality. The schema of the category of *substance* is said to be *permanence in time*, and the corresponding principle is that in all changes of empirical objects the quantity of substance remains unaltered. The schema of the category of *ground and consequent* is said to be *succession subject to a rule*, i.e. regular sequence. The corresponding principle is that all changes in empirical objects are causally determined by previous changes. The schema of the category of *community* is said to be the *regular coexistence* of a certain state of one empirical object with a certain state of another empirical object. The corresponding principle is that empirical objects coexisting in space mutually determine each other's contemporary states. The schema of the category of *possibility* is existence at *some time or other*. The schema of the category of *actuality* is existence at a *certain determinate time*. The schema of the category of *necessity* is existence *at all times*. The three corresponding principles may be ignored for the present purpose.

(2) It is queer that the schema of the categories of *quantity* should be said to be *number*, when the corresponding principle is, not that all perceptible objects are enumerable, but that they all have *extensive magnitude*.

(3) The connexion with time seems to be much more external and artificial in the case of the schemata of *quantity* and *quality* than in that of the schemata of the categories under *relation* and *modality*. The ordinary notions of substance and of causation are essentially bound up with such temporal characteristics as permanence and change, sequence and coexistence. And in the physical world existence at some time or other is a criterion for possibility, and existence at all times is a criterion for necessity. But Kant brings in the reference to time in regard to number or extensive magnitude only by reference to such facts as that counting is a successive process, or that measuring involves performing, actually or imaginatively, some such process as repeatedly laying down and taking up a measuring-rod. And he brings in the reference to time in regard to intensive magnitude only in a still more artificial and external way. He does this only by referring to the fact that we can regard any sensation as having reached its present intensity by gradual increase from zero, and

conversely can think of it as gradually fading away and vanishing when its intensity becomes zero.

(4) On the other hand, Kant's talk of a synthesis performed by the mind on originally unconnected elements seems to fit such processes as counting or measuring fairly well, but to have very little obvious bearing on the regular sequence or regular coexistence of certain attributes, which he takes as the schemata of the categories of relation.

(5) When we look at Kant's proofs of the three most important of his principles, viz. the so-called *Analogies of Experience*, which correspond to the schemata of the three categories of relation, what we notice is this. He is obviously concerned there with the following very important question. What is implied in the fact that we distinguish dates, the durations, and the temporal order of our presentations from the dates, durations, and temporal order respectively of the empirical things and events which we perceive or remember by means of them? E.g. the presentation by which I perceive the front of a house always either precedes or follows that by which I perceive the back of it, yet I believe that the back and the front coexist and not that they exist successively. Again, I always hear thunder after I see lightning, but I believe that the physical events which I thus perceive successively are simultaneous. Then, again, I distinguish between the order in which my memory-images of a series of events happen to occur and the order in which the remembered events took place.

2.6.3 Comments on the notion of schematism

It is now possible to get a rough idea of what Kant meant in practice by a transcendental schema, as distinct from a pure category, and of why the schemata are important in his system. As usual, the doctrine is much more plausible in connexion with the categories of ground and consequent and substance and attribute than with any of the rest. I will take ground and consequent as the best example.

Let us start with the conditional or hypothetical form of judgment 'If *p* then *q*'. One would use this to express an ordinary causal law, e.g. 'If the temperature of a body is raised it thereupon expands'. But it obviously covers a great deal beside ordinary causal laws. It would be used, e.g., to express propositions of pure mathematics which have nothing to do with things or events. Thus: 'If an equation is of the *n*-th degree it has *n* roots'. So the first restriction which we might impose would be to consider the conditional form as confined to *actual or possible existents*. We thus get the general notion of the existence of one particular being a necessary consequence or a necessary condition of the existence of another. This is the *pure category* of ground and consequent. It involves no reference, explicit or implicit, to space or to time. Kant must presumably be thinking of the pure category when he asserts, as he constantly does, that our sense-impressions depend upon or are due to foreign things-in-themselves. He cannot here be thinking of causation in the ordinary sense, which involves the notion of *events* or *processes*, and of their coexistence or *immediate sequence*. For he is quite certain that things-in-themselves have no temporal characteristics. Finally, then, we come to the notion of ground and consequent restricted to *things and events in time*. This is the notion of the *necessary immediate sequence* of a certain kind of event either in the same substance or in another substance which stands in a certain relation to the former. This is the ordinary notion of *cause and effect*. This would be the *schematised category* of ground and consequent. Now even in the schematised category there is a feature which cannot be literally presented to us in sense-perception or literally illustrated by any image or set of images. This is the element of *necessity*, which obviously is purely intellectual and conceptual. But we can still raise the following question: Is there any feature in what we literally can perceive which, so to speak, *represents and symbolises* the necessity which we cannot literally perceive? I understand Kant's answer to be the following. We can literally perceive such a fact as that every observed instance of X has been followed immediately by an instance of Y in a certain relation R (e.g. in an adjoining region of space) to it. This kind of observable fact represents and symbolises the non-perceptible necessity of sequence involved in a causal law. The general form of such observable facts, viz. regular sequence of an event of one kind on an event of a certain other kind in a certain relation to the former, is the *transcendental schema* of the category of ground and consequent. If we generalise from this example we reach the following conclusion. The transcendental schema of a category is a certain type of perceptible temporal pattern in the world of phenomenal objects, which symbolises that feature in the category which can only be conceived and cannot literally be perceived or imaged.

To this I would add the following remarks. (1) The account just offered of a transcendental schema is independent of Kant's own special view that a category is the concept of one of the innate rules of synthesis which the imagination follows in creating our perceptual experience of a world of independent empirical objects in a single objective space and time. But it could be combined with that or any other view of the nature of categories. (2) Suppose we admit that observable regularity of sequence is the schema of the category of ground and consequent, and suppose we admit that it is the product of an *a priori* synthesis. Then it seems to me highly misleading to say that this synthesis is performed on *purely temporal* elements. An absolutely essential factor in the product is the notion of the manifestation of a certain *perceptible quality* being regularly followed by that of a certain other *perceptible quality* in a certain *non-temporal* relation (e.g. spatial adjunction) to the former. Naturally the *general* schema does not involve a reference to any *particular* perceptible qualities or any *particular* non-temporal relation. But, without a reference to such qualities and such a relation in general, all talk of a *rule* of sequence becomes meaningless.

In conclusion we must note the following significant remark which Kant makes on pp. 186–7 (B 185–7/A 145–7). He says that, whilst the substitution of schematised categories for pure categories is in a sense a restriction, yet in practice this comes to very little. If we omit the restriction to things and events in time, nothing definite remains in the concept except some notion belonging to pure logic. Suppose, e.g., that we try to go back from the schematised category of persistent substance and variable states to the pure category of substance and accident. We find that nothing definite remains except the purely logical notion of a subject which *has* attributes but *is not itself* an attribute of anything else. Kant remarks: 'Such a presentation I can put to no use, for it tells me nothing as to the nature of that which is thus to be viewed as a primary subject' (p. 187, B 186/A 147).

In view of this, and in view of the fact that Kant operates entirely with schematised categories and schemata in his proofs of the principles of pure understanding, one might be inclined to ask whether the pure categories are not idle subtleties which might with advantage have been omitted altogether. I can think of two answers which Kant might give. Whether either of them is valid is another question. One answer is that he wants to be sure that he has got a complete list of categories. He thinks that he can do so, if and only if he starts with the various possible distinctions of form among judgments, and makes this the clue to the discovery and enumeration of the categories. This way obviously leads through the pure categories to the schematised categories, however useless the contents of the halfway house may be in themselves. Another answer is that he needs at any rate the pure category of ground and consequent at two points at least in his system. He needs it for his doctrine that our sense-impressions stand to foreign things-in-themselves in the relation of consequent to ground. And he needs it for the distinction between noumenal and empirical determination which is the basis of his solution of the antinomy of determinism and freedom.

3 The Transcendental Deduction of the Categories

We can now turn to the chapter which Kant entitled *Transcendental Deduction of the Categories*. This is one of the most important and the most obscure parts of Kant's work. It is plain that Kant was not altogether satisfied with the exposition which he gave in A. For he largely rewrote the *Transcendental Deduction* in B, and omitted altogether certain parts to which he had attached considerable importance in A. Between the two editions he wrote and published the *Prolegomena*. This is supposed to be a simplified and semi-popular account of the doctrines of the *Critique of Pure Reason*. Where it differs from the *Critique* it cannot claim the same authority as the latter. But it will be worth while to say a little about the doctrine of the *Prolegomena* in due course, for it seems to differ, in regard to the Deduction of the Categories, from both A and B. Lastly, we cannot safely neglect Deduction A and say that Deduction B represents Kant's more mature views. For some of the sections in A which Kant omitted in B are of great interest and importance, and it is doubtful whether B can be understood without reference to A. I shall therefore deal in turn with Deduction A and Deduction B and then say a little about the part of the *Prolegomena* which treats of the same topic as they. But before going into detail I shall state in my own way what I believe to be the problem with which Kant was concerned in this part of his philosophy.

3.1 Independent statement of Kant's problem

(1) I will first introduce some terminology which will be convenient. (1) In this part of the lectures I shall use the word 'intuitive presentation' to cover both sense-data of all kinds and mental images of all kinds. (2) Kant held the following opinions about intuitive presentation. (a) Any intuitive presentation is an event in, or state of, the mind of a certain *one* person for a certain *one* period of time. According to him it would be nonsensical to suggest that the sensibly brown and sensibly circular colour-expanse which was presented to me when I looked at a certain penny on a certain occasion existed before, or will exist after, being presented to me. It would be nonsensical to suggest that it could be presented to anyone but me, or that it could be presented to me on several occasions separated by intervals during which it was not presented to me. (b) Nothing in the least like an intuitive presentation could exist except as a state of some person's mind. To talk of a sensibly brown and sensibly circular colour-expanse which was not presented to someone either in sensation or in imagination is nonsensical. We can sum this up as follows. It is nonsensical to talk of a sensibile which is not an actual sense-datum to someone, and it is nonsense to suggest that one and the same sensibile might be a sense-datum to more than one person or to the same person on several separate occasions. And similar remarks apply if we substitute 'imaginabile' for 'sensibile' and 'image' for 'sense-datum'. (3) We can consider any intuitive presentation under two different headings. (a) We can consider it as an event which begins at a certain date in a certain person's mental history and then lasts for so long. In this respect it stands in various direct temporal relations to his other experiences and in specifically psychological relations to them.

This may be called the '*occurrent* aspect' of an intuitive presentation. (b) We can consider it as being a presentation of such-and-such a kind, e.g. a sensibly brown circular colour-expanse or a loud squeaky noise, and so on. This may be called its '*qualitative* aspect'. (4) Presentations, in their qualitative aspect, may stand in certain relations to each other which could not possibly relate them in their occurrent aspects. E.g. the visual sensum *B* might be intermediate in shape and in colour between the visual sensum *A* and the visual sensum *C*. But in their occurrent aspect these presentations would not have figures or colours and therefore could not be comparable in these respects. On the other hand, they would have direct temporal relations. *A* and *B* might occur in the same specious present, and *C* might not begin until *A* and *B* had ceased. (5) An intuitive presentation may become the *object* of a *reflective* cognition on the part of the person whose presentation it is. This might be directed specially to its occurrent aspect or specially to its qualitative aspect. In the former case I should say that it is made an object of *psychological introspection* and in the latter an object of *phenomenological inspection*. But one is, no doubt, generally aware vaguely of one's own presentations while they are occurring in one without specially attending to them in either aspect. I shall express this by saying that an intuitive presentation is often the immediate object of a state of simultaneous *indiscriminating reflective awareness*. (6) Many intuitive presentations, and in particular sense-data, are ingredients in those cognitive experiences which we call *sense-perceptions*. And every sense-perception contains one or more intuitive presentations as an essential ingredient. When a person is having a sense-perception he seems to himself to be directly aware of a certain *physical thing* (e.g. a chair or a tree) or a certain *physical event* (e.g. a flash of lightning or a clap of thunder). And he takes this to be manifesting perceptibly to him certain of its qualities and relations. An essential factor in determining the particular qualities and relations which he perceives the object as having on a given occasion is the qualitative aspect of the sense-data which are ingredients of his perception on that occasion. E.g. if his visual sense-datum is of a certain kind, and certain other conditions are fulfilled, he will perceive the object as a uniformly coloured sphere. If his visual sense-datum is of a certain other kind, and the other conditions are similar, he will perceive the object as a cube with variously coloured faces; and so on.

We may now sum all this up as follows. (1) According to Kant a sense-datum or image in itself is an event in a person's mind. (2) It can be considered in two different aspects, viz. *occurrent* and *qualitative*. We consider it in its *occurrent* aspect when we ask: 'When and in whom did it occur, how long did it last, and how was it related psychologically to his other mental states?' We consider it in its *qualitative* aspect when we ask: 'What are the sensible qualities of this sense-datum or image, and in what determinate forms are they present in it?' (3) An intuitive presentation can be the *immediate object* of a simultaneous state of reflective awareness. (4) Whether it is *itself* an object of reflective awareness or not, it can be an ingredient in a cognitive experience which essentially refers to an object, viz. a *sense-perception*. If so, the qualitative aspect of the presentation is an essential factor in determining the qualities and relations which the perceived physical object is perceived as having.

(II) We must now go more fully into the notion of a physical object. This term covers both a physical *thing*, i.e. a body, and a physical *event*, e.g. a flash of lightning. For the present we can confine ourselves to the notion of a body, for Kant does not specially concern himself with the notion of a physical event. I have already stated in dealing with Kant's doctrine of imaginative synthesis (2.4.1.1) the main features in the concept of a body. All that is needed here is to summarise this briefly and to make some additions. A body is thought of as something which has the following characteristics. (1) It is a *substance* which persists for a considerable time. At any moment it has a number of different determinable *qualities* in certain determinate forms. In course of time the determinate forms of these may alter or may remain unaltered. (2) It has a store of *causal or dispositional properties*, e.g. a certain mass, elasticity, melting-point, etc. These manifest themselves in the characteristic ways in which its qualities change under the influence of other bodies, and also in the characteristic ways in which the qualities of other bodies change under its influence. (3) It is bounded by a closed surface, and therefore has a back as well as a front, an inside as well as an outside, and so on. Of course it may be either solid or hollow inside. (4) Each body at any moment has a certain *position*. In course of time this may remain constant or change. If it changes it will do so *continuously*. This means that, if it occupies different positions p_1 and p_2 at two different moments t_1 and t_2 it must have occupied a continuous series of positions intermediate between p_1 and p_2 at the moments intermediate between t_1 and t_2. (5) All bodies at every moment occupy positions in one and the same unchanging three-dimensional spatial system.

The above may be described as the *ontological* characteristics which are involved in the notion of a body. We must next consider what might be called the *epistemological* characteristics which are involved in it, i.e. the relations of bodies to human and other percipients. (1) A body is not dependent for its *existence* on being perceived either by a certain particular human observer or by some human observer or other. It would have existed if it had never been observed and it would continue to exist if all human observers were eliminated. Nor does becoming perceived or ceasing to be perceived make any difference to the qualities or dispositions of a body. (2) A body has qualities which are not at the moment being perceived and it may have qualities which no human observer can perceive because we lack the appropriate senses. Thus a lump of snow is cold when it is only being seen and not felt, and is white when it is only being felt and not seen. (3) A body has *simultaneously* spatial parts which can be perceived only *successively*. The back and the front of a house coexist, and so do the outside and the inside of a glove, but no one can see them at the same time. (4) One and the same body, though unchanged in respect of a certain perceptible quality, may yet *present different appearances* in respect of that quality. It may do so to the same observer at different times and to different observers at the same time. (5) In spite of this the only direct evidence which anyone can have for the existence of a body is *his sensations*. And the only direct evidence which he can have for ascribing such-and-such qualities and dispositions to any particular body is his sensations and their variations under assigned conditions. (6) One and the same body can be perceived by the same person on two or more occasions separated by an interval during which he has not been perceiving it. And he can often *recognise* it on the second occasion as the *same* body which he had perceived on an earlier occasion. (7) One and the same body can be perceived by any number of persons, either simultaneously or successively. (8) A person who perceives a body can often *identify* it as being of a certain *kind*, e.g. a tree, a dog, etc.

(III) It is now easy to state in outline what is the problem with which Kant is wrestling in the *Transcendental Deduction*, and to see that it is genuine and important. It can be put as follows: How do we get the notion of a body? Is it a valid notion, which has application, even though we may occasionally make mistakes of detail in applying it, e.g. in dreams, hallucinations, etc.? If it is valid, how can we establish its validity? On the one hand, each person's sense-data are scrappy, fleeting, variable, and inactive by-products, and (if Kant is right) private to himself. On the other hand, the notion of a body is the notion of something public, neutral, independent of observers, persistent, and replete with active and passive powers. Yet a person is never directly acquainted with any physical object, as he may be through introspection and inspection with his own experiences and sense-data and images. All that he can ever know or believe about physical objects is based on his sensations. How then can he even have the notion of a physical object? And, since we cannot have got it from being acquainted with instances of it, how do we know that there are any instances of it?

3.2 Transcendental Deduction A

The *Transcendental Deduction* in A is highly obscure and repetitive. Some critics think that it embodies notes which Kant had made at various stages of his philosophical career and then mixed up with each other when writing the *Critique of Pure Reason*. Some of them go so far as to profess to be able to divide the argument into four strata of various dates, and to be able to say precisely at what line of what page a fragment of a certain stratum begins and at what line of what page it is followed by a fragment of a certain other stratum. I regard all this with extreme scepticism and shall not trouble you further with it. What can be said with certainty is this. (1) Kant tries to analyse the notion of physical object and the notion of perceiving a physical object. It looks as if he offers two different analyses of the notion of physical object, but it is possible that they are supplementary rather than contradictory, and that he stresses sometimes one aspect and sometimes the other. (2) He tries to distinguish a number of mental processes, other than merely having sensations, which he thinks are essential to sense-perception. Here again there is a great deal of repetition. It is uncertain whether he is stating several alternative views which are incompatible in detail or is stating a single view and stressing and elaborating certain details in one place and others in other places. However this may be, the following seems to be certain. In the case of each faculty which he considers to be involved in sense-perception he distinguishes an empirical and a transcendental function. Sometimes he talks as if there were an empirical and a transcendental use of each of these faculties. Sometimes he talks as if there were in each case two faculties, one empirical and the other transcendental, closely connected with each other. On the former alternative he argues that the empirical use of any of these faculties presupposes the transcendental use of it. On the latter he argues that the functioning of an empirical faculty presupposes the functioning of the corresponding transcendental faculty. (3) On the basis of his analysis of the notion of physical object and of sense-perception, and of his account of the various faculties other than sensation involved in sense-perception, he proceeds to his justification. He professes to justify the application of the notion of physical object and of the various categories involved in it *within* human experience. The argument is highly obscure, but it is certain that an essential factor in it is an appeal to something which he calls the *transcendental unity of apperception*. And it is certain that this phrase refers to the characteristic kind of unity which there is among all the experiences which can be described as the experiences of a single self-conscious person.

I shall now try to explain what seem to be the most important points in the *Transcendental Deduction* A, though I do not pretend to be able to give a single coherent picture of it.

3.2.1 Why do the categories need a transcendental deduction?

Kant explains that he is here using 'deduction' in a technical sense in which

it is used in Roman law. It means establishing a right – in this case the right
to use the categories, e.g. cause and substance, in the way in which we do
use them. Kant holds it to be certain that these concepts are *a priori*, in the
sense that they cannot have been derived by abstraction from instances
which manifest them to us in sensation, as e.g. the concept of redness is.
Yet we take for granted that they do apply to every object which we ever
have perceived or ever will perceive. We take for granted that every such
object will be a substance, that it will exercise causal influences and be
subject to causal influences, and so on. Moreover we accept as necessary
truths certain general principles involving these concepts, e.g. that every
physical event is causally determined by other physical events, that in
all physical changes the quantity of material substance remains unaltered
and so on. It is our right to these convictions which needs to be justified.

It would no doubt be possible to trace the conditions under which these
concepts become explicit in the mental history of each individual or of the
human race. Such a psycho–genetic enquiry is interesting and important in
its place, but it cannot provide any answer to the question about justification. If our use of the categories needs to be justified and can be
justified, it must be on quite different lines.

Kant then raises the question: Does it, after all, need justification?
According to him, the concepts and principles of pure geometry are just as
non-empirical as categories like cause and substance. We all assume without question that the concepts and laws of geometry will apply to everything that we shall ever perceive. Yet this does not seem to need justification. Why then should the categories, and the principles which
involve them, need it? To this Kant's answer seems to be as follows. *Prima
facie* there is nothing absurd in the supposition that our sensations might
come to us in such a complete jumble that we could never have regarded
them as appearances of persistent material substances interacting causally
with each other. But, even if this had been so, it need not have worried the
geometer. He could still have formed the concepts of pure geometry, e.g.
the straight line, the circle, and so on. He could still have recognised the
axioms of pure geometry. And he could still have found approximate
instances of his pure concepts in his visual and tactual sense-data or have
constructed instances in imagination. If there are material substances,
geometry applies to them because they are extended. But it applies to them
in virtue of what they have in common with sense-data and images, viz.
their extension and figure, and not in virtue of what distinguishes them
from sense-data and images, viz. their substantiality, their causal properties, and so on. So the fact that the concepts and laws of geometry,
although *a priori*, do not seem *prima facie* to need a transcendental deduction, does not show that no such deduction is needed for the *a priori*

concepts of cause and substance and the *a priori* principles which involve them.

To this Kant adds the following remark. Once a person sees that our use of the categories of cause, substance, etc. needs justification, he will begin to feel doubts about the application of the notion of space and will want a transcendental deduction for this also. For philosophers and theologians have applied spatial concepts, just as they have applied the concepts of cause and of substance, to objects which could not possibly be perceived by the senses, e.g. to God and the soul and the material universe taken as a collective whole. And one might fairly wonder whether this is justifiable, even if we did not know that all sorts of difficulties and contradictions have arisen in such applications. Now Kant claims to have supplied a trans-cendental deduction for spatial concepts and principles by showing that space is the *a priori* form of human intuition, and thus applies to *all* objects that one will ever be able to perceive with the senses and *only* to such objects. But it is obvious that no such deduction can be applied to the categories, for they are essentially *discursive* and not intuitive.

There are three comments to be made on this distinction which Kant draws between the categories and the principles which involve them, on the one hand, and the concepts and principles of geometry on the other. (1) I am very doubtful whether we should have formed certain fundamental geometrical concepts, e.g. that of the straight line, unless sensation had presented us with approximate instances, e.g. edges that look and feel straight, rays of light, and so on. Would an intelligent jellyfish, floating about in the water and never meeting with anything that presented the appearance of a rigid body, have formed the concepts or discovered the principles of Euclidean geometry, even if these be *a priori* in Kant's sense? (2) I am doubtful whether it is true that the concepts and principles of geometry would at any rate apply to our visual sensa or images, and that it would not matter to geometry if our sensations came in such a jumble that we could not base upon them perceptions of a world of persistent solid bodies. For, although geometry is not concerned with the causal prop-erties and the sensible qualities which distinguish a body from an empty region of the same shape, size, and position, it *is* concerned with idealised bodies considered in their purely extensional and positional aspect. It is not concerned with mere sensa and images as such, and it would be difficult or impossible to apply the concepts and principles of geometry to them. (3) Kant's suggestion that we could be aware of our sense-data and images even if they came in such a jumble that no perception of a world of bodies could be based on them is certainly not in accordance with his final view. In the course of the *Transcendental Deduction*, and still more in the second edition form of the *Refutation of Idealism*, he reaches a fundamentally different conclusion. He seems to argue that a person could not be introspectively or inspectively aware of his own sense-data and images unless they were so interconnected that he could and did base upon them percepts of a world of bodies, which are conceived as substances, causes, etc., and are subject to the law of causation, the conservation of mass, and so on.

3.2.2 General principles of a transcendental deduction

We can now consider the preliminary sketch which Kant gives of the general lines which a transcendental deduction must follow. He starts by distinguishing 'experience', in a certain technical sense, from merely having a number of simultaneous and successive sensations, images, and feelings. The essential point is this. If a person says that he is seeing or hearing or remembering, it is always sensible to ask: '*What* are you seeing?' '*What* are your hearing?' '*What* are you remembering?'. And we expect him to mention some name or descriptive phrase which ostensibly denotes or describes some thing or event other than this experience of seeing or hearing or remembering. We may call such experiences 'epistemologically objective'. An experience may be epistemologically objective even if it should be delusive. E.g. a dream of a man pointing a revolver at one is just as much an epistemologically objective experience as a sane person's waking-perception of a similar incident. In fact it is only with regard to epistemologically objective experiences that the question 'Is it veridical or delusive?' is significant. For the question comes to this. 'Is there in fact a thing or event answering exactly or approximately to the description of the epistemological object of this experience and standing in certain assignable relations to it as a mental occurrent?' If there is, the experience is veridical; if not, it is delusive. So by 'experience', in his technical sense, Kant means experiences which are epistemologically objective, i.e. which ostensibly present to us objects other than themselves, and ostensibly provide us with information about these objects. It will be best to substitute the phrase 'epistemologically objective experience' for 'experience' here. For we need a general name to cover both states of mind like perceptions and memories, which *are* epistemologically objective, and mere isolated sensations, feelings, etc., which are not. And it is often convenient to use the word 'experiences' in this wider sense.

Kant now proceeds to state the conditions which must be fulfilled if a person is to have an epistemologically objective experience which ostensibly presents to him a particular thing or event. There must be (1) an intuitive experience, e.g. a sensation, and (2) a conceptual experience. The latter consists in thinking of an object of such-and-such a description and judging that it is now present to one's senses. The details of the description under which one thinks of the object will be determined by the nature of the sensation which one is having. But there will be factors in it which are not sense-given.

Kant's position may be summed up as follows. Unless and until I base upon a sensation a perceptual *judgment,* which is determined in part by it but goes beyond anything that is given in it, I do not begin to have an epistemologically objective experience. And unless I make this transition from merely having sensations to having perceptions, my experience cannot significantly be called 'veridical' or 'delusive'.

Now all perceptual judgments involve certain very general concepts, viz. those which are part of the notion of a physical thing or event. These general concepts may therefore be said to make epistemologically objective experiences possible. We can be certain *a priori* that they will apply to any object which we ever can ostensibly perceive. For ostensibly to perceive an object just consists in having certain sensations and in basing upon them perceptual judgments which involve these concepts. If I were ever to have a sensation on which I could not base such a judgment, I should *ipso facto* not ostensibly perceive any object in connexion with that sensation. This, Kant says, gives us the general principle for the transcendental deduction of all the *a priori* factors in our cognition, whether they belong to the intuitive or to the conceptual department of our minds. We justify their application by showing that they are necessary conditions without which epistemologically objective experiences would be impossible. Without the *a priori* factors of space and time, which belong to the intuitive side of the mind, there could be no visual, tactual, or other extensive sense-data, and so the sensuous factor in sense-perception would be impossible. Without the *a priori* concepts involved in the notion of a physical thing or event no perceptual judgments could be based on our sensations, and so the conceptual factor in sense-perception would be impossible (pp. 125–7, B 124–7/A 92–4).

The next question is: How does all this concern the categories, which Kant is claiming to deduce? In this connexion we may quote the following statement. The categories 'are concepts of an object in general. . .' (p. 128, B 128). Evidently Kant held that the various categories, substance, cause, etc. are all involved in the notion of physical thing. Therefore when we make, on the basis of our sensations, a perceptual judgment to the effect that there is such-and-such a physical thing, e.g. a cow out yonder, we are implicitly predicating all the categories which are involved in the notion of a physical thing. It seems to follow that Kant held that the concept of physical object is, in his sense, an *a priori* concept. This may seem odd, but it fits in with certain explicit statements which he makes about *a priori* concepts and their relation to experience on pp. 129–30 (A 96–7).

What he says there amounts to this. Although an *a priori* concept contains no factors *derived from* experiences, yet it would be completely without application unless it applied to objects of actual or possible experiences. If the categories apply to anything, then, they apply neither to the things-in-themselves of the metaphysicians, nor to the sense-data and images of the epistemologists and psychologists, but to the chairs and tables and atoms of ordinary sense-perception and natural science. And they apply of necessity to all these empirical objects, because to perceive such an object just consists in having a sensation and basing upon it a perceptual judgment, which involves the categories because they are involved in the notion of physical object.

Before going further I will make some comments on this. I agree with Kant that the experience of ostensibly perceiving a physical object involves having a sensation and also involves something more of a different kind. I agree that the moment you begin to say anything about the epistemological object, e.g. to describe it as a tree or a cow, or to ascribe such-and-such a colour or shape to it, you are certainly making a perceptual judgment. I agree that, unless you either *actually* did make such judgments or would be *prepared* to do so, you could hardly be said to be perceiving anything in particular. I agree further that such judgments, when reflected upon, are seen to involve particular applications of the notions of persistent substance and variable states and qualitites, of active and passive causal properties, of the contrast between physical reality and sensible appearances, and so on. And I agree that these notions certainly cannot be exemplified by our sensations and derived from them in the plain straightforward way in which the notions of red or hot no doubt are. At this stage the two critical comments which I would make are these. (1) I feel sure that one often has the experience of ostensibly perceiving a certain object without *actually* making any explicit perceptual judgment about it. I think we must admit that in many cases there is no more than adjusting one's body and mind as one would do *if* one had made certain perceptual judgments. I would not go further than to say that there must be *either* an actual judgment *or* a state of what Price calls 'perceptual acceptance',[1] which would develop into a perceptual judgment if any relevant question were raised about the object either by oneself or by another. (2) Suppose, however, that we were to grant that an actual perceptual judgment is always present as an essential constituent of the experience of ostensibly perceiving an object. In what sense precisely would this justify the application of the categories of substance and cause and so on? I think that Kant's argument up to this point would warrant only the following conclusion. It is as certain that we do apply the categories of cause and substance, and probably some others too, as that we have experiences in which we ostensibly perceive physical objects. And we certainly do have such experiences. If any of these experiences are *veridical*, then our use of

[1] [H. H. Price, *Perception* (London, 1932).]

these categories is justified. But the question remains whether any of our perceptual experiences *are* veridical. Unless this can be established, we cannot pass to the categorical conclusion that our use of these categories *is* justified. And, even if we can do this, nothing that has been said so far would show that the general principles involving such categories, e.g. the law of universal causation, must hold for perceptible objects. For it certainly seems *prima facie* possible that part of the notion of a physical object is that it is a relatively permanent *substance* with active and passive *causal* properties, and that we do from time to time perceive such objects, and yet that the law of universal causation and the principle of the conservation of matter do not hold of these objects. We shall have to consider in due course whether anything that Kant says later gets us beyond this point.

The next stage in Kant's account of the general principles of a transcendental deduction is this. On p. 138 (A111) he opens chapter 4 with the following statement. 'There is one single experience in which all perceptions are represented as in thoroughgoing and orderly connexion, just as there is only one space and one time in which all modes of appearance . . . occur.' A little lower down he says that the categories are simply the *conceptual* conditions of a possible experience, just as space and time are its *intuitional* conditions. He also says: 'The *a priori* conditions of a possible experience in general are at the same time conditions of the possibility of objects of experience' (p. 138, A111). On the next page he takes the concept of cause as an example and makes the following remark. 'The concept of cause is nothing but a synthesis . . . [of appearances] . . . according to concepts. Without such unity, which has its *a priori* rule and which subjects the appearances to itself, no thoroughgoing . . . unity of consciousness would be met with in the manifold of perceptions. These perceptions would not then belong to any experience and consequently would be without an object. They would be merely a blind play of presentations, less even than a dream' (p. 139, A112).

What does all this come to? I think that three things are plain. (1) When Kant talks of 'one single experience', of 'a possible experience in general', and of a 'thoroughgoing unity of consciousness' what he is thinking of is this. He is thinking of that characteristic kind of unity which unites all the experiences of a single self-conscious person, in virtue of which that person and no one else can say of each of them 'This is an experience of *mine*'. Each of us regards all the *things* which he has perceived or ever could perceive as located in a single *spatial* system, and all the *events* which he has perceived or introspected or ever could perceive or introspect as dated in single *time*-system. Similarly each of us regards all *experiences* which he has had or ever could have as so interrelated that he would be able to say of each of them 'This is an experience of mine'. (2) In this part of his argument Kant seems to be considering something more than the synthesis of a number of sense-impressions and images into a percept of a particular object at a particular moment from a particular point of view. He seems to be considering the interconnexion of a vast number of simultaneous and successive percepts to constitute an individual's perceptual and conceptual experience of a world of persistent interacting solid objects in a single spatio-temporal system. (3) In consequence of this, something more than the mere *category* of cause, e.g., is supposed to be involved. It seems plain that the notion of *causal laws* is supposed to enter; and also the *a priori* principle that every perceptible event is completely determined, in accordance with some particular causal law, by certain earlier events which could in principle have been perceived. I think that this must be what Kant has in mind when, in taking the example of causation, he talks of such unity as 'having its *a priori* rule'. I take it that the '*a priori* rule' in this case is the principle of universal causation.

On these assumptions as to Kant's meaning his argument could be put as follows. Of all the sensations that I have had in the past and can ever have in future it must be true that I could say of them 'These are *my* sensations'. This is almost an analytic proposition. But it can be reinforced by considering what is involved by saying that such-and-such experiences of mine were perceptions of various parts or aspects of a certain physical thing from various points of view. For certainly part of what I mean is that, if *I* were to do or were to have done certain things, *I* should have had certain sensations, related in their qualitative aspect in certain assignable ways to the sensations which *I* in fact have had. Now, if a number of mental events have the common property of being *my* experiences, they must *ipso facto* be interrelated in certain very general but characteristic ways. No future mental event which was not related in those ways to the past mental events which were *my* experiences could itself count as an experience of *mine*. It might belong to another person, or perhaps to no person at all, or be what might be called an 'unconscious' mental event arising from the stimulation of some part of my body. But it could be no part of *my* experience as a self-conscious person. I can therefore be certain that any sensation which I can ever count as mine will have to be related to my present and my past sensations by that relationship *R*, whatever it may be, which relates my present sensations to each other and to my past sensations, and which is involved in their all being experiences which I can call *mine*. This relationship is no doubt concerned primarily with these sensations in their *occurrent* aspect. But it involves certain relations between them in their qualitative aspect; for it is a question of sense-data of such-and-such *qualities* occurring in such-and-such a temporal order. Now my present and my past sensations have been so interrelated that I could and did regard them as various appearances of physical things in a single spatio-temporal system, interacting with each other according to certain laws of sequence. These relations among my sensations in their qualitative aspect are entailed by the relationship R among them which makes them all *my* sensations. I can therefore be certain *a priori* that any future sensation which could possibly be mine would be related to my present and my past sensations by these same relations. Hence I can be certain that I shall be able to regard all future sensations that I may have as so many appearances of physical things in a single spatio-temporal system interacting with each other according to certain laws of sequence.

The point is that it is not a merely contingent fact that my sensations have so far come in such groups that I could regard them in this way. My mind is a selective agent, and no sensation could possibly enter into *my* experience and be a sensation of *mine* unless it had such relations to my other experiences that I could regard it in this way. As Kant puts it, the 'empirical affinity of phenomena', i.e. the fact that all my sensations up to now *have* come in such groupings, is not just contingent. It is a consequence of what he calls 'transcendental affinity', i.e. of the fact that no set of mental occurrents which were not so related could be the experiences of any one self-conscious person.

This an extremely ingenious argument. It seems to me to be sound in outline but doubtful in detail. The fact that a number of mental occurrents are all experiences of a single self-conscious person does no doubt entail that they all have some very general relation R to each other. And it no doubt follows that every mental occurrent which can ever count as an experience of that same person will have to stand in this relation R to the other mental occurrents which have been experiences of his. But even Kant would admit that the mental occurrents which have been experiences of mine have plenty of relations which are not entailed by the mere fact that they were all mine. And he would admit that they have the general relationship R in certain specific forms which are not entailed by the mere fact that they were all mine. For he does not pretend that we can know *a priori* what perceptible substances there are or even what kinds of perceptible substances there are. And he does not pretend that we can know *a priori* any of the particular causal laws which in fact hold in nature. Now it is not necessary that future experiences, merely in order to be mine, should have these *other* relations which my past experiences had. And it is not necessary that future experiences, merely in order to be mine, should have the relationship R in the *special determinate form* in which my past experiences had it. How can he be sure that the relations among my present and past sensations which enabled me to regard them all as appearances of bodies in a single spatial system, interacting with each other according to invariable laws, are really involved in the relation R which they had in virtue of being all experiences of mine? Might they not have been so interrelated in their *occurrent* aspect as to count as experiences of mine and yet not interrelated in their *qualitative* aspect in the very special ways which would make me regard them as appearances of bodies in a single spatial system interacting in accordance with invariable laws? Up to this point it seems to me that Kant has produced an argument which might justify us in holding that *some categories or other* must apply to all the objects which I could ever ostensibly perceive. And it might be suspected that *some* very general principles involving these categories would hold for all such objects. But he has not justified the use of any particular category, such as cause, or of any particular principle, such as the principle that every perceptible event is completely determined by earlier events which could in principle have been perceived. We shall have to consider whether he can get beyond this point when he goes into further detail.

Before leaving this topic I will refer to an interesting passage on p. 140 (A114), which shows, I think, that I have not been misinterpreting Kant and that he was well aware that his doctrine seems at first sight highly paradoxical. 'That nature should direct itself according to our subjective ground of apperception, and should indeed depend upon it in respect of its conformity to law, sounds very strange and absurd. But when we consider that this nature is not a thing-in-itself but is merely an aggregate of appearances – so many presentations of the mind – we shall not be surprised . . .' I think that this may be paraphrased as follows. Nature for each person is just the totality of all the objects which are or could conceivably be presented to him in sense-perception. It is therefore not surprising that there should be in it certain types of order and unity which arise from the following two interconnected sources: (1) From those relations between various sensa and images which generate from them perceptions of physical things and events. (2) From those further relations between perceptions which are involved in their all being experiences of a single self-conscious person. On this view of nature it is intelligible that we could show *a priori* that it would inevitably conform to certain very general principles of unity. But, on any other view of it, it would simply be an empirical fact that, so far as our observations go, nature has up to date conformed to these principles.

3.2.3 The processes involved in epistemologically objective experiences

We will now consider Kant's detailed account of the processes involved in generating out of sense-impressions what he calls 'experience', i.e. perceptual cognition of a world of physical things and events subject to causal laws.

On p. 143 at the bottom (A120) he says that he will start from the empirical. What immediately follows is an elaborate bit of empirical, though hypothetical, psychology. Then he tries to show that certain transcendental conditions are presupposed by the empirical processes which he has been describing. The details of Kant's argument are obscure and confused; so I think it will be best for me to state in my own way what he probably had in mind.

3.2.3.1 The functions of 'imagination'

(1) The ultimate data of all human cognition of objects are sense-impressions of various kinds, e.g. visual, tactual, auditory, and so on. A sense-impression is something essentially private and subjective. It is meaningless to suggest that it, or anything like it, could exist except as an event in a certain person's mind at a certain moment of his history. (2) In the case of any human being past his first infancy the sense-impressions which he is getting at any moment from the stimulation of various parts of his various sense-organs are integrated into what may be called 'sense-fields'. His visual sense-impressions at any one moment are integrated into a visual field, his tactual sensations at any one moment are integrated into a tactual field, and so on. Moreover these various contemporary sense-fields of the same person are integrated with each other. Obviously my visual field and my tactual field at each moment are united with each other in a characteristic way in which my visual field is not united with the tactual field of any other person. Kant ascribes this integration of sense-impressions to a faculty which he calls *imagination*. As we shall see, he ascribes various functions to imagination. The particular function of integrating contemporary sense-impressions of the same sense into a sense-field and integrating the various contemporary sense-fields of a single person seems to be what Kant calls *apprehension*. (3) The successive sense-fields of the same person do not just vanish without a trace, giving place to a successor which in turn vanishes without a trace. Obviously, e.g., one's successive visual fields are integrated with each other to form what might be called a visual 'sense-*history*'. The same is true for one's successive auditory, tactual, and other sense-fields. Kant ascribes this kind of integration also to imagination. This function of it seems to be, or to be included in, what he calls *reproduction*. It would be a mistake to suppose that it always or usually consists in the production of images which coexist with the present sense-field and resemble the immediately past one. All that one can say is that the present field is felt as continuing an immediately previous field, that most features in it are felt as familiar, that many appear as qualitatively unchanged, that others appear as continuing a change already begun, and so on. (4) The two processes which I have so far described are concerned with the integration of all a person's simultaneous sense-impressions into a total sense-field and all his successive total sense-

fields into a single total sense-history. They might be described as processes of *collective* integration. I think that they might fairly be called
transcendental and non-empirical in the sense that they are not concerned
with the particular qualities of particular sense-impressions and are minimal conditions without which no kind of unitary personal experience
would be possible. (5) We must next consider processes which might be
described as *selective* integration. In the case of any human being past his
first infancy, his total visual field at any moment is nearly always differentiated into a number of outstanding coloured patches of various
shapes and sizes against a comparatively undifferentiated coloured background. Each such outstanding patch is taken by him to be a visual
appearance from his present point of view of a certain part of a certain
body, e.g. of the top of a table, of the hind-quarters of a cow, and so on.
Similar remarks apply, though the differentiation is generally much less
definite, to other kinds of sense-field. E.g. a person's auditory field at a
certain moment might consist of a vague background of sound with
certain outstanding auditory data, one of which he refers to the ticking of
his clock, another to the tolling of a distant bell, and so on, as heard from
where he now is. Now, in order for this to be possible, at least the
following conditions must be fulfilled. (a) Any such outstanding patch of
colour consists no doubt of a large number of simultaneous visual sense-
impressions integrated into a special pattern and differentiated from the
rest of the contents of the same visual field. (b) The presence of this
outstanding patch must call up in his mind the idea of certain correlated
series of *possible* visual appearances. It must make him take for granted
that, if he were to occupy any one of a certain series of positions and were
to fulfil certain other conditions, he would be presented with a certain one
of this series of correlated possible visual appearances. (c) It must also call
up in his mind the idea of certain possible correlated appearances in his
non-visual sense-fields, e.g. the characteristic *feel* of a smooth cool shining
surface, the characteristic *sound* which it would give if tapped, and so on. It
must make him take for granted that he would be presented with these
correlated non-visual appearances if he were to fulfil certain conditions. (6)
Now the second and third of these necessary conditions evidently depend
on at least the following factors. (a) On certain *empirical* facts. In the past he
must actually have been presented with such a series of correlated visual
appearances on occasions when he actually did successively occupy a
certain series of positions. And he must actually have been presented with
such correlated non-visual appearances on occasions when he was presented with this kind of visual appearance and when he actually did fulfil
these further conditions. (b) On his possession of certain *mental faculties*. (i)
Each such series of correlated sense-experiences must leave some kind of
trace, and the traces left by different series must remain distinct from each

other and not just fuse into a single blurred trace. (ii) The trace left by any one such series must be capable of being excited on future occasions when the person again has a sensation which resembles qualitatively any one of the terms in that past series. (iii) When the trace is thus excited it must give rise to images which in fact resemble the other terms in the series of sensations which originally left the trace. (iv) There need be no experience of *remembering* the occasions on which one had such a series of sensations. But the excitement of the trace must give rise to a state of taking for granted that the present images would be replaced by corresponding sensations *if* one were to fulfil certain conditions. These conditions are the ones which actually were fulfilled in the past when one actually had the series of sensations which left the trace. We might describe the four powers just mentioned as *retentiveness, re-excitement of similarity, reinstatement in imagery*, and *uncritical acceptance of reinstatability in sensation*. (7) The next point to notice is this. In each one of a series of my successive visual fields there may be a visual appearance which I ascribe to one and the same object, e.g. a certain cat. Then there may come a series of my visual fields in each of which there is no visual appearance which I can ascribe to that object. And then there may come a series of my visual fields in each of which there is a visual appearance which I ascribe to the *same* object. (This would happen, e.g., if I were to turn my head away for a while and then look back in the former direction and the cat had not moved appreciably. It would also happen if I were to continue to look in the same direction and the cat were to run into some bushes and then to run out again.) Now I do not believe that the object ceases to exist and then starts to exist again. I think that Kant's view would be that, on the basis of past *continuous* series of sensations and the traces left by them, the missing visual sensations are replaced by corresponding images. Each such image is accompanied by a state of uncritically taking for granted that one *would* be having a corresponding sensation *if* one were now fulfilling certain conditions, e.g. if one were still looking in the same direction instead of having turned one's head. Kant describes all these processes which I have been discussing as 'empirical reproduction'.

3.2.3.2 The 'affinity' of appearances

The next stage of the argument appears to be as follows (pp. 144–6, A 120–4). (1) We might have all the mental powers which we have been considering. But they would remain latent and could not get to work unless the following conditions were fulfilled. Let $s_1, s_2, \ldots, s_n$ be a series of successive sense-fields in a person's mental history. In any one of them, e.g. s_r, there will be a number of items which stand out from the innumerable others which are presented along with them, e.g. a certain coloured patch, a certain ticking noise, and so on. Let us call these x_r, y_r, z_r, etc. Now certain outstanding items in any sense-field are specially connected with certain outstanding items in the sense-fields which are adjacent to it in the series. Thus to the item x_1 in s_1 there may correspond an item x_2 in s_2, an item x_3 in s_3, and so on. And to the item y_1 in s_1 there may correspond an item y_2 in s_2 and an item y_3 in s_3, and so on. In this way there are within a person's total sense-history various outstanding *strands* which go on side by side, e.g. the strand x_1, x_2, x_3 . . . and the strand y_1, y_2, y_3 . . . Now it is such strands within one's total sense-history which leave traces and provide the materials for re-excitement by similarity, reinstatement in imagery, and so on. I think that Kant is referring to this when he says at the bottom of p. 144 (A 121), 'This subjective and *empirical* ground of reproduction according to rules is what is called the *association* of presentations.' (2) Kant now makes the following essential step. He argues that although it is contingent that there should be this, that, or the other strand of associated sensations in the mental history of a particular self-conscious individual, yet it is necessary that there should be *some* such strands in the mental history of *any* such individual. For otherwise, he says, 'there might exist a multitude of perceptions . . . in which much empirical consciousness would arise in my mind, but in a state of separation and without belonging to a consciousness of myself' (p. 145, A 122). It seems to me that he goes further than asserting that there must be *some* outstanding strands in the mental history of any self-conscious individual. He seems to assert that *every* sense-datum must be capable of being regarded as an item in *some* such strand if a person can say of it: 'This is a sense-datum of *mine*' (cf. remarks on p. 145, A 122). He gives the name of *affinity* to this property which he holds must belong to all the sense-data of which an individual could say: 'These are mine'. (3) And now finally he seems to assert the following proposition. The fact that every sense-datum which I can call mine is such that it can be regarded as one of a series of actual or possible sense-data of mine subject to certain rules is not just a contingent fact. It must be due to the fact that I myself have unconsciously imposed upon all these sense-data such properties as fit them to answer to this condition. Cf., e.g., the following statement: '. . . the affinity of all appearances, near or remote, is a necessary consequence of a synthesis in imagination which is grounded *a priori* on rules' (p. 145, A 123). It appears that Kant ascribes this process to what he calls the *productive*, as distinct from the *reproductive*, imagination. The following is a characteristic statement of Kant's doctrine. 'Thus the order and regularity in the appearances, which we entitle *nature*, we ourselves introduce. We could never find them in appearances, had not we ourselves or the nature of our minds originally set them there' (p. 147, A 125). The whole subject is developed on pp. 147–9 (A 126–8), and there is no doubt that Kant was fully aware that he was asserting something which would shock his readers. I will quote the following passages. 'Thus the understanding is something more than a power of formulating rules through comparison of instances; it is itself the lawgiver of nature' (p. 148, A127). 'However exaggerated and absurd it may sound to say that the understanding is itself the source of the laws of nature . . . such an assertion is none the less correct' (p. 148, A127).

Kant tries to mitigate the paradox as follows. He admits that every particular law of nature, e.g. the law that metals expand when heated, is contingent and empirical and established only by induction. But he says that all empirical laws 'are only special determinations of still higher laws; and the highest of these, under which the others all stand, issue *a priori* from the understanding itself' (p. 148, A126). He says that it is through the latter that 'appearances take on an orderly character, just as the same appearances, despite the differences in their empirical forms, must none the less be in harmony with the pure form of sensibility', i.e. with the properties of the innate spatio-temporal system in which they present themselves (pp. 148–9, A128).

3.2.3.3 The understanding and its categories

Hitherto we have been talking of what Kant calls 'imagination'. But he is claiming to deduce the *categories*, and they are supposed to be concepts of the faculty called 'understanding'. We have at last come to this in connexion with affinity and the law-abidingness of nature. We must now consider in more detail what Kant says about it.

(1) As regards the understanding Kant says on p. 147 that he has described it in various ways in various places. It has been contrasted, e.g., as an *active* cognitive power with *sensibility* as purely passive and receptive. Again, it has been described as the department of the mind which is concerned with *concepts* or with making *judgments*. He says that he will now describe it as the *faculty of rules*. He asserts (what seems to me to be extremely doubtful) that all these different descriptions can be seen on reflection to be identical. But he says that the description of understanding as a faculty of rules is more fruitful, and approximates more closely to its essential nature. One p. 146 he says that the pure or productive imagination is the essential mediating link between the two extremes of sensibility and understanding.

(2) As regards the categories Kant makes the following statements in this connexion. 'In the understanding there are . . . pure *a priori* modes of knowledge, which contain the necessary unity of the pure synthesis of imagination in respect of all possible appearances. These are the *categories* . . .' (p. 143, A119). On p. 128 (B128) he says that the categories are concepts of an *object in general*. On pp. 146–7 (A124–5) he says that actual

experience contains, in its highest empirical forms, 'certain concepts which render possible the formal unity of experiences and therewith all objective validity of empirical cognition'. He says that it is these concepts, 'in so far as they concern solely the form of an experience in general', which he calls *categories*.

(3) If we put this together and bring it down from the clouds, it seems to me to come to something like the following. (a) The categories are the concepts of the most general structural features in the notion of a world of bodies and physical events located in a single space and time, interacting with each other, and subject in all its changes to complete determination in accordance with universal laws. (b) Each human mind has implicit in it an innate conception of such a world and therefore innate conceptions of all the fundamental structural features involved in the notion of such a world. This innate conception belongs, as being conceptual and not intuitive, to that department of the mind which we call *understanding*. (c) In order that such a world may be *perceived as actual*, and not merely *conceived as possible*, one's sense-data must have such qualities and come in such temporal and spatial relations that one can regard them all as appearances of bodies or physical events which fit into the innate scheme conceived by one's understanding. (d) Now one's sense-impressions are due to the action of foreign things-in-themselves upon that thing-in-itself which is one's own mind as it really is. There can be no guarantee that they will fit into the innate scheme conceived by one's understanding unless there be some part of one's mind which 'doctors' them, in accordance with that scheme, in such a way that they shall fit in with it. The part of one's mind which does this is called *productive imagination*. It may be said to mediate between understanding and sensibility for the following reason. It is concerned with *sensibility* because it operates upon sense-impressions, supplements them by appropriate images, and so on. It is concerned with *understanding* because its operations ensure that one's sense-impressions shall have such qualities and relations that we can regard them all as so many different appearances of a system of law-abiding interacting bodies such as the understanding conceives.

3.2.3.4 The doctrine of a 'synopsis' and three 'syntheses'

Before leaving the general topic of *processes involved in epistemologically objective experience* there is one other thing to be mentioned. From the last paragraph on p. 130 to the end of the second paragraph on p. 134 (A 97–104) Kant puts forward an elaborate preliminary account of these processes. He says that these sections are intended 'rather to prepare than to instruct the reader'. And he makes little further reference by name to the various mental powers and processes which he here distinguishes. The main interest of these sections is that they introduce us to a topic which plays a very important part later on. This may be described as the distinction between (1) merely having a number of sensations which do *in fact* occur in a certain sequence, and (2) perceiving by means of a sequence of sensations either the coexisting parts of a physical thing or an objective sequence of physical events. An example of the first would be perceiving by means of a sequence of visual sensations the coexistent front, sides, and back of a house. An example of the second would be perceiving by means of a sequence of auditory sensations a certain objective sequence of sounds as having a characteristic pattern, e.g. as a rendering of a certain tune.

In these sections Kant asserts that for this kind of thing to be possible there must be first a process which he calls 'synopsis' and then on top of that three processes which he calls 'syntheses'. He ascribes the synopsis to the senses, but says that the syntheses are spontaneous acts of our own. To the three syntheses he gives the names *apprehension in intuition, reproduction in imagination*, and *recognition in concepts*. The whole doctrine here is so obscure and confused that it is not worth while to consider in detail what each of these various processes is supposed to do. I think that *synopsis* perhaps corresponds roughly to what I have called *collective integration*.

It will be worth while however to add a remark about the so-called *synthesis of recognition in concepts*. I doubt whether it can properly be called a *synthesis*, in the sense in which the other processes may properly be so called. What I suspect to be at the back of Kant's mind is this. When the other processes are completed, and not till then, one is in a position to make a perceptual judgment, e.g. 'This is a house' or 'This is a tune'. Such a judgment may be still more concrete and determinate, e.g. 'This is the Master's Lodge' or 'This is *God save the King*'. Or it may be extremely abstract and indeterminate, e.g. 'This is a physical thing' or 'This is a physical process'. In any case one may be said to be recognising the perceived object as an instance of a certain concept. The predicates of the more concrete judgments are certainly empirical concepts. The predicates of the most abstract of such judgments are, according to Kant, *a priori* concepts, involving certainly the categories of cause and substance, and Kant would probably hold involving all the categories. Any empirical concept which can be a predicate in a perceptual judgment is a more or less determinate specification of the *a priori* concepts which constitute the formal structure of every possible perceptual judgment.

3.2.4 The notion of physical object

Kant's description of the notion of physical object occurs in the part of *Transcendental Deduction* A from the middle of p. 134 (A 104) to the end of the first paragraph on p. 138 (A 110). It opens with the remark: 'At this point we must make clear to ourselves what we mean by the expression "an object of representations".' What Kant says is extremely obscure, but certain points emerge fairly plainly.

(1) If we take together the third paragraph on p. 134 and the paragraph in the middle of p. 137 we get a doctrine which might be paraphrased as follows. (a) Every perception as such *has* an epistemological object. (b) Every perception can also in turn *become* an object of reflective cognition. It can be introspected psychologically and inspected phenomenologically by the person whose perception it is. (c) Such reflective inspection or introspection is a case of *direct acquaintance* with its object. The only particulars with which anyone can ever be directly acquainted are *his own experiences*, and the only kind of direct acquaintance possible to him is reflective inspection or introspection. It follows at once that, even if a sense-perception be completely veridical, it is never a case of direct acquaintance with the physical object of which it is a perception. (d) When a person inspects one of his own perceptions what he becomes acquainted with is a sense-datum or image or a complex of these. In this he intuits a certain sensible quality, e.g. sensible redness, sensible coldness, and so on, and a certain sensible shape, extension, and position in his visual or tactual sense-field. (e) What he *judges* about the *physical object* which he is ostensibly perceiving is correlated with the sensible and the spatial qualities which he would *intuit* in his perception if he were to inspect it. (f) From all this it follows that the concept of a physical object is the concept of something utterly different in kind from the sense-data which we take to be appearances of it to us. For *they* are private, subjective, and fleeting, and are possible objects of direct acquaintance to the person whose sense-data they are. But *it* is something public, neutral, and persistent, which presents various appearances but cannot be an object of direct acquaintance to anyone at any time. No property of it can be *intuited* by anyone at any time. Kant therefore describes it as 'an object which cannot itself be intuited by us and which may therefore be named the non-empirical, i.e. transcendental, object, *x*' (p. 137, A 109). This is one side of Kant's doctrine. It might be described as the *agnostic realistic* aspect of it.

(2) If we now return to that with which a person can be acquainted, viz. his own sense-data and images, we can ask ourselves: Under what circumstances does one regard a number of different sense-data, occurring perhaps at different times and perhaps very dissimilar in quality, as so many different appearances of one and the same physical thing? Again, under what circumstances does one regard a number of different sense-data, occurring at different times, as appearances of different *coexisting parts* of one and the same physical thing? And again, under what circumstances do we regard them as manifestations of different *coexisting qualities*, e.g. the colour and the temperature, of one and the same physical thing? Obvi-

ously the answer must be on the following lines. We do this when these sense-data are interrelated by certain relations in which they do not stand to our other sense-data. These characteristic interrelations among a set of sense-data, which entitle them all to be called appearances of the same physical object, could be described to some extent, though Kant never attempts to do so. E.g. one important relation would be that the shapes of certain visual sense-data in such a set are projectively or perspectively related. Another important relation would be that the areas of certain visual sense-data in such a set could be regarded as together making up the surface of a solid. Kant states the general doctrine quite clearly at the bottom of p. 134 and top of p. 135. In so far as a number of sense-data all relate to an object, he says, 'they must necessarily agree with one another, i.e. must possess that unity which constitutes the concept of an object' (A 104–5).

(3) We have now to connect this with the previous remarks about the non-empirical or transcendental object x. Kant's view appears to be this. The concept of a physical object is *not* just the concept of a set of actual and possible sense-data interrelated by certain characteristic relations which do not relate them to our other sense-data. It involves the concept of something which *imposes* this kind of order upon our sense-data. This is the concept of something which ensures that, when certain sense-data occur, certain others, related to them in these peculiar ways, *will* occur if we *do* certain things and *would* have occurred if we *had* done certain things. Cf. the following remark: 'The object is viewed as that which prevents our cognitions from being haphazard or arbitrary and which determines them *a priori* in some definite fashion' (p. 134, A 104). If we put all this together, it seems to come to this. From the nature of the case one cannot be *acquainted with* a physical object, as one can be acquainted with one's own sense-data and images through introspection and inspection. And one cannot *intuit* any characteristic of a physical object, as one intuits the sensible colour, the sensible shape, etc. of a sense-datum if one inspects it. An essential part of the notion of an ordinary physical object, e.g. the fountain in the Great Court of Trinity, is the notion of a *transcendental* object. A transcendental object can be cognised only as something answering to a certain description which one conceives and understands. And the only description under which one can think of a transcendental object is as the something which imposes upon a certain group of one's actual and possible sense-data those characteristic kinds of interconnexion which lead us to call them all so many different appearances of a certain one physical object. Thus, e.g., in the thought of that physical thing which we call the Trinity Fountain there are two different and equally essential factors, viz. (a) the thought of a certain set of actual and possible sense-data interconnected in certain characteristic ways, and (b) the thought of a some-

thing which imposes these characteristic interconnexions, but about which nothing further can be said except by further specifying the interconnexions which it imposes.

(4) Kant continually insists that the notion of a physical object involves the notion of *rules* and involves the notion of *necessity*. The following is a typical passage. 'A concept is always . . . something universal which serves as a rule. The concept of body, e.g., . . . serves as a rule in our knowledge of outer appearances . . . The concept of body . . . necessitates the representation of extension and therewith representations of impenetrability, shape, etc.' (p. 135, A 106). I think that all this is very obscure and ambiguous in detail. But there is one important point which may have been in Kant's mind. The characteristic kinds of interconnexion among a set of sense-data which lead us to count them all as appearances of a certain one physical object cannot be reduced to mere facts of actual regular sequence or regular co-existence. Suppose I am presented with a certain sense-datum of such a group. It is not enough for me to remember that in the past such a sense-datum *has* always been followed by such-and-such another sense-datum *whenever* I behaved in a certain way. What is required is that I shall believe certain propositions about the sense-data which *would* have been presented to me *if* I *had* done certain things which I did not in fact do, or which *would* be presented to me in the immediate future if I *were* now to do certain things which I have no intention of doing. Now the notion of the consequences which would have followed from conditions which were not in fact fulfilled, or of the consequences which would follow from conditions which will not in fact be fulfilled, does involve the notion of some kind of *necessity*. And another point about it is that this notion cannot plausibly be supposed to have been derived by abstraction from anything presented to us in sensation. If any notion might plausibly be held to be non-empirical in origin, it is the notion of a consequence which would necessarily have followed on the fulfilment of a condition which was not in fact fulfilled.

I have now considered the main points which seem to me to be fairly certain. If Kant had confined himself to these and had stuck to them throughout, the situation would have been much simpler than it in fact is. I will now make some comments on what has already been stated.

(1) On my interpretation Kant's complete account of the notion of a physical object involves two aspects, both of which he regards as essential. One is the doctrine of the transcendental object. This is what I will call the *agnostic realistic* aspect. The other is the account of the conditions under which we regard each of a number of different sense-data as so many different appearances of one and the same physical object. This may be called the *phenomenalist* aspect. Only we must remember that Kant held a view which many modern phenomenalists would ignore or reject, viz.

that the notion of *causal necessity* is involved in any adequate account of these conditions. Now very often Kant seems to forget the agnostic realistic aspect altogether and to talk as if he thought that the phenomenalist aspect were sufficient in itself. He often talks as if he held that the notion of physical object could be reduced entirely to the notion of a set of actual and possible sense-data interconnected in accordance with certain rules of necessary sequence and coexistence. Perhaps that is not very surprising in view of the fact that the phenomenalist aspect can be developed and specified in detail, whilst nothing further can be said of the agnostic realistic aspect.

(2) I think that Kant is quite right in holding that the commonsense notion of physical object involves something beside the phenomenalist aspect. To put it in logical terms, common sense is not content to believe that the hypothetical propositions about the sequence and coexistence of sense-data, which *would* occur under conditions which may or may not be fulfilled, are ultimate. Part of the notion of a physical object is that it is the *categorical* basis of all these conditional facts. But I think that Kant waters down this aspect of the commonsense notion of a physical object far too much in his very agnostic account of the transcendental object. I am sure that common sense thinks of the parts of a physical object which are not being seen or felt at a certain moment as then existing in precisely the same literal and categorical sense as the parts of it which are then being seen or felt. It thinks of the unseen and unfelt parts as continuous with those which are being seen or felt, and as completing with them a closed three-dimensional contour. It therefore thinks of that which determines the various interconnected appearances which we ascribe to a certain physical object as something very much more determinately specifiable than the mere x which is Kant's transcendental object. Kant himself came to much the same conclusion, whether consistently with the rest of his system or not, in the *Refutation of Idealism* in B.

(3) Kant is here merely *analysing the concept* of physical object. For that purpose it is irrelevant whether there really are any existents answering to the descriptions of transcendental objects. But it would be of interest to know whether he held that there were or not. If he did not hold this, we must suppose that he held that the notion of an x which corresponds to a certain group of interrelated sense-data and imposes upon them the characteristic rules of interconnexion is a kind of innate fiction of the human mind. All that really exists on that view is the groups of interconnected sense-data and the rules of necessary sequence and coexistence in accordance with which they are interconnected. But when a human mind is presented with such a group it cannot help conceiving and believing in an x which lies at the basis of it and imposes these rules upon it.

(4) Some commentators regard the passages in which the transcendental

object occurs as very early in date, and identify the transcendental objects with the foreign things-in-themselves which Kant held to be the ultimate sources of our sense-impressions. This latter interpretation seems to me both incredible and quite unnecessary. Kant is obviously trying to analyse the ordinary notion of this or that physical object, e.g. this tree or that house. To drag in a reference to foreign things-in-themselves would be completely irrelevant in the context. Moreover a transcendental object is thought of as something which imposes a certain kind of law-abiding *interconnexion* upon a certain group of actual and possible sense-data. Now I do not think that Kant ever ascribes *order* and *interconnexion* to the action of foreign things-in-themselves. He always thinks of them as just the source of the unordered manifold of sense-impressions, which have to get both their spatio-temporal and their causal order from elsewhere.

(5) I think it might plausibly be said that Kant ought to identify the transcendental objects with the *percipient himself* as performing certain *transcendental* activities. For he asserts that in some way each person unwittingly imposes upon all his sense-data such interrelations, rules of sequence and coexistence, etc., as enable and compel him to treat them all as various appearances of a world of bodies subject in all their changes to causal laws. His alleged ground for this is that a set of sense-data could not all count as the experiences of a single self-conscious person unless they were interrelated in this way. In a similar way, if one were a Berkeleian, one would have to identify the transcendental objects with God as performing certain *telepathic* activities. For the Berkeleian asserts that what gives to our sensations the kind of order and coherence which enables and compels us to regard them as appearances of a world of interacting bodies is the action of God who produces these sensations in us telepathically in accordance with certain rules of sequence and coexistence.

3.3 Transcendental Deduction B

The *Transcendental Deduction* B occupies pp. 151–75 (B 130–69). It is divided into sections numbered from §15 to §27 both inclusive. It is extremely obscure. I shall not go into it in detail, but shall mention the main points in which it differs from *Transcendental Deduction* A by omission, addition, or further development.

(1) Very little is said in detail about the various processes involved in sense-perception. But there is no reason to suppose that Kant had altered his views about them. They are referred to, though so briefly that it would be almost impossible to understand what Kant had in mind unless one had read Deduction A. Thus in §24 he distinguishes between what he calls *intellectual* synthesis and what he calls *figurative* synthesis. It is through figurative synthesis that the categories get their application to perceptible

objects. Figurative synthesis is ascribed to the imagination, and imagination is defined as 'the faculty of representing in intuition an object that is *not itself present*'. Imagination can mediate between understanding and sensibility for the following reason. On the one hand, it resembles thought in being active and spontaneous. The mind can, so to speak, create images for itself at will within certain limits, whilst it is entirely dependent on external stimulation for sensations. On the other hand, it resembles sensibility in that its products, viz. images, are particular existents and more or less resemble actual sense-data. The transcendental function of imagination is to operate upon sense-data and to supplement them with images under the guidance of the understanding. As a result of this one's sense-data are arranged in such groupings and are so supplemented that one can and does have the experience of ostensibly perceiving a world of physical things and events, which exemplify the various categories, and are subject to certain *a priori* principles involving the categories, e.g. the law of universal causation. In a footnote (pp. 171–2, B161) Kant goes even further. He says there: 'It is one and the same spontaneity, which, in the one case under the title of "imagination" and in the other case under the title of "understanding", brings combination into the manifold of intuition.' Then, again, in §26 there is a reference to an old friend, viz. 'synthesis of apprehension', and a definition is given of this process.

(2) All reference to the notion of transcendental object, as an essential factor in the notion of physical object, seems to have vanished. Kant seems to consider that a purely phenomenalistic analysis of the concept of physical object is adequate.

(3) The fundamental importance of the synthetic unity of apperception is stressed even more strongly than in Deduction A. It becomes the ultimate ground for the deduction of the categories.

(4) Kant leads up to this, and introduces the whole subject, by a general discussion of the *conjunction* or *combination* of a manifold. The main points which he makes are these. (a) The data of sense, as they arise in us, are a mere plurality of items without any particular order or arrangement intrinsic to them. Any order that one *finds* in them must have been *put* into them by oneself, whether consciously or unconsciously, by an act or process of ordering or arranging or combining. (b) Any such process of combining and arranging must be ascribed to the intellectual part of the mind, i.e. to the understanding. For it is something that we *do*, and not something which we just passively *receive*. (c) Every form of mental analysis presupposes a previous synthesis of the analysandum by the person who performs the analysis.

Now, as regards all this, I can only say that Kant offers no reason for it and that I do not find it self-evident or even particularly plausible. Nor is it clear to me that, because the processes of synthesis have to be ascribed to a part of the mind which is active and not merely receptive, that part can be identified with the *understanding*, in the sense of the faculty which uses concepts and makes judgments. Yet it is important for Kant to make this identification if he is to maintain that the categories which he professes to deduce transcendentally are those which he discovers and enumerates by reflecting on the classification of judgments by formal logicians.

(5) The transition from these general remarks about combination to the transcendental unity of apperception is the following. (a) It is impossible for me to combine mentally a set of items unless they are all either experiences of *mine* or at any rate objects of experiences of mine. If an item is neither one of *my* experiences nor an object which I perceive or remember or imagine or think about or cognise in some other way, it is nothing to me and I cannot combine it with anything else. Therefore a necessary condition for any particular process of synthesis by a person is that the items to be synthesised should be so interconnected that he can count them all as *his* experiences or as objects of *his* experiences. (Kant does not clearly distinguish the two alternatives, but it seems necessary to do so.) (b) Kant ascribes this primary synthesis to something which he calls 'transcendental apperception'. The unity thus produced, which is the precondition of all more determinate forms of combining and arranging, is called the 'transcendental unity of apperception'. (c) It is an analytic proposition that any experience which can be counted as *mine* must be one of which *I* could be conscious and could recognise as mine. But it is a synthetic proposition that such-and-such relations must hold among all the experiences which could count as those of a single self-conscious person. (d) Starting from the premiss that all the items which I could possibly combine in any way must have to each other those relations which are involved in their all being my experiences Kant jumps to the following conclusion. He concludes that my sense-data and images must be so combined and arranged as to constitute an organised system of ostensible perceptions of a world of persistent extended substances subject in all their changes to the law of universal causation. I cannot see that this follows and I cannot find any adequate argument for it. I think it is very plausible to hold that there is a *strong positive correlation* between preserving one's sense of personal identity and living in what appears to be a reason-ably stable world of fairly persistent recognisable things whose changes take place in a fairly regular way. But there are certainly other factors involved in personal identity, e.g. ostensible memories of experiences which may not have been perceptions of physical things or events. And, on the other hand, I should think that personal identity could be preserved even if one lived in a world which appeared to be much less stable and law-abiding than the actual world appears to be. Certainly the occasional sudden creation and annihilation of perceptible objects, and the occasional

occurrence of incompletely determined events, would not be fatal. For *prima facie* this does appear to happen, and yet those who witness it do not cease to be self-conscious persons. It is no answer to say that scientists hold that in principle all such *prima facie* appearances can be accounted for without abandoning the principles of the permanence of substance and of universal causation. For savages and uneducated men, who take the appearances at their face value and have never consciously formulated these principles, manage to maintain their personal identity. And it would be highly unconvincing to say that they must be recognising these principles unconsciously and unwittingly supplementing and arranging their sense-data in accordance with them.

(6) In §19 and §20 Kant attempts to do something which he does not attempt in Deduction A. He tries to show that the unity of apperception is a necessary condition of every kind of *judgment*, beside being a necessary condition of the perception of a world of persistent law-abiding objects. And he tries to justify, by this means, the contention that the categories which he is here deducing are the same as those which he claimed to discover by means of the classification of judgments in formal logic. I accept the premiss, but I cannot follow the argument. Certainly anyone who makes a judgment of any kind must be either perceiving or thinking of the subject and must be thinking of the predicate, and must be thinking of some relation between the two. Unless all these different experiences were *his* experiences *he* could not make a judgment. I agree too that in making a judgment, as distinct from merely having one idea which calls up another by association, a person is asserting an *objective* connexion between the subject which he is perceiving or thinking of and the predicate which he is thinking of. But I cannot follow the argument from these premisses in §20. What Kant says about judgment in §19 is closely connected with certain doctrines in the *Prolegomena* which we shall consider later.

(7) In §22 and §23 Kant brings out very clearly the point that, although the categories are not *derived from* experience, yet they can properly be *applied* only to objects of actual or possible sense-perception. A category in itself is the concept of an *a priori* plan for synthesising sense-given data so as to produce epistemologically objective experiences. In theory the categories would apply to *any* kind of sense-given data, even if they were quite unlike ours. I suppose that they would apply even to a being whose innate forms of intuition were unlike ours. But in practice they provide *knowledge* of objects, as distinct from mere unverifiable speculation, only when employed to synthesise the acutal sense-data of human beings subject to our actual forms of intuition, viz. a one-dimensional time and a three-dimensional space. The objects, about which they supply knowledge, are not things-in-themselves, but empirical objects. And here at any

rate Kant takes a purely phenomenalist view of empirical objects. They *are* just groups of actual and possible human sense-data, interconnected in accordance with rules which are particular empirical specifications of an *a priori* ground-plan.

(8) In the latter part of §24 and in §25 Kant deals with the question of one's empirical knowledge of oneself and one's own experiences, in terms of his general theory about synthesis and the transcendental unity of apperception. In particular he tries to remove the *prima facie* objections to his doctrine that a person knows himself and his own experiences only as these appear to him under the form of time. I shall defer this until I deal with Kant's doctrine of the self and of self-consciousness.

(9) There is an important footnote to §26 on p. 170 (B 161). Kant here applies his general doctrine of combination to the special case of pure space. Geometers treat space as a peculiar kind of *object*. Now space is certainly in some sense a complex whole with a characteristic kind of unity. For it can be thought of as consisting of sub-regions adjoined to each other along their boundaries. In accordance with Kant's general principles we must have synthesised it, and this synthesis must have been performed by the productive imagination working on a plan inspired by the understanding. Kant admits that in the *Aesthetic* he talked as if space were *given* as a whole by *a priori* intuitions independently of conceptually guided synthesis. He now says that this was merely a rough preliminary statement which must be corrected. The only comment that I will make is one that has been made by A. H. Smith in his *Kantian Studies*.[1] Kant's statements here imply that the understanding has *a priori* concepts of types of synthesis *other* than the categories. For geometers certainly do not think of space as a persistent *substance* with variable *states* or as something which has active or passive *causal* properties. I suspect that Kant thought that the kind of synthesis which is involved here is an *unconscious* process analogous to that which we consciously and deliberately perform when we construct a figure in imagination by calling up an image of a point moving and tracing out a line or the contour of an area. Here, it might be said, you have an introspectible instance of the understanding acting upon the imagination. You have a concept of a certain kind of figure, e.g. a circle, and you deliberately construct in imagination an image answering to that concept by imaging a point moving in accordance with a rule. He discusses this topic on p. 167 (B 155-6). In a footnote he draws an interesting distinction between two kinds of motion, viz. the motion of a body in space and the kind of imaged motion of an imaged point in tracing out the image of a geometrical figure. He says that *physical motion* can be known about only empirically. But the imaginative motion used by geometers is 'a pure act of . . . successive synthesis of the manifold . . . by means of productive

[1] [A. H. Smith, *Kantian Studies* (Oxford, 1947).]

imagination, and belongs not only to geometry but even to transcendental philosophy'.

(10) In various places in Deduction B (notably in §16 and §17) Kant tries to bring out the peculiarities of the human understanding, which works by imaginative synthesis in accordance with categories, by contrasting it with a different kind of understanding which we can conceive to be possible. This he calls an *intuitive understanding*. This notion occurs in many parts of Kant's writings. It plays a very important part in his account of internal teleology and the concept of a living organism in the *Critique of Judgment*. I will defer discussion of it until we consider that subject.

(11) In the last two paragraphs, i.e. §26 and §27, Kant reverts to the notion of the human understanding as the source of the laws of nature. He puts the difficulty very fairly in the middle paragraph of p. 172 (B 163). How is it conceivable 'that nature should have to proceed in accordance with categories which . . . are not derived from it and do not model themselves on its pattern. . . .?' His attempted answer is on the same lines as in Deduction A. If by 'nature' we meant the totality of things-in-themselves, this would be quite inconceivable. But this is not what we mean by 'nature'. We mean by it the totality of *empirical* objects, i.e. objects which we actually do or conceivably may perceive with our senses, and objects, such as atoms, whose existence can be inferred by ordinary scientific reasoning from these. Now, according to Kant, these objects are what we should now call 'logical constructions', made in accordance with certain innate principles of synthesis which the human understanding imposes upon human sense-data through the agency of the productive imagination. And unless my sense-data were organised in these ways they would not be *mine*, i.e. they would not be so interconnected that they could count as the experiences of a single self-conscious person who can recognise his identity and his common ownership in reference to them. On that hypothesis, which Kant claims to have established, it is not particularly paradoxical that the categories, and certain general principles involving the categories, should apply to everything in nature. Even so Kant does not assert that we impose upon nature the *particular* laws which in fact hold in it, e.g. the law that metals expand when heated. All such laws might be discovered by observation and induction. What we impose is only such highly general principles as, e.g., the following: To every change there corresponds a certain immediately previous change, such that the one follows upon the other in accordance with *some* empirical causal law or other.

3.4 Concluding comments on certain points in the two Deductions

In expounding the two Deductions I have incidentally commented upon what I consider to be the strong points and various weak points in the arguments and the conclusions. I will now consider in rather more detail two very fundamental points, viz. the notion of *conjunction* or *combination* of the items of a manifold, and the notion of the human understanding as the source of the law-abidingness of nature.

3.4.1 The notion of conjunction

Is it really intelligible to suppose that there could be a plurality of items entirely devoid of all intrinsic order or interrelations? And, if there were such a plurality, is it intelligible to suggest that we could impose any kind of order or arrangement upon it? It seems to me that we must distinguish two cases, viz. (1) where the items are supposed to exist *independently* of us and our activity of ordering, and (2) where we ourselves *produce* the items in a certain order. In the first case I think that in all known instances what we do is not to *impose* an arrangement on something which had none at all, but to substitute a new, and it may be more intimate and significant, arrangement for one that already existed. That, e.g., is obviously all that we are doing if we build a house with bricks. It is less obvious, but no less true, that this is all that one is doing when one paints a picture or draws a figure with pencil or pen and ink. Take, e.g., the case of drawing a figure with pen and ink. The ink already existed aggregated on the surface of the nib and in the inkpot. This ink already was in certain spatial relations to the blank sheet of paper. All that one does is to bring the ink by means of the pen into a new spatial relation to the paper, viz. that of contact, and then to alter the state of aggregation of the ink, viz. to spread out in a line on the paper the ink which was previously aggregated in a blob on the surface of the nib. Now, according to Kant, we just *receive* sense-impressions; we do not *create* them, though we may fairly be said to create images. It seems to me, then, unintelligible to suggest that sense-impressions as such have no intrinsic order, and that we literally impose relations altogether *de novo* upon them. At the most, I think, the understanding might, through the productive imagination, *alter* the determinate form of order which they already possess, modify some of their qualities, and supplement them with certain suitably related images.

The second alternative might be illustrated by speaking a sentence or by drawing a line in imagination. Here one does create a whole, consisting of parts which have a certain order. But one does so by creating the parts successively in that order, and not by imposing the order on items which exist independently of one's creative action. Now this alternative cannot be analogous to the supposed ordering of intrinsically unordered sense-impressions by the understanding. For we do not create the sense-impressions which we are said to arrange; they are supposed to be produced in us by foreign things-in-themselves.

I am therefore doubtful whether any acceptable meaning can be attached to Kant's doctrine of conjunction, which is fundamental in Deduction B.

3.4.2 The human mind as the source of the law-abidingness of nature

The best description that I have read on this topic is to be found in Joseph's essays *Comparison of Kant's Idealism with That of Berkeley* and *The Syntheses of Sense and Understanding* in his *Essays in Ancient and Modern Philosophy*.[1] Kant and Berkeley agree that our various sensations occur in such groupings as they *would* occur in *if* they were produced in us by a world of bodies in a single three-dimensional spatial system, all of whose changes are subject to causal determination. Berkeley held that in fact there are no bodies, except in the sense of what we should now call logical constructions out of interrelated human sense-data. Kant appears to take the same view of bodies in Deduction B, though he seems to take a much more realistic view in the Refutation of Idealism in B. Now Berkeley holds that the sense-data which we take to be appearances of bodies and events in bodies are produced in us telepathically by God, and that the characteristic order and grouping in which they occur in us is due to the deliberate intention and action of God. Kant holds that the sense-data are produced in us by foreign things-in-themselves. He holds that the ordering and grouping of them in such ways that one can take them as appearances of a world of law-abiding bodies is done by one's own understanding operating through one's own productive imagination upon the sense-data thus produced in one. Thus Berkeley assigns to God two different functions, viz. producing and arranging sense-data, which Kant divides between foreign things-in-themselves and the human individual's understanding. On Berkeley's view God is like a person expressing his own thoughts by uttering appropriate words in an appropriate order, and human percipients might be compared to God's audience. On Kant's view each individual is like a person who has a lot of type, all jumbled up together, handed to him. He has to make a suitable selection from this and then arrange it in such a way that it expresses in print, in some language which he understands, a certain complex thought which he has.

If we now leave illustrations and metaphors, which are always in part misleading, the difficulty about the understanding imposing law-abidingness upon nature is this. There is no way of imposing law-

[1] [H. W. B. Joseph, *Essays in Ancient and Modern Philosophy* (Oxford, 1935).]

abidingness in the *abstract*. The only way of ensuring that nature shall be law-abiding throughout is to impose *determinate* laws of some kind or other upon it. Now this is just what Kant denies that we do, and it would certainly be very paradoxical indeed to hold that we do it. Yet nothing else would suffice. I think that Kant may have made the following mistake. He saw no doubt that nature could be completely law-abiding no matter what the determinate laws might be. It would be just as law-abiding if metals always *contracted* or always *exploded* when heated as if they always expanded, which is the actual law. I suspect that he inadvertently passed from the fact that the law-abidingness of nature does not involve any *one* set of determinate laws rather than any *other*, to the fallacy that one could impose complete law-abidingness without imposing *any* set of determinate laws. It is as if one should pass from the true premiss that a person can express himself grammatically without obeying the rules of English grammar, and without obeying the rules of Greek grammar, and so on, to the conclusion that he could express himself grammatically without obeying the laws of grammar of any particular language.

Suppose, however, we make the fantastic assumption that each of us has, concealed in his understanding, a *detailed* concept of a system of bodies subject to a *particular* set of determinate laws. Suppose, further, that he has immense powers of arranging his sense-data and supplementing them with appropriate images so as to produce a set of ostensible perceptions of a world of bodies subject to those laws. He might still be unable to carry this out. For the qualities of the sense-data supplied to him by foreign things-in-themselves might be such that no amount of arrangement would fit them into this plan. Or, again, there might be so many gaps in his sense-data that no amount of supplementation by images would fit them into this plan.

Kant would say, no doubt, that if that were so the sense-data in question would not be so interrelated as to belong to a single self-conscious person who could recognise himself as their common owner. This, if it could be proved, would certainly be very important. But it does not remove the difficulty. It would show only that to be a self-conscious person, and to ostensibly perceive a world of bodies subject in all their changes to causal laws, mutually entail each other. It would not show that *both* conditions might not break down together at any moment, through foreign things-in-themselves supplying sense-data which could not be arranged according to the plan or failing to supply sense-data which are essential to the plan.

There are two remarks which I will make before leaving this topic. (1) Kant's theory seems to take no account of the existence of a plurality of intercommunicating persons. He ignores the fact that an essential feature in each person's notion of the external world is that it is perceptible not only by himself but by others, and that each person's knowledge of it is based jointly on what he perceives himself and what other persons report to him that they have perceived. If we take Kant's theory literally, each person has his own private time and space and physical world, which he has constructed for himself. Even if Kant has accounted for the *internal* coherence and law-abidingness of each such private world, he has given no explanation of their coherence with *each other*. Here Berkeley's theory is in a much stronger position.

(2) In talking of the ways in which the understanding operates on the crude data of sense by means of the productive imagination I have assumed that this operation consists in doing something *positive* to them, as when a builder rearranges stone in the form of a house, and perhaps has to chip and cut the rough blocks supplied from the quarry in order to make them fit. But it is fair to remember that order might be introduced simply by the negative process of *rejecting* anything that does not fit into the scheme. Suppose one had a metal plate with a design cut in stencil on it, and one pressed it down hard on a lump of putty or plasticine. Then the material which got through would have a certain pattern simply because the uncut background of the plate kept out all that did not conform to this pattern. Similarly the function of the productive imagination might be to suppress into the unconscious all those sense-impressions which did not fit into the scheme which is latent in the understanding. This alternative is worth considering, but it does not remove the main difficulty. Unless *enough* plasticine is provided, and it is spread out over a sufficient area, the stencil plate will not be able to impress its design by mere rejection. Moreover, it may be part of the intention of the designer that different items in the pattern shall be of certain colours, e.g. that the roses shall be pink, the leaves green, the sky blue, and so on. If so, it will be useless to press the stencil plate on to the plasticine unless the latter is already appropriately variegated in colour. In the same way things-in-themselves might not provide enough sense-impressions or sense-impressions of suitable varieties of quality. In that case what remained, after all the sense-impressions which did not fit into the understanding's scheme had been suppressed into the unconscious, would be insufficient in amount or unsuitable in quality to constitute an exemplification of the scheme.

3.5 The theory in the Prolegomena

Before leaving the *Transcendental Deduction* I will give a very brief sketch of the theory which Kant put forward in the *Prolegomena*. This theory is stated in the section entitled *How Is Pure Natural Science Possible?* By 'pure natural science' Kant means certain synthetic *a priori* principles about all the things and events in nature. An example is the law of universal causation. The general line which Kant takes here is the same as in the *Critique of Pure Reason*. There is no hope of establishing such universal propositions about nature unless you define 'nature' as the sum total of objects of possible human sense-perception. And, if you define 'nature' in this way, the principles can be established only by showing that, unless they held of all the objects of possible human sense-perception, the most characteristic features of specifically human experience would be impossible. It would be impossible to have epistemologically objective experiences at all, as distinct from mere feelings. It would be impossible to be a self-conscious individual, recognising one's identity throughout one's various experiences and knowing oneself as their common owner. And so on. Kant sums this up in the sentence 'The *a priori* conditions of the possibility of experiences are at the same time the sources from which all the universal laws of nature are derived.'[1]

3.5.1 'Judgments of perception' and 'judgments of experience'

The peculiarity of the detailed argument in the *Prolegomena* is that is starts from a distinction between two kinds of empirical judgment which he calls *judgments of perception* and *judgments of experience*. This distinction is not explicitly drawn in the *Critique of Pure Reason,* but it is plain that Kant has it in mind in §19 of Deduction B (p. 159, B 141–2). He gives as examples of judgments of *perception* 'The room is warm', 'Sugar is sweet', and 'The stone gets hot whenever the sun shines on it'. His examples of judgments of *experience* are 'Air is elastic' and 'The sun's light causes the stone to get hot'. He says that judgments of perception involve *no category* and claim only *subjective validity*, whilst judgments of experience involve a category and claim objective validity.

As usual, Kant has got hold of an important point. But neither his terminology nor his examples are altogether satisfactory. All his examples, e.g., involve at least the category of *substance*. Again, he would have done better to take as examples 'The room *feels* warm to me', 'This stuff *tastes* sweet to me', and to have contrasted them with 'The room *is* warm' (as indicated by the thermometer), 'This stuff *is* sweet' (i.e. would taste sweet to any normal person in normal health), and so on. Then, again, his examples of judgments of perception cover two very different cases, viz. (1) *singular* judgments like 'The room feels warm to me', and (2) *general* judgments of regular sequence or coexistence, e.g. 'The stone gets hot whenever the sun shines on it'. Kant wishes to contrast the latter with causal judgments, e.g. 'The sun's light *causes* the stone to get hot'.

To avoid these objections I shall substitute for Kant's term 'judgments of perception' the two terms (1) judgments of *autobiographical inspection*

[1] [P. 56.]

and (2) judgments of *regular concomitance*. The former are singular, e.g. 'The room feels hot to me'. The latter are general, e.g. 'On all occasions known to me on which a metal has been heated it has expanded'. We may keep Kant's term 'judgments of experience'. But we must notice that it covers at least two different kinds of judgment, viz. (1) *perceptual* judgments, e.g. 'The room is hot', 'The dish is round', etc., and (2) *causal* judgments, e.g. 'Heating a metal causes it to expand'. The contrast is between (1) judgments of autobiographical inspection and perceptual judgments, and (2) judgments of regular concomitance and causal judgments.

Now the essential points are these. (1) Both judgments of autobiographical inspection and judgments of regular concomitance contain an essential reference to the *person* who makes the judgment and to the *time* at which he makes it. When I say that this looks round or feels hot to me, I admit that the very same particular may, at another moment and without having undergone any internal change, look elliptical or feel cold to me. And I admit that at this very moment the same particular may look elliptical or feel cold to *you*. Again, suppose I say that an all occasions known to me on which a metal has been heated it has expanded. I admit that on future occasions *I* may meet with a contrary instance. And I admit that even now *you* may have met with contrary instances.

(2) As regards judgments of experience, Kant says that the judge claims that his judgment is (a) valid for *everyone*, and (b) valid for him *at all times*. There is no difficulty about the first claim, either as regards perceptual judgments or causal judgments. 'This *is* round' or 'This *causes* that' has no reference to the speaker himself or to any other person. It is just neutral as between persons. Nor is there any difficulty about the second claim as regards *causal* judgments. A causal judgment asserts that *whenever* an event of a certain kind happens at any place an event of a certain other kind *necessarily follows* in the same or an adjacent place. But it is not so obvious in what sense a singular perceptual judgment, e.g. 'That thing is round', claims to be valid at all times. The person who makes such a judgment certainly does not claim that this thing always has been and always will be round. The real point is this. If I make the judgment 'This looks round to me' that form of words may cease to express a true judgment without any change in *the thing in question*. I might, e.g., merely have altered my position relative to it, so that it now looks elliptical to me. But if I make the judgment 'This *is* round' and it is true, then that form of words will continue to express a true judgment unless and until there is a relevant *change in the thing*. E.g. the thing which was round may become bent into some other shape.

The next step in the argument is this. Kant alleges that we start with mere judgments of autobiographical inspection and judgments of regular concomitance and that we then *convert them into* or *replace them by* judgments of experience. This seems to me to be false if taken as expressing a psychological fact. And it is certainly not Kant's usual view. We obviously begin with ordinary perceptual judgments such as 'That is round'. We begin to distinguish between 'being round' and 'looking round to me here and now' only when we notice and reflect upon the variations in the sensible appearances of what we take to be the same unchanged physical object. No doubt a case could be made for holding that to perceive an object involves being presented with a particular appearance of it in sensation and basing a non-inferential judgment about the object on the presented sense-datum. On that view one might say that having a sense-datum of a certain kind is a necessary precondition of making a perceptual judgment. But it would not follow, nor is it true, that to make an autobiographical inspective judgment about a sense-datum is a necessary precondition of making a perceptual judgment about the object which presents itself to one by that sense-datum. So I should deny that autobiographical inspective judgments are either psychologically or logically prior to perceptual judgments. On the other hand, I think we may grant that judgments of regular concomitance are both logically and psychologically prior to causal judgments. They are the premises of the inductive arguments which lead to causal judgments.

3.5.2 Introduction of the notion of necessity

The next step in Kant's argument is this. He alleges that the transition from judgments of autobiographical inspection and judgments of regular concomitance to judgments of experience always involves introducing the notion of *necessity*. As usual we must take in turn the transition to perceptual judgments like 'This is round' and the transition to causal judgments like 'Heating a metal causes it to expand'.

Prima facie it is difficult to see where the alleged element of necessity comes in in an ordinary perceptual judgment like 'This dish is round'. Kant admits that the fact corresponding to the judgment is contingent. The very same object might have been elliptical. If it were made of plastic material, it might actually become elliptical in future or have been so in the past. I think that what Kant has in mind here might be described as *necessary agreement* between the true judgments of different observers perceiving the same object at the same time and between the true judgments of the same observer perceiving the same object at different times. If I judge that a certain object is round, and this is true, then anyone else who judges about the shape of that same object at the same time will have to ascribe the same shape to it as I do or else judge falsely. Similarly if I judge about the shape of the same object at any other time I shall have to ascribe the same shape to it as before unless there has been some change in its shape. On the other hand suppose that a number of persons are looking at the same penny at the same time from different positions and are making autobiographical inspective judgments about how it looks to them. Then the predicates of their judgments will not necessarily agree even though all their judgments are true. It will be true for one to say 'This looks round to me' and for another in a different position to say 'This looks elliptical to me'. And similar remarks apply to judgments made by the same person at different times if he shifts his position whilst the object remains unchanged in shape.

This difference between perceptual judgments and autobiographical inspective judgments about the same physical object is an immediate consequence of the following fact. The predicate of an autobiographical inspective judgment involves a reference to the person who judges and the time at which he judges. Therefore no two autobiographical inspective judgments, made by different persons or by the same person at different times, can have the same predicate or refer to the same fact, even if they have a common subject. But the predicate of a perceptual judgment involves no references either to the person who judges or to the time at which he judges. Therefore a number of perceptual judgments, made by different persons or by the same person at different moments, *can* have the same predicate as well as the same subject. They *can* all refer to the same fact; and they will necessarily agree with each other if they all accord with that fact, i.e. they *will* necessarily have the same predicate.

Let us now consider the contrast between a judgment of regular concomitance and the corresponding causal judgment. In the case of the causal judgment, as in the case of a perceptual judgment, there is necessitated agreement between all true judgments which refer to the same fact. But there is also an entirely different kind of necessity. A causal judgment *asserts* a necessary connexion. It asserts, e.g., that if a metal is heated it is necessitated thereby to expand. The necessity here is in the *content* of *each* such judgment, and not merely in the agreement *between* all such judgments which refer to the same fact and concord with it. This kind of necessity is absent, not only in judgments of regular concomitance and judgments of autobiographical inspection, but also in perceptual judgments.

In this connexion it is very important to distinguish between a *necessary judgment* and a *judgment of necessitation*. Every causal judgment is a judgment of necessitation. It asserts that the occurrence of an event of a certain kind at any time and place necessitates the immediately subsequent occurrence of an event of a certain other kind at the same or an adjacent place. But, according to Kant and to most philosophers since Hume, no causal judgment is a *necessary* judgment. That is, no such judgment is either self-evident or can be inferred deductively from premises all of which are self-evident. The only available evidence for any causal judgment is observed regularity and inductive generalisation. Failure to draw this distinction is a source of much confusion in philosophical discussions about causation.

3.5.3 Necessity and empirical objectivity

We can now pass to the next stage in Kant's argument. He asserts that the two notions of *objective validity* and *necessitated agreement* are logically equivalent. 'If one judgment agrees with an object, all judgments about the same object must agree with each other.' So objective validity entails necessitated agreement. 'Conversely, if we find reason to regard a judgment as holding of necesity for everyone, we must regard it as objective, i.e. as expressing a property of the object and not merely a relation of a percept to a subject.'[1] So necessitated agreement entails objective validity.

He then goes on to make some very important statements in §19 about 'objects' in this sense and 'objects' in the sense of things-in-themselves. The following quotations are typical. 'Although we are not acquainted with the object in itself, yet objective validity is understood whenever we regard a judgment as necessarily valid for everyone.' 'We recognise the object through such a judgment even though it remains unknown to us as it is in itself.' 'Judgments of experience do not get their objective validity through direct acquaintance with the object (for this is impossible), but simply from the fact that the empirical judgment is valid for everyone.' 'The object, as it is in itself, remains forever unknown; but, when the connexion of presentations which are impressed in our sensibility by it is regarded as valid for everybody, the object is determined and the judgment is objective.'[2]

Kant's problem here may be put as follows. Even though all my sense-impressions be in fact due to things-in-themselves, I am never acquainted with any thing-in-itself. I am acquainted only with my sense-impressions or images or groups of them. Yet I certainly do claim to perceive this, that, and the other external independent object. And I certainly do make judgments which assert that such-and-such a perceived object has such-and-such a quality. How then do I get the very notion of external independent objects? And under what circumstances do I claim to be perceiving such an object and to be making judgments about its qualities?

Kant's answer seems to come to the following. (1) When I should commonly be said to be 'perceiving a certain physical object' I am having a certain group of sense-data, memory-images and other images, inter-

[1] [Pp. 56–7.]   [2] [P. 57.]

connected in certain characteristic ways. (2) On such occasions there are two kinds of judgments which I may make. (a) I may confine myself to judgments like 'This looks round to me', 'This feels cold to me', and so on. In that case I admit that another person, who would commonly be said to be 'perceiving the *same* object at the *same* time as I', might correctly make a dissimilar judgment of the same kind. He might judge 'This looks elliptical to me' or 'This feels warm to me'. And he might be quite correct. (b) I might instead make a judgment like 'This *is* round' or 'This *is* physically hot'. In that case I hold that any other person, who would commonly be said to be 'perceiving the same object at the same time as I', will be mistaken if he makes a judgment referring to the same property of the same object and it does not agree in its predicate with my judgment. I do not assert that his perceptual experiences must be exactly like mine. If that were so, his autobiographical inspective judgment would have to agree with mine, and I do not assert this. But I do assert that there must be that kind and degree of correlation between his perceptual experiences and mine which will oblige him to make a perceptual judgment in agreement with mine if he makes one at all and it is to be correct. Now Kant's view seems to be this. The concept of an empirical object is the concept of a something which necessitates such a similarity between the percepts of all human observers who would commonly be said to be 'perceiving the same object at the same time' that their perceptual judgments would agree with each other. If this is Kant's theory, it seems to be open to the following criticisms.

(1) *Prima facie* the definition is circular. This definition of a *physical object* involves the notion of a number of persons who would commonly be said to be perceiving *the same physical object* at the same time. Unless this latter phrase can be analysed in some way which eliminates all references to the notion of physical object, the definition is plainly circular. Whether this could be done seems highly doubtful. At any rate Kant has not attempted to do it.

(2) Let us suppose that this can be done and the definition can thus be made non-circular. The question then arises: How does any of us come to have these beliefs about the judgments which everyone else would make under certain hypothetical conditions? If this question can be answered, a second question at once arises. Has anyone any good *reason* for holding such beliefs about the judgments which other persons would make under the supposed conditions? Do we not, as a matter of fact, *start* from the belief that sense-perception makes us aware of independent external objects, in a *non-phenomenalistic* sense, and that these are in principle common to all percipients? Do we not in fact *derive* our beliefs as to the judgments which other percipients would make under the supposed conditions from this belief?

3.5.4 Introduction of the categories

We can now pass to the final stage in Kant's argument. This is where the categories come in. He thinks that the transition from judgments of autobiographical inspection to judgments of perception involves the use of the categories. In §18 he says that our ground for regarding a judgment as valid for everyone 'never depends on the percept but always on the pure conception of the understanding [i.e. the category] under which the percept is subsumed'. He repeats the same statement in almost the same words in §19 and in §20. Then come a number of general statements which are difficult to follow until we reach §§27–30 inclusive. Here Kant explicitly mentions and professes to solve Hume's problem about our knowledge of causation. He makes it plain in §27 and §28 that he is largely in agreement with Hume about our knowledge of causal propositions and that he thinks that his view should be extended to the notion of substance. He puts this side of his case as strongly as possible at the beginning of §28. 'I have no notion of such a connexion of things-in-themselves that they can either exist as substances or act as causes or stand in community with others as parts of a real whole.' We may sum up this part by saying that Kant thinks that nothing can be made of the notions of substance, cause, and reciprocity if you try to apply them to things without reference to their actual or possible relation to human percipients. Kant would say that Hume failed to see this point. He assumed that, if the notion of cause applies to anything, it must apply to things regardless of their being or not being possible objects of human sense-perception. He was quite right in denying its validity when so applied. But he did not notice the possibility that it might be valid within the more restricted sphere of objects of actual and possible human sense-perception, or that we might be able to prove that it *must* apply to all such objects.

In §28 we come to the other side of Kant's doctrine on this point. He says here that, just as the concepts of cause, substance, etc., do not apply to things-in-themselves, so too they do not apply to appearances as such, i.e. to sense-data and images or to groups of actual sense-data and images. They apply to empirical objects, i.e. the chairs and tables of common sense and the atoms and molecules of the natural scientists. It follows that these concepts cannot be empirical, in the sense in which concepts of sensible qualities, e.g. redness, hotness, etc., are so. All that one can be acquainted with and can inspect is one's own sense-data and images. But neither an individual sense-datum or image nor any actual group of sense-data and images is an instance of the concept of substance or the concept of cause. Therefore we cannot have derived these concepts by abstraction from instances of them with which we have been acquainted and which we have inspected. Kant concludes, at the end of §27, that 'these concepts are not derived merely from experience, and the necessity represented in them is not to be regarded as a mere fiction engendered in us by custom'.

3.5.5 Empirical objects and the categories

At this stage the following two questions become pressing. (1) On Kant's view what exactly is an ordinary empirical object, such as a chair or a tree; i.e. what is the nature of the objects to which alone the categories apply? (2) Since the categories are said to have an intelligible meaning only when applied to such objects, what is their meaning when they are so applied? I think that Kant's answer to both these questions in the *Prolegomena* might be stated as follows.

(1) Let us begin with a perceptual judgment. I see a certain object and I make the perceptual judgment 'That is a penny and it is round'. What precisely is happening on Kant's view? (a) I am having a certain group of sense-data and associated images with certain characteristic qualities and interrelations. (b) I am impelled by this to judge that I or any other human percipient *would* have (or *would* have had) sense-data of certain characteristic qualities, following each other in a certain characteristic order, *if* he were to fulfil (or *if* he had fulfilled) certain conditions after or before the present moment. So sentences which contain names of physical objects can, on this view, be replaced without loss of meaning by sentences which do not contain such names. The new sentences are entirely about the sense-data which anyone *would* have *if* he were to fulfil certain conditions. If circularity is to be avoided these conditions must themselves be statable entirely in terms of actual and possible sense-data and images. And what they assert is that these hypothetical sense-data would have or would have had such-and-such sensible qualities and would follow or would have followed each other in such-and-such an order.

(2) Let us next take a causal judgment, e.g. 'Heating a metal causes it to expand'. What precisely does this come to on Kant's view? (a) A group of my sense-data and associated images has constantly been followed in my experience by a group which is similar in the main but has certain characteristic differences. (b) I am impelled by this to judge that *any* human percipient who at any time had a group of sense-data and images of the first kind *would* necessarily have one of the second kind *if* he were thereupon to fulfil certain conditions. If circularity is to be avoided, these conditions must themselves be statable entirely in terms of actual and possible sense-data and images. So causal judgments, on this view, are really about the hypothetical sequences of certain hypothetical groups of sense-data and images. And what they assert is that, if a group of one kind were to occur at any time and in any person, it *would* necessarily be

followed by one of the second kind, *if* he were thereupon to fulfil certain conditions.

It seems to me that this interpretation is consistent with nearly all Kant's statements in the *Prolegomena*. (1) If the concepts of substance and of cause are concepts of necessitated groupings and sequences of groupings of sense-data in human minds, they plainly do not apply to things-in-themselves. (2) It is also true that perceptual and causal judgments are not about any actual groups or sequences of sense-data. They are *based upon* actual groups and actual sequences. But they go beyond these, and make conditional statements about the hypothetical groupings and sequences of sense-data which have not actually occurred and may never occur. (3) All such judgments involve the notion of what *would* necessarily have happened *if* conditions which were not in fact fulfilled *had* been fulfilled. This involves the notions of possibility, of necessity, and of conditions and consequences. The senses cannot possibly supply these notions. They are confined to the actual and the contingent. (4) Our perceptual judgments and our causal judgments are determined in detail by the actual qualities, groupings, and sequences of our sense-data and images. These *might* be noticed for their own sake, though in actual fact they very seldom are. If we did pay attention to them for their own sake, and did express the results of our inspection, we should express them by autobiographical inspective judgments and by judgments of regular concomitance. Thus the perceptual and causal judgments which we do in *fact* make are correlated with the autobiographical inspective judgments and the judgments of regular concomitance which we *might* make, but generally do not make, on the same occasion. This is the fact which Kant expresses in a most unsatisfactory way by saying that we start with 'judgments of perception' and transform them into 'judgments of experience' by subsuming them under the categories.

3.5.6 Relevance of the theory to Hume's problem

I have already said that I doubt whether this kind of theory about physical objects can be stated without logical circularity. But let us suppose that it can. Then we can ask how far it is relevant to the problem which Hume raised about causation.

Hume's difficulty was threefold. (1) What do we *mean* by saying that any event of one kind *would necessarily* be followed by an event of a certain other kind? (2) What justification have we for asserting, with regard to an event of a given kind K (e.g. heatings of metals) that it would necessarily be followed by an event of a certain other kind K' (e.g. expansion of the same bit of metal)? (3) What ground is there for believing that *every* event is a necessary sequent of a certain earlier event? These three problems may be described respectively as (1) the analysis of the *notion of causal necessity*, (2) the evidence for *particular causal laws,* and (3) the evidence for the *law of universal causation*.

(1) As regards the question of *analysis* Kant has drawn a number of very necessary distinctions and seen a number of important connexions which Hume ignored. He has distinguished between our sense-data and our percepts of physical objects and has shown that the latter involve a great deal in addition to the former. He has distinguished between empirical objects and things-in-themselves, and has tried to analyse the notion of empirical object. He has shown that the notion of cause cannot be treated in isolation from the notion of empirical object; for the latter, on his analysis, involves the notion of necessary sequence and concomitance.

(2) As regards the evidence for *particular causal laws* Kant has made no attempt to answer Hume in any of his writings. He agrees with Hume that the evidence is empirical and inductive, and he has not attempted to solve the problem of the justification of induction.

(3) As regards the evidence for the *principle of universal causation*, Kant's position is as follows. (a) He agrees with Hume that it is not self-evident. (b) He holds that the principle cannot be proved, and that it is barely intelligible, if it be applied to things-in-themselves. But he thinks that it is intelligible and that it can be proved by transcendental arguments if it is confined to objects of actual and possible human sense-perception. His attempts to prove it under these restrictions are to be found in the section of the *Critique of Pure Reason* entitled *Analogies of Experience*.

I suspect that Kant may have thought that the proof of the *principle of universal causation* for objects of actual and possible human sense-perception would contribute to solving the problem of the evidence for particular causal laws. If he did think this, he was certainly mistaken. The problem of the evidence for 'This causes that' is in no way lightened by knowing that *every* event is caused by *some* other event.

4 The principles of pure understanding

We come now to Kant's attempted proofs of what he calls the *principles of pure understanding*. These are certain very general synthetic propositions, involving the schematised categories, which Kant claims to prove by transcendental arguments for all objects of actual and possible human sense perception. The general line of argument is the same as that used in the Transcendental Deduction of the Categories. It consists in trying to show that, unless these principles held for every object that a person could possibly perceive, then some of the most general features of human experience would be impossible. It would be impossible to have epistemologically objective experiences at all, to recognise one's identity throughout one's various experiences, to say of each of them 'This is an experience of mine', and so on. But in trying to prove these principles Kant appeals to somewhat more special, though still extremely general, features of human experience. He lays great stress on certain *temporal* features of it. In particular he appeals to the fact that we all draw a distinction between the *subjective* temporal order in which we happen to get our sensations, or in which our memory-images happen to arise, and the *objective* temporal order of the things or events which we perceive or remember by means of them.

4.1 The mathematical principles

Corresponding to all three categories of quantity is a single principle, and corresponding to all three categories of quality there is also a single principle. These two principles Kant calls *mathematical principles*. They are not themselves a *part* of mathematics, like the axioms of geometry or the rules of arithmetic. They are required in order to guarantee that the axioms and theorems of pure mathematics will be *applicable* to every thing or event that we could possibly perceive. The principle corresponding to the categories of quantity is generally referred to as the 'axiom of intuition', and that which corresponds to the categories of quality as the 'anticipation of perception'. This is not strictly accurate. The former should be called the 'principle of the axioms of intuition', and that is how Kant describes it in B. The axioms of intuition themselves are the axioms of pure geometry. The principle is what guarantees their applicability to all possible objects of sense-perception. In the same way the other principle would better be called the 'principle for anticipating perceptions'. That is how Kant describes it in A. We will now take the two mathematical principles in turn.

4.1.1 The principle of the axioms of intuition

Kant formulated this principle slightly differently in A and in B. And in B he prefixed a new paragraph to the proof which he had given in A. We may take the statement of the principle which he gave in B. It runs as follows: 'All intuitions are extensive magnitudes.' The formulation in A was: 'All phenomena are, in their intuition, extensive magnitudes' (p. 197, A 162/B 202).

The proof in A begins with a definition of 'extensive magnitude'. Kant defines it as follows. An entity has extensive magnitude if it is composed of parts, and 'the presentation of the parts makes possible and therefore precedes the presentation of the whole'. (p. 198, A 162/B 203). He alleges that this is the case with every line and every stretch of time, however short. This seems to me to be plainly false; though it is doubtless true of lines and other spaces which are too big to be taken in at a single glance, and of stretches of time which are too long to fall within a single specious present. But Kant says that we cannot think of any line without generating it in imagination by the movement of a point. However that may be, the definition seems to me to be open to several objections. (1) It is unsatisfactory to define a characteristic by reference to a quite contingent fact about the way in which human beings come to perceive or to conceive instances of it. Now, even if it were true that we can perceive or conceive extensive quanta only by a process of successive synthesis, this would seem to be a purely contingent fact. (2) In the *Aesthetic* Kant has asserted that, in the case of *pure* space and *pure* time, at any rate, the whole is logically prior to its parts. We have to think of any region of space or stretch of time as *marked out* in some way from the rest of the whole. We do not think of any part as something which could conceivably have existed in the absence of the rest of the whole. Now, if space and time were held to be *independent* existents, there would be no difficulty in combining the view that the whole is logically prior to the parts with the view that our *perception* or *conception* of the whole is psychologically or even logically dependent on our successive *perceptions* or *conceptions* of the parts. But if we hold, as Kant does, that space and time exist only as objects of intuition to the individual human mind, it becomes very difficult to combine these two propositions. (3) I should have thought that the proper definition of an extensive quantum would be on the following lines. It is a whole composed of parts which are *homogeneous* in kind with itself and which compose it by being *adjoined* to each other at their common boundaries. I think that the notions of homogeneity between parts and whole and *adjunction* of parts at a common boundary are essential. If we leave them out we get only the notion of an *enumerable* quantum, i.e. what we might call a *quotum*, i.e. a whole whose parts can be *counted*. E.g. the population of Cambridge in 1950 is a quotum, but it is not an extensive quantum. In connexion with any continuous extensive quantum there is an indefinite number of alternative quota. E.g. a given straight line can be regarded as equivalent to n lines of one foot each placed end to end, as equivalent to $12n$ lines of one inch each placed end to end, and so on.

Kant's argument comes to this. No external object can be perceived except by intuiting a visual or tactual sense-datum. All such sense-data are constructed by a process of successive synthesis. But the process of synthesis by which we construct deliberately geometrical figures in imagination by synthesising elements of the *pure* manifold is precisely the same process by which we unconsciously construct sense-data of various shapes and sizes out of isolated sense-impressions. Now the laws of pure geometry are the laws of this process of synthesis. Hence they apply equally to the pure figures which we produce deliberately in imagination, and to every sensible appearance by which a physical object can ever present itself to us in sense-perception.

If this is the argument, it seems to me to be irrelevant for Kant's purpose, even if it be valid. What he wants to prove is that the axioms of pure geometry apply to every *physical object* which we can ever perceive. What the argument proves, if it is valid, is that they will apply to every *sense-datum* by means of which we can perceive a physical object. It is no answer to this to say that physical objects are not things-in-themselves. For they are also not to be identified with any of the sense-data by which they manifest themselves to us. Even if we take a purely phenomenalistic view of physical objects, as Kant seems to do in the *Prolegomena* and in Deduction B, a physical object is a set of suitably interconnected actual and possible sense-data and images. On this view we need to do what Kant has never attempted to do, and *define*, in terms of the qualities and relations of sense-data, what we mean by ascribing a certain size and shape to a *physical object*. E.g., no sense-datum is cubical, and the various visual sense-data which we take to be the appearances which a certain cube would present to the same person or to various persons from different positions do not fit together over common boundaries to give a cubical surface. Therefore even if the laws of pure geometry apply, for the reasons given by Kant, to every possible appearance of a cubical object, it does not follow that they will apply to the cubical object itself. All that we are justified in saying is this. If a physical object is a logical construction out of visual and tactual sense-data, then the spatial properties of a physical object will be a logical construction out of the spatial qualities and relations of such sense-data. It follows no doubt that every geometrical proposition about physical objects must be *analysable* in terms of geometrical propositions about sense-data and their sensible relations. But it by no means follows, and is almost certainly false, that the former are *identical with* the latter.

There is one further comment to be made. The principle under discussion is supposed to correspond to the schema of the categories of quantity. Now this schema is said to be *number*, not *extensive magnitude*. We should therefore have expected that the principle would state that all phenomena are *enumerable quota*, not that they are all *extensive quanta*. If so, it would be concerned with the applicability of pure arithmetic and not with that of pure geometry.

4.1.2 The principle for anticipating perceptions

This is formulated slightly differently in A and in B. In A it runs: 'In all phenomena sensation, and the real which corresponds to it in the object (*realitas phaenomenon*), has an *intensive magnitude*, i.e. a degree' (p. 201,

A 166). In B Kant leaves out the word 'sensation' and substitutes 'the real which is an object of sensation' (p. 201, B 207).

We may begin by noticing the following points. (1) Kant is much clearer here than in the formulation of the first mathematical principle that he has to prove something about empirical objects and not merely about the sense-data by which we perceive them. The phrase in brackets – *realitas phaenomenon* – in A is no doubt added to make it quite clear that he is also not concerned with things-in-themselves. (2) The principle is supposed to correspond to the three categories of quality, and the schema of these has been asserted to be *intensive magnitude* (p. 184, A 143/B 182). (3) Kant defines 'intensive magnitude' as follows. It is 'a magnitude which is apprehended only as unity and in which multiplicity can be represented only through approximation to negation, i.e. zero' (p. 203, A 168/B 210). I think it is worth pointing out that an *extensive* quantum is always a particular existent, which can be regarded as a whole composed of parts, e.g. a body, a geometrical figure, etc. An *intensive* quantum is always a quality or a relation, e.g. colour, temperature, loudness, etc. The notion of whole and parts does not apply to it. Of course one and the same particular might have extensive magnitude as a particular and intensive magnitude in respect of one or more of its qualities. E.g. a flash of lightning has extensive magnitude in respect of occupying a certain region in the sky and intensive magnitude in respect of the brightness of its colour. (4) Kant prefixed in B a new first paragraph to the proof which he had given in A.

Kant explains as follows why he calls this a principle for *anticipating* perceptions. We cannot anticipate *a priori* the perceptible qualities of future perceived objects. For the qualities which we shall perceive in them depend upon the sensible qualities of our future sense-impressions. Now these are determined only partly by the nature of our sensibility; for they are also conditioned by the external influences which may happen to act on our senses in future. Nevertheless, if Kant is right, we can know one thing beforehand about the perceptible qualities of all empirical objects. We can know that, whatever these qualities may be, they will be capable of different degrees of intensity and will be present at any moment in some one determinate degree. To this extent, and to this alone, we can anticipate the perceptible qualities of empirical objects.

Kant seems to give two proofs. One starts at the bottom of p. 202 and continues to the end of the paragraph on the top of p. 204 (A 167–9/B 209–11). The other is contained in the new paragraph prefixed in B (pp. 201–2, B 208). In each case Kant begins by trying to prove his principle for the sensible qualities of sense-data, and then goes on to argue from this to the perceptible qualities of the physical objects which we perceive by these sense-data.

First proof. This seems to amount to the following. If we consider any sense-impression, e.g. an impression of a certain shade of red or of a certain sound, we can always conceive of it as being replaced by another of exactly the same shade or the same note but of weaker intensity. This becomes particularly obvious when we notice that we can always imagine this impression as having arisen gradually and continuously from zero intensity, or can imagine it gradually and continuously fading out to zero intensity, without altering its character in any other way. We must therefore ascribe a certain kind of magnitude to all our sense-impressions. But this magnitude is not extensive. If it were, a sense-impression of a given intensity would actually be composed of sense-impressions of weaker intensity. In order to have it we should need actually to have a series of sense-impressions of greater and greater intensity and then synthesise them, as Kant thinks we do whenever we perceive or imagine a line of finite length. But we certainly do not do this. A sense-impression of any intensity might be of *momentary* duration. So the magnitude possessed by sense-impressions is not extensive but intensive. It is not apprehended by an actual process of successive synthesis, as extensive magnitude is. But its intensive character is recognised on subsequent reflection, when we recognise that the actual sense-impression *might* have been more or less intense though otherwise unchanged, and that it *might* have reached its present intensity through a continuous intensification from zero.

I think we should all be prepared to accept this as regards the sensible qualities of our actual sense-impressions. But the question is whether this justifies us in being certain that there will always be some perceptible quality in the perceived empirical object, and that this also will have intensive magnitude. At this crucial point Kant's argument is vague and unsatisfactory. The transition seems to be made in the following sentence near the top of p. 203. 'Now what corresponds in empirical intuition to sensation is reality (*realitas phaenomenon*); what corresponds to its absence is negation, i.e. zero.' I will leave this question until we have considered the second proof, where it also arises.

Second proof. This argument turns on a distinction which Kant makes between 'empirical' and 'pure' consciousness. What he has in mind is this. When I perceive any object by sight or by touch I can distinguish the following two features in it. (1) Its spatio-temporal characteristics, i.e. its size, shape, position, duration, and date. (2) Certain qualities, e.g. colour, temperature, etc., which I perceive as pervading its area or volume throughout its duration. My awareness of the spatio-temporal characteristics, according to Kant, is *pure* or *formal* consciousness. It is an intuition of a certain region of my innate space throughout a certain stretch of my innate time. My awareness of the pervading sensible qualities, which mark out this area or volume during this period, is *empirical* consciousness. For the nature of this sensible filling depends on the action of foreign things-in-themselves upon my sensibility. If the empirical consciousness is removed one ceases to *perceive* anything, though on Kant's view one would continue to have a *pure formal intuitive awareness* of the empty spatio-temporal framework. 'Phenomena, as objects of perception, are not pure, i.e. merely formal *intuita,* like space and time. For in and by themselves these latter cannot be perceived' (p. 201, B 207).

Now the notion of physical reality just is the notion of *filled,* as distinct from empty, volume and duration. In any particular case of sense-perception it is the sensible qualities of my sense-impressions which tell me that a certain volume is filled during a certain period, and give me all the information that I can get about the nature of the filling. Now I find that, without any change in the pure or formal intuitum, the empirical consciousness may have any degree above zero. I.e. I could continue to be aware of the same area or volume, pervaded throughout by a certain sensible quality, whilst that sensible quality could have any degree of intensity above zero. It is because every sense-quality can be conceived as gradually increasing from zero to its actual intensity, whilst pervading the same intuited area or volume, that we must ascribe intensive magnitude to all our sensations. And it is because the qualities which distinguish perceptible phenomena from mere empty regions of space are perceived only by means of the sensible qualities of our sense-data that we must ascribe intensive magnitude to these perceptible qualities.

Here again the last step of the argument is vague and inconclusive. What Kant actually says is this: 'Corresponding to this intensity of sensation an *intensive magnitude,* i.e. a degree of influence . . . on the special sense involved, must be ascribed to all objects of perception, in so far as perception contains sensation' (p. 202, B 208). This seems to involve an appeal to causation. In so far as it does so, it is open to the following criticisms. (1) On p. 203 (A 168–9/B 210) Kant makes a somewhat similar reference to causation. But there he immediately adds the remark: 'This, however, I touch on only in passing; for with causality I am not at present dealing.' (2) The argument presupposes the principle that if an effect has an intensive magnitude, then its cause must also have an intensive magnitude. This is certainly not obvious. Why should not sensations which have *intensive* magnitude be caused by features in the perceived object which have only *extensive* magnitude, e.g. the number, size, figure, and arrangement of its particles? (3) If Kant's account of physical objects be correct, what precisely is meant by saying that events in a perceived physical object cause the sensations by which one perceives it? The physical object is itself a group of actual and possible sense-data subject to rules of necessary sequence and coexistence. So any such statement plainly needs very elaborate interpretation, and this Kant has not attempted to give. On the other hand, he always holds that our sense-impressions are ultimately due, not to physical objects, but to foreign things-in-themselves. But, even if this kind of dependence can properly be called 'causal influence', it is quite irrelevant for the present purpose. For we are concerned here with empirical objects and not with things-in-themselves.

Perhaps all that Kant means is that the perceptible qualities which we ascribe to physical objects are logical constructions out of the sensible qualities of the sense-data which we take to be appearances of those objects. As the latter have intensive magnitudes we ascribe to the former an intensive magnitude which is a logical construction out of these intensive magnitudes. I think that this is true and that it would have been well worth while to have developed it in detail. For, just as we draw a distinction between the various *apparent* shapes and sizes which a perceived object presents under various conditions and its *real* shape and size, so we distinguish between the various colours and temperatures which it presents under various conditions and something which we could call its 'real' or 'standard' colour or temperature. We regard many of the variations in intensity of our colour-sensations or temperature-sensations as merely subjective, and others of them as indicating a variation in the objective colour or temperature of the perceived object. The conditions under which we draw this distinction could no doubt be stated, and these could be regarded as giving the meaning of such a statement as 'This thing which I am now perceiving is really hot though it feels cold to me'.

The rest of this section is taken up with some interesting, but not very relevant, remarks about continuity, the notion of a vacuum, and an alternative possible explanation of the different density of different materials, e.g. gold and silver. The following are the main points:

(1) Space and time are essentially *continua*. This implies that their parts are themselves volumes or durations respectively. Points and lines and surfaces are not really *parts* of space, and instants are not really *parts* of time. They are only *limits*.

(2) Every intensive quantum is also continuous, in the sense that it is capable of having any one of a continuous series of degrees from zero upwards.

(3) The most general concept of a perceptible phenomenon is the concept of a region of space pervaded throughout a certain period by one or more physical qualities of a certain intensity. It is therefore the concept of something which is in principle capable of continuous variation both in shape and size and in what Kant calls its degree or intensity of reality.

(4) Kant is careful to add that it does not follow that all actual change must be continuous. For that introduces questions of causality. Whilst every variation of extension and intensity is *logically* possible, it may be that only a discontinuous selection out of this continuous range of logi-

cally possible values is *causally* possible. There is, e.g., nothing logically impossible in the notion of halving or quartering an electron. But it might be that nothing which occupied half the space occupied by an electron would have any property that could be connected, however indirectly, with anything that we can perceive.

(5) From the nature of the case there could never be any conclusive evidence, direct or indirect, for the existence of empty regions of space. For there is no theoretical minimum to the intensity of a physical quality, whilst there is no doubt a practical minimum to the susceptibility of our senses and the delicacy of our instruments of measurement. Hence it is always possible that a region which seems to be empty is in fact pervaded by a physical quality of too low an intensity to be detected.

(6) This introduces Kant's own private opinion about matter, which he worked out in detail in his *Metaphysical Foundations of Natural Science.* Scientists have commonly assumed that, when a body, e.g. a gas, can be compressed and rarefied, this *must* imply that it has pores like a sponge. The process *must* consist simply in increasing or diminishing these pores without altering the volume of the actual material of which the body is composed. This view is, e.g., strongly and explicitly asserted by Descartes. Leibniz pointed out that it is compatible with the denial of a vacuum, because the pores in body *A* may be filled with material of a different kind, like the air or water in the pores of a sponge, and this may go on *ad infinitum.* Now Kant says quite truly that the common scientific theory rests simply on a metaphysical dogma, viz. that nothing which *continuously* occupies a certain volume could possibly occupy continuously a greater or a smaller volume. Kant here suggests an alternative theory, which he worked out in more detail in the *Metaphysical Foundations.* It is that each ultimate constituent of a perceptible body is simply a region of space, continuously pervaded by a field of repulsive force which increases rapidly as you approach the centre of the region from any direction. When you compress such a body all that happens is that a smaller volume is continuously pervaded by a more intense repulsive force. Conversely when you expand it. This type of theory is certainly quite possible. It was worked out in elaborate mathematical detail by Boscovich in the eighteenth century and by Clerk Maxwell in the nineteenth.

4.2 The dynamical principles

Kant gives the name 'dynamical' to the principles which correspond to the categories of relation. In this case there is a different principle corresponding to each different category. They are called by Kant 'Analogies of Experience'.

Kant draws the following distinction between the mathematical and the dynamical principles. He says that the former 'are concerned with phenomena and their empirical intuition', whilst the latter are concerned 'only with the *existence* of such phenomena and their *relation* to one another in respect of their existence' (p. 210, A 178/B 220). I think that what Kant means is the following. The mathematical principles are involved in our perceptions of each individual physical thing or event, and they guarantee that pure geometry and arithmetic will apply to these objects. But the dynamical principles are concerned with those interconnexions between one's perceptions of different things and events which enable one to regard their objects as forming a single spatio-temporal and causal system. We must remember, of course, that Kant held that both are equally necessary in order that a person should have epistemologically objective experiences and should be able to recognise himself as the common owner of a number of different experiences.

Kant describes the mathematical principles as 'constitutive' and the dynamical ones as merely 'regulative'. He says that the principles which correspond to the categories of modality, i.e. the *postulates of empirical thought*, are also merely regulative. I think that the difference which he has in mind is this. When we assert that every perceptible object must have extensive magnitude, in respect of occupying a certain region of space for a certain period of time, we are saying something about the *constitution* of any and every physical object. So too when we say that, in order to count as occupied by a physical object, a region must be pervaded by qualities which can have any degree of intensity above zero. But, when we say that every perceptible event must be the state of some perceptible substance and must be caused by some earlier perceptible event, we are simply asserting very general *rules of connexion* which all perceptible events must obey. (I think that Kant uses the word 'regulative' in a different, though connected, sense when he talks, in the *Transcendental Dialectic*, of the 'regulative use of the ideas of reason'.)

We must next consider why Kant calls the three dynamical principles 'Analogies'. His explanation occurs on p. 211 (A 179–80/B 222–3). It is most obscure, but I think it may come to the following. If we know that $x : a :: b : c$, where a, b, and c are numbers and the relation is that of numerical ratio, we can calculate the value of x from the formula $x = (a \times b)/c$. But suppose that we are given a perceived event a. Then the principle of causation assures us only that there must have been *some* earlier event x which stands to a in the relation of cause to effect. It does not enable us to determine the qualities of x or its spatial or other non-causal relations to a. In order to do this we need to know and to apply the relevant *particular* causal laws. Now these can be known only by observation and inductive generalisation and not *a priori*. On the other hand, the principle of causation does assure us that *something or other* in the state of affairs immediately before *a* must have caused *a*. It therefore encourages us to look for the *particular event* which stands in the causal relation to *a*. If we were not certain of this *a priori*, we might well be content just to accept the occurrence of *a* as an ultimate fact and to look no further, if its cause did not stare us in the face or if we failed to find it after a merely superficial search for it. I suppose that somewhat similar remarks might be made *mutatis mutandis* about the principle that every perceptible event must be a state of *some* perceptible substance or other.

Finally, Kant insists that the dynamical and regulative principles, though completely certain when confined to their proper subject-matter, are not self-evident and require proof. This proof can be supplied if and only if we confine their application to objects of possible sense-perception. If you try to assert the law of universal causation or the principle of the permanence of substance without this restriction, they are neither self-evident nor capable of proof. I think that Kant would go further and say that they are not even intelligible.

This suggests the following reflection. If Kant is correct, no member of the human race had the slightest ground for believing the principle of universal causation until 1781, when Kant published the first edition of the *Critique of Pure Reason*. And since that time no one has had the slightest ground for believing it except the tiny minority who have read, understood, and accepted the extremely obscure argument in the second Analogy of Experience. Yet, unless people had accepted the principle, they would have had no adequate motive for continuing to seek for the cause of an event if they failed to find a cause for it after superficial investigation. It is fortunate that the whole human race, or at any rate all scientists, have acted under the delusion that the principle is self-evident.

Before treating the three Analogies in detail I will make some remarks about the premisses common to all the proofs. One premiss is that we cannot perceive the moments or stretches of empty time, but only things and events in time. Another premiss is that each of us believes that every event which he could ever perceive has its date and duration in a single objective time-system, and that his own experiences and those of other persons also have their dates and durations in this same objective time-system. This latter premiss is not ultimate for Kant. His ultimate ground for it is the synthetic unity of apperception. He holds that, unless all the objects of a person's various perceptions could be so regarded, he would not have epistemologically objective experiences at all, and therefore no perceptions. And, moreover, these various perceptions would not be so related to each other and to his other experiences that they would all be the experiences of a single self-conscious person. I cannot see that Kant has ever established this extremely important proposition; but it is absolutely fundamental to his philosophy.

Kant gives the following reason why there are three Analogies of Experience. He says that there are three *modes* of time, viz. duration, succession, and coexistence, and therefore there are three principles governing all relations of phenomena in time (p. 209, B219). There are two remarks to be made about this. (1) This is quite a new explanation of why there should be three principles. One would expect Kant to hold that there are three principles because there are three categories under the head of relation, viz. substance, cause, and reciprocity. (2) The more important point is this. In many places Kant seems explicitly to deny that there are *three* modes of time. Thus in the second sentence of the proof of the first Analogy in A (p. 213, A182) he says that 'time can determine phenomena as existing in a *twofold* manner, either as in succession to one another or as coexisting'. Again, on p. 214 (A183/B226) he says explicitly: 'Coexistence is not a mode of time itself; for none of the parts of time coexist, they are all in succession to each other.' Thus he first takes duration, succession, and coexistence as the three modes of time; then drops duration; and finally drops coexistence. And all this happens within a few pages.

I think that the solution is as follows. We must distinguish in the first place between the relations of moments of time and the relations of events or processes in time. There is only one possible relation between two moments of time, viz. that one of them must succeed the other. But a pair of instantaneous events may be either simultaneous or successive. And a pair of processes, each of which goes on for a finite time, may have a number of different temporal relations to each other. One may wholly succeed the other, or they may partially overlap, or both may begin at the same moment and end at the same later moment. Finally there is the property of *enduring through* a period of time, as distinct from *taking up* a period of time. This applies only to substances, which have a history, and not to events or to processes.

4.2.1 The first Analogy: substance and its permanence

The first Analogy is formulated somewhat differently in A and in B. In A it is: 'All phenomena contain the permanent, i.e. substance, as the object itself, and the transitory as its mere determination, i.e. as a way in which the object exists' (p. 212, A182). In B it is: 'In all change of phenomena substance is permanent; its quantum in nature is neither increased nor diminished' (p. 212, B224). If we take the two together they seem to amount to the two following propositions. (1) All perceptible events are varying states of perceptible permanent things. (2) The aggregate of these things is a quantum which is neither increased nor diminished by any of the changes which take place in them. The second proposition seems to be logically independent of the first, and it is explicitly formulated only in B.

But Kant's example about apparent changes of mass when a body is burned (p. 215, A185/B228) shows clearly that even in A he either identified the transcendental principle of the permanence of substance with the physio-chemical principle of the conservation of mass, or at any rate thought that the former entailed the latter.

I think we can dispose of this latter part of the principle at once. The only argument that I can find for the conservation of a certain quantum throughout all changes is in the last sentence of the first paragraph of the proof in B. 'As it [i.e. empirical substance] is thus unchangeable in its existence, its quantity in nature can be neither increased nor diminished' (p. 213, B225). Now the following comments may be made on this.

(1) Even if this argument is valid, the utmost that it would prove is that there must be *some* measurable characteristic of substances, which can be summed up for all the substances in nature, such that the sum total in respect of this characteristic remains constant throughout all changes in nature. Now mass is an empirical characteristic which we learn about through experiences of setting bodies in motion or stopping them when they are in motion or changing their velocity or direction of motion. We might tentatively identify the magnitude which has to be conserved with mass, on finding that mass is in fact conserved. But we certainly could not make the identification on the grounds of a transcendental argument from the necessary conditions of perceptual experience.

(2) Even this more modest conclusion does not follow from anything that Kant has proved. The utmost that he claims to have proved in A and in the earlier part of the proof in B is that every perceptible event must be a state of a perceptible substance, and none of these substances can come into existence or cease to exist in the course of nature. All that could legitimately be deduced from this is that the total *number* of ultimate substances in nature is constant. It does not follow that there must be some magnitude possessed by every ultimate substance, such that the aggregate value of this magnitude, when summed for all of them, must be the same at all times.

We can now consider Kant's proofs of the first part of the principle, viz. that all perceptible events are states of permanent perceptible substances. There are two of them.

4.2.1.1 First proof

The first occupies the first paragraph on p. 213 (B225).

(1) It opens with the statement 'All phenomena are in time; and in it alone, as *substratum*, can either coexistence or succession be represented.' I take this to amount to the following. When we say that two events or processes are simultaneous we mean that they occupy *the same* moment or

stretch of absolute time. When we say that they are successive we mean that they occupy *different* and therefore successive moments or *different* and therefore wholly or partly successive stretches of absolute time.

(2) The next step is the statement 'Thus the time in which all change of phenomena has to be thought of as occurring, remains and does not change.'[1] There are three remarks to be made about this. (a) As the sentence opens with the word 'Thus' it looks as if Kant thought that the second statement was a logical consequence of the first. I think that the point may be that to say that time changes would imply that there was a second time in which the changes of the first time occur, and that this is nonsensical. (b) I agree that it is nonsensical to say that time changes, in the sense in which we say that the water in a kettle changes as its temperature rises. But it is equally nonsensical, and for the same reason, to say that time remains *unchanged,* in the sense in which the water in a kettle remains unchanged if nothing happens to it. For this would equally involve a second time in which the first time remained unchanged. (c) Perhaps what Kant had in mind when he said that time remains and does not change is this. In one sense we do regard past, present, and future moments as constituting a serial whole, comparable to the number series . . . $-2, -1, 0, +1, +2, ...$, which exists equally at *every* moment. Yet in another sense we should say that at *any* moment the moments which preceded it have *ceased* to exist and the moments which will follow it have not yet *begun* to exist.

(3) The next step is the statement that, since time itself cannot be perceived, there must be something in what we do perceive to represent to us this peculiar unchangeableness which we have to ascribe to the time-series. Kant concludes that the unchangeableness *of* the time-series, which we cannot perceive, must be represented in what we can perceive by something which we conceive as unchanging *throughout* time. Successive perceptible events make up the history of a perceptible permanent substance, as successive moments make up that serial whole which is pure time. It is only by perceiving the former that we are able to conceive the latter.

I cannot say that I find this argument at all convincing. The only comment that I will make is this. It is an essential part of Kant's doctrine that there is one and only one objective time-system, in which all perceptible events and processes are dated. One would therefore expect the conclusion of an argument on the above lines to be that there is one and only one perceptible material substance, corresponding to the one time-system as a whole, of which all perceptible events are states, corresponding to the successive moments in the one time-system. But this does not appear to be his conclusion. He seems to accept the ordinary commonsense view that there are many material substances.

[1] [P. 213, B 225.]

4.2.1.2 Second proof

This is to be found in the second paragraph of p. 213 (A 182–3/B 225–6). (1) It starts with the statement 'our *apprehension* of the manifold of appearance is always successive and therefore always changing'. (2) Nevertheless we do distinguish in the objects which we perceive between items which are objectively successive and items which are objectively simultaneous. E.g. the sense-datum by which I perceive the front of a house and the sense-datum by which I perceive the back of the same house are always successive, but I judge that the back and the front *coexist*. Again, the auditory sense-datum by which I perceive the discharge of a distant gun is always later than the visual sense-datum by which I perceive it. Yet I judge that the corresponding physical events in the gun are *simultaneous*. On the other hand when I have successively a red and a green sense-datum in looking at traffic-lights I judge that they correspond to objectively *successive* physical events. Another set of facts which Kant may have had in mind, but which he does not explicitly mention, is the following. We regard certain changes in our sense-data as indicating mere changes in *appearance* of a physical object which has *not* changed in any relevant respect. An example is the changes in sensible size and shape of our visual sense-data when we view the top of a penny from different distances and directions. We regard other changes in our sense-data as indicating an objective change in a perceived physical object, e.g. when we judge that an air-balloon swells out or that a penny gets bent.

(3) The question therefore arises: How do we determine whether sense-data, which are always successive and may be qualitatively dissimilar, correspond to objectively successive events, on the one hand, or (a) to *different but coexistent parts* of the same perceived object, or (b) to mere changes of *appearances* in the same unchanged part of the same unchanged object, or (c) to objectively *simultaneous* physical events, on the other hand? I will give Kant's answer in his own words. 'For such determination we require an underlying ground which exists *at all times*, i.e. something *abiding* and *permanent,* of which all change and coexistence are only so many ways in which the permanent exists.' (4) This is the whole of the argument. Immediately afterwards Kant reverts to statements which are mere repetitions of points made in the first proof.

I will now make some comments. (1) As usual, Kant has got hold of something extremely important. And, so far as I know, no philosopher before him had paid any explicit attention to these facts. (2) As regards his first premiss, that 'our *apprehension* of the manifold... is always successive and therefore also changing', I would make the following comments. (a) We must distinguish between the kind of change which consists in the fact that our consciousness takes the form of a series of successive spacious presents, and the kind of change which consists in the fact that the contents of different specious presents may differ wholly or partly in *quality*. Suppose I lie on my back on a summer day and gaze up into a cloudless sky. Then the contents of my successive specious presents for a considerable period may not differ appreciably in *quality*. On the other hand, if I suddenly shut my eyes or turn my head there will be an almost complete difference in the quality of the contents of two adjacent specious presents. In most cases the contents of two adjacent specious presents are predominantly alike in quality with minor differences in certain details. But whether the contents are exactly alike, or wholly unlike, or partly alike and partly unlike in quality, there is equally a succession of specious presents. This is the only sense in which I could admit that our apprehension is always *successive*, and I think that it is somewhat misleading to add 'and *therefore* also changing'. (b) I think that all that Kant really needs are the following facts. (i) That the contents of successive specious presents nearly always differ more or less in the quality of their content and that they may differ profoundly, as when we shut our eyes or suddenly turn our heads. (ii) That sometimes we ascribe this change of content to objective changes in perceived objects and sometimes regard them as merely subjective, in the various ways which I have indicated above. (c) Surely Kant cannot have meant to deny the perfectly obvious fact that within one and the same specious present one is aware of a plurality of simultaneous contents, e.g. that my pen, my hand, the paper on which I am writing, and the ticking of my clock, present themselves sensibly to me by various simultaneous sense-data in each of a series of successive specious presents. It would be absurd to deny this, and it does not seem relevant to his argument to do so. (d) It seems to me that Kant omits to notice one very important and relevant fact about our sensible experience. There is an actual *sensible* quality of motion or of change and an actual *sensible* quality of rest or quiescence. Within a single specious present certain items present themselves as in motion or as changing in quality. E.g. when one looks at a flickering flame. Others present themselves as at rest or as quiescent in quality; e.g. when one looks at the top of a table in steady illumination.

(3) Kant does not imagine that he is stating the *sufficient* conditions for determining whether a sequence in our sensations does or does not correspond to an objective sequence or change in the objects which we perceive by means of them. He is concerned with precisely the same problem in the second and third Analogies, and he argues there that a reference to *causation*, as well as to *substance*, is involved. At most he would claim to be stating in the first Analogy a condition which is necessary but not sufficient.

(4) The final step in the argument seems to me to be deplorably weak. Indeed the sentence which I have quoted seems not to contain any appreci-

able *argument* at all. It seems to be a mere dogmatic statement of the conclusion which Kant claims to be proving.

(5) The last remark which I will make about both the attempted proofs is this. Is not the conclusion which Kant claims to have proved contrary to the facts? We certainly do somehow manage to distinguish between the subjective temporal sequence of our sense-data and the objective temporal coexistence or sequence of the things or events which we perceive by means of them. But do we take any of the objects which we perceive to be absolutely permanent? Surely we know perfectly well that none of them are so. Now Kant must have been perfectly well aware of this. What then are the substances, to which he thinks we must ascribe all perceptible events as states, and which he thinks we must regard as neither coming into existence nor ceasing to exist in the course of nature? They must be in some sense actual or possible objects of human sense-perception. Yet none of the ordinary perceptible substances answers to the conditions. All that I can suggest is this. Kant might say that we regard all the substances that we actually perceive as composite, and that we have no difficulty in conceiving the generation of a new composite substance or the annihilation of an old one. This consists simply in certain pre-existing substances coming into new and more intimate interrelations and then remaining in them for some time; or in their ceasing to stand in such interrelations after they have been intimately interrelated for some time. But, he might say, we must hold that all substances which are composite and can begin or cease to exist are composed of others which cannot begin or cease to exist in the course of nature. These latter may not be perceptible severally, but they are perceptible collectively. And it is *they* to which all perceptible events must be ascribed as states. This seems to be the only interpretation of Kant's phrase 'perceptible substances' which avoids a flagrant contradiction with obvious facts. Suppose, then, that we do put this interpretation on it. Is it not then fantastic to hold that no one could draw the distinction, which we all do draw, between the subjective temporal sequences of sense-data and the objective temporal relations of perceived things and events, unless he regarded all perceptible events as states of permanent perceptible substances in this very 'highbrow' sense?

4.2.1.3 General remarks about permanence and change

The rest of Kant's remarks under the title of the *First Analogy* consist merely of remarks about permanence and change, and not of any new argument. The following are the main points.

(1) He draws a distinction between *alteration* and *change*. We say only of a persistent substance that it *alters*; and its alteration consists in some state of it *changing*. In this sense it would be improper to speak of a *thing* as *changing*

or to speak of a *state* of a thing as *altering*. I think that this distinction is valid and important, though I doubt whether Kant himself or other people consistently use the words 'alteration' and 'change' in these particular ways.

(2) The permanence of substance, in the sense in which Kant claims to have proved it, is alleged by him to be quite consistent with the theological doctrine that all substances were originally created by God and might at any time be annihilated by him. For all that Kant claims to have shown is that *we* could not determine whether a subjective sequence in our sensations represented an objective sequence in perceptible objects unless we could regard every perceptible event as a state of some permanent perceptible substance. Now I suppose that what God would create and what he might annihilate would be things-in-themselves. Obviously Kant's doctrine is compatible with the view that all things-in-themselves were originally created by God. Suppose God were to create some additional things-in-themselves. I suppose that, unless the additional sense-impressions supplied by these could be synthesised by our imaginations and understandings in such a way as to fit into our present scheme of perceptions and its conceptual elaborations, they would simply be repressed into the unconscious and would never become sense-*data* for anyone. Suppose, on the other hand, that God were to annihilate some of the existing things-in-themselves from which we ultimately derive our present sensations. This might, I should think, leave such gaps in our sense-impressions that no amount of synthesis and supplementation by images would enable us to go on having sense-perceptions of an orderly world of permanent empirical objects, all of whose changes were determined in accordance with causal laws. But, if Kant's doctrine of the synthetic unity of apperception is true, there would in that case be no self-conscious persons left to be aware of the change. There would remain only such streams of sensations and feelings as we might imagine constitute the mental histories of jellyfish or tapeworms or amoebae.

4.2.2 The second Analogy: universal causation

In A the second Analogy is stated in the form 'Everything that happens, i.e. begins to be, presupposes something upon which it follows according to a rule' (p. 218, A 189). In B it is stated in the form 'All alterations take place in conformity with the law of the connection of cause and effect' (p. 218, B 232). I do not think that there is any fundamental difference between the two formulations.

Both Kemp Smith[1] and Paton[2] profess to detect six different proofs. But

[1] [N. Kemp Smith, *A Commentary to Kant's Critique of Pure Reason*, 2nd ed. (London, 1923).]
[2] [H. J. Paton, *Kant's Metaphysics of Experience* (London, 1936).]

Smith admits that the first three are almost identical, and that the fifth is very much like the proof in B which he counts as the sixth. The fourth is unique and peculiar. I shall therefore take it that there are at most three proofs which are distinct enough to be worth distinguishing. What I shall call the first proof begins at the second paragraph on p. 219 and goes on to the end of the first paragraph on p. 225 (A 189–99/B 232–44). What I shall call the second proof is to be found on p. 218 and the first paragraph of p. 219 (B 233–4) and again in the passage which begins with the last paragraph of p. 226 and ends at the end of the first paragraph of p. 227 (A 201–2/B 246–7). What I shall call the third proof begins at the second paragraph of p. 225 and ends at the end of the second paragraph on p. 226 (A 199–201/B 244–6).

4.2.2.1 First proof

Kant starts, as in the first Analogy, with the premiss that all one's experiences are successive. Nonetheless one sometimes bases upon them a perceptual judgment of objective coexistence and sometimes a perceptual judgment of objective sequence. He takes two examples to illustrate this. (1) Suppose I look at any large opaque object such as a house. I cannot possibly see the whole of the outside surface at once from any one position. I may first look at the roof and then turn my head downwards until the ground floor comes into view. I may first look at the left side of the front and then turn my head sideways till the right-hand side of the front comes into view. Finally I may walk round it until I have seen the sides and the back as well as the front. Here the sensations by which I perceive the various parts of the house are certainly *successive*. But I take them to reveal successively to me *coexisting* parts of the surface of a single physical thing. (2) Suppose I look at a boat sailing down a river. The sensations by which I perceive the boat are again successive. But now I judge that I am perceiving a series of objectively *successive* events, viz. the successive occupation by the boat of a series of different positions relative to the banks of the river. There is no doubt about the facts. And there is no doubt that anyone who could not draw this kind of distinction between the order in which he gets his sensations, and the objective temporal order of the things and events which he perceives by means of them would lack something which is quite fundamental in normal human experience. Kant's problem here is 'How do we come to make such distinctions, and what is implied by the possibility of doing so?'

(1) He begins by raising a fundamental question. He accepts the view that the only particulars with which any person can be acquainted are his own experiences, including under this heading his own sense-data and images. Now these are successive. But the very fact that I draw a dis-

tinction between the order in which I get my sensations and the order which exists in perceived objects implies that I regard my sensations as signs of something other than and different in kind from themselves. What can this be, and how can I know anything about it?

Kant begins by making it quite plain that no reference to things-in-themselves is here relevant. We are talking about *empirical* objects, such as houses and boats sailing on rivers. So the objects of which sense-data are signs are not things-in-themselves. On the other hand, these objects cannot be unsensed sensibilia for that is a meaningless phrase. A sensibile must, from the nature of the case, be the actual sense-datum of some one person on some one occasion. It is something essentially private, mind-dependent, and fleeting. Yet these characteristics are the exact antithesis of all that we understand by a physical object. What then can the empirical object be, of which our sense-data are signs?

Kant's answer on p. 220 is a form of phenomenalism. The empirical object, of which a certain sense-datum is a sign, is a whole set of actual and possible sense-data interconnected in accordance with certain rules. Each sense-datum in such a set of regularly interconnected actual and possible sense-data counts as a percept of the object which is the set as a whole; but it is a percept of it from a special point of view and under special limitations. This account of an empirical object and its various sensible appearances is very similar to that given by Russell in his *Analysis of Mind*.[1] But there are at least two important differences. Russell talks of unsensed sensibilia; Kant regards all such talk as nonsensical. And for Kant the rules, which are an essential factor in the concept of an empirical object, involve *a priori* concepts, such as that of causal necessitation.

(2) Having settled the question of what is meant by an empirical object, Kant passes to his main questions. (a) Under what conditions do we in fact regard two successive sense-data which differ in quality as indicating an objective *sequence*, and under what circumstances do we regard them as indicating different coexisting parts of a perceived physical thing? (b) What do these conditions imply?

(a) As regards the first question Kant's answer is this. In the case of perceiving the various parts of a house I believe that I could have had the relevant sense-data in the reverse order. Suppose that in fact the sense-datum which I take to be an appearance of the front preceded the sense-datum which I take to be an appearance of the back. I fully believe that a sense-datum exactly like the latter *could* have occurred in my experience *before,* instead of after, one exactly like the former. But in the case of perceiving the boat moving downstream the opposite is the case. I have a certain sequence of sense-data which I take to be appearances of the same boat at a series of positions further and further downstream. I believe that

[1] [B. Russell, *The Analysis of Mind* (London, 1921).]

it would then and there have been impossible for me to have had a sequence of similar sense-data in the reverse temporal order.

If we generalise from Kant's two examples, the conditions may be stated as follows. Suppose that on a certain occasion a sense-datum x is followed immediately in my experience by a certain qualitatively dissimilar sense-datum y, and that they are so interconnected that I regard them as referring to the same perceived thing. I may believe that it would have been possible for me then and there to have had instead a sense-datum x' exactly like x and a sense-datum y' exactly like y, but in the temporal order y', x' instead of the temporal order x, y. If so, I take x and y to be appearances of different *coexisting parts* of the same perceptible object. On the other hand, I may believe that it would have been impossible for me there and then to have had anything but a sense-datum exactly like y immediately after having the sense-datum x. If so, I take x and y to be appearances respectively of an earlier and an immediately later state of a certain perceived physical thing. And so I take their sequence in my experience to be a perception of an objective alteration in that thing from the former to the latter state, i.e. to be a perception of a physical event.

Now I suspect that Kant would go further than to say that this is a *criterion* for deciding that one is perceiving a physical event. I suspect that he would wish to say that it is an *analysis* of the notion of perceiving a physical event. After all, if one is to give a phenomenalistic analysis of the notion of physical *thing*, one must also give a phenomenalistic analysis of the notion of physical *event*. So I am inclined to ascribe the following doctrine to Kant. To say that I am witnessing a physical event is *equivalent* to saying (i) that I have two immediately successive sense-data x and y, which differ in quality but are so interconnected that I take them to refer to the same physical thing T; and (ii) that the immediate sequence of y upon x in my experience on this occasion is inevitable.

(b) We come now to the implications of this. What Kant actually says is this. 'In this case . . . we must derive the *subjective succession* of apprehension from the *objective succession* of phenomena' (p. 221, A 193/B 238). But he adds a little further on in the same paragraph the following statement: 'The objective succession will therefore consist in that order of the manifold of appearance according to which, *in conformity with a rule*, the apprehension of that which happens follows upon the apprehension of that which precedes' (p. 222, A 193/B 238).

It is not easy to reconcile these two statements. The first of them would, in a sense, be admitted by everyone. We should say the earlier state ζ of the perceived thing T determines the earlier sense-datum x in the percipient. The immediately subsequent state η of the perceived thing T determines the immediately subsequent sense-datum y in the percipient. Since η objectively follows immediately upon ζ, y, which is an effect of η, inevitably follows immediately on x, which is an effect of ζ. But obviously this will not do for Kant's purposes, even if we admit that it is true. In the first place, it presupposes a non-phenomenalistic view of the physical thing T and of its successive states ζ and η. Secondly, although it does bring in causation, it does not bring it in in the place where Kant is trying to show that it must be held to be present. What he wants to prove is that the transition from the physical state ζ to the physical state η must be causally necessitated either by ζ itself or by some other perceptible physical state objectively simultaneous with ζ. But the causation here is between ζ and x and between η and y; and this might exist even if the transition from ζ to η were completely undetermined. We must therefore either ignore this remark, as completely irrelevant, or assume that it is a rough preliminary statement which needs to be reinterpreted phenomenalistically. We will therefore pass on to the second statement.

Remembering that Kant is giving a purely phenomenalistic analysis of physical thing and physical event, and that he does not allow the possibility of unsensed sensibilia, I think that we must ascribe the following view to him here. Anyone who holds that the actual sequence of sense-datum y on sense-datum x in his experience was inevitable must *ipso facto* hold the following belief. He must believe that either x itself or some other sense-datum of his simultaneous with x *causally necessitated* the immediately subsequent occurrence of sense-datum y in his experience.

(3) On this interpretation we can now sum up the argument as follows. (a) The notions of physical thing and physical event must be analysed entirely in terms of actual and possible sense-data and their interconnexion within experience. Therefore the notion of the causation of one physical event by another must also be analysed entirely in these terms. (b) To say that a sequence x, y of sense-data in a person's experience is a perception by him of an event in a physical thing is to say (i) that these two sense-data differ in quality but are so interconnected as to count as appearances to him of the same physical thing T; and (ii) that the immediate sequence of y upon x in his experience on that occasion was *inevitable*. (c) To say that the sequence was *inevitable* involves saying that either x itself or some other sense-datum of his simultaneous with x *causally necessitated* the immediately subsequent occurrence of y in his experience. (d) On the phenomenalistic analysis of physical event and physical causation this in turn is equivalent to the following statement. The physical state η, of which y is an appearance, is causally necessitated by an immediately previous physical state, of which either x itself, or some other sense-datum of his simultaneous with x, is an appearance. (e) Therefore, whenever a sequence x, y of sense-data in a person's experience can be counted as a perception by him of an objective transition from one state of a perceived thing to another, the later of these physical states is causally necessitated

either by the earlier of them or by some other perceptible physical state simultaneous with the earlier of them.

I think that the argument is logically coherent when interpreted in this way. The question whether it proves its conclusion depends on whether we can accept Kant's phenomenalistic analysis of certain ordinary notions, viz. of physical object, physical event, and the causation of one physical event by another. Now it may be doubted whether *any* purely phenomenalistic analysis of these notions is satisfactory. The general formula of such attempts at analysis is this. You start with what common sense regards as a *criterion* for the truth of a certain type of proposition, e.g. for the truth of a proposition of the form 'This physical event objectively follows that one'. And then you assert that this is not a mere criterion but is the *analysis* of such propositions. Now most attempts on these lines are open to at least the two following criticisms. (1) That they start by being vague, and end by becoming circular when you try to make them precise. The typical circularity is a reference to a percipient's *body*, to its position in a *public space*, and to its adjustments and orientation at certain moments in a *public time-system*. All these notions are used without receiving a phenomenalist analysis. It is just airily asserted or implied that this could easily be done if it were worth while to take the time and trouble. But it is very doubtful whether it can be done. (2) That it is often impossible to admit that the set of propositons which is offered as the phenomenalistic analysis of commonsense statements of a certain type even is *materially equivalent* to the latter, still less that it expresses what one *means* by the latter.

Now, even if these *general* objections can be met, it would not of course follow that Kant's particular phenomenalistic analyses of the notions involved in the second Analogy are acceptable. It seems to me that they are all far too *individualistic* to be at all plausible. E.g., if the notion of physical event is to be analysed phenomenalistically, it must surely be analysed, not only in terms of the sequence of sense-data which one individual did have or would have had, but in terms of the sequence which *any* individual would have had under assignable conditions. Again, whatever I may mean by saying that a physical event which I perceive is caused by some immediately previous physical event, which was in principle perceptible, I surely do not mean something which relates merely to *my own* sensa and to their causal determination by *each other*.

4.2.2.2 Second proof

The principle of the second proof is quite different from that of the first. Kant is no longer concerned with the distinction between the successive perception of *coexisting parts* of an object and the perception of an *objective sequence* of qualitatively dissimilar states of an object. He now considers what is involved in the fact that we *know* or *believe* that a certain change takes place in the order ζ, η, whilst we can quite well *imagine* a change taking place *either* in the order ζ, η *or* in the reverse order η, ζ. The argument occurs both in the two new introductory paragraphs which Kant prefixed in B (pp. 218–19, B 232–4) and in a part which is common to A and B (pp. 226–7, A 201–2/B 246–7). I find it extremely obscure.

I think it will be best to begin with a case where there is a short but finite gap between the two successive sense-data which are one's basis for judging that a certain objective change has taken place in a certain direction. An example would be the sequence of a green round sense-datum *a* followed after a short interval by a red round sense-datum *b* in a similar position in one's visual field. This leads one to judge that there has been an objective sequence from a green light to a red light in a certain signalling apparatus.

Taking this as our example, I think that Kant's argument would be as follows.

(1) The question of a change does not arise until one has the red sense-datum *b*. But at that time one is no longer having the green sense-datum *a*. If there is to be any question of judging that there is a change, the vanished green sense-datum *a* must be replaced by an image *a* which coexists with the red sense-datum *b* and is specially linked with *it* as contrasted with the numerous other sense-data which are contemporary with it. This is part of the process which Kant calls synthesis by the productive imagination.

(2) Now merely to say that the present red sense-datum *b* is selectively linked with a contemporary green image *a* is not enough. For this is a *necessary* condition of various alternative kinds of belief-attitudes, and is not a *sufficient* condition of any one of them. One *may* judge that the image represents a certain physical state which objectively preceded the physical state which the sense-datum *b* represents. But one might not judge that the image represents any actual past physical state at all. One might simply be led to *imagine* a green physical state as *having preceded*, or to imagine a green physical state as *about to follow*, the red physical state which the present sense-datum represents. Sometimes one has the one kind of experience and sometimes the other, when one has a sense-datum and a contemporary image selectively linked with it. The following question therefore arises. Suppose one has a sense-datum *b* and a contemporary image *a* selectively linked with it. Under what conditions does one take *a* to represent an *actual* physical state which *objectively preceded* the physical state which one takes *b* to represent? It is evident that in these cases and in these only some kind of *compulsion* is exerted upon the otherwise free play of the imagination. Apart from this compulsion you need not take *a* to represent any physical

state that ever has been or ever will be *actual*. And apart from this compulsion you need not date the state represented by *a* before rather than after the state represented by the sense-datum *b*.

(3) Kant's answer appears to be the following. This compulsion will be exercised upon my imagination if and only if I believe that the image *a* represents a physical state which either (a) itself causally necessitates the state which the sense-datum *b* represents or (b) is contemporary with some other physical state which causally necessitates the state which the sense-datum *b* represents.

(4) We may now sum up the argument as follows. (We must remember that I am at present restricting it to cases where there is a short but finite gap between two successive sense-data which refer to the same physical thing.) (a) In order to judge that a physical alteration has just taken place in a certain physical thing *T* I must have a present sense-datum *b* and an image *a* which is selectively linked with *b*. The sense-datum and the image must be so interrelated that they are taken as referring to the same physical thing *T* and perhaps to the same part of it. (b) This, though necessary, is insufficient. I shall not judge that a physical alteration has just taken place in *T* unless I feel compelled to take the image *a* as representing an actual past state of *T* which objectively preceded the state of *T* which my present sense-datum *b* represents. (c) I shall not feel compelled to regard the image *a* in this way unless the following condition is fulfilled. I must believe that the state of *T* which is represented by my sense-datum *b* is causally determined, either by a state of it which is represented by my image *a* or by some other state of it which is contemporary with that represented by *a*. (d) It follows that no one could ever be in a position to judge that he had just witnessed a physical alteration unless he believed that the later of the two physical states which constitute that transition was causally necessitated, either by the earlier of them itself or by some other physical state contemporary with the earlier of them. (e) Suppose we now bring in Kant's phenomenalistic account of physical things and events and of the causation of one physical event by another. Then I suspect that the belief mentioned in (d) above would come to this. The person in question must believe that his image *a* was causally necessitated by a sense-datum *a* of his which either itself causally necessitated his sense-datum *b* or was simultaneous with some other sense-datum of his which did so. I will now make some comments on the argument.

(1) I do not think that it would have any plausibility if it were applied to cases where the two successive sense-data *a* and *b* are adjoined to each other without any temporal gap in the same specious present. These are the cases where one can talk literally of *perceiving a change as happening*, as opposed to merely judging that a change has just happened. Examples are looking at a flickering flame, seeing the second-hand of a watch jumping, and so on.

Kant always ignores such experiences. Yet here the transition is actually *given* as taking place in a certain direction. These experiences must surely be of quite fundamental importance in all discussion of our notions and beliefs about sequence and change. But it would surely be absurd to say that they involve images and a reference to the principle of universal causation.

(2) On the other hand, a similar argument to Kant's could be applied to the case of remembering a series of events. Suppose I remember that x was followed by y. It may quite well happen that the image of y arises in my mind on this occasion *before* the image of x. So I am able somehow to distinguish between the subjective order in which my memory-images happen to occur on a certain occasion and the objective order in which I believe the original experiences to have happened. Then again, in whichever order the images happen to occur, I can *imagine* y to have preceded x, though I fully believe that x in fact preceded y. So I am able somehow to distinguish between an imagined order of events and what I take to have been the real order of events. This is a very important fact, which needs explanation and presumably has important epistemological implications even if we do not accept Kant's particular conclusions.

(3) An absolutely vital step in Kant's argument is that which I have numbered (c) in the summary. It comes to this. I shall not feel compelled to regard my image a as representing an actual state of T which *objectively preceded* that state of T which my present sense–datum b represents, except on the following conditions. I must believe that the state which my present sense–datum b represents was causally necessitated either by a state of T which my image a represents or by some other state of T simultaneous with that one. Why should Kant be so sure of this? So far as I can discover the only reason that he gives is a negative one, viz. that I cannot perceive the moments of time. 'Time cannot be perceived in itself, and what precedes and what follows cannot therefore be empirically determined by reference to it in the object' (p. 219, B233).

Now about this there are three remarks to be made. (a) It would not really help if we could perceive moments of time. For the image a occurs at the *same* moment as the sense–datum b. What would help would be if one or other of the following two alternatives could be admitted. (i) If at a later moment I could be *directly acquainted* with something that happened at an earlier moment, and could be aware of it as having such–and–such a *degree of remoteness* from the present. Or (ii) if a present image, which is in *fact* due to a certain past event, should, so to speak, carry on its face some *inspectable mark* by which one could know this fact about it and could estimate the degree of remoteness of that past event from the present. I am quite sure that Kant would deny both of these alternatives. (b) But it is not enough to deny these alternatives in order to establish the particular alternative which

Kant adopts. E.g. some images certainly have a characteristic, not possessed by others, which might be described as 'feeling of familiarity'. We
refer such images to the past. Then, again, among such images there are
differences in liveliness, in amount of detail, and so on. I might regard a
livelier and more detailed image as generally representing a less remote
event than a less lively and vaguer image. There are almost certainly many
different signs which we use in judging the objective order of events, and
probably none of them by itself is sufficient. (c) We do undoubtedly often
use a causal criterion of the objective order of events, when we believe that
we have established particular causal laws. E.g. if I find that I recorded a
certain event in my diary, I can conclude on causal grounds that the event
itself objectively preceded my making the record of it. But it is plain that
causal considerations could not be one's only criterion for determining the
objective order of events. No causal law could be established unless we
already had some other criterion for dating events. For the only empirical
evidence for holding that X causes Y is that X-like events have always been
found *to be followed by* Y-like events.

(4) If we accepted every step of Kant's argument, his conclusion would
only come to the following. In every case where I judge that I have
witnessed a physical alteration in a thing I *cannot but believe* that the later
state was causally necessitated either by the earlier state itself or by some
other state contemporary with this. He would not have proved that this
belief, which I cannot help having on any such occasion, is *always, or indeed
ever*, true. I think that Kant is often inclined to think that he has proved a
proposition of the latter kind, when the utmost that he could plausibly
claim to have proved is one of the former kind.

4.2.2.3 Third proof

The third proof is utterly unlike the rest, but it is somewhat analogous
to the first proof of the first Analogy. It begins in the middle of p. 225
and continues to the end of the second paragraph of p. 226
(A 199–201/B 244–6). So far as I can see, the essence of the argument is this.
We know certain things *a priori* about time. We cannot have learned these
by contemplating moments of time themselves, and reflecting upon
them; for they are imperceptible. Therefore these properties of *time* must
be represented to us by certain features which necessarily belong to the
series of *perceptible events in time*. Kant argues that the property of being
causally necessitated by some previous event must belong to every event
in time, if we are to be able to ascribe to time itself certain properties which
we do in fact regard as necessarily belonging to it.

The properties of time which Kant takes as the basis of his argument are
stated very obscurely. In the opening lines of the proof he says that it is 'a

necessary law of our sensibility that the preceding time *necessarily deter-mines* the succeeding time'. But at the end of the same paragraph he describes what he has just been talking of as 'this *continuity* in the con-nexion of times' (p. 225, A 199/B 244). Continuity can hardly be identified with necessary determination. The continuity of time means that there is a moment between any two moments. If this is to be represented by some fact about perceptible events, the fact would presumably be that there is a total state between any two successive total states of the physical world. The 'necessary determination of the succeeding time by the preceding time' must presumably mean that, if the instant t in fact *precedes* the instant t' then it is inconceivable that t should have instead *followed* t'. If this is to be represented by some fact about perceptible events the fact would pre-sumably be something about its being inconceivable that an effect should precede its cause.

I shall now make up and then criticise an argument on these lines. It may or may not be precisely what Kant had in mind, but I have little doubt that it corresponds roughly to what he meant.

(1) We should all agree that, if the moment t *in fact preceded* the moment t', then it is *logically* impossible that t' should instead have preceded t. The question then arises: How do we come to know this fact about moments of time, since they are imperceptible?

(2) Kant answers that we can know this property of the series of *moments* only because it is represented by a certain property of the series of *events*. What property of events represents this property of moments? Suppose that every event were causally determined by some earlier event. Then if e' in fact succeeded e it is *causally* impossible that e' should not have succeeded e. For, if every event is causally determined by earlier events, then either e itself or some other event contemporary with e must have been either the direct cause or a causal ancestor of e'. Hence, if e was *in fact* followed by e' after a certain interval, it is *causally impossible* that e' should not have followed e after that interval.

(3) We may sum this up as follows. (a) If all events be causally deter-mined by earlier events, and we take any total state of affairs as our datum, then it is *causally* impossible that any of the total states of affairs which *in fact* followed should not have followed. (b) It is only by recognising this *causal* necessity in the actual order of perceptible *events* that we can con-ceive and know the *logical* necessity of the actual order of *moments*. (c) Since we do know the latter, we must recognise the former.

(4) An argument about continuity could be constructed on similar lines. If t and t' be any two moments, we know that, however near together they may be, there must be another moment between them. In order to know this fact about *moments*, which we cannot perceive, we must know some corresponding fact about *events*, which we can perceive. Now if e' be any

event, we know that it must have a causal ancestor in every earlier state of the world's history. And we know that, if e be a causal ancestor of e', then, however near together these two events may be, there must be a continuous series of events connecting them, such that each event in the series is a causal descendant of e and a causal ancestor of e'. The argument would be that, unless we knew this fact about the *causally* necessary continuity of the series of *events*, we could neither conceive nor know the *logically* necessary continuity of the series of *moments*. Since we do know the latter, we must know the former.

Supposing this to be Kant's argument, we can make the following comments on it.

(1) If we accept both the premisses and the reasoning, it proves only that we must *believe* that every perceptible event is causally determined by some earlier perceptible event, and that there is a continuous causal chain of events between them. It does not follow that these beliefs are *true*.

(2) I think we can explain how we know that two moments of time cannot but stand in the temporal relation in which they do in fact stand without any appeal to the principle of universal causation. By definition, a *moment*, as distinct from an *event*, is something which has no characteristics except a certain determinate temporal position. Now any moment which had stood to t in a different temporal relation from that in which t' stood to it would necessarily have had a different temporal position from that which t' in fact had. It would therefore, by definition, have been a different moment from t'. It is therefore a purely *analytic* proposition that two moments could not have stood to each other in a different temporal relation from that in which they did in fact stand. Obviously we do not need to know that all events are causally necessitated by earlier events in order to know this purely analytic proposition about moments.

4.2.2.4 General remarks about causation

We will consider finally a few general remarks which Kant makes about causation.

(1) He remarks on p. 223 (A 195–6/B 240–1) that the general principle that every event is causally determined by some earlier event cannot be based on observation and induction, as empiricists assert. According to them we first observe regular sequences; then prove by induction from them particular causal laws; and finally prove, by a further induction from these, that every event is connected with some causal law. Now, if Kant be right, this procedure would be circular. For, according to him, we could not perceive any objective sequence at all, and be sure that it was objective, unless we already accepted the general principle that every perceptible event is causally determined by previous events which are in a wide sense

perceptible. On his view we can discover laws in nature only because we have unconsciously put law-abidingness into nature. We have done this by so supplementing, connecting, and repressing the sense-impressions supplied by foreign things-in-themselves that we end by ostensibly perceiving a world of permanent interacting substances, all of whose varying states are causally determined. I do not accept Kant's reasons for his rejection of the empiricist view. But I think that his conclusion follows from his premises and that it is in fact true. I do not believe for a moment that our belief in the principle of universal causation does in fact rest on induction, or that it could be established by induction in the sense in which particular causal laws can be.

(2) On pp. 227–8 (A202–4/B247–9) Kant discusses cases where cause and effect seem to be *simultaneous*. He points out that we have to consider *order* in time and not *lapse* of time. There is never any lapse of time between the completion of the causal conditions and the beginning of the effect. When a weight is hanging on a spring and stretching it the cause, viz. the presence of the weight, and the effect, viz. the extension of the spring, seem to be simultaneous. But we must go back to the beginning of the transaction. We find that the bringing of the weight into position ended at the moment when the extension of the spring began. Afterwards each successive infinitely short phase of the state of being stretched depends on the immediately preceding infinitely short phase of the state of supporting the weight.

(3) From the beginning of the last paragraph on p. 228 to the end of the first paragraph on p. 230 (A 204–6/B 249–52) Kant considers the relation of cause to substance. (a) He begins by saying that 'causality leads to the concept of action, this in turn to the concept of force, and thereby to the concept of substance'. He remarks that, although *permanence* is the essential and peculiar characteristic of an empirical substance, yet the most convenient practical criterion of substantiality is often *activity* rather than permanence. (b) He reiterates that he is concerned with empirical or phenomenal substances and not with things-in-themselves. And in discussing causation he is concerned with *alterations* in the states of phenomenal substances, and not with the *generation* or *annihilation* of such substances themselves. In fact he has shown in the first Analogy that they cannot be generated or annihilated in the course of nature. We can indeed think, or at least talk, of the generation or annihilation of things-in-themselves. But the kind of causation which would be involved there is *creative*, and could be exercised only by God. This is not the sense in which we talk of causation in ordinary life or in natural science, and it is not the sense of it with which he is concerned in the *Analogies of Experience*. (c) He asserts that all alteration must take place *continuously*. If a later state of a thing differs from an earlier state of it by a finite amount, either quan-

titatively or qualitatively, there must be a series of intermediate states in which this quantity or quality occurs in all intermediate values. This continuity in alteration requires continuity of action in the cause which is responsible for the alteration. Kant admits that we ought to feel suspicious about all such claims to know things *a priori* about the course of nature. But he claims to be able to prove this proposition within the range of possible experiences by a transcendental argument.

It is worth noting that both the doctrine that force or activity is characteristic of substance, and the principle of continuity, are favourite doctrines of Leibniz's. Kant no doubt inherited them in his dogmatic days, retained them, and then tried to work them into his new critical philosophy.

4.2.3 The third Analogy: universal interaction

Kant prefixed a new paragraph in B to what was the first paragraph in A. He also formulated the Analogy slightly differently. The formulation in B is that all substances, '*in so far as they can be perceived to coexist in space*, are in thoroughgoing reciprocity'. The formulation in A omits the reference to space, and has 'mutual interaction' instead of 'thoroughgoing reciprocity'. I do not suppose that the latter difference is of any importance. The former might be. Kant might have held in A that his argument applied both to mental and to material substances, and in B he may wish to confine it to perceptible material things. I shall assume that this is his intention.

Norman Kemp Smith[1] professes to discover no less than four proofs in the four pages which Kant devotes to this subject. It seems to me that there are two distinguishable proofs, viz. that in A and that in the new paragraph which Kant prefixed in B. What Kemp Smith counts as the third proof is contained in the concluding paragraph, viz. the second paragraph of p. 236. Kant describes this as 'remarks which may be helpful in further elucidation of my argument'. I do not find them helpful and I shall ignore them.

This is the most obscure of the three Analogies, and that is saying a good deal.

(1) In the first place, one may ask: Why should Kant need to deal specially with the coexistence of substances? He claims to have proved that *every* perceptible substance exists throughout the *whole* of time. If so, surely *all* substances *always* coexist. I think that the answer must be as follows. We have noted that this is so obviously false with regard to all ordinary perceptible substances, chairs, trees, human bodies, etc., that he cannot have been referring to them in the first Analogy. These substances are all composite, and they plainly do begin to exist and cease to exist.

[1] [*Commentary*, pp. 381ff.]

What he must claim to have proved is that there are *ultimate* substances which neither begin nor cease to exist in the course of nature, and that all substances which do begin and cease to exist are composed of these. Now it is clear from his examples that he is not concerned with these ultimate substances, but with composite ones which do begin and cease to exist. For he takes as an example the earth and the moon. I think we may take it that he is concerned with the coexistence of two or more perceptible substances, each of which can be perceived by a person separately, but no two of which can be perceived by him together. The same question would presumably arise about different parts of what we count as a single composite substance, e.g. the back and the front of a house.

(2) The next question is: What does Kant mean by 'thoroughgoing reciprocity' or 'mutual interaction'? This is far from clear. On the top of p. 234 he seems to identify this with what he calls 'the reciprocal sequence of the determinations' of the substances in question. I think it is plain that by the 'determinations' of a substance Kant means simply states of it or alterations in it. Now, if this statement is taken literally, to say that two substances A and B are in mutual interaction would seem to have the following meaning. Every alteration a_1 in A causally necessitates a later alteration β_1 in B; this in turn causally necessitates a later alteration a_2 in A; this causally necessitates a later alteration β_2 in B; and so on. In the first paragraph of p. 235 he says: 'Each substance . . . must contain in itself the causality of certain determinations in the other . . . and at the same time the effects of the causality of that other.' He there adds the important qualification that this causal relation need not be *immediate*. And in the next paragraph he gives the following example. 'The light, which plays between our eye and the celestial bodies, produces a *mediate* community between us and them.' This is an odd example. One sees what he means by 'mediate', viz. that the light from the celestial body travels through a medium to one's eye. But does he really think that some causal influence also travels back from one's eye to the celestial body? Probably a better example would have been light emitted from body A, travelling to body B, then being reflected back from B to A, and so on. I think that the accurate definition of the statement that A and B are in 'thoroughgoing reciprocity' would be this. (a) *Every* alteration in A is a factor in the total cause of an alteration in B, and is itself the effect of a total cause in which an alteration in B is a factor. (b) If we substitute B for A and A for B throughout the first statement the new statement is also true. I shall take this to be what Kant ought to mean.

(3) Whatever obscurity there may be in the details of Kant's arguments, it is plain that he is raising a very important question, and that he is right in thinking that a reference to causality is relevant to the answer. (a) The question may be put as follows. If I can no longer perceive A when I am

perceiving B, and can no longer perceive B when I am perceiving A, how can I ever know that B exists while I am perceiving A or that A exists while I am perceiving B? And, unless I can know such things, how can I ever know that A and B coexist? It seems to me that the essential point is what we *mean* by saying, and what *evidence* we ever have for saying, that a person can perceive one and the same thing on two separated occasions and that it continued to exist during the interval when he was not perceiving it. This question is particularly pressing for anyone who accepts a purely phenomenalistic analysis of the notion of a material thing. It is still more pressing if he holds, as Kant does, that it is meaningless to talk of a sensibile which is not the sense-datum of one particular individual on one particular occasion. (b) The relevance of causality to the answer is this. It would generally be admitted that, when I am no longer perceiving B, the only evidence that I can have for its continued existence is that I perceive some state a, in some other thing A, which I am now perceiving, and that I take a to be an effect of some state β of B. No doubt this needs a good deal of qualification in detail. Causal influences from very distant things take a long time to travel, and so B may have ceased to exist by the time that the state a has been produced in A. And it is a far cry from this to Kant's conclusion about 'thoroughgoing reciprocal interaction'. Nevertheless, it is true that the only available evidence for the continued existence of what one is no longer perceiving is its perceived effects on something which one still is perceiving. And it is true that the phenomenalist must, as usual, translate what ordinary men count as a mere *criterion* for the *truth or falsity* of a proposition into an *analysis* of its *meaning*. With these preliminary remarks we may pass to Kant's arguments.

4.2.3.1 The proof in A

The proof in A begins with the second paragraph of p. 234 and ends at the end of the first paragraph of p. 236 (A 211–14/B 258–61). I shall assume that we are concerned with two perceptible things A and B each of which is composite and therefore can begin or cease to exist, even if we accept the conclusion of the first Analogy. And I shall assume that a person cannot perceive both A and B together, though he can perceive each of them successively. As we know, one does sometimes hold under such circumstances that A and B coexist.

(1) The first question for Kant is: Under what conditions does one judge that A and B coexist under such circumstances? To this he repeats the answer which he gave in the second Analogy. I believe that A and B coexist if and only if I believe that my perception of A might equally well have preceded or followed my perception of B on a given occasion.

(2) The next step is the transition from the alleged possibility of the

perceptions occurring in the reverse order on the same occasion to the conclusion that A and B must reciprocally exert causal influence on each other. I must confess that I cannot understand what Kant has in mind here. The following two points are presumably significant. (a) He twice speaks of the existence of a *medium* of some kind, occupying the space between A and B, as if this were involved in the argument. E.g. at the bottom of p. 234 he says that, if two substances were altogether indifferent causally to each other, 'they would be separated by a completely empty space'. And he concludes from this that, if one first perceived A and then ceased to do so and began to perceive B, one 'would not be able to distinguish whether the second follows objectively on the first or whether it is . . . coexistent with it'. Then, again, on p. 235 in the second paragraph, he says: 'We may easily recognise from our experiences that only the continuous influences in all parts of space can lead our senses from one object to another. The light, which plays between our eye and the celestial bodies, produces a mediate community between us and them, and thereby shows us that they coexist.' (b) The other remark which is presumably important occurs at the beginning of the first paragraph of p. 235. 'There must therefore, besides the mere existence of A and B, be something through which A determines for B its position in time, and also conversely B for A. For only on this condition can these substances be empirically represented as *coexisting*.'

I do not understand the argument, but I will make the following comments.

(1) I should agree that the occurrence of some kind of causal influence of both A and B *on the body of the percipient* is necessary if he is to perceive *either* of them. And of course he must have perceived *both* of them before the question whether they coexist or exist only successively can arise for him. But (a) what is primarily required is an influence of each of them on a certain *third* thing, viz. the percipient's body, and not a mutual influence on each other. *Unless* they influence the observer's body, it is not *sufficient* for them to influence each other. And *if* they influence the observer's body, it is not *necessary* for them to influence each other. The utmost that I could admit here is that, since there is nothing unique about an observer's body, considered as a physical thing, it is unlikely that A and B would both influence it without also influencing each other in some way. (b) It is not essential that the influence on the observer's body should be reciprocated, though it is possible that it always is in fact reciprocated to some infinitesimally slight degree. (c) The influence of A and B on the percipient's body cannot be what Kant has in mind here. For it is a necessary condition for perceiving A and B at all, whilst he is concerned with the necessary and sufficient condition for judging that A and B coexist when they can be perceived only successively.

(2) I should agree that, if you are to have any reason for judging that A

still exists when you are no longer perceiving it and have begun to perceive B, it must take the following form. You must now be perceiving a certain state ζ of a certain thing X, and you must judge that ζ is an effect of a nearly contemporary state a of A. But X need not be identical with B. It might be anything else that you perceive simultaneously with B. E.g. X might be a mirror standing beside B, and ζ might be a reflection of A in it. There might also be a mirror Y standing beside A and η might be a reflection of B in it. If, whenever I looked at A, I saw also a reflection of B in X, and, whenever I looked at B, I saw also a reflection of A in Y, I should judge that A and B coexist. But there need be no action of A on B or of B on A. Kant's requirements would be fulfilled only in some such very exceptional case as when A and B are both themselves mirrors, and A reflects B and B reflects A.

(3) I do not understand what Kant can mean by A determining for B its position in time and also conversely B for A. In the whole of this argument A and B are supposed to be ordinary composite substances or parts of the same composite substance, e.g. the Great Gate and the Wren Library at Trinity. The position in time of such a substance could only mean the stretch of time occupied by its history from its beginning to its end. It is surely quite obvious that in general neither of two coexisting composite substances determines the position of the other in time.

Kant's remark would have been more intelligible if he had said that one's *perception* of A determines for one's *perception* of B its position in time, and conversely. Suppose that A and B coexist, that I first look at A, then look away from it to B, and then look away from B and back to A. Call the perceptions a_1, β_1, a_2. Then it is roughly true to say that the date at which β_1 begins is determined jointly by the date at which a_1 ends and the time taken to make the appropriate movement of my head or my eyes. And it is roughly true to say that the date at which a_2 begins is detemined jointly by the date at which β_1 ends and the time taken to make the reverse movement of my head or my eyes. But now suppose instead that B objectively begins after an interval following on the cessation of A. Then the first moment at which I can possibly perceive B is the moment at which it begins to exist. And the last moment at which I can possibly perceive A is the moment at which it ceases to exist. Thus the date of my first possible perception of B is in no sense determined by the date of my last possible perception of A or vice versa. I cannot help thinking that Kant must have had something of this kind in mind.

(4) We must remember that he is trying to give an analysis of the statement 'The substances A and B coexist although I can perceive them only successively' in terms of a phenomenalist analysis of the notion of a perceptible substance. And we must remember that this phenomenalist analysis is extremely individualistic. May he not be saying that the right

analysis is somewhat on the following lines: 'The date at which I can begin to have a perception of B after ceasing to have a perception of A is determined by the date at which I cease to have a perception of A and the duration of a certain series of kinaesthetic sensations which I thereupon initiate'? May he not be going even a step further than this and asserting the following proposition: 'In such cases the occurrence of an experience which I count as a perception of A, followed by a certain series of kinaesthetic sensations which I thereupon initiate, is a *sufficient* causal condition for the occurrence of an experience which I count as a perception of B. And conversely with B substituted for A and A for B.' No doubt this proposition sounds highly paradoxical. But we must not be afraid of ascribing paradoxical opinions to Kant. And it is not incredible that he may have held this paradoxical opinion, if we remember the analogy, pointed out by Joseph,[1] between Kant and Berkeley. For Kant one's own imagination, under the unconscious guidance of one's own under-standing, has to produce, out of sense-impressions generated by foreign things-in-themselves, the appearance of a world of coexisting independent material things. For Berkeley God produces this appearance in each of us by deliberately generating telepathically in us sense-impressions in appro-priate regular sequences.

4.2.3.2 The proof in B

The new proof which Kant added in B is contained in what became the opening paragraph of the third analogy (pp. 233–4, B 257–8). Its premisses are the same as before, viz. (1) that we judge A and B to be coexistent only if we believe that the actual order in which we perceived them could have been reversed on that occasion, and (2) that we cannot perceive moments of time and thus date perceived objects directly. The novelty, if it be a novelty, is in the transition from these premisses to the conclusion. It occurs on the top of p. 234. 'Consequently, in the case of things which coexist externally to each other, a pure concept of the reciprocal sequence of their determinations is required, if we are to be able to say that the reciprocal sequence of the perceptions is grounded in the object, and so to represent the coexistence as objective.' By 'pure concept' here Kant no doubt means a category, viz. the category of reciprocity. If this step is different from that which we have already discussed in the proof in A, I must confess that I do not understand what it is supposed to be. Norman Kemp Smith suggests that Kant is trying to develop an argument analog-ous to those which he used in what I have called the third proof of the second Analogy and the first proof of the first Analogy. This would make it an argument from some feature which is *logically necessary* in pure space

[1] [H. W. B. Joseph, *Essays in Ancient and Modern Philosophy* (Oxford, 1935).]

or pure time, which we cannot perceive, to some kind of *causal necessity* in the contents of space and time which we can perceive. The latter feature would be for us a representative of the former. I must confess that I cannot see any sign in the actual text that he has such an argument in mind. So I can only leave the matter unexplained.

4.2.4 Concluding remarks on the Analogies

However obscure and inconclusive the arguments in the *Analogies of Experience* may be, there is no doubt that Kant was attacking for the first time an extremely important problem, and that he has pointed out some facts which are essential to any solution of it. The problem is the meaning and the implications of the proposition, which we all in some sense take for granted, that all perceptible things and events have their places and dates in a single spatio-temporal system. An important part of this problem is the fact that we distinguish between the temporal order in which our perceptions or our memories happen to occur and the objective temporal positions and relations of the things or events which we perceive or remember. Kant is right in holding that the criteria by which we distinguish subjective and objective temporal order, and the methods by which we date events in an objective time-system, involve an essential reference to space and to the concepts of cause and substance. He may even be right in holding that they are closely bound up with certain tacit assumptions about the persistence of substances and the causal determination of their alterations of state. Lastly, he gave at least one important criterion, which we do in fact use, for judging whether a sequence in our perceptions represents an objective sequence of events or merely the successive perception of objectively coexisting things or parts of the same thing. And he saw that the use of this criterion implies certain general assumptions involving the notions of cause and substance

Now this problem exists, and these contributions to it are important, on *any* view of the nature of sense-perception and of its objects. But suppose that you accept a *phenomenalistic* analysis of all statements about sense-perception and about perceptible objects. And suppose, in addition, you hold it to be meaningless to suggest that there could be a sensibile which was not an actual sense-datum for a particular individual on a particular occasion. Kant seems to be presupposing both these doctrines in the *Analogies*, and certainly many philosophers since his time have explicitly asserted them. In that case all the problems with which Kant has been dealing become still more pressing and still more difficult. A meaning has to be attached, compatible with this kind of analysis, to the notion of a thing existing when it is not being perceived, to the notion of an unperceived event in either a perceived or an unperceived thing, and to the statement that a perceived event in a perceived thing is caused by an unperceived event in it or in some unperceived thing.

Now the three principles which Kant claimed to prove *are* taken for granted by natural science, or at any rate *were* taken for granted by all scientists in their professional capacity until quite lately. What Kant claimed to show was that even the most ordinary everyday perceptual experiences would be impossible unless these general principles hold for all objects of possible sense-perception. Now it seems to me that, even if we accepted his proofs, the utmost that he would have shown is that each of us must *believe* or *proceed as if he believed* that these principles hold for all objects of possible sense-perception. But I am sure that he has not proved even this, and I not think that it is true. Everyday experience would be quite possible, provided that there was a reasonable amount of persistence, of regular sequence, and of systematic coherence. It does not require that every perceptible substance should be either *absolutely* permanent itself or composed of *absolutely* permanent constituents. It does not require that *every* perceptible event shall be *completely* determined by earlier events which were in principle perceptible. And it does not require that *every* perceptible substance shall act upon and be acted upon by *every* other perceptible substance that coexists with it in space. Nor does everyday experience require that each of us should *believe* or *proceed as if he believed* these very sweeping principles. But I think that this much must be admitted. Even in everyday experience there would be much less permanence and regularity of sequence if we just took our sense-impressions as they came, and did not constantly act on the assumption that there is far more permanence and far more regularity in nature than there appears *prima facie* to be. And probably natural science would have made very little progress in discovering the laws of nature and their interconnexions in a single system of law, unless it had proceeded on something like the very sweeping assumptions which Kant claims to have proved.

4.3 The Postulates of Empirical Thought

Kant gives the name 'postulates of empirical thought' to the three *a priori* principles which he thinks correspond to the three categories of modality. They may be described as the postulates of *possibility*, of *actuality*, and of *necessity*. At the end of his treatment of the postulate of actuality in B he inserts a short but very famous and important passage, which he calls *Refutation of Idealism*.

The general question with which the postulates are concerned is this. We take some concept *C*, which is internally consistent and therefore is the concept of something which is at least *logically* possible. We then ask: (1) Is it the concept of something which is in other respects possible? E.g. the concept of telepathy involves no contradiction. But is it the concept of a mode of human cognition which is in other respects possible? (2) Suppose that we can answer the first question in the affirmative. We can then ask: Is it the concept of something which is *actual*? E.g. the concept of an aeroplane was the concept of something causally, and not merely logically, possible in the days before any aeroplane had been constructed. But it was not the concept of anything actual until the first aeroplane was made. (3) Suppose that we can answer the second question in the affirmative. We can then ask: Is it the concept of something which is *necessary*? E.g. if the law of universal causation is admitted, then the concept of any event that has actually taken place is the concept of something whose occurrence was causally necessitated. Suppose, on the other hand, that indeterminism holds for certain human volitions. Then the concept of a certain volition which actually took place might be the concept of something which was *causally contingent*. The three postulates are supposed to give the principles on which such questions can be answered. The criterion is in every case *epistemological*; it refers always to the conditions under which a term can be an object of human experience. So it will be useful to talk of 'experiential' possibility, actuality, and necessity.

4.3.1 The postulate of possibility

When Kant is being careful he talks of a concept *itself* as possible or impossible only when he means that it *does not* or that it *does* involve some internal logical contradiction. In that sense all the concepts with which we are to be concerned are 'possible' concepts. The question with which the postulate of possibility is concerned is whether a concept which is itself possible, in the sense of internally consistent, is the concept of something experientially possible. When Kant is being careful he describes a concept of which this can be affirmed as having 'objective reality'. But he does not consistently keep to this terminology.

The postulate of possibility states that a concept is the concept of something experientially possible if it is the concept of something which is compatible with the *formal* conditions of experience, i.e. with the properties of space and time, on the one hand, and with the categories and pure principles of the understanding, on the other. This amounts to saying that it is the concept of something which would not conflict with the laws of arithmetic and Euclidean geometry, or with the principles established in the three Analogies. What Kant calls 'empirical concepts', i.e. those derived by abstraction from perceived instances of them, are obviously concepts of experientially possible objects. Again, the categories, or at any rate the pure schemata of the categories, answer to the test. For, although they are not derived by abstraction from perceived instances of them, they are involved in the very notion of a perceptible object as such. Ideal geometrical concepts, e.g. the concept of a perfect circle or an exact straight line, are in a somewhat different position. Certainly we can be sure that they conform to the formal conditions of *intuition*; for, according to Kant, we can *construct* instances of them by pure imaginative synthesis in the pure *a priori* spatial manifold. But the question might still be raised whether they conform to the formal conditions of the understanding. Can we be certain that there could be a *physical object* which had an exactly circular contour or exactly straight edges? Kant holds that we can. His ground is that the same processes and the same principles of synthesis are involved in synthesising sense-impressions into perceptible extended objects as are involved in synthesising the elements of the pure spatial manifold into geometrical figures. I think we should have to admit that the sense-impressions provided by foreign things-in-themselves might be such that we *could* not synthesise them into an object of a certain determinate simple geometrical form. But I think that, even if Kant would admit this, he would say that it is irrelevant for the present purpose. Lastly we come to *factitious* concepts, i.e. concepts which we make up by arbitrarily connecting in imagination items which have been presented separately but never in this particular combination in our perceptual experience. An example would be the concept of a mermaid. Kant says that the only way to show that a factitious concept is the concept of a possible object is to wait and see whether experience presents us with an actual instance. The postulate of possibility is not concerned with such cases. The examples which Kant chooses are more remote from actual experience than my example of the concept of a mermaid. They are the concept of telepathy, of non-inferential precognition, and of a substance which has a position in space but does not occupy a volume by exercising a repulsive force. I suspect that he would doubt, or positively deny, that anything answering to these concepts would be compatible with the principles of pure understanding. If so, it is doubtful whether these concepts have objective reality or it is certain that they have not. I think that Kant would have had to deny that certain concepts which occur in modern atomic physics have objective validity. For the notion of the jumping of an electron at a certain moment from one orbit to another as a causally undetermined event conflicts with the second Analogy.

4.3.2 The postulate of actuality

The postulate of actuality states that a concept is the concept of something experientially actual if either (1) an instance of it is or has been actually perceived by someone, or (2) the existence of an instance of it has to be postulated in order to account causally for something which someone actually is perceiving or has perceived. In this connexion Kant says that, when he talks of an object of possible sense-perception, he does not exclude objects which no human being could perceive because his senses are not acute enough. It is evident from his example about magnetic attraction that he thinks that this covers the hypothetical entities of physics, such as atoms, electrons, light-waves, etc.

It seems to me that the position is not nearly so simple as Kant makes out. I think that we ought to distinguish at least three cases. (1) Objects which we could perceive with our present senses if only we could be in a suitable position to observe them, e.g. the other side of the moon. (2) Objects which are of the same kind as objects which we can perceive but are too small to be perceived by our senses, e.g. filter-passing viruses. (3) Scientific objects, such as atoms, electrons, light-waves, etc. Kant evidently identifies the third class with the second. This is certainly a mistake. No conceivable increase in the acuteness of our present senses, and no additional senses which we can conceive, would enable us to perceive these scientific objects. The analysis of propositions about them presents a special problem to phenomenalists which they have never, so far as I know, satisfactorily solved.

4.3.3 The postulate of necessity

The formulation of this in Kant's own words is as follows. 'That which, in its connexion with the actual, is determined in accordance with universal conditions of experience, exists as *necessary*' (p. 239, A218/B266). The meaning of this is made plain in Kant's explanations on pp. 247–9. A concept is the concept of something whose existence is experientially necessary, if it is the concept of something which would be causally necessitated, in accordance with a known law of nature, by the existence of something else which is experientially actual. Kant makes several remarks about this.

(1) It applies only to concepts of events and not to concepts of substances. For, according to him, it is only alteration in substances, and not the coming to be and the ceasing to be of substances, which is causally determined. No substance can be either generated or annihilated in the course of nature. To this I must make the usual comment. Ordinary perceptible composite substances, e.g. eggs and chickens, certainly do come into and go out of existence in the course of nature, and we assume that this is causally determined. It is only their hypothetical ultimate constituents to which the first Analogy could possibly apply. And Kant ought to have found more difficulty than he appears to have done in giving a phenomenalistic account of these supposed ultimate constituent substances.

(2) Kant mentions four principles, which he asserts to be *a priori* and capable of transcendental proof, which would make it *impossible* for any concept which conflicts with them to be objectively valid. These are (a) that every alteration in a substance is *completely determined* by some previous alteration. (b) That this determination always takes place in accordance with some *general rule*. (c) That all change is *continuous* in time. And (d) that there are no *empty spatial gaps* between any two coexisting substances in nature. In connexion with the fourth of these he makes the following remark. He does not claim here to be able to prove *a priori* that there may not be empty space *beyond* the confines of the material world. (This is a question which he discusses later on in the first antinomy.) What he claims to prove *a priori* is that there can be no empty space *within* the material world. Any concept or theory which conflicts with this, e.g. what Leibniz called the theory of 'atom and the void', can be rejected at once as involving something which would be experientially impossible.

(3) At the bottom of p. 250 Kant makes a very startling statement, which, if interpreted literally, seems to confirm my view that he is not only attempting a phenomenalistic analysis of propositions about perceived objects, but is doing this on an extremely *individualistic* basis. 'That yet another series of phenomena, in thoroughgoing connexion with that which is given in perception, is possible, and consequently that *more than one* all-embracing experience is possible, cannot be inferred from what is given . . .' (p. 250, A 231–2/B 284). All that I can say is that everyone does assume this to be not only possible but actual. For no one believes himself to be the only self-conscious individual, and everyone believes that the experiences of others cohere with, and to some extent fill up the gaps between, his own.

4.3.4 Refutation of Idealism

Kant added in B, at the end of his discussion of the postulate of actuality, a new section entitled *Refutation of Idealism* (pp. 244–7, B 274–9). Although there is no section with that title in A, Kant did deal with the same topic in a section much further on in the book, entitled the *Fourth Paralogism: Ideality* (pp. 344–52, A 366–80). He omitted this altogether in B. I shall refer to the *Fourth Paralogism* as Refutation A and to the *Refutation of Idealism* as Refutation B. The best account that I have found of these two refutations of idealism is in A. H. Smith's book.[1]

4.3.4.1 Refutation A

The Refutation of Idealism in the *Fourth Paralogism* is perfectly straight-

[1] [A. H. Smith, *Kantian Studies* (Oxford, 1947).]

forward and easy to follow. To begin with we may feel surprised to find
Kant claiming to refute idealism. Is he not commonly regarded as an
idealist philosopher? He provides the answer to this in Refutation A by
distinguishing certain different forms of 'idealism' and 'realism', and
stating which he accepts and which he claims to refute. The distinctions
which he draws are as follows.

He defines an 'idealist' as a person who denies that anyone is ever
directly acquainted with an object which occupies a position in space and
exists independently of being perceived by him. Now idealists may be
subdivided in the first place into two classes, viz. (1) *sceptical* and (2)
non-sceptical. Suppose that a person in normal waking life is having an
experience which he would naturally express by saying 'I am perceiving
such-and-such an external object'. Then the *sceptical* idealist would admit
that there *may* be an existentially independent object occupying a position
in space and corresponding in some special way to this experience. He
would deny only that the experience consists in being directly acquainted
with such an object, if such there be. And he would conclude that belief in
its existence, and beliefs about its qualities and relations, can be only more
or less probable inferences from the occurrence and the characteristics of
the perceptual experience.

The *non-sceptical* idealist would deny that there is or can be an existentially independent object, occupying a position in space and corresponding to the perceptual experience. Now non-sceptical idealists can
be subdivided into two classes in accordance with the primary reason
which they have for their negative attitude. (a) One's primary reason for
holding that there cannot be an existentially independent object occupying
a position in space and corresponding to a perceptual experience might be
that one had accepted Kant's view of space. One might have been per-
suaded, e.g., that one's *a priori* knowledge of geometry would be impossible unless space itself were an innate form of intuition in which one
locates one's various sense-impressions. Kant calls a non-sceptical idealist
of this kind a *transcendental* idealist. He himself is, of course, a transcendental idealist. (b) On the other hand, one's primary reason for being a
non-sceptical idealist might be that one thought that there were contradictions in the notion of space or of extended objects existing independently of being perceived. Kant calls a non-sceptical idealist of this
kind a *dogmatic* idealist. A good example would be Leibniz. Of course it is
quite possible that a person might be driven into transcendental idealism
by way of dogmatic idealism. For he would have to account for the
appearance of a world of independent extended located objects somehow.

The position can now be stated clearly in these terms. Kant was a
transcendental idealist. He is not at present concerned with *dogmatic* ideal-

ism. That question comes up later, in the first and second antinomies. What he is concerned with here and now is to refute *sceptical* idealism. This doctrine he ascribes to Descartes. Kant never examines the doctrine which might be described as *non-idealism*. This would hold that a normal waking perceptual experience consists in being directly acquainted with an existentially independent object occupying a certain position in an existentially independent space. He would have claimed to have refuted this in establishing the subjectivity of space in the *Aesthetic*. And, quite apart from that, he would no doubt have held that it would be too absurd for any instructed philosopher to take seriously after the work of Descartes and Locke and Berkely and Hume.

Before considering Kant's refutation of the sceptical idealism of Descartes we must notice a further distinction which he is careful to draw. He points out that such phrases as '*outside* the percipient', '*external* object', etc. are ambiguous. In the empirical sense an 'external object' means simply an object located in space and spatially related to other such objects. In this sense the percipient's own body would be an external object. In the metaphysical sense it means a foreign thing-in-itself, i.e. a thing-in-itself other than the one which is the percipient as he really is. Now Kant is concerned here entirely with *empirical* objects and *empirical* externality, and not at all with *things-in-themselves* and *metaphysical* externality. 'It is not of this [latter] that we are here speaking, but of the empirical object, which is an *external* object if it is represented in *space*, and an *inner* object if it is represented only in its *time-relations*' (p. 348, A 373).

We can now deal with the refutation of sceptical idealism. The position to be refuted may be stated as follows. Each of us is directly acquainted with himself and his various experiences, but with nothing else. Among the experiences with which one is acquainted are perceptual experiences, i.e. such as their owner would naturally express by saying, e.g., 'I see a white round plate on top of a shiny square black table'. Now it is possible that there may be a thing now existing in space independently of the percipient and his perceptual experience which answers more or less to the description which he would give on the basis of that experience. But, since the perception does not consist in being acquainted with any such independent object, if such there be, there can be only one possible ground for believing in its existence and ascribing such-and-such characteristics to it. These beliefs can be justified only as *inferences* from the occurrence and the inspectable qualities of the perception and its inspectable relations to other experiences owned by the same person. Such inferences can only be from the perceptual experience and its inspectable features, as *effect*, to the independent object as its hypothetical remote *part-cause*. And any such inference is highly uncertain. The cause might be some non-introspectible process in the percipient himself. And, even if it were something external to him in the metaphysical sense, it need not resemble its effect in having spatial qualities and relations.

Kant's refutation may be stated as follows. (1) It has been shown by various arguments in the *Aesthetic* that space and time are not entities which exist independently of the percipient. They are private innate mind-dependent intuita, which exist only in so far as they are actually intuited by a particular individual. Nothing could possibly be located in space or dated in time independently of a particular percipient; for there is no space and no time, independent of each particular percipient, for anything to be located or dated in. (2) It must be admitted that the only entities with which anyone could possibly be acquainted are either (a) his own experiences, or (b) the immediate objects of certain of his experiences, e.g. visual sense-data, images, etc. And it must be admitted that it is meaningless to suggest that any of the latter entities could possibly exist except as the object of one particular experience in the mental history of one particular person. (3) Every one of a person's experiences has a date and a duration in his private mind-dependent *time-system*. And the immediate object of any of his experiences which has an immediate object has the same date and duration in his private time-system as the experience whose immediate object it is. From the nature of the case nothing but his own experiences and their immediate objects can have dates and durations in his private time-system. And there is no *public* or *neutral* time-system in which they, or anything else, could have dates and durations. (4) None of a person's experiences have any extension or location in his private *space-system*. But the immediate objects of some of his experiences, in particular those of his normal waking visual perceptions, have extension, shape, and location in his private space-system. From the nature of the case nothing but the immediate objects of his experiences can have extensions and locations in his private space-system. And there is no *public* or *neutral* space-system in which they, or anything else, could have extensions or locations. (5) Now the only empirical external objects which there are or could be are those immediate objects of a person's experiences which have extension and location in his private space-system. He is just as immediately aware of these and of their extension and location in space as he is of his own experiences and of their duration and location in time. There is no question of being immediately aware of the latter only, and then precariously inferring the former from them by a process of inference from effect to cause. So knowledge of one's own experiences and knowledge of *empirically* external objects are logically and epistemologically precisely on a level. (6) Suppose, finally, that you raise the *metaphysical* question of things-in-themselves. Then, again, the two kinds of knowledge are exactly on a level. Introspective knowledge of oneself and one's own experiences is knowledge only of *phenomena*, since its objects are presented under the subjectively imposed form of *time*. And perceptual knowledge of empirically external things and events is also knowledge only of *phenomena*, since its objects are presented under the subjectively imposed form of *space*. We know that there must be a thing-in-itself underlying the introspectible mental phenomena, and we know that there must be a thing-in-itself underlying the perceptible physical phenomena. But we have no reason to hold that the former is mental and not material and that the latter is material and not mental. We do not even know whether two different things-in-themselves are involved or only a single one for both sets of phenomena.

There is one thing to be added to this refutation. Kant is concerned to show that it is just as possible for him as for anyone else to distinguish between normal waking sense-perception, on the one hand, and mere imagination or dreaming or waking delusions, on the other. As regards imagination the essential points are these. (1) It is not an independent function. It presupposes actual sense-perception and could not start to work unless and until a person had had a good deal of actual sense-perception. The same remark applies to dreaming. (2) Although visual images are extended and have shapes, they are not located in the one private space in which visual and tactual sense-data are located. As regards the tests for waking or dreaming and for veridical or delusive waking sense-perception, there is only one method which anyone can use, whatever his philosophical opinions may be. You must start with a basis of what you take to be veridical waking sense-perception and then see whether the experience to be tested does or does not cohere with this in accordance with accepted empirical laws.

I will now comment on this refutation of sceptical idealism. (1) It of course presupposes Kant's conclusions as to the nature of space and time in the *Aesthetic*. Now, whatever we may think about the arguments regarding space, the arguments regarding time are most unconvincing. But it is only if we accept his view of time that there is any reason to hold that in introspection we are acquainted only with *appearances* of ourselves and our states. Apart from this there is no reason to doubt that introspection makes us aware of ourselves and their states precisely as they would be if we did not introspect them. That was no doubt Descartes' view. If we accepted Kant's doctrine of space and rejected his doctrine of time, the objects of sense-perception would be phenomena and not things-in-themselves whilst the objects of introspection would be things-in-themselves and their states. (2) Even if we accept Kant's doctrine of time, there is not complete parallelism between a person's experiences and the objects which are located in his private space-system. The latter, according to Kant, are the immediate objects of certain of his experiences, e.g. of his visual perceptions. And according to him it is impossible that any such

entity should exist except as the immediate object of a certain one experience of a certain individual. But would Kant be prepared to say the same of
the visual perceptions themselves, or of any other experiences? Would he
be prepared to say that it is impossible that an *experience itself* should exist
except as the immediate object of a certain one other experience, viz. an
introspection, in the same individual? Such a doctrine would obviously be
absurd; for *that* introspection could then exist only as the object of an
introspection of a higher order, and so on without end. Thus it would
seem that it must be admitted, on any view, that *experiences of perceiving*
and other experiences exist in their own right; whilst on Kant's view the
objects which are located in a person's private space-system can exist *only*
as the objects of certain of his experiences. (3) Much the most important
objection to the refutation is this. It assumes an extremely crude analysis of
the notion of external object and of perceiving an external object. This is
not only obviously incompatible with the way in which these notions are
in fact used, but is also inconsistent with the analysis which Kant gives or
presupposes in the most important parts of the *Critique of Pure Reason*.
What Kant does in this refutation is to *identify* a physical object with the
particular sense-datum by which that object manifests itself to one or more
of the senses of a particular person on a particular occasion. Now we can
say at once that physical object words, such as 'chair', 'stone', 'explosion',
and so on, are not used in that way and are constantly used in ways which
are quite incompatible with any such analysis. No analysis is worth
considering unless it is compatible with the significance of such statements
as 'This object existed while I was not perceiving it', 'This object, which I
am now perceiving, has parts and properties which I am not now perceiving', 'This object is really flat but it looks solid to me here and now', and so
on. Now elsewhere Kant is fully alive to this; and it is one of his great
merits to have seen that it raises very difficult problems and to have tackled
them. They are precisely those problems with which he has been concerned in the *Transcendental Deduction* and in the *Analogies of Experience*.
There he gives or presupposes a species of phenomenalistic analysis, in
terms of groups of actual and possible sense-data interconnected in accordance with rules of sequence and coexistence. Now it is important to
notice that even with a phenomenalistic analysis of the notions of physical
object and sense-perception, something like Descartes' problem recurs,
though in a greatly modified form. A person who claims to be perceiving
on a certain occasion a physical object answering to a certain description is
claiming much more than merely to be presented with a sense-datum of a
certain kind. He is claiming that he *would* be presented with certain other
sense-data if he were now to do certain things; that he *would have been*
presented now with certain different sense-data if he *had* done certain
things immediately beforehand; and so on. Unless these beliefs are true he

is not in fact perceiving the physical object which he claims to be perceiving. If they are wildly false he is not in fact perceiving a physical object at all. But he may obviously know that he is being presented with such-and-such a sense-datum and that he is having such-and-such beliefs in connexion with it, and yet these beliefs may be partly or completely false. It is therefore true, even on the phenomenalist analysis, that one can be quite certain that one is having an experience which one would describe as 'ostensibly perceiving an object of such-and-such a kind' whilst one is never justified in being quite sure that there is an object answering to that description. So something faintly analogous to Descartes' 'sceptical idealism' remains, even if we accept a phenomenalistic analysis of the notions of physical object and sense-perception.

4.3.4.2 Refutation B

It is not surprising that Kant was dissatisfied with Refutation A and that he omitted it in B and wrote a new refutation. Unfortunately Refutation B is very obscure. And it certainly looks as if Kant here went to the other extreme and professed to prove things which are inconsistent with the phenomenalistic analysis which he elsewhere asserts or presupposes. Even when he had rewritten the refutation he could not let it alone. For in the preface to B he adds a long footnote about it, and proposes a change of wording in the third sentence of the new refutation (pp. 34–6, B xl–xli).

In the introduction to Refutation B (p. 244, B274–5) Kant definitely ascribes *dogmatic* idealism to Berkeley. He says that Berkeley maintains that 'space . . . is something which is in itself impossible'. And he ascribes to him the doctrine that 'things in space are merely imaginary entities'. It seems to me that this is a rather questionable account of Berkeley's position. However that may be, Kant then passes to the sceptical idealism of Descartes. In order to refute that, he says, we need to show that 'we have *experience* and not merely imagination of outer things'. And the only line of argument which is of any use is to show that, unless one had experience and not merely imagination of outer things, one could not have what Descartes and everyone else admits that one has, viz. awareness of oneself and one's own experiences. So this is what Kant is going to try to prove. Before considering the argument in detail it is important to notice the following facts.

(1) Kant constantly talks here of the difference between the *perception* of outer things and the mere *imagination* of them. It seems to me plain that what he has in mind is the following. From the purely introspective standpoint normal waking sense-perceptions, waking hallucinations, and dreams are indistinguishable. In each case the experient is presented with certain data manifesting certain sensible characteristics. In each case he

would naturally express his experience by saying 'I see (or feel or hear) such-and-such a thing'. And in each case he would take for granted that he is now acquainted with a thing answering to this description, and that it exists in space independently of the experience which he is now having. Let us say that in all such cases a person is having an 'ostensible sense-perception'. Now ordinary common sense would hold that, if the person in question is awake and in a normal state, he is *in fact* acquainted with a thing which answers exactly or approximately to the description which he would give and which exists in space independently of his present ostensible sense-perception. We may describe this by saying that in such cases the *ostensible* sense-perception is *veridical*, and that it *really is* a perception. As we say, 'He really *is* seeing a table, not just dreaming that he sees one'. But ordinary common sense also holds that, in the case of dreams and of certain waking ostensible sense-perceptions, the claim which the experient would make at the time is mistaken in *principle* and not merely more or less incorrect in detail. It holds that in such cases the experient is not acquainted with any object existing in space independently of his ostensible perception and answering even remotely to the description which he would give. We may describe this by saying that in such cases the ostensible sense-perception is in principle *delusive*, and that it is *not really* a perception. As we say 'He is not *really* seeing a table or anything else, he is only dreaming that he sees one'. When Kant says that Berkeley holds that things in space are merely imaginary entities the view which he ascribes to him may be stated as follows. *All* our ostensible sense-perceptions have the character which common sense ascribes to dreams and waking hallucinations, and *none* of them have the character which common sense ascribes to normal waking ostensible sense-perceptions. In fact all are in principle *delusive* and therefore none of them are *really* perceptions. Kant ascribes to Descartes the same view with 'may possibly be' substituted for 'are'. What Kant claims to prove is that *some* at least of our ostensible sense-perceptions must be veridical and therefore really be perceptions. In some at least of them the experient *is* acquainted with an object which exists in space independently of his present ostensible sense-perception and which answers at least approximately to the description which he would give of it.

(2) Kant does not profess to be giving a test by which one can decide with regard to any particular ostensible sense-perception whether it is veridical or delusive. He would use the same tests which common sense and natural science would use. But he holds the following two propositions. (a) All these tests presuppose that *some* of these experiences are veridical. (b) The occurrence of delusive ostensible sense-perceptions, i.e. dreams, hallucinations, etc., is causally dependent on the occurrence of veridical perceptual experiences.

(3) Kant thinks that the bare proposition 'I exist' is known to each of us independently of his having veridical sense-perceptions. But he claims that all *concrete* knowledge of facts about oneself, e.g. knowing that one had such-and-such an experience at such-and-such a time, would be impossible unless one had veridical sense-perceptions.

The question then comes to this. Why did Kant hold that a person could have no concrete introspective knowledge of himself and his own experiences unless some of those experiences were states of acquaintance with things existing in space independently of being perceived by him, and answering more or less accurately to the descriptions which he would give of them? The following things can be said with certainty here.

(1) All concrete introspective knowledge of oneself and one's own experiences is knowledge of oneself as having such-and-such experiences at *various times*. Now Kant asserts that a person cannot be aware of anything as beginning at a certain date, going on for so long, and then stopping and being followed either immediately or after a lapse or with partial overlapping by something else, except on the following conditon. He must be acquainted with something *permanent*.

(2) Kant asserts that this permanent something, with which a person must be acquainted, cannot be anything that he can intuit in *himself*. The reason which he gives in the new passage which he substituted in the preface to B runs as follows. (I am expanding it slightly in order to remove merely verbal obscurities.) 'All grounds of determination of my existence which are to be met with in me are *representations*. As such, they themselves require something permanent, distinct from them, in relation to which their change may be determined. And so something permanent, distinct from my representations, is required, in relation to which my existence in the time in which these representations change may be determined.'

Immediately after this in the footnote on p. 34 Kant remarks that it will probably be objected that, after all, I cannot be directly acquainted with anything except my own states. Therefore at most I can be acquainted with my representations of external things, and not with external things. Before considering his answer to this objection we will consider the light which it throws on the passage just quoted. I suggest that what Kant had in mind is this. He took for granted that no one would suppose that the permanent something which a person must be acquainted with could be any of his own *experiences*. For these are so obviously just transitory states of himself. But, if this permanent something is to be a state of himself, and cannot be any of his experiences, the only other suggestion is that it might be the *sense-data* which present themselves to him when he ostensibly perceives an external object. To this I understand Kant to answer that these, which he describes as 'representations of external things', are just as obviously transitory states of oneself as one's own experiences. Therefore the permanent somethings, with which one must be acquainted, cannot be one's sense-data, but must be the independent material things which one's sense-data present in a fragmentary and intermittent way to one.

(3) We can now return to the objection which Kant thinks will be made, and consider the answer which he makes to it in this footnote. The objection is that, after all, the only existents that anyone *can* be acquainted with are his own experiences and his own sense-data. The answer is most obscure. It runs as follows. 'Through inner *experience* I am conscious of *my existence* in time and consequently of its determinability in time. This is more than to be conscious of my representation. It is identical with the *empirical consciousness of my existence* . . . This consciousness of my existence in time is identically bound up with the consciousness of a relation to something outside me . . . The inner intuition, in which my existence can alone be determined, is sensible and is bound up with the condition of time. This determination, and therefore the inner experience itself, depends upon something permanent, which is not in me, to which I must regard myself as standing in relation . . . This something permanent must therefore be an external thing, distinct from all my representations, and its existence must be included in the *determination* of my existence, constituting with it but a single experience . . .'[1] To this Kant adds one further remark, which may be important. 'The representation of something *permanent* . . . is not the same as *permanent representation*. For, though the representation . . . may be very transitory and variable . . . it yet refers to something permanent.'[2]

(4) I suggest that what Kant may mean is this. In ordinary self-consciousness I think of my empirical self as something which persists through time and has now this and now that experience and is presented now with this and now with that sense-datum. It is meaningless to suggest that *this* kind of cognitive experience might be merely a dream or a hallucination, as has been suggested with regard to all our ostensible sense-perceptions. But I am not directly acquainted with my empirical self as such. When I introspect I am directly acquainted only with this or that experience or sense-datum. I can *think of* myself as something which persists through time, only because I am *acquainted with* certain things, other than myself and my experiences and my sense-data, which persist through time, and because I think of myself as standing in certain relations to these things. To be acquainted with these permanent things other than myself and my experiences, and to think of myself as standing in certain relations to these, is an essential part of the experience known as empirical self-consciousness.

Supposing that this or something like it is what Kant meant, I would make the following comments.

[1] [Pp. 34–6, B xl–xli.]   [2] [P. 36, B xli.]

(1) It is certainly *logically* possible, even if it be not causally possible, that all one's ostensible perceptions should be non-veridical, i.e. that they should all be of the nature of dreams and waking hallucinations. If Kant is right, it would follow that a being whose ostensible perceptions were all of this nature could not possibly be aware of himself as persisting through time and having now this and now that experience and being presented now with this and now with that sense-datum. Now it seems to me that this is not in the least obvious, provided that his dreams and hallucinations were reasonably coherent and consistent with each other, that he could remember them, and so on.

(2) At the most would Kant have shown more than that a person would need to *believe* or take for *granted* that some of his ostensible perceptions are states of acquaintance with persistent independent external objects? We all do take this for granted at the time, even in the case of ostensible perceptions which other persons or we ourselves at other times believe to be non-veridical. Is anything more needed?

(3) I do not doubt that consciousness of oneself as a persistent subject is very closely bound up with having ostensible perceptions which one can and does take to be states of acquaintance with persistent independent objects existing in space. But Kant ought to have considered in detail the connexions and the possible disconnexions between the two kinds of cognitive experience. It seems to me not to be a matter that can be settled by *a priori* reasoning. Yet it is difficult to discuss it empirically, for want of negative instances. The possible negative instances would occur in cases of lunacy, delirium, brain injuries, etc. But patients cannot give any very coherent account of their experiences while they are suffering, and, if they recover, it is seldom possible for them to remember and to report accurately about either their consciousness of objects or their consciousness of themselves while they were ill.

(4) Supposing that Kant's arguments were sound, could his conclusions here possibly be reconciled with the rest of his doctrines? We must remember that the external objects with which we are said to be acquainted in normal waking sense-perception are *not* supposed to be things-in-themselves. They are *phenomenal* objects, and the space in which they exist is something *private* to the mind of the individual percipient and *dependent* upon it. Similarly the self, of which one is conscious as persisting through time and owning a succession of various experiences and being presented with various sense-data, is not a thing-in-itself. It too is a *phenomenal* object, and the time through which it perists and in which its various experiences come and go is something private to the individual and dependent upon him. The arguments and conclusions of Refutation A are much easier to reconcile with this part of Kant's doctrine than are those of Refutation B. It was greatly to Kant's credit to see that the conclusions

of Refutation A will not do; and that we must somehow give a meaning to the statement that a physical object exists when a particular person is not perceiving it, to the distinction between the dates and durations of our perceivings and rememberings and the dates and durations of what we perceive and remember, and so on. But I cannot believe that he ever got this and the other features of his doctrine into one focus. The conclusions of Refutation B seem too realistic to fit the rest of his system, whilst the conclusions of Refutation A are too subjectivist to fit the admitted facts.

4.4 Phenomena and noumena

The last chapter of the *Transcendental Analytic* is devoted to a discussion of the ground of the distinction of all objects into phenomena and noumena. Kant omitted several longish passages which are to be found in A when he revised the *Critique*; and he added four new paragraphs in B.

I will take what is common to both A and B together with the four new paragraphs in B. I shall omit the paragraphs in A which were omitted in B. The main points are these.

4.4.1 Empirical and transcendental uses of concepts and principles

Kant distinguishes between the *empirical* and the *transcendental* use of a concept or of a principle which involves a concept. In its empirical use it is applied only to *phenomena*, i.e. to objects of actual and possible sense-experience. In its transcendental use it is applied to objects in general without any such restriction. Kant reiterates here his doctrine that, although there are certain essential elements in human cognition which are native to the mind and are not derived by abstraction from perceived instances of them, yet they can never be significantly applied except to objects of actual or possible sense-experience. He considers in turn the concepts of pure geometry and arithmetic and the categories and the principles which involve them.

He says that the concepts and principles of pure geometry would mean nothing to us unless we could construct intuitable instances of them. This, he thinks, we can do *a priori* in pure imagination; but the result is an intuitable particular analogous to a sensible object. Somewhat similar remarks apply to the concepts and formulae of arithmetic. We cannot make anything of them until we have instantiated the concepts of the various numbers by collections of dots, etc. and the concept of arithmetical addition by imagining two such collections as mixed to form a single collection, and so on. Thus a transcendental use of these concepts and principles would deprive them of all meaning for us.

He then considers the categories and principles which involve them. He argues that it is only the schemata of the categories in time, and not the pure categories, which have any concrete meaning for us. He tries to show this in turn for several important categories. (1) The concept of *extensive magnitude* becomes concretely intelligible only when we think of a whole composed of so many units. But this notion involves the notion of *successively* synthesising homogeneous parts, e.g. unit lines end-to-end, unit squares edge-to-edge, unit cubes face-to-face, and so on. And this is unintelligible except in relation to our experience of time and sequence. (2) The concept of *reality*, as opposed to non-entity, can be given a concrete meaning only be contrasting a period of *time* during which some process is going on or some thing is persisting with a period during which no process is going on and no thing is persisting. (3) If you leave out from the notion of *substance* the thought of something which persists through time, it reduces to the purely logical notion of something which *has* predicates but is *not* predicable of anything. (4) If you leave out from the notion of *cause* the thought of a sequence in accordance with a rule, it reduces to the purely logical notion of something from whose existence one could deduce the existence of something else. (5) Lastly, suppose you leave out reference to consistency or inconsistency with the formal conditions of possible experience, i.e. the laws of geometry and arithmetic and principles like the permanence of substance and the law of causation. Then the notion of *possibility* reduces to the purely logical notion of non-self-contradiction. If you leave out reference to the fact of being actually perceived by someone or being a factor in causing some effect which is actually perceived by someone, the notion of *actuality* loses all concrete meaning. And if you leave out reference to being causally necessitated by something that has already happened, the notion of *necessity* reduces to the purely logical notion of entailment. Kant draws the following conclusions. From the nature of the case the pure categories, as distinct from their schemata, cannot be used *empirically*. But we also cannot use them *transcendentally*, for, if we try to do so, we find that they have lost all concrete meaning. So the conclusion is that we cannot use them at all. Suppose, e.g., that you profess to be thinking of a non-spatial non-temporal substance or cause, which could not possibly be an object of sense-perception. Then you will find that you have nothing positive before your mind except something describable in purely logical terms, e.g. a subject which is not a predicate, a term whose existence entails the existence of some other term, and so on.

It is not clear to me that Kant always takes the same view of the pure categories. It seems to me that he sometimes talks as if a category were essentially the notion of a fundamental principle of *synthesis*, and sometimes as if it were one of the fundamental factors in the most general notion of a possible *existent thing*. When the reference to synthesis is prominent, the distinction between a pure category and a schematised category is this. The pure category is the concept of a certain fundamental principle for synthesising a manifold of some kind or other, whilst a schematised category is the concept of a certain fundamental principle for synthesising *sense-impressions*, presented *successively* under the form of time, and, in the case of some of them, under the form of *space* also. Now we cannot in fact conceive of any but a *sense-given* manifold, or of any forms of intuition except *time* and *space*. So we cannot in pratice make anything of the concept of a principle for synthesising a manifold in general. On the other hand, when the reference to synthesis is not prominent, Kant seems to say that we can *think* of things which would be instances of the pure categories, but could not conceivably present themselves to our senses. But he holds that these are mere idle speculations, which could never by any possibility be converted into *knowledge* or even *rational conjecture*.

4.4.2 The notion of a noumenon

This bring us to the notion of *noumenon*. Kant begins by remarking that we are liable to think that the *categories* have a wider range of possible application than the *forms of intuition*, i.e. space and time. Since the categories are forms of *thought*, they seem to be less closely bound up with sensation than space and time, which are forms of *intuition*. We are thus more tempted to think that the categories may have an application beyond the range of possible sense-perception. Now here Kant says that, in point of fact, the categories have even less meaning in abstraction from the data of sense than have the pure forms of intuition. For the latter do at least present a kind of object to us, though a very queer one, about which we can have scientific knowledge, viz. the pure space of geometry and pure time. But a category is nothing but the concept of one of the fundamental ways in which the imagination synthesises *some* kind of manifold under the guidance of thought. Still we are very liable to overlook this fact; presumably because such syntheses are not deliberate operations conducted in accordance with a plan of which one is explicitly aware.

4.4.2.1. Positive and negative senses of 'noumenon'

The next point is this. We describe certain entities as 'sensible' or 'perceptible'. E.g. we call a chair or a tree a 'sensible' or a 'perceptible' object. This language suggests two things. (1) It suggests a distinction between an object as it is in itself and the same object as it manifests its existence and presence to us by affecting our senses. This suggests that perhaps the *very same object* might be intuited in an entirely different way, viz. *non-sensuously*. (2) Even if it be held that no object which could be perceived by the senses could ever be non-sensuously intuited, the phraseology suggests that there might be *other* objects which could be non-sensuously intuited but never perceived by the senses. Now the notion of 'noumenon' is closely connected with speculations of this kind.

Now Kant points out that there is a dangerous ambiguity in all this. We might define a 'noumenon' in either of the two following ways. (1) An existent particular which either (a) is not a possible object of sense-perception at all, or (b) which, though it can present itself to the senses, cannot be known *as it is in itself* by sense-perception. This may be called the *negative* sense of 'noumenon'. (2) An existent particular which either (a) can be an object only of a kind of non-sensuous intuition or (b) which, though it can present itself to the senses, can be known as it is in itself only by means of such non-sensuous intuition. This may be called the *positive* sense of 'noumenon'. The positive sense presupposes the actual existence, or at least the possibility, of a special kind of intuitive cognition of particular existents, viz. *non-sensuous*, or, as Kant calls it, 'intellectual' intuition. Human beings certainly do not possess this, and Kant says that we can form no concrete notion of the possibility of it. Therefore the word 'noumenon', in the positive sense, expresses no intelligible concept.

But, when used in the negative sense, it expresses something intelligible and, in Kant's opinion, highly useful. He describes it as 'a merely *limiting concept*, the function of which is to curb the pretensions of sensibility' (p. 272, A255/B311). On p. 270 he makes a still stronger statement: 'Doubtless, indeed, there are intelligible entities corresponding to the sensible entities; there may also be intelligible entities to which our sensible faculty of intuition has no relation whatsoever' (B309).

4.4.2.2 Noumenon and thing-in-itself

This brings us to the question of the connexion between the notion of 'noumenon' and the notion of 'thing-in-itself'. When Kant says that there are doubtless intelligible entities corresponding to the sensible entities, he is certainly thinking of foreign things-in-themselves. He always assumes that the sense-impressions which we synthesise into percepts of empirical things and events outside us in space are ultimately derived from things which exist independently of us and our senses and forms of intuition and categories. He also always assumes that there must be a real non-temporal self corresponding to the empirical persistent self which each of us is aware of by introspection. This plays an important part in his ethical works, under the name of the 'noumenal self'. Now a thing-in-itself is a noumenon in the negative sense. It must have some *intrinsic* nature. Its nature cannot just consist in and be exhausted by the purely *extrinsic* property of manifesting itself by such-and-such sense impressions to a mind provided with such-and-such senses and forms of intuition. But this intrinsic nature could be known only by a kind of non-sensuous direct acquaintance, which we can talk about but cannot form any positive conception of. Kant sums up the position quite fairly at the end of the first paragraph on p. 273. Our understanding, he says there, 'limits sensibility by applying the term "noumena" to things-in-themselves, i.e. to things not regarded as appearances. But in so doing it at the same time sets limits to itself, recognising that it cannot know these noumena through any of the categories, and that it must therefore think of them only under the title of an unknown something' (B 312).

I think that this is probably the consistent view for Kant to take. But one wonders whether he has any good ground for continuing to believe so firmly in the existence of foreign things-in-themselves, 'corresponding to sensible entities', when the notion of thing-in-itself has become so completely eviscerated. I suspect that he started with a fairly commonsense view of independent extended substances in an independent space, which act on the minds of various percipients through their sense organs, and produce in these various minds correlated sensible appearances of themselves from various points of view. But gradually more and more of this has been given up. There is no common space and time independent of each percipient, for space and time are forms of intuition imposed by each percipient on his sense-impressions. The foreign things-in-themselves can no longer properly be regarded as substances or as causes. For the notions of substance and of cause are innate forms of synthesis, in accordance with which each individual's imagination synthesises and supplements his sense-impressions under the guidance of his understanding, to produce a coherent experience. What connexion then is left between one's sense-impressions and a foreign thing-in-itself which makes it plausible to go on postulating the latter in connexion with the former?

4.4.3 The sensible world and the world of theoretical physics

The last point that Kant makes is this. It is not uncommon to say that the *senses* present us with objects as they *appear*, whilst in mathematical physics we come to know by means of *reason* about things as they *are*. The world, as it really is, is the world of molecules, atoms, electrons, light-waves, etc., and we learn about this by using understanding and reason and rejecting notions derived from the senses. Kant remarks that, in the only sense in which this is true, it does not conflict with anything that he has said about the emptiness of the concepts and principles of the understanding when used transcendentally. The only legitimate contrast is between objects of sense-perception considered separately and superficially, and objects of sense-perception considered in their interrelations, as a coherent causal system subject in all its changes to the particular laws of nature and the general principles of pure understanding.

4

TRANSITION FROM EPISTEMOLOGY TO ONTOLOGY

Hitherto we have been dealing with that division of transcendental logic which Kant calls 'transcendental *analytic*'. We now pass to that division of it which he calls 'transcendental *dialectic*'. In this he is concerned with the nature and validity of speculative philosophy and natural theology. This is supposed to be the special department of pure reason. The epistemological conclusions reached in the *Transcendental Aesthetic* and the *Transcendental Analytic* are now made the basis for a critique of the exercise of pure reason in the realm of ontology.

1 The ideas of reason

We have already seen that Kant distinguishes two fundamental cognitive faculties, viz. intuition and thought, and holds that both are essential to knowledge. He now distinguishes two different faculties under the head of thought, and calls them *understanding* and *reason*. The categories and the pure principles which involve them belong to understanding, and have been dealt with in the *Transcendental Analytic*. Kant holds that there are other concepts peculiar to reason. He calls them *ideas*. The *Transcendental Dialectic* is concerned with reason and its ideas, and with the *a priori* arguments, involving these ideas, by which speculative philosophers and natural theologians profess to prove important ontological propositions.

It must be understood that Kant is here using the words 'reason' and 'idea' in a special technical sense. The first thing is to see what he means by them, and how he supposes reason and its ideas to be related to understanding and its categories.

The essential point seems to be this. In ordinary practical thinking and in natural science we are continually presented with certain series of terms, which we seem to be able to pursue as far as we like in thought without coming to any natural end-term or limit. The two most important types of such series are the spatio-temporal and the causal. Each of these gives rise to two cases. (1a) Any extension or duration seems to be part of a larger extension or longer duration, and there seems to be no intrinsic maximum or upper limit. (1b) Any extension or duration seems to be composed of smaller extensions or shorter durations, and there seems to be no intrinsic minimum or lower limit. (2a) Every event seems to be the effect of some earlier event, and we seem never to reach back to any event which is a cause but not an effect. (2b) The existence of any substance seems to be intrinsically contingent. We may be able to say that it is a necessary consequence of the existence of some other substance, as e.g. the existence of a person depends on the previous existence of his parents. But the existence of these other substances is just as contingent intrinsically. We seem never to come to any substance whose existence is intrinsically necessary.

Now in ordinary life and natural science these various unending series give us no trouble. We follow each one just so far as we need for the purpose in hand, whilst we recognise that it could have been followed further in the same direction if necessary. But the human mind is so constituted that it cannot help reflecting philosophically on such series, and when it does so it finds them profoundly unsatisfactory. It cannot help thinking that they must in fact be completed somehow, that they must have first and last terms, and so on. Now Kant means by 'reason' that factor in our intellectual make-up which will not let us rest content with the various unending series which the understanding presents to our notice, and which tries to think of each such series as somehow ended or completed in a characteristic way. By 'ideas of reason' he means the concepts of such last terms and completed wholes. Thus the notion of a first event, or the notion of the world as a completed spatio-temporal whole, is an idea of reason. So too is the notion of an event which is a cause of later events but not an effect of earlier events. So too is the notion of a perfectly simple substance with no parts. So too is the notion of a substance whose existence is intrinsically necessary.

Now not only are there such ideas. Speculative philosophers and natural theologians have tried to prove that they have actual application. It is alleged, e.g., by indeterminists that human volitions are events which have effects but are not completely determined by earlier events. Many philosophers have argued that the human soul must be a simple substance, and have tried to prove from this that it is immortal. Again, theologians regard God as an existent whose existence is intrinsically necessary; and they have put forward various arguments to prove that there must be an entity answering to this description. Thus speculative philosophy and natural theology are specially concerned with ideas of reason.

Now we know that no agreement has been reached on these subjects; so we may suspect that there is something wrong somewhere. Moreover, there is the following interesting fact to be noticed. If we compare and contrast mathematics, natural science, and speculative philosophy, we notice two things. (1) No one in his senses doubts that the principles and methods of mathematics are sound, that its results are certain, and that it continually advances. No one seriously doubts that the principles and methods of natural science are sound, that its results are at least highly probable and are corrigible if mistaken in detail, and that it continually advances. But there are no agreed results, and there is no steady advance in speculative philosophy and theology. (2) Yet speculative philosophy and theology use the same concepts and the same *a priori* principles as mathematics and natural science. They use the notions of space and time, cause and substance, and such principles as the permanence of substance and the law of universal causation. It is therefore very important to discover and to state clearly the limits within which these concepts and principles are valid and fruitful, and outside which they have no valid use.

Kant claims to have done this in the *Transcendental Aesthetic* and the *Transcendental Analytic*. For he claims to have shown there that space, time, and the categories and the principles which involve them, cannot from their very nature be significantly used outside the range of possible human sense-perception. But he is not content with this. He is quite certain that the fallacies into which speculative philosophers and natural theologians have fallen are not simply chance mistakes which they might have avoided if they had been cleverer or luckier. They are intrinsic to the nature of the human mind. It is natural to any intelligent man to speculate on these topics, and, if he does so, to use arguments of this kind about them. Moreover there are *negative* as well as *positive* ontologists, and Kant holds that their arguments are no less fallacious. E.g. there are persons who claim to prove *a priori* that the world *cannot* have a beginning in time or be limited in space. There are persons who claim to prove that there *cannot* be simple substances, that the soul *must* come to an end with the death of the body, that there *cannot* be incompletely determined volitions, and that no such entity as the God of natural theology is possible. According to Kant their arguments are as baseless as those of their opponents and for the same reasons.

Now Kant always assumes as evident that men could not have a cognitive faculty, with a characteristic innate equipment, which served no useful purpose at all and was incapable of leading to anything but fallacies. He takes it for granted that there must be a right and a wrong use for the ideas of reason. He therefore devotes himself in the *Transcendental Dialectic* to a two-fold task. One is to show in detail that the use made of the ideas of reason by speculative philosophers and natural theologians, and by those who attempt to reach opposite conclusions by similar *a priori* arguments, is mistaken. The other is to discover and to state the right use of the ideas of reason in human thinking.

2 The problems of speculative philosophy

Owing to Kant's passion for taking the divisions of formal logic as a clue to the divisions of transcendental philosophy, there is a good deal of artificiality in the arrangement of the material in the *Transcendental Dialectic*. It seems to me that in some cases what is essentially the same problem is discussed several times under different headings. E.g. the arguments for and against the proposition that there is an intrinsically necessary existent on which the existence of everything else depends are discussed twice over. For I cannot see any real difference between the fourth antinomy and the cosmological argument for the existence of God. However, the essential points are these.

(1) On Kant's view, the misuse of the ideas of reason leads to three bogus *a priori* sciences, which he calls *rational cosmology*, *rational psychology*, and *speculative theology*. Rational cosmology claims to prove *a priori* that the world did or that it did not have a beginning, that it is or that it is not limited in extent, that it is or that it is not composed of simple substances. Rational psychology claims to prove *a priori* that the human soul is a simple substance, that it survives the death of the body, and so on. Speculative theology claims to prove *a priori*, without using specifically ethical or religious premises and without appealing to any alleged divine revelation, that there is a being which exists of necessity and that the existence of everything else is derived from it.

(2) According to Kant one of the ideas of reason, viz. the idea of freedom, is in a quite peculiar position. In the *Critique of Pure Reason* we are given the *a priori* arguments for complete determinism and the *a priori* arguments for free will. But the solution offered by Kant is that *both* conclusions may be true. The same person may be completely determined in all his actions when considered as a phenomenon, but may be undetermined when considered as a noumenon. Now in his ethical works Kant takes in the additional premiss, which seems to him obvious, that a man is a *moral* agent, subject to obligations, and responsible for his deliberate actions. He argues that this entails that a man is free as regards his noumenal self, though completely determined as regards his phenomenal self. So we can conclude that the idea of freedom certainly does apply within the world of noumena.

(3) As regards *rational cosmology* the results of Kant's discussion are purely destructive, and they are not supplemented by anything positive in the two later *Critiques*. The only positive feature is this. Kant tries to explain the useful part which is played in human thought by the *proper* use of these ideas of reason which lead to the fallacies of rational cosmology when misused.

(4) As regards *rational psychology* the results of the discussion in the *Transcendental Dialectic* are again purely destructive. And the same can be said of *speculative theology*. Kant never went back on the conclusion that all such arguments for the simplicity and immortality of the soul or for the existence of God are simply fallacious. But he also concluded that any

arguments of the same type *against* the simplicity or immortality of the soul or *against* the existence of God are equally fallacious. The *a priori* arguments for and against simply prove nothing and leave an open field. Now in the *Critique of Practical Reason* Kant argues that, when certain ethical facts are taken into account as premises, we have positive grounds for accepting the immortality of the soul and the existence of God. In the *Critique of Judgment*, which is largely concerned with the nature and validity of the notion of teleology, the question of the argument from design is reverted to and discussed at a considerably deeper level than in the *Critique of Pure Reason*.

(5) The discussion of the soul in the *Transcendental Dialectic* must be taken along with Kant's many statements about the self in other parts of the *Critique of Pure Reason*, as well as with his doctrine in the ethical works. It is a very complicated story indeed, and of very doubtful consistency.

In view of all this the course which I shall take is the following. I shall first discuss *rational cosmology*, where the conclusions are purely negative and there is no positive supplement to be made from the later *Critiques*. I shall then deal with what I will call *problems of ontology other than cosmology*. Under this heading I shall discuss (1) *the self and self-consciousness*, (2) *freedom and determinism*, and (3) *God*. Here I shall take together the negative results of the *Dialectic* and the positive doctrines contained in other parts of the *Critique of Pure Reason* and in the *Critique of Practical Reason* and the *Critique of Judgment*.

5

ONTOLOGY

1 Rational cosmology

The second chapter of the second book of the *Transcendental Dialectic* is occupied with what Kant calls *The Antinomy of Pure Reason* (pp. 384–484, A 405–567/B 432–595). Kant holds that there are four antinomies, two about space and time and their contents, and two about causation. The two former are called the *mathematical* antinomies, and the two latter are called the *dynamical* antinomies. The dynamical antinomies are concerned with the problem of freedom versus determinism and with the problem of a first cause of nature versus the view that nature as a whole is an unconditioned infinite series of mutually conditioning events. We are not concerned with them at present. But the two mathematical antinomies are the whole content of the bogus science of rational cosmology, and we will now deal with them.

1.1 The general notion of an antinomy

Before going into detail I will give a general account of what Kant means by an 'antinomy'. This will cover both the mathematical and the dynamical antinomies.

Kant held that human reason comes into an inevitable conflict with itself whenever it is presented with anything that depends on a series of conditions all of which are of the same nature. We cannot rest intellectually content with passing endlessly backwards in thought from one condition to another, which in turn depends on a previous condition. The human intellect seeks to discover something *unconditioned* as a resting-place. Now it tries to do this in two different ways. One way is to seek for a certain outstanding term in the series of conditions, viz. one which is itself unconditioned, so that we can stop at it as a first and self-explanatory term. The other way is to take the whole endless series of conditioned and conditioning terms as a single unconditioned self-explanatory whole. These two opposite ways of trying to pass from the conditioned to the unconditioned are called by Kant respectively the *thesis* and the *antithesis* of an *antinomy*. One seems to be able to produce equally cogent *refutations* of both thesis and antithesis, or equally cogent *proofs* of both of them. And yet they seem to be mutually exclusive and collectively exhaustive alternatives. Evidently there must be something radically wrong somewhere. Yet it remains a fact that intelligent men, when they begin to speculate on these topics, cannot help getting involved in these antinomies. For it is of the essence of human reason to seek the unconditioned and the self-explanatory and to try to devise and explain the conditioned in terms of it. So there remains a task which philosophy cannot shirk, viz. what Kant calls the *solution of the antinomies*. This consists in showing what is true and what is false in the thesis and in the antithesis, and pointing out the precise function in human knowledge which is performed by reason in its natural yet hopeless search for the unconditioned.

We can now state in general terms the nature of an antinomy and of its solution. You have two sentences 'S is p_1' and 'S is p_2'. These seem to express propositions which are mutually exclusive and collectively exhaustive, i.e. such that both of them cannot be true and both of them cannot be false. Yet it seems that both of them can be *proved* by equally cogent reasoning, or that both of them can be *disproved* by equally cogent reasoning, from equally evident premises.

Now assuming that the reasoning on both sides of an antinomy really is cogent, there are two and only two possible types of solution. (1) Suppose you seem to have *disproved* both 'S is p_1' and 'S is p_2', although they seem to be collectively exhaustive alternatives. Then the solution may be that S does not really have the determinable characteristic P under which p_1 and p_2 are the two collectively exhaustive determinates. You have tacitly assumed that it had this determinable characteristic. Once you give up that assumption you will have no difficulty in admitting that *both* 'S is p_1' and 'S is p_2' are false. E.g. if the world is not really temporal at all, we can admit that it is equally false to say that there was a *first* event in its history and to say that every event in its history had a *predecessor*. (2) Suppose you seem to have *proved* both 'S is p_1' and 'S is p_2', although they seem to be mutually exclusive alternatives. Then the solution may be that the name 'S' is ambiguous and that it stands for a different subject in the two sentences. In that case the two propositions are really of the forms 'S_1 is p_1' and 'S_2 is p_2'. In that case there may be no difficulty in admitting that both are true. E.g. if the word 'man' may mean either 'man as he appears to himself on introspection' or 'man as he is in himself', then the sentences 'A man is free in some of his actions' and 'A man is completely determined in all his actions' are ambiguous. If you substitute one sense of 'man' in one of them and the other sense of 'man' in the other, each may express a true proposition. Kant adopts the first type of solution for the mathematical antinomies and the second for the dynamical.

1.2 The mathematical antinomies

We can now pass to the mathematical antinomies. There are two of these. The first is concerned with the infinite or finite extension of the world in space and with the infinite or finite duration of the world's history backwards in time. The second is concerned with the infinite or finite divisibility of matter in respect of its spatial extension.

1.2.1 First antinomy

The thesis of the first antinomy is that the world had a beginning in time and is limited in space. The antithesis is that it had no beginning in time and is unlimited in space, being infinite both in its duration backwards and in its extent. Kant does not attempt to prove either the thesis or the antithesis directly. What he claims to do is to refute in turn the antithesis and the thesis. On the assumption that the two are collectively exhaustive alternatives, a refutation of either would be an indirect proof of the other. I will now consider in turn the argument as applied to duration and the argument as applied to extension.

1.2.1.1 Argument as applied to duration

(1) *Refutation of antithesis.* If the world never began, it must have been going on for an infinite time up to any event in its history that we choose to take, e.g. the Battle of Waterloo. This means that an infinite sequence of successive phases in its history would have elapsed before the Battle of Waterloo. Kant says that this is impossible.

The only reason which he gives is this: 'The infinity of a series consists in the fact that it can never be completed through successive synthesis' (p. 397, A 427/B 455). Before commenting on this it will be well to consider the additional remarks which Kant makes in his *Observations on the Thesis* (pp. 399–403, A 430–4/B 458–62). He says there that he might have made the argument easier for himself by taking a different defintion of an infinite quantum, which is very commonly accepted, but which he regards as unsatisfactory. The unsatisfactory definition comes to this. A quantum is infinite if it contains a number N of equal units (e.g. years or cubic feet) adjoined to each other, where N is such that no number greater than N is possible. On this definition the very notion of an infinite quantum could be rejected offhand as self-contradictory. For there can be no number N such that a greater number is impossible; the sequence of integers has and can have no greatest term. In a footnote (p. 401, A 433/B 461) Kant states what he considers to be the mathematical notion of an infinite quantum. It comes to this. A quantum is infinite if for every number N it contains a greater number of equal adjoined units than N. Thus, e.g., a duration is infinite if for every number N it contains a greater number of successive years than N. This definition does not, like the other, rule out the possibility of an infinite quantum at the start by making it involve the impossible notion of a greatest cardinal number. But it is not the definition which Kant states in the text itself. This runs as follows: 'The true transcendental concept of infinitude is this, viz. that the successive synthesis of units required for the enumeration of a quantum can never be completed.' In the footnote he says that this entails the 'mathematical concept of the infinite', which I have given in my own words above. In the text he says that it follows from the 'transcendental concept' that 'an infinity of actual successive states leading up to a given moment . . . cannot have elapsed'.

The question is whether this 'transcendental concept' of the infinity of a quantum is satisfactory, and whether it really does entail the consequences which Kant says it does.

It seems to me to be unsatisfactory, for the following reason. It drags in a reference to an operation to be performed by someone in a sequence of steps, and it defines the infinity of a quantum in terms of the impossibility of completing that operation in any time, however long.

In order to take the simplest possible concrete case, let us apply the definition to the notion of a straight line L, which has one end A, but is supposed to stretch out to an infinite length in one direction from A. I take it that what Kant would say is this. Suppose you were to lay down a unit measure of length, e.g. a foot-rule AB, with its end A coinciding with the end A of the line L, and its end B coinciding with another point of the line L. Then turn AB through $180°$ about its end B, so that its end A now coincides with a point two feet along the line L. Then turn it in the same direction through $180°$ about its end A, so that its end B now coincides with a point three feet along the line L. And so on. Then, if and only if the line L is of infinite length, there will always be a part of it which remains unmeasured however long you may continue this process.

Now the reference to the series of operations with the measuring-rod, and to the time taken in performing it, seems to me to be irrelevant. It does not really matter that it would take a certain time to turn the foot-rule on each successive occasion. The relevant fact is that, even if each turn could be performed literally *instantaneously* and there were no *interval* between successive turns, no *number* of such adjoined units would constitute a line as long as L. Here all reference to temporal sequence has disappeared. The only way left to drag it in would be by the absurd expedient of saying that number involves *counting,* and that counting is essentially a sequence of acts.

The question that remains is whether this definition of an infinite quantum makes it impossible that an infinite time should have elapsed up to a given event.

I can only suppose that what Kant had at the back of his mind is something like the following. The successive phases of the history of the world, e.g. the contents of successive years of world history up to a given moment, e.g. up to 1 January 1900, *have* automatically *synthesised themselves* by adjunction to a completed whole, viz. the total history of the world up to that date. (We can ignore the fact that the history of the world continued after that date. For the present purpose it would do just as well if the universe had been completely annihilated on 1 January 1900.) So, Kant would say, the history of the universe up to that date does *not* answer to the definition of being infinite in duration. For, if it did, *no* successive adjunction of one year to another, however often repeated, would give a duration as long as the actual duration of the world up to a given date. Yet in fact that is exactly what has automatically happened through the lapse of successive years. Therefore the past duration of the world must be *finite*, and therefore the world must have had a *beginning*.

It seems to me plain that there is something wrong with this argument, though I think that there is at the back of it a genuine and important distinction between time and space. The distinction is this. In the case of an *extended* object any synthesis that may be performed is *extrinsic* to the quantum itself. The synthesis consists, e.g., in seeing different parts of the object successively, remembering at each stage what one is no longer seeing, and joining in imagination what one is now only remembering. Or, again, it may consist, e.g., in successively laying down a measuring-rod and keeping a record of the number of times one has turned it through 180° or shifted it parallel to itself. It is always taken for granted that the *spatially* extended object exists at every moment as a complete whole, quite independently of the process of synthesis and of the stage which that has reached at any moment. But, in the case of a *temporal* process, successive synthesis seems to be *intrinsic* to the process. The history of the world just consists of the totality of the phases which have successively *adjoined themselves* to each other in a series; and process just *consists in* such successive synthesis of new phases to old ones.

Now this is an important peculiarity of time and duration. But just for that reason it seems to me that Kant makes here an unjustified use of his definition of infinity in terms of the impossibility of completion by successive synthesis of adjoined units. Obviously the successive synthesis of units which is contemplated in this definition is the kind of *extrinsic* synthesis which we perform when we survey a spatially extended object part by part, or when we measure it by repeatedly laying down a rod, and so on. What Kant does here is to substitute for this the *intrinsic* synthesis which is uniquely characteristic of temporal process, and then to apply the definition, which is in terms of *extrinsic* synthesis, to show that the history of the world cannot be infinitely long *a parte ante*. It seems to me that the substitution of this new and unique sense of 'successive synthesis' for the old one has robbed the definition of all meaning.

I think that one can see the invalidity of the argument and the doubtfulness of the conclusion, if one imagines oneself starting, as before, from a given date in the world's history, e.g. 1 January 1900, and measuring *backwards* from it in years. Here we can apply the original definition, for it is now *we* who are performing an *extrinsic* synthesis of units. Now here either of the following two alternatives seems to be equally conceivable. (a) That there is a number N, such that further than N years back from 1 January 1900 neither matter nor minds nor anything else existed. (b) That for *every* number N there was matter or minds or something else existing further than N years back from 1 January 1900.

I suspect that the conclusion of the thesis, viz. that the world must have had a beginning, may derive a certain plausibility from a kind of spatial picture or metaphor which is very hard to avoid. One tends to think of the history of the world by analogy with a strip of toothpaste which is being continually and steadily pressed out of a tube. One then takes any actual phase in the world's history as analogous to a cross-section of this strip, and one takes the length of the strip between the mouth of the tube and this cross-section as representing the duration of the world's history up to that particular phase. Then one asks oneself: How could the strip ever have got to this, or to any other, determinate point if the mouth of the tube has been infinitely remote?

However seductive this picture may be, one can see that it is nonsensical by making the following elementary reflection. It is sensible to ask: How *fast* is the paste coming out of the tube? And it is sensible to say that it might be coming faster or slower. But it is meaningless to ask: How quickly do the contents of successive years succeed each other? And it is meaningless to say that they might do so faster or slower. It is most important to realise that time is something absolutely unique, and that no metaphors from the movements or other changes of particular things can be anything but misleading if used to elucidate the notion of 'absolute becoming', which they all presuppose.

(2) *Refutation of thesis.* In refuting the thesis Kant begins by asserting that to say that the world had a beginning implies the existence of empty time before the world began. He then argues that there is nothing in any moment of empty time to determine why the world should begin at that moment rather than at any other. He then tacitly assumes Leibniz's principle of sufficient reason. Since there would be no sufficient reason why the world should have begun at one rather than at another moment of absolute time, it cannot have begun at any. Therefore it never began.

I cannot see that Kant is justified in saying that the supposition that the world began involves the notion of a previous empty time, if that means an existent entity of a peculiar kind. Suppose, e.g., that the relational theory of time were correct, and that time and instants are logical constructions out of direct temporal relations between events. Then to say that the world had a beginning is simply to say that there was a certain event which was followed by others but was not preceded by any other event. To say that this event would 'have been preceded by empty time' would come to this. It would amount to saying that it is logically possible that there should have been events which preceded the event which was *in fact* the first event.

On this relational view of time the question 'Why did the world begin when it did, and not at some earlier or later moment?' would reduce to the question 'Why did the particular event, which in fact had no predecessors, not have predecessors?' Certainly this question could always be asked, however far back from the present we suppose the first event to have been. And it certainly would not arise if there were no event without predecessors. But I cannot help doubting whether it is a significant question, except in a rather special theistic context; and in that context the only answer is 'God knows!' So I am not prepared to accept Kant's argument as a conclusive objection to the possibility that the world had a beginning.

Before passing to Kant's arguments about spatial extension I will make two general remarks about the first antinomy in respect to time.

(a) Kant does not explicitly distinguish the following two questions. (i) Was there, or was there not, a *first event* in the world's history? (ii) Is the *duration* of the world's history backwards from any assigned phase in it *finite or infinite*? These are certainly different questions, though they are no doubt logically connected.

One logical relation between them would seem to be this. If there was a first event in the world's history, then the duration of that history backwards from any assigned phase in it is finite. But does the converse of this hold? Can we say that, if there was *not* a first event in the world's history, then the duration of that history backwards from any assigned phase in it is *infinite*? If we are prepared to press the analogy between a continuous temporal sequence of instants or instantaneous events, on the one hand, and a continuous sequence of rational fractions in order of magnitude, on the other, the answer would seem to be in the negative.

Consider, e.g., the sequence of rational fractions, in ascending order of magnitude, and take, e.g., the segment of it up to and including the fraction ½. This certainly has no first term, since there is no smallest fraction. Yet one would certainly say that the segment up to and including ½ is of finite 'length', and that its 'length' is in fact one half of that of the segment up to and including the fraction 1/1. Suppose now that we are willing to press the analogy between instants and their temporal sequence, on the one hand, and rational fractions and their sequence in order of magnitude, on the other. Then we shall have to admit the possibility that the world's history had no first phase and yet that its duration backwards from the present is finite. For my own part I regard analogies between actual existents (such as events and their temporal relations) and abstract entities (such as pure numbers and their arithmetical relations) as an extremely shaky foundation for any conclusions about the former. But I mention for what it is worth the consequence of pursuing the analogy here.

(b) If we admit the possibility just mentioned, we have the following three alternatives about the world's history: (i) A first event and therefore a finite duration backwards from the present. (ii) No first event, but a finite upper limit of duration backwards from the present. (iii) No first event and an infinite duration backwards from the present.

Now it seems to me that, when these alternatives are evisaged, one sees that the fundamental question is about the possibility or impossibility of a *first event* and about the possibility or impossibility of there being *no first event*. The question of finite or infinite duration backwards from the present seems to be of interest only in so far as an answer to it carries with it one or other of the alternatives, a first event or no first event.

Now (if I may make some personal confessions) I find no difficulty in supposing that the world's history had no beginning and that its duration backwards from its present phase is infinite. Nor do I find any insuperable difficulty in supposing that the world's history had no beginning, but that its duration backwards from its present phase does not exceed a certain finite limiting value. But I must confess that I have a very great difficulty in supposing that there was a first phase in the world's history, i.e. a phase immediately before which there existed neither matter, nor minds, nor anything else. I note the following two autobiographical facts here for what they may be worth. (a) I have no difficulty in supposing that there might be a *last* phase in the world's history, i.e. one immediately *after* which there will exist neither matter nor minds nor anything else. (b) I have no difficulty in supposing that the material world may have an *outer spatial boundary*.

Both these facts suggest that the difficulty which I feel is connected with something peculiar to *time*, as distinct from space. The first of them suggests that it is not just a psychological difficulty due to the fact that I have had no experience of absolute beginnings. For I have equally had no experience of absolute endings. To speak more accurately, I *have* had plenty of experience of what seemed *prima facie* to be absolute beginnings, e.g. when dew was precipitated; and I *have* had plenty of experience of what seemed *prima facie* to be absolute endings, e.g. when a volatile liquid totally evaporated. But in spite of this I find myself taking an entirely different attitude towards the suggestion of an absolute beginning of the world's history and the suggestion of an absolute end to it.

I suspect that my difficulty about a first event or phase in the world's history is due to the fact that, whatever I may *say* when I am trying to give Hume a run for his money, I cannot really *believe in* anything beginning to exist without being *caused* (in the old-fashioned sense of *produced* or *generated*) by something else which existed before and up to the moment when the entity in question began to exist. That this principle has no trace of self-evidence when 'cause' is interpreted in terms of *law*, and not in terms of *generation*, is, of course, irrelevant. When 'cause' is interpreted in terms of generation I do find it impossible to give up the principle; and with that confession of the intellectual impotence of old age I must leave this topic.

1.2.1.2 Argument as applied to extension

(1) *Refutation of antithesis.* What Kant proves, if he proves anything, is stated as follows (p. 398, A429/B457): 'An infinite aggregate of actual things cannot . . . be viewed as a *given* whole, nor consequently as *simultaneously* given.' He proceeds without further argument to say: 'The world is therefore, as regards extension in space, not infinite . . .'

Now it is surely plain that the second proposition does not follow from the first. The most obvious meaning of the first proposition is that, if the world did consist of an infinite aggregate of coexistent things, we could at no moment perceive it as such. It may perhaps be stretched to mean that we could not know conceptually that it was such. Supposing this to be true, it would not follow that the world cannot *be* an infinitely extended whole. The utmost that would follow is that we could never *know* it to be so, if it were so.

The argument to prove the first proposition may be stated as follows. It is obvious that any extended object which can be perceived at one glance is of *finite* extent. Hence an *infinite* whole could not be presented on any *one* occasion to sense-perception. Now any whole which cannot be perceived at one glance can be cognised perceptually only by a process of *successive synthesis*, i.e. by perceiving successively different parts, which are in fact adjoined to make up the whole, and holding in memory one's perceptions of the parts which one is no longer perceiving. But it is obvious that in this way one could not in any finite time cognise perceptually any infinitely extended whole.

Kant then continues as follows: 'In order therefore to conceive as a whole the world which fills all regions of space, the successive synthesis of the parts of an infinite world must be viewed as completed, i.e. an infinite time must be viewed as having elapsed in the enumeration of all coexisting things' (p. 398, A428-9/B456-7).

This argument seems to me to be invalid. All that Kant has proved is the trivial proposition that, if the world were infinitely extended, it would take an infinitely long time to perceive successively an exhaustive set of adjoined parts of it. He then argues that, in order to *conceive* of the world as infinitely extended, one must conceive of someone as completing this infinitely long sequence of successive perceptions. But surely that is required only in order to conceive of an infinitely extended world *being perceived* by a finite observer whose field of view at any moment is limited and who therefore has to perceive very large objects piecemeal. It does not seem to be required in order to conceive of *the world as infinitely extended*. I do not see why it is necessary to bring in a reference to perception at all. But, even if the only way of conceiving an infinitely extended world were to conceive it as something which it would take an infinite time for an observer to perceive piecemeal, Kant's conclusion would not follow. For it does not take an infinite time to *conceive of* a process which would take an infinite time to *perform*.

(2) *Refutation of thesis*. Kant begins the argument in the same way as he began the refutation of the thesis about time. If the world be of finite extension, he says, it must be situated somewhere within an unlimited empty space. But he continues the argument differently. He does *not* argue that there is no sufficient reason why it should be in one region of absolute space rather than another, and therefore that it must be in *every* part of space if it is in *any* part of it. Instead he argues as follows. There would have to be a certain relation (presumably the relation of 'being bound by') between the world as a whole and the empty space outside it. But this, he says, would be a relation to *nothing*, and therefore no relation. So he concludes that the world cannot be limited in its spatial extension.

This is surely a very queer argument. The only way in which I can make sense of it is to recast it as follows. To say that the world is limited in spatial extent implies that it is situated somewhere in absolute space. But there can be nothing answering to the description of absolute space. Therefore the world cannot be limited in spatial extent. If this is what Kant meant, he might have used a similar argument to show that the history of the world cannot be of finite duration.

Supposing this to be the argument, it seems to me to be a failure. Either we accept or we reject the possibility of an entity answering to the description of absolute space. If we accept it, then a relation of the world as a whole to the space outside it is *not* a relation to *nothing*. It is, indeed, not a relation to any *thing*. It is a relation to a peculiar kind of non-material extended existent. Suppose, on the other hand, that we reject the possibility of absolute space, and accept a relational view, such as Leibniz put forward. On that view space and regions in space are logical constructions out of spatial relations which hold directly between bodies. On that alternative, the statement that the world is of finite extension means simply that there is a number N, such that the distance between any two particles in the actual world is less than N units of length, e.g. less than N miles. The statement that, if the world is of finite extent, it must be situated in empty space, would have the following meaning. It would mean that, although *in fact* there is a number N, such that no two actual particles are further than (say) N miles apart, yet there is no impossibility in supposing that there *might be* particles further apart than this or than any other number of units which could be mentioned.

1.2.1.3 Concluding comments

The following further remarks seem worth making before leaving this topic.

(1) Kant naturally assumed without question that the geometry of absolute space, if there were such an entity, would be Euclidean. No other alternatives had been seriously contemplated or worked out in his day.

Now a feature of Euclidean geometry, which it shares with some but not with all alternative geometries of homaloidal space, is that the straight line in it is an *open* sequence of points extending indefinitely in both directions. In some, but not all, alternative systems of geometry for homaloidal space, the straight line is a *closed* sequence of points, analogous to a great circle on a sphere. On the first alternative, absolute space would be intrinsically unlimited in all directions, and Kant naturally assumes this. On the second alternative, absolute space would be intrinsically finite. There would be a kind of natural maximum of *length*, as there is in ordinary Euclidean geometry a natural maximum of *angular deviation*, viz. the angle through which a line would have to be turned about one end in order to bring it back into coincidence with itself after completing a circle.

It is idle to speculate on what Kant would have said about such alternative possibilities. But it is important for us to notice that the spatial finitude of the material world would be in a different logical position according to whether the geometry of nature is supposed to be of the 'open' or of the 'closed' type. If it is of the closed type, the material world *must* be of finite extent. The only alternatives would be: (a) that there are material particles which are at the intrinsically maximal distance apart, or (b) that every pair of material particles is at less than that distance apart. If, on the other hand, the geometry of nature is of the open type, the material world might be either of finite or of infinite extent. Relative to the 'closed' alternative the finitude of the material world is necessary; relative to the 'open' alternative it is contingent. But it is important to notice that the necessity of finitude on the first alternative is *only* a relative necessity. For, if it be a fact that the geometry of nature is of the closed type, it is a contingent fact and the evidence for it would be empirical. What can be said, however, is this. The evidence for the geometry of nature being of the closed or of the open kind would consist of empirical facts of a *higher order of generality* than the facts which would serve as evidence for the world being finite or being infinite in extent *given that* the goemetry of nature is of the open kind.

(2) It is important to notice that Kant never makes the *infinity* of absolute time or of Euclidean absolute space an objection to their possibility. Hence he cannot have held, as many philosophers (e.g. Hegel) have done, that there is some kind of logical contradiction in the notion of infinite quanta as such. This is, indeed, pretty clear from his observations on the thesis of the first antinomy, which I have already quoted. He refuses to make things easy for himself by using a certain common, but mistaken, definition of infinity, viz. one which involves the self- contradictory notion of a greatest cardinal number. The implication is that he regarded what he calls in the footnote (p. 401, A433/B461) 'the mathematical concept of the infinite' as free from contradiction.

(3) Kant here produces no independent arguments for or against the possibility of absolute space or absolute time. He is concerned with the extension of the *material world*, and with the duration *a parte ante* of it and of any minds which there may be in it. But, as we have seen, he does use as a premiss in one of his arguments that empty space outside the boundaries of the material world would be 'nothing'. Now the only ground that he gives for this is in footnote (b) to B457 (p. 398). There he simply reasserts the doctrine of the *Aesthetic* that space and time are merely forms of intuition.

Now there are two things to be said about this. (a) The arguments in the antinomies are supposed to be such as would occur naturally to any intelligent man, with philosophic interests and training, who reflects and reasons on these topics. They ought not, therefore, to involve a premiss for which the only support is a special doctrine of Kant's critical philosophy. (b) Later on Kant uses the contradictory results of the mathematical antinomies to *support* his doctrine that space and time are merely forms of intuition. This is circular, if that doctrine is the only ground for accepting a certain premiss which is used in one of the arguments in these antinomies.

1.2.2 Second antinomy

The thesis of the second antinomy is that every compound substance consists of simple parts, and therefore that every substance is either itself simple or is composed of a set of parts which are simple. The antithesis is that no compound substance is composed of simple parts, and therefore that there are no simple substances. Kant is here confining his attention to material objects in space. The alleged proof that a human soul must be a simple substance is considered elsewhere, viz. in the section entitled the *Paralogisms of Pure Reason*.

(1) *Proof of thesis*. The argument turns on a fundamental assumption, which Kant states as follows: 'Composition, as applied to substances, is an *accidental* relation, independently of which they must still exist as self-subsistent entities' (p. 403, A 435/B 463). I think that what this comes to is the following. If S be a genuine substance, then it is logically possible that it should have been *the only* genuine substance; i.e. the existence of any genuine substance is logically independent of the existence of any other substance.

The other premiss in Kant's argument is that a compound substance would be a whole, composed of a set of parts each of which is itself a substance.

If we combine these two premisses, we see that it follows that what is called a '*compound* substance' cannot be a genuine *substance*. For the existence of any whole is logically dependent on the existence of its parts. The existence of a compound substance would therefore be *logically dependent* on the existence of the parts of which it is composed, and those parts would be themselves substances. But the existence of any genuine substance is *logically independent* of the existence of any other substance. It follows that the expression 'compound substance' involves a contradiction. If there are any genuine substances, they must all be simple; what is called a 'compound substance' is not really a substance, but is simply an aggregate of interrelated simple substances.

I think it must be admitted that we are entitled to draw from the premisses and the definitions the hypothetical conclusion '*If* there are any genuine substances, they are none of them compound substances'. But we are not entitled to draw the categorical conclusion 'There *are* genuine substances, and they are all simple'. For it might be that there is nothing in the world answering to the conditions which Kant lays down for a genuine substance.

There are two points worth noting in Kant's *Observations on the Thesis* (p. 405, A 438/B 466). (a) He says that this argument would not apply to absolute space or absolute time. The reason is that they would not be wholes composed of accidentally associated parts. In absolute space, e.g., the whole would be logically prior to the sub-regions which are its parts; it would not be related to them as a stack of bricks is to the individual bricks which together compose it. Nor would the various sub-regions be related to each other as the various bricks which together compose a stack are interrelated. For each brick might have existed even if none of the others had done so. But each region of space presupposes space as a whole, and therefore all the other sub-regions of space.

I think that this contrast is correct and important. But it raises the question whether the material world (or rather the old-fashioned 'luminiferous ether', in which material particles are perhaps vortices) may not really be a whole of the same kind as absolute space would be, and not an aggregate of accidentally interrelated simple substances.

(b) At the end of these *Observations* Kant remarks that the thesis is really the principle with which Leibniz begins his *Monadology*. That remark is true, so far as it goes. But it seems to me that there is one important difference. Leibniz tried to make us see that the notion of a whole composed of parts, which are themselves composed of parts, which are themselves composed of parts . . ., and so on without end, involves a regress which is vicious. Kant shows merely that a 'compound substance' would not answer to his definition of a 'substance'.

I must confess that I cannot but find myself agreeing with Leibniz here. But I am well aware that many contemporary philosophers, at least as intelligent and acute as myself, profess to find no difficulty in the regress which Leibniz felt to be obviously vicious. That there is no formal contradiction in it, is, I think, plain. But that does not seem to me to settle the question.

(2) *Proof of antithesis.* The antithesis may be divided into two assertions, which we will call (a) and (b). Assertion (a) is that no composite thing is made up of *simple* parts. Assertion (b) is that there can be *no* simple existents in the world. We will take them in turn.

Assertion (a). Kant begins by saying that the notion of a compound substance applies only to extended objects. For a compound substance is an aggregate of *externally* related parts, and it is only in space that external relations are possible. We must therefore think of each compound substance as occupying a volume in space.

The next step is this. If a whole occupies a volume, every part of it must occupy some part of that volume. But the parts of a volume are themselves volumes. Therefore, if a compound substance consisted of simple parts, each of these simple parts would occupy a volume.

So far there is no difficulty. But, in order to be fair to Kant, I will quote his own words for the next step. 'Everything real which occupies a volume contains in itself a manifold of constituents external to each other, and is therefore composite. And . . . a real composite . . . is made up . . . of substances . . .' (p. 403, A436/B464). So what Kant asserts is that each of the allegedly *simple* substances, of which a body is alleged to be composed, would have to be a *compound* substance, in order to occupy the volume which it must occupy if it is to be part of that body. Now that is of course a contradiction. So he concludes that an extended substance cannot consist of simple parts. But all compound substances are extended. Therefore no compound substance can consist of simpe parts.

Before commenting on the main argument I will remark that I do not accept Kant's statement that the notion of a compound substance applies only to extended objects. I can quite well conceive of an unembodied mind, and such a mind might fairly be called an unextended substance. I can also quite well conceive of a group of such minds, communicating with and influencing each other telepathically, and closely interrelated by certain emotional relations, common interests, etc. Such a group of closely interrelated unembodied minds might fairly be called a compound spiritual substance, though not of course a compound *mind*. And it would be unextended.

Passing now to the case of extended compound substances and to Kant's argument about them, I think that there is a fallacy. The phrase 'to occupy a volume' is ambiguous. It needs to be redefined according to the various alternative views which may be held about the nature of bodies. If we are to be fair to the thesis, we must remember that, on its view, a body will just be a collection of intimately aggregated *unextended* particles, e.g. mass-points or centres of repulsive or attractive force. Next, we must remember that to 'occupy a volume', in the case of an unextended particle, can only mean to *fall within* that volume. Kant does not say whether the thesis supposes a finite body to consist of a finite, or of an infinite, number of unextended particles. So I will consider each of these alternatives in turn.

(i) *The finite alternative.* If a body B consists of a *finite* number of unextended particles, it can occupy a region V only *discontinuously*. What this would come to is the following. Every particle of B falls within some sub-region of V and every sub-region of V which exceeds a certain small volume v contains at least one particle of B. Some sub-regions of V, which are smaller than v, would fail to contain any particle of B. I do not see the slightest objection to the view that every body occupies the region which it does occupy *only discontinuously*.

(ii) *The infinite alternative.* What I have to say under this head pre-supposes that we can safely apply the notions of infinity and continuity, developed in pure mathematics for real numbers and sequences of such numbers, to concrete particular existents in the space and time of nature. As I have already remarked, I do not feel at all sure that this is legitimate. Let us, however, suppose for the sake of argument that it is.

Then we could combine the view that a body consists of *unextended* particles with the view that it occupies a volume *continuously*, by assigning a high enough order of infinity to the number of particles of which the body consists. I should say that a body B continuously occupies the region V, if the following two conditions are fulfilled. (A) Every sub-region of V, however small, contains at least one particle of B. (B) Every particle of B falls within some sub-region of V. There is no doubt that these conditions could be fulfilled, provided that the number of particles composing the body is as great as the number of points in the number-continuum.

The place at which Kant's argument goes wrong is where he says that 'everything which occupies a volume contains in itself a manifold of constituents external to each other, and is therefore composite'. He here uses 'occupy' in the sense of *fill*, and not merely in the sense of *fall within*. An unextended particle could not occupy a volume in the former sense; it could do so only in the latter. It seems to me that he failed to recognise that the supposition that a body is composed of *unextended* particles is compatible with at least the two following alternatives, neither of which is intrinsically impossible. (A) That the number of unextended particles composing a finite body is *finite*, and that the body occupies a volume *discontinuously*, as a crowd occupies Trafalgar Square. (B) That the number of unextended particles composing the finite body is *infinite*, and that an aggregate of a sufficiently great infinite number of unextended particles may *continuously* occupy a volume, although no individual particle can do more than fall within a volume.

Assertion (b). Finally, we come to the second assertion of the antithesis. This is much stronger than the first. It says that there are no simple substances at all, and not merely that no extended substance is composed of simple substances.

We need not spend much time on this. For in his proof (p. 403, A 437/B 465) Kant explains that he is not really claiming to establish this. He claims only to show that 'the existence of the absolutely simple cannot be established by any experience of perception, outer or inner'. This is an entirely different assertion, and I have no wish to question it.

1.3 Solution of the antinomies

The main arguments in the antinomies are not specially characteristics of Kant's philosophy. But the solutions which he offers are highly characteristic. On his view the questions which are raised in the antinomies are natural and inevitable questions for human reason to ask, and the arguments on each side are natural and inevitable arguments for it to use. But, when we find that we can refute each of two alternatives which seem to be collectively exhaustive, or prove each of two alternatives which seem to be mutually exclusive, we know that there must be something wrong with the question. Kant thinks that reason ought to be able to find out what is wrong with a question which it has put to itself. So he holds that the demand for a solution of the antinomies is one which reason rightly makes and which can certainly be met. Kant's solution is contained in sections VI to IX inclusive of the *Transcendental Dialectic* (pp. 439–84, A 490–567/B 518–95). Up to the middle of p. 455 the argument is quite general and applies to all four antinomies. The detailed solution of the mathematical antinomies is contained in p. 455 (middle) to p. 464 (middle). I will begin with the general argument.

1.3.1 General principles of solution

According to Kant the difficulty in each case arises through treating phenomena as if they were things-in-themselves. This part of the *Critique of Pure Reason* embodies very early stages of Kant's critical thinking and he did not rewrite it in terms of the later developments. Phenomena are taken to be simply presentations, i.e. entities such that it is meaningless to suggest of any one of them that it could have existed except as presented to one particular individual on one particular occasion. The thing-in-itself is called the 'transcendental object', and it seems to be regarded as the unknown cause which produces phenomena by affecting human sensibility. Space and time are relations between the various presentations produced in one's mind by the action of the transcendental object upon it.

Kant calls this doctrine 'transcendental idealism'. As usual, he resents its being identified with Berkeley's view, which he calls 'the decried empirical idealism'. But it is in fact very much like Berkeley, with the reference to God as the cause of our ideas left out. Apart from that omission the main difference is that Kant makes time, as well as space, be a form which the mind imposes upon its presentations. He therefore holds that each of us knows himself and his states only as phenomena, whilst Berkeley held that each of us knows himself and his states as they are. Kant claims that on his view external objects are just as real as the space in which they are located, and that he can distinguish dreams, waking hallucinations, and mere imaginations, on the one hand, from veridical sense-perceptions, on the other. But Berkeley makes exactly the same claims and with just as good grounds. The essential point is that all this belongs to a stage of Kant's development at which he had no notion of a third kind of entity, viz. the *empirical or phenomenal* object, distinct both from this, that, and the other presentation, and from the thing-in-itself.

Now, Kant says, all the antinomies rest on the following general principles. If something which in fact depends on conditions be given, then all these conditions are given along with it. I will now continue the argument in my own words, but I think I shall be stating what Kant had in mind.

We must distinguish between conditions of *existence* or *occurrence* and conditions for forming part of a *certain person's experience*. It is true that, if something exists or happens, every condition on which its existence or occurrence depends must have been fulfilled. This, Kant says, is a merely analytic proposition.

Next we come to a point which Kant does not quite clearly express, but which I have no doubt that he wishes to make. One *phenomenon* does not depend for its existence or occurrence on another *phenomenon*. With his present interpretation of 'phenomenon' this means that one *presentation* does not cause another *presentation*. This is just Berkeley's principle that all ideas are prefectly inert and inactive. Each phenomenon is determined, not by other phenomena, but by the non-temporal and non-spatial action of the unknowable thing-in-itself on the mind of the person whose presentation it is. But this is not what people who use the antinomies are thinking about when they talk of conditions of things and events. They are thinking of other things or events earlier in time and adjacent in space, and they are thinking of ordinary causal laws such as we deal with in science and daily life.

Now, on Kant's view, the *phenomenal* conditions of a phenomenon are not conditions on which its *existence* or *occurrence* depends. They are just other phenomena, connected with this one in accordance with such rules as are entailed by or are compatible with the fact that the two phenomena do or might fall within the experience of a single self-conscious individual. But, in this sense of 'condition', the fact that a certain phenomenon is presented does not imply that all its conditions must actually have been fulfilled. Since this presentation does in fact fall into the experience of a certain individual, it must no doubt be connected with certain rules. And, if he is to go on being conscious of objects and of himself, it is no doubt true that his future presentations will have to be connected with this one in accordance with the same rules. These earlier presentations are the *phenomenal* conditions of this phenomenon, and it is one of the *phenomenal* conditions of these later presentations. And the relations of regular sequence, in which they must stand if they are to fall into the experience of a single self-conscious person, are the laws of nature. But the *existence* of a phenomenal thing or event depends in no way on the fulfilment of its *phenomenal* conditions.

There is a sense in which the series of phenomenal conditions of a given phenomenon can be carried backwards in time before the birth of the individual in whom this phenomenon is a presentation. In the same sense this series of phenomenal conditions can be carried outwards and inwards in space beyond the limits of his actual perceptions. The sense is this. We can conceive of *possible* presentations connected with this presentation in accordance with the rules which govern the connexions of our *actual* presentations. In so doing we are merely conceiving certain presentations which we infer that this individual *would* have had *if* he had been born earlier or had had stronger or finer sense-organs, etc. We infer this from the presentations which he is actually having and the empirical rules which we have found to govern sequences of presentations within an individual. Thus the series of phenomenal conditions of a given phenomenon comes simply to this. It is the series of other presentations which we can infer, from the occurrence of this presentation and the rules governing sequences of presentations in an individual, that this individual *would* have or *would have* had under certain conditions. (It is, of course, assumed that these conditions, e.g. being born earlier, having better sense-organs, being differently situated in space, and so on, can themselves be described purely in terms of actual and possible presentations.)

Now, Kant argues, such a series is not intrinsically *finite*, as the theses of the antinomies allege. For, from the nature of the case, one would never arrive on these lines at the notion of some unique phenomenal condition beyond which no further phenomenal condition could be conceived. On the other hand, such a series is not intrinsically *infinite*, as the antitheses allege. At any moment it actually extends just so far as someone has actually carried his observations and his inferences from them in accordance with established empirical rules of sequence. We may sum this up as follows. The series of phenomenal conditions of a phenomenon is indefinitely *extensible*, and therefore not intrinsically finite in the sense contemplated by the theses. But at any moment it is only of *finite* length, and therefore it is not actually infinite in the sense contemplated by the antitheses.

This is the essence of Kant's solution. But there remains one other point to be added. Kant says that the principle of reason which starts us on these antinomies is valuable, provided we take it simply as a *maxim for our scientific procedure* and not as a law about the nature of things-in-themselves. The principle is always to seek for the totality of the conditions of any phenomenon. In actual fact this search must be vain, if Kant is right. But the natural desire which we have, as rational beings, to reach this impossible goal keeps us always investigating and trying to carry our researches further back in time, further outward in space, and deeper into the minute parts of matter. The principles of reason involved in the antinomies are valuable, but not as telling us anything about the nature of reality, which they claim to do. They are valuable only as the stick on which nature perpetually dangles a kind of transcendental carrot before the noses of scientists. Kant expresses this by saying that the principles of reason involved in the antinomies are *regulative* only and *not constitutive* (p. 450, A 509/B 537). It will be remembered that Kant drew a distinction among the principles of pure understanding between the axioms and anticipations, on the one hand, and the Analogies and post-ulates, on the other. He called the former 'constitutive' and the latter 'regulative' principles. It seems to me plain that he is using 'regulative' and 'constitutive' in different senses when he says that the principles of reason are only regulative and not constitutive, and when he says that the Analogies and postulates are only regulative and not constitutive. Nevertheless, I think it is easy to see the point of resemblance which he had in mind.

Suppose we compare, e.g., the second Analogy, i.e. the law of universal causation within the world of phenomena, with the principle that there must be a completed totality of conditions for any phenomenon. The fundamental difference is that the second Analogy states and proves a general fact about the world of phenomena, whilst the principle of completed conditions only seems to do so. The resemblance is this. The second Analogy does not tell you *what* causes *what*; it tells you only that every phenomenal event is determined in accordance with some empirical rule or other by earlier phenomenal events. But in so doing it does give rise to a positive mental attitude in the search for causes. It encourages one to go on looking for them, even where they are not at all obvious, by assuring one that they are there somewhere to be found. The principle of the totality of conditions acts in the same way by encouraging continued research into phenomenal conditions. But, according to Kant, the encouragement here rests on a delusion. There is not in fact a completed condition or set of conditions to be found in the phenomenal world.

1.3.2 Application to the mathematical antinomies

I will now consider, with special reference to the *mathematical* antinomies, how far this type of solution is satisfactory.

(1) One might object to the extremely subjectivist view of phenomenal objects which the solution presupposes. E.g., take the statement that the sun existed before there were any men. On the present view this would simply mean that *if* there had been men before there actually were any, they *would* have had presentations like those which we have when we say that we see the sun, feel its warmth, and so on. Again, take the statement that there may be stars beyond the furthest that have been seen through the strongest available telescope. On the present view this means merely that *if* men were situated on some very remote star of *if* they had stronger telescopes, they might have presentations like those which we have when we say that we are seeing a star.

Now there are at least three comments to be made on this. (a) It seems very doubtful whether this is all, or indeed a part, of what we mean when we say that the sun existed before there were men or that there may be stars so distant that no one has seen them. These statements about the presentations which *would* be had or would *have been* had, if certain conditions *were to be* or *had been* fulfilled, seem to be rather *consequences* of existential propositions about physical objects than *analyses of the meaning* of these propositions. (b) This kind of analysis can be of no use unless the hypothetical unfulfilled conditions can themselves be stated wholly in terms of actual and possible presentations. It seems very doubtful whether this could be done. The fundamental difficulty is not the endless complexity of detail which would be needed for a full analysis on these lines. It is the question whether the conditions can be intelligibly stated without presupposing a common objective time-system, and a common objective system either of absolute space or of independent bodies in spatial relations to each other and to the bodies of human percipients. (c) This difficulty is hard enough for *any* kind of phenomenalist. But it is particularly hard for a phenomenalist who holds the Kantian doctrine that time and space are merely a system of relations imposed by each individual on his own presentations. On such a theory what can be meant by talking of the presentations which I should have had *if* I had lived at any earlier period? What is to be understood by the supposition of my having lived at an earlier period than I did? My time-system begins with my first presentation and ends with my last presentation. The same is true *mutatis mutandis* of the time-system of any other individual. And there is no more sense in talking of a *common* time-system, in which the time-systems of various individuals are located, than in talking of presentations which are common to several individuals or which do not occur in any individual.

(2) Suppose we ignore these difficulties. Suppose that a meaning can be given, in terms of the theory, to the antecedents of the conditional propositions which are essential to the theory. Then we might ask whether similar questions will not arise, in terms of Kant's theory of phenomena, to those which originally led to the mathematical antinomies. It surely must be the case either that a man would or that he would not have had visual, tactual and auditory presentations if he had existed more than ten million years ago. Suppose it is true that he would have had such presentations no matter how long ago he might have lived. Then, in terms of the phenomenalist theory, we could say that the material world had no beginning. Suppose, on the other hand, it is true that there is a certain date in the past before which a man would have had no such presentations if he had lived then. Then, in terms of the phenomenalist theory, we could say that the material world began to exist at a certain date in the past. So it seems to me that, if Kant's phenomenalist theory could be stated so as to be consistent and intelligible, the question whether the world did or did not begin at some date in the past could be stated in terms of it. Each alternative would be intelligible, and they would be mutually exclusive and collectively exhaustive. Similar remarks apply to the question whether the world is limited or unlimited in space. And the same is true of the second antinomy. It must be the case that an observer who used stronger and stronger means of magnification either *would* always go on getting more and more detailed visual presentations, or that a point would be reached after which his visual presentations would *not* become more detailed. On the first alternative, we could say, in terms of the phenomenalist theory, that a bit of matter is infinitely divisible. On the second alternative, we could say, in terms of the same theory, that a bit of matter consists of ultimate parts which are simple.

(3) Now it seems to me that Kant sometimes sees this point quite clearly and gives the right answer. But sometimes he seems not to see it, and then he gives the wrong answer. In particular, he tries to distinguish the cases of the first and the second antinomies; and I think that he gives the right answer for the first and the wrong one for the second.

(4) The right answer is as follows. Both alternatives can be stated in terms of Kant's theory of phenomena, if that theory itself can be stated consistently. And one or other of them must be true and one or other must be false. But, when the alternatives are thus restated, there can be *no arguments a priori* for or against either of them. Whether a man would or would not have had visual, tactual, and auditory sensations whenever or wherever he had lived depends on the nature of things-in-themselves, about which we neither know nor can know anything *a priori*. Similarly, whether a man would or would not continually go on getting more and more differentiated presentations as the strength of his optical instruments was increased, depends on the nature of things-in-themselves. Now the trouble about the antinomies was not that we could not decide between the alternatives, but that it seemed possible to prove both of them or to disprove both of them. The correct answer is for Kant to show that, on his view of matter and space and time, the *questions* can be restated and are unanswerable *a priori*, whilst the *arguments* collapse, because founded on considerations which do not apply to mere presentations. All that remains is the practical maxim never to treat the earliest or the remotest or the minutest phenomenal condition which you have yet discovered as being really ultimate. For you can always *conceive* the possibility of an earlier or remoter or minuter phenomenal condition. And you can always ascribe the fact that you have not yet found it to defects in your senses, or your instruments of observation, or your powers of reasoning from phenomena to their phenomenal conditions.

Kant takes the correct view in the following passages. (a) p. 442 (A496/B524). 'The cause of the empirical conditions of this advance, i.e. that which determines *what* members I shall meet with, or how far I shall meet with *any* members, in my regress, is transcendental. It is therefore necessarily unknown to me.' (b) In the solution of the first antinomy (pp. 455ff, A517ff/B545ff) he again takes the correct view, except in the second and third paragraphs on p. 457, which are inconsistent with that view.

The incorrect view, which Kant continually slips into, first appears in the last sentence of the second paragraph on p. 444. Here he certainly seems to say that we can be sure that we *always shall* be able in principle to find earlier, remoter, and minuter empirical conditions. The correct doctrine is that we can never be sure that *we shall not* be able to find such empirical conditions. The other doctrine would imply that we know something very definite and positive about things-in-themselves, viz. that they would supply presentations to a person at every date and every place at which he might be. This would imply that we know the world to be infinite in time and space, when that statement is interpreted in terms of Kant's view of phenomena.

Kant suddenly reverts to this incorrect view in the middle of his solution of the first antinomy (p. 457, second and third paragraphs). Kant ends the third paragraph with the sentence 'Consequently an absolute limit of the world is impossible empirically and therefore also absolutely.' The correct doctrine is that, whether the regress of phenomenal conditions in space and time be in fact capable of unlimited extension or not, we never have any right to treat the last phenomenal condition which we happen to have reached as being the last which things-in-themselves will supply.

(5) The incorrect view seems to me to pervade the solution of the second antinomy, and to be involved in Kant's opinion that there is an essential difference between the two mathematical antinomies. This is connected with a distinction which he draws between an *infinite* and an *indefinite* regress (pp. 451–4, A 511–16/B 539–44). I will now try to explain this.

The distinction comes to this. In the case of the extension of the world in space and its duration in time we start by intuiting a fragmentary part. We then expand our concept of the world by a series of steps outward and backward from this intuited basis. We never *intuit* the world as a spatial whole or its history as a temporal whole. We can only *conceive of* it as a whole, and we have to do so in terms of this series of actual or possible steps from an intuited basis. This is what Kant calls an *indefinite* regress.

In the case of a bit of matter and its division into parts, the whole is given in intuition from the start. Kant says: 'Not only is there never any empirical ground for stopping in the division, but the further members of any continued division are empirically given *prior to* the continuation of the division' (p. 452, A 513/B 541). This is what Kant calls an *infinite* regress.

(6) Now it seems to me that Kant's notion of infinite, as opposed to indefinite, regress is inconsistent with his solution of the antinomies. On his view the question of division into parts is concerned with *phenomena,* and a phenomenon is a *presentation* which exists only in so far as it is presented to one particular individual on one particular occasion. Now the following two criticisms may be made.

(a) Let us admit that it is intelligible to hold that a presentation may contain parts which are not discriminated by the person whose presentation it is. We could then admit that all these parts are 'empirically given', even before the owner of the presentation has discriminated them, provided that this means no more than the tautology that they are parts of a whole which exists only in being presented to this person on this occasion. But, even so, what right has Kant to assume that, *however* far a person carries the process of discriminating parts in a presentation of his, there must *still* be further parts in it which he might discriminate? This is to assume that the presentation really does consist of parts within parts without end. All that Kant is justified in saying is that a person has never any positive reason for believing that any part which he has discriminated in one of his presentations is simple. But this makes the regress *indefinite* and not infinite.

(b) A still more radical criticism might be made. Is it intelligible to suggest that a presentation contains any parts except those which the person whose presentation it is discriminates in it at the time when he is having it? Suppose I look at an object first with the naked eye, then with a magnifying glass, then with a microscope, and so on. Suppose that I distinguish more parts at each of these stages. Then I am not by this process discovering more and more parts in *my original presentation*. What I am doing may be described as follows. At each stage I replace my previous presentation by a numerically different and more differentiated presentation. The various presentations in such a series are so interrelated that they are called more and more detailed presentations of the same object. On this view there is no reason to admit that any one of these presentations has any more parts than I actually discriminate in it at the time when I am having it. We could then simply reject Kant's contention that the parts which will be discriminated later are empirically given from the very first. The parts which are empirically given when I look through the microscope are parts of the presentation which begin to exist only when I begin to look through the microscope. They are not parts of the presentation which I had when I was looking through the magnifying glass. When I was still looking through the magnifying glass neither these parts nor the presentation of which they are parts had begun to exist, and therefore these parts cannot have been empirically given at that stage.

(7) Kant argues on pp. 448–9 (A 506–7/B 534–5) that the mathematical antinomies serve indirectly to prove the doctrine of the *Aesthetic* that space and time are forms of our intuition and apply only to phenomena. For it is only on the latter view that the contradictions which are developed in these two antinomies can be resolved. This contention suggests the following comments. (a) The arguments in these antinomies are extremely shaky, so that it is by no means certain that there is any contradiction to be resolved. (b) In so far as the arguments in certain places appeal to the conclusions of the *Aesthetic* it would be circular to use the solution of the antinomies as a support to those conclusions. (c) Even if the arguments were valid, and the appeals in some of them to the conclusions of the *Aesthetic* could be avoided, it is not obvious that the contradictions would not be resolved by some less drastic means than the extreme subjectivism which Kant here assumes.

2 The self and self-consciousness

Kant's account of the nature of the human self and of its knowledge of itself is extremely complicated, and it is doubtful whether a single consistent doctrine can be extracted from his various utterances. In the first place, we must distinguish between two views, which I will call the *critical view* and the *ethical view* of the self. There are certain features common to both of them. (1) In both Kant distinguishes between the *empirical or phenomenal* self, on the one hand, and the *noumenal or real* self, on the other. One's noumenal self is oneself as it really is, one's empirical self is oneself as it appears to one under the form of time. (2) In both Kant distinguishes two different cognitive faculties which are concerned with a person's awareness of himself and his own experiences and activities. These he calls *inner sense* and *apperception*. Inner sense, as its name implies, is a faculty belonging to the passive receptive department of one's mind, and it is concerned with particular existents. Apperception is a faculty belonging to the active intellectual department of one's mind. (3) In both views Kant holds that through inner sense a person can be aware of himself and of his states only as they appear under the subjectively imposed form of time, i.e. he can be aware only of himself as a phenomenon. The fundamental difference between the two views is concerned with apperception. In the *critical view* Kant consistently holds to his general doctrine that the human intellect is purely discursive. It enables us only to *think of* a particular, as something answering to such-and-such a description. It does not enable us to be *acquainted with* any particular. Nor does it enable us to know whether there is or is not a particular answering to a certain description. To settle such questions an appeal must always be made to the data of sense, either inner or outer. The other function which Kant ascribes to apperception, consistently with his general doctrine in the *Critique of Pure Reason*, is that of synthesising sense-given data in accordance with certain *a priori* concepts. Perhaps a better way of putting this would be to say that it provides the *a priori* scheme in accordance with which the imagination synthesises sense-given data and fills in gaps between them with appropriate images. In the *ethical view* it certainly seems as if Kant ascribes a very different function to apperception. It looks as if he takes it to be a kind of non-sensuous intuition, whereby a person can actually be acquainted with himself and certain of his activities, viz. the rational ones, as they are in themselves. This view of apperception is very much the same as Leibniz's. It is therefore not at all surprising that it should occur in Kant's pre-critical works. But it is surprising that it should occur both in certain passages in the *Critique of Pure Reason* and in the ethical works which were written still later.

As the *ethical view* is very closely bound up with Kant's doctrine of freedom and determinism, it will be best to treat it under that heading. For the present I shall confine myself to the *critical view*. This may itself be divided into two parts, viz. *epistemological* and *ontological*, though they are closely connected with each other. The former deals with the ways in which a human being cognises himself and his own experiences and activities. The latter is concerned with such questions as these: Can a human self be known to be a *substance*? Can it be shown to be *simple* and *indivisible*? Can anything be determined *a priori* as to its relation to the *body* of the human individual whose mind it is?

2.1 Epistemological part

The epistemological part of the *critical view* may be divided into the *theory of inner sense* and the *theory of transcendental apperception*. The former is treated in the *Aesthetic* in connexion with Kant's doctrine of time and in certain sections of the *Transcendental Deduction* B. The latter is treated mainly in the same sections of *Transcendental Deduction* B, but something is said about it also in the *Refutation of Idealism* which was added in B.

2.1.1 Inner sense

(1) The first account of inner sense is in the part of the *Aesthetic* where Kant is explaining and defending his doctrine of time (pp. 77–81, A 33–9/B 49–56). Time, Kant says, is 'nothing but the form of inner sense, i.e. of one's intuition of oneself and one's inner states' (p. 77, A 33/B 49). He goes on to say that this doctrine about time has caused much more difficulty than the corresponding doctrine about space. He tries to deal with the difficulties in §7 (pp. 79–80, A 36–9/B 53–6). He thinks that people feel the two following difficulties.

(a) They say: There is no doubt that our *experiences* come and go in a perpetual succession, whether or not there be independent external things or events corresponding to any of them. Therefore *they* at least must really be in time. If so, time cannot be merely a subjective form which a person imposes upon his own mental states.

To this Kant's answer is as follows. Certainly your experiences present themselves to you, when you are reflectively aware of them, as having temporal characteristics. But I never denied this; on the contrary, I have asserted it. What I say is that, *as they are in themselves*, they have no such characteristics. The temporal characteristics are projected into them by yourself in the act of being reflectively aware of them. 'If. . . I could intuit myself or be intuited by another being, without this condition of sensibility, the very same determinations which we now represent to ourselves as alterations would be known as something into which the notion of time, and therefore of alteration, would not enter' (p. 79, A 37/B 54).

(b) The second difficulty is this. People readily admit that a distinction must be drawn between their presentations and the external things and events of which these are appearances. For there are all the facts about sensory illusions and variation which idealists and sceptics have adduced from time immemorial. But a person does not see why he should distinguish between his own mental states as they are in themselves and as they appear to him when he is relectively aware of them. He simply takes for granted that this reflective awareness is a pure act of acquaintance, which neither adds anything to its object nor distorts it in any way.

To this Kant answers as follows. People have failed to recognise that external objects, as perceived by sight, touch, etc., and oneself and one's states, as revealed to reflective awareness, are both in the same position. 'In neither case can their reality as representations be questioned, and in both cases they belong only to appearance . . .' (p. 80, A 38/B 55). Once this is realised we can assert that our mental states, as they are in themselves, are non-temporal, and yet admit that, as they appear to us in our reflective awareness of them, they are temporal.

(c) On p. 77 (A 34/B 50) Kant says that time is an *a priori* condition of all appearances whatever, whilst space is an *a priori* condition only of a certain sub-class of appearances. The reason that he gives is this. 'All representations, whether they have for their objects outer things or not, belong . . . as determinations of the mind to our inner state.' He adds that time is 'the *immediate* condition of inner appearances, and thereby the *mediate* condition of outer appearances'.

(2) Kant returned to this topic in certain new sections of the *Aesthetic* which he added in B (pp. 87–9, B 66–71). These contain some very obscure statements. Kant opens the discussion by saying that he will now produce an argument in confirmation of the doctrine that the objects of both inner and outer sense are mere appearances. He begins with the objects of outer sense, i.e. of sight, touch, hearing, etc. He asserts that all that we can learn about such objects by *intuition* concerns their *relations*. We can perceive their *relative* positions at any moment, and the changes and rates of change of their *relative* positions from moment to moment. We can discover laws governing the *relative* motions of perceived objects. On the basis of these we can ascribe to certain perceived objects certain inherent moving forces, e.g. such-and-such elasticity, inertia, gravitational attraction, magnetism, and so on. But these forces are describable only in terms of the effects in the way of relative motion which these objects would produce or would suffer if they stood in certain spatial relations to certain other objects. 'What it is that is present in this or that location, or what it is that is operative in the things themselves apart from change of location, is not given through intuition' (p. 87, B 66–7).

Kant then argues as follows. To know a thing as it is in itself cannot consist in merely knowing its relations to other things. Therefore what we learn by intuition about the objects of the external senses is not knowledge about them as they are in themselves. Kant then makes a step which seems to me to be a *non sequitur*. 'We may therefore conclude that . . . outer sense . . . can contain in its representation only the relation of an object to the subject . . .' (p. 87, B 67). I cannot see any justification for passing from the premiss that intuition informs us only about the relations of one object to another *object* to the conclusion that it informs us only about the relations of objects to the *subject*, i.e. to the person who intuits these objects.

However that may be, Kant now passes from the objects of outer sense to those of introspection. He says that the same conclusion must be drawn about them too, i.e. we can know them only as they appear to us under the subjectively imposed form of time. The argument is extremely obscure, and I do not pretend to understand it as a whole. But the following points seem to emerge.

(a) Kant says that the 'proper materials' which constitute the contents of one's mind and are therefore objects of introspection are the representations of the *outer senses*. This would seem to imply that what one is presented with when one introspects are always visual, tactual, auditory, and suchlike sense-data, and perhaps also images of similar kinds. I do not know what Kant means by 'proper' in this context. He certainly did not deny that emotions, desires, bodily feelings, etc. are also part of the content of the empirical self and are presented to one when one introspects. I suspect that he is mainly concerned to deny that emotions, desires, bodily feelings, etc. are also part of the content of the empirical self and are presented to one when one introspects. I suspect that he is mainly concerned to deny that introspection ever presents to us our own *mental acts*, e.g. acts of perceiving, attending, inferring, etc.

(b) Space, as an innate system of intuitable relationships, exists in one's mind prior to one's ostensible perceptions of this or that particular external object. But one intuits particular spatial relations only when the external senses present one with this or that external object located in one's innate spatial system. Similarly time, as an innate system of intuitable relationships, exists in one's mind prior to one's introspective awareness of this or that particular experience. But one intuits particular temporal relations only when introspection presents one with this or that experience located in one's innate temporal system. Now it is admitted that ostensibly perceiving a certain external object cannot consist in being directly acquainted with an independently existing thing and in intuiting the qualities which belong to it as it is in itself. Similarly it must be admitted that introspecting a certain experience cannot consist in being directly acquainted with an independently existing state of oneself and in intuiting the qualities which belong to it as it is in itself. Even if this introspection were as veridical as such a cognition possibly could be, it would consist in perceiving as *temporal* a state of oneself which is in itself *non-temporal*.

(c) A man cannot have the experience of ostensibly perceiving an external object except through having various sense-impressions, arranging them unconsciously in his innate spatial system, supplementing them by appropriate images, and synthesising them in accordance with certain innate intellectual principles. Similarly he cannot become conscious of himself except through being introspectively aware of a manifold of particular experiences which are contents of himself, arranging them unconsciously in his innate temporal system, and synthesising them in accordance with certain innate intellectual principles.

(d) When Kant describes the power of becoming aware of one's own experiences as a *sense* he implies that it is a *passive* power of the mind. The mind has to be acted upon by something, and its states of introspective awareness are what it produces when so stimulated. If we ask: '*What* acts on the mind in this case?', Kant's answer is as follows. It is the *mind itself* in the exercise of certain of its active powers. If we now ask: '*Which* of its active powers?', Kant's answer seems to be this. The mental activity which calls forth states of reflective awareness in a mind is its unconscious activity of arranging in itself its own presentations derived from the outer senses. Presumably this activity of arranging must be *non-temporal*, and it is certainly non-introspectible. And presumably the arrangement which it brings about must be in itself some kind of *non-temporal* and *non-spatial* pattern. But that arrangement appears to the mind, under the stimulation of its own non-temporal activity of arranging, as a *temporal* pattern of sense-data, images, etc. constituting its own mental history.

This is the best sense that I can make of the extremely obscure subsection II (pp. 87–8, B 66–9).

(3) Kant returned once more to the same topic in §24 of *Transcendental Deduction* B (pp. 165–8, B 152–7). He says there that there is a paradox, which everyone must have felt, in his account of time and inner sense in the section of the *Aesthetic* which we have just been considering. His doctrine is that each of us intuits himself only as he is inwardly *affected*. Now Kant says: 'This would seem to be contradictory, since we should then have to be in a passive relation to ourselves' (p. 166, B 153). Kant thinks that it was in order to avoid this contradiction that most psychologists have regarded introspective awareness, not as a form of sensibility, but as an act of direct acquaintance with oneself and one's experiences as they are in themselves.

I take it that the difficulty is that, if a person acts on himself, then he is at once active and passive in respect of the same transaction, and that this seems contradictory. If this were the only or the main difficulty in Kant's doctrine of inner sense, I do not think he need have worried much about it. The main interest is in what he says in solution of the alleged difficulty, for this throws light on his doctrine. He asserts definitely that what *acts* in this case is the mind in its synthesising capacity, i.e. the understanding operating as productive imagination. What is *acted upon* is the same mind in its passive receptive capacity, i.e. the sensibility.

(4) Then come some very difficult remarks about the inner sense. Kant says that it 'contains the mere form of intuition, but without combination of the manifold in it, and therefore so far contains no *determinate* intuition'. A determinate intuition of inner sense becomes possible only through 'a transcendental act of imagination, i.e. the synthetic influence of the understanding on the inner sense' (pp. 166–7, B 154). I think that this becomes more intelligible if we compare it with the statement about space in the footnote on pp. 170–1 (B 160–1) which I referred to when commenting on *Transcendental Deduction* B. Kant says there that pure space, considered as a peculiar kind of object contemplated by geometers, is not presented to us by pure intuition alone, as he had suggested in the *Aesthetic*. Pure intuition alone provides only a pure unorganised spatial manifold. To make space into an object this manifold must be synthesised by the productive imagination, working on a plan imposed by the understanding. Now I am fairly sure that Kant is here putting forward a similar view about pure time considered as an object. In the *Aesthetic* he talked as if pure time were presented to us as a whole by intuition alone. What he is now saying is that pure intuition alone supplies only an unorganised manifold of purely temporal elements. These must be synthesised by the productive imagination, working on a plan imposed by the understanding, if pure time is to be presented as an object, comparable to the pure space which is the object considered by geometers.

On p. 167 (B 154–5) Kant goes into further detail about this synthesis which produces time as an object. He says that, in order to represent time to ourselves, we must first in imagination *draw* a straight line. Then we must concentrate our attention, not on the *product*, i.e. the resulting imagined line, nor on the items synthesised, i.e. the elements of the purely *spatial* manifold, but on the *process* of synthesising. This he describes as 'motion, as an act of the subject and not as a determination of an object' (p. 167, B 155). He says explicitly that 'the synthesis of the manifold in space first produces the concept of succession'. So far as I can understand his doctrine, it comes to this. It is this act of imaginatively drawing geometrical lines, and thus synthesising purely *spatial* elements, which reacts upon the inner sense. This effects a synthesis of the unorganised purely *temporal* elements, which are all that inner intuition by itself can provide. As a result of this synthesis of these purely temporal elements one is presented with stretches of pure time. In these we locate the sense-data, images, etc. which are presented to us when we introspect.

(5) At the end of this same §24 (p. 168, B156) Kant gives an argument which professes to show that inner sense enables a person to intuit himself only as he is *inwardly affected* by himself and therefore only as a *phenomenon*. It is easy to state the premisses of the argument. They are the following. (a) We can present time to ourselves as an *object* only under the image of a line which we draw in imagination. (b) We can date our own experiences and assign various durations to them only by reference to changes which we perceive in external things, e.g. the apparent movement of the sun, the movement of the hands of a clock, and so on. From these two premisses Kant draws the conclusion that 'the determinations of inner sense have . . . to be arranged as appearances in time in precisely the same manner in which we arrange those of outer sense in space'. He then adds as a third premiss that space is a subjective form in which we arrange the data supplied by the outer senses. From this he draws the following conclusion. in introspection a person is aware of himself only as affected by himself, just as in sense-perception he is aware of external objects only as they affect him.

2.1.2 Apperception

The most important passages dealing with apperception, in connexion with self-consciousness, are §24 and §25 of *Transcendental Deduction* B. It is also mentioned in *Refutation of Idealism* B, and particularly in the corrective note to the refutation which Kant introduced near the end of the preface to B (pp. 34–6, B xl–xli).

I suppose that Kant took over the word 'apperception' from Leibniz. For Leibniz it means acquaintance by a person with himself and his own states of mind. It will be remembered that Leibniz held that there is no reason why a mind should not have perceptions and other experiences with which it is not acquainted; that in fact every human mind has a vast number of such states; and that no mind below the human level is ever acquainted with itself or with any of its states. A mind below the human level has infinitely many *perceptions* but no *apperception*, according to Leibniz. Now Leibniz held the following two views. (1) Sensation and intellectual cognition do not differ in kind. Both are cognition, and they differ only in respect of a feature which he calls 'confusion'. Sensation is cognition which is *very confused*; intellectual cognition is cognition which is *clear and distinct*. (2) A mind is aware of itself and its own states so far and only so far as its cognition is *clear and distinct*. Therefore Leibniz would count apperception as combining the following two characteristics. (1) It is *intellectual* cognition, since it is clear and distinct cognition. (2) It is acquaintance with *particular existents*, viz. oneself and its states.

Now Kant could not possibly accept this. He holds the following three views. (1) Sensation and intellectual cognition are radically different in kind. In sensation one is passive and receptive. A sensation is a state evoked in one's mind by the action of something upon it. In intellectual cognition one is exercising a spontaneous activity of one's mind. (2) In order to have knowledge of any particular existent, whether it be a substance or an event, both sensation and intellectual cognition are needed. (a) Sensation is needed to provide concrete particular data. The *human* intellect is incapable of doing this; though Kant holds that we can conceive the possibility of a non-human intellect which would supply or create its own data. (b) The human mind, under the guidance of the intellect, must unconsciously *synthesise* the data provided by sense, in accordance with certain innate concepts, and supplement these data with appropriate images. (c) Finally the mind must make explicit judgments. The *form* of the judgment expresses the innate principles and concepts, in accordance with which the synthesis has been conducted. Its particular subject and predicate are determined by the special data which sensation has provided for synthesis. (3) Sensation is never acquaintance with substances or events as they are in themselves. There is a certain structural characteristic, viz. temporality, common to *all* sensations, which they derive from the mind in which they occur. And there is a certain other structural characteristic, viz. spatiality, common to a whole important class of sensations, though not to all sensations, which they derive from the mind in which they occur.

It is evident, then, that Kant cannot accept apperception in Leibniz's sense. For it would combine characteristics which he holds to be incompatible. In the first place, it would be purely *intellectual* cognition and yet would provide knowledge of *particular existents*, viz. oneself and one's various experiences. Secondly it would reveal these particular existents as they are in *themselves*, and not as tinged with certain structural features supplied by the percipient's mind. The upshot of the matter in this. (1) Kant keeps Leibniz's term 'apperception', and he uses it as Leibniz had done to denote a form of purely intellectual cognition. But, consistently with his general view, he denies that it is acquaintance with particular existents. (2) He introduces another faculty, viz. *internal sense*, which Leibniz never contemplated. This resembles Leibniz's apperception, in so far as it supplies the particular data which are essential for any concrete knowledge of one's empirical self and its various states. But in every other respect it differs from Leibniz's apperception. Consistently with his general view, Kant denies that it presents ourselves and our states to us as they are in themselves. It provides only unorganised data; and knowledge of oneself and one's states does not arise until these have been synthesised under the guidance of the understanding. Moreover, these data are not one's own states as they are in themselves. They are the effects of certain

activities of oneself upon oneself, and they are all marked with the characteristic of temporality. This is a subjective form supplied by the mind itself
in reacting to the stimulus of its own activities. It does not belong to the
self and its activities in themselves. Therefore, when the data of inner sense
have been synthesised by apperception, the result is not knowledge of
oneself and one's states as they are in themselves. It is knowledge of them
only as they appear to oneself under the temporal form which has been
imposed upon them by oneself.

I think that this comes out fairly clearly in the following quotations. 'In
the synthetic original unity of apperception I am conscious of myself, *not*
as I appear to myself, *nor* as I am in myself, but only *that* I am. This
representation is a *thought*, not an intuition. In order to *know* myself there is
required (in addition to the act of thought which brings the manifold of
every possible intuition to the unity of apperception) a *determinate mode of
intuition*, whereby this manifold is given . . . It follows that . . . the
determination of my existence can take place only in conformity with the
form of inner sense, according to the special mode in which the manifold
which I combine is given in inner intuition. Accordingly I have no *knowledge* of myself as I am, but only as I appear to myself' (*Transcendental
Deduction* B, §25, pp. 168–9, B 157–8). (In this and other passages when
Kant talks of the 'determination of my own existence' he means simply
getting concrete determinate knowledge of myself and my states.)

'Just as for knowledge of an *object distinct from me* I require, beside the
thought of an object in general [viz. the category of thinghood], an
intuition by which I can determine that general concept, so for *knowledge of
myself* I require beside the thought of myself an intuition of the manifold in
me, by which I determine this thought . . . I exist as an intelligence which is
conscious solely of its *power of combining*. But, in respect of the manifold
which it has to combine, I am subjected to a limiting condition . . . viz.
that this combination can be made intuitable to me only according to
relations of *time* . . . Such an intelligence therefore can know itself only as it
appears to itself in respect of an intuition . . . which cannot be supplied by
the understanding itself' (*Transcendental Deduction* B, §25, p. 169, B 158–9).

In the footnote to preface B xl (p. 35) Kant talks of the '*intellectual
consciousness of one's existence*'. He says that this is 'prior to the empirical
consciousness of it. But the inner intuition, in which alone my existence
can be determined, is *sensible* and is bound up with the condition of time.' I
think it is obvious that Kant means by the 'intellectual consciousness of
one's existence' what he elsewhere calls 'apperception'. And when he says
that it is 'prior to' empirical consciousness of one's existence he is thinking
of *logical* priority, not temporal priority. He means that apperception
provides the general notion of a self owning a vareity of states, but that
inner intuition provides all the concrete data and the form of temporality.

Empirical consciousness of oneself and its states arises only when these data have been synthesised as a set of simultaneous and successive experiences of determinate characters, in accordance with the general plan which is innate in the understanding.

There is an important footnote on p. 169, B158 (*Transcendental Deduction* B §25). It is somewhat obscure, and I will state what I take to be the meaning of the main points in it. It opens with the sentences 'The "I think" expresses the act of determining my existence. Existence is already given thereby, but the mode in which I am to determine that existence, i.e. the manifold belonging to it, is not thereby given.' The interpretation which I would suggest for this is the following. Suppose a person makes a judgment which he would naturally express in English by saying 'I am thinking'. Then the mere *occurrence* of that judgment guarantees its *truth*. For judging is a mode of thinking. Now in making this judgment the person who does so is ascribing a certain activity, viz. *thinking*, to a certain object, viz. to that entity, whatever it may be, which he denotes by the word 'I' on that occasion. Since such a judgment is true whenever it occurs, its occurrence guarantees the existence of its subject. Whenever such a judgment occurs it is certain that there is something answering to the word 'I' as used by that person on that occasion, and it is certain that this something is exercising the activity described as 'thinking'. But that is absolutely all that the occurrence of such a judgment guarantees. I think that Kant may have had Descartes' *Cogito ergo sum* in mind, and that he may want to point out that this is all that it amounts to. Descartes obviously thought that the occurrence of such a judgment on any occasion guarantees a great deal more than this, viz. the existence of a persistent mental substance, which is acquainted with itself and uses 'I' as a proper name for itself. Kant is concerned here to point out that nothing of the sort is guaranteed by the mere fact that a person on a certain occasion makes the judgment which he would express by saying 'I am thinking'. All concrete knowledge about oneself requires concrete data, which have to be supplied to one's intellect from elsewhere and worked up into determinate introspective judgments. In that respect knowledge of oneself is in exactly the same position as knowledge of any foreign object.

The remainder of the footnote may be paraphrased as follows. The data, by means of which I make determinate judgments about myself and my states, are presented to me intuitively under the form of time, which is innate in my mind. But my acts of synthesising these data, and thus determinately specifying myself and my states, are *not* presented to me under any innate form of intuition. They are not presented to me *intuitively* at all. As regards my mental *activities* all that I can do is to *conceive* myself as something which actively synthesises data passively received. I have no special data by which I can further specify these activities. The only way in which I can specify them is by reference to the various products of their action on sense-given data. I can cognise them only descriptively, and the descriptions are in terms of their products.

2.1.3 Comments

I will now make some comments on Kant's critical theory of self-consciousness.

(1) It is evident that Kant held that empirical consciousness of oneself and one's states is closely analogous to perception of external things and events. Now this might be true even if Kant's main epistemological doctrines were false, and it might be false even if his other epistemological doctrines were true. So it will be worth while to begin by considering it on its own merits or demerits. In order to do this we will begin by reminding ourselves of the main admitted facts about our ostensible perceptions of external objects. I shall take the word 'object' to cover both things and events here.

(a) To have an ostensible perception of an external object involves as an essential factor having a visual, tactual, or auditory *sensation*. (b) But it involves something more than and quite different from this. It involves having certain non-inferential and uncritical *beliefs* or *quasi-beliefs*. The *details* of these on any occasion are determined partly by the nature of the present sensation and partly by the traces of past experiences which it excites by association. It may well be, as Kant would assert, that the characteristic *determinable outline* of all such beliefs depends on factors which are innate in the human mind. But, however that may be, one thing is certain about such perceptual beliefs or quasi-beliefs. Each of them goes beyond anything that is or could possibly be given in the sensation which occasions it. One believes, e.g., that one is being presented by sight with a thing that has an inside as well as an outside, a back as well as a front, temperature and hardness as well as colour, causal properties as well as perceptible qualities, and so on. One believes that it existed before one began to perceive it and that it will not cease to exist merely because one ceases to perceive it. One believes that it is perceptible to other persons. And so on. It is because ostensible perceptions of external objects involve these beliefs or quasi-beliefs that they can be either veridical or delusive in *detail,* as everyone admits. And it is because of this that it is at least *prima facie* intelligible to suggest, as some eminent philosophers have done, that *all* ostensible perception of external objects is *delusive in principle*. (c) It is commonly held, on empirical grounds, that the sensations of sight and touch and hearing, which are essential constituents in our ostensible perceptions of external objects, are causally conditioned in the following way. (i) The *immediate* necessary and sufficient *bodily* condition of each of them is a certain contemporary physical alteration in a certain part of the percipient's brain. (There may also be contemporary *mental* conditions which must be fulfilled if a sensation is to arise. But, if so, we know little or nothing about them.) (ii) In general this immediate necessary and sufficient bodily condition of a sensation is a rather remote causal descendant of a certain physical process in a certain material thing outside the percipient's body. This sets up a transmissive process in the physical medium between the external thing and the percipient's body; this in turn causes a disturbance in certain parts of certain of his receptor sense-organs; and this in turn sets up a transmissive process in certain of the nerves which connect those organs with his brain.

(2) Let us next consider one's empirical awareness of oneself and one's own experiences, and compare and contrast this with ostensible perception of external objects.

(a) One very important part of the content of one's mind at any moment when one is awake and in normal surroundings is those very same visual, tactual, and auditory sensations which are constituents of one's ostensible perceptions of external objects. Normally one just *has* these sensations and ostensibly perceives external objects and their qualities, relations, and alterations *by means of* them. But one *can* direct a special act of inspective attention upon this, that, or another of them. When one does so one observes its intrinsic qualities and relations to one's other sensations. One may then notice, e.g., that the visual sense-datum by which one is ostensibly seeing a *circular* external object is itself *elliptical*. And so on. This kind of inspective attention to one's sense-data is a comparatively rare and sophisticated activity. It is performed deliberately and carefully only by psychologists, philosophers, and artists in the course of their professional business. But it no doubt occurs occasionally and carelessly in all of us, especially when there is something notably odd in one's sense-data, e.g. when one 'sees double' or is presented with the peculiar appearance of a stick half in air and half in water.

(b) Another important part of the content of one's mind at any moment is the sensations and feelings by which one ostensibly perceives, not external objects, but certain states located within one's own body. Examples are twinges of toothache, itchings, feelings of strain, etc. These are occasional outstanding items in a vague and fairly constant background of what may be called 'bodily feeling'. These two may be inspectively attended to, as, e.g., when one tries to describe a painful bodily feeling to a doctor or dentist.

(c) A third important part of the content of one's mind at most times is *images*. These occur in at least the following different ways. (i) In association with sensations. Such images are an essential factor in ostensible perceptions of external objects and of one's own body. They co-operate with the associated sensations in determining the details of our perceptual judgments or quasi-judgments. (ii) As constituents of ostensible memories. (iii) As constituents of anticipations. (iv) As constituents of imaginings and reveries. (v) More or less loose, and not as constituents of any experience which involves believing or entertaining propositions.

(3) As regards awareness of one's empirical self, I think that it is necessary to draw a distinction analogous to the distinction between *having a sensation* and *ostensibly perceiving* by means of it an external object. One certainly thinks of oneself as a persistent something, which had various experiences before the present moment and will have other experiences after that moment. Even at the present moment it is held to be having a whole background of experiences beside the particular out-standing experience which one happens then to be specially noticing and inspecting. Then, again, it is held to have had innumerable experiences beside the comparatively few and comparatively isolated ones which one ostensibly remembers at any moment. Lastly, one thinks of oneself as something which has certain very general innate mental powers, e.g. the power of forming associations, of making abstractions, of producing images, and so on. And one thinks of oneself as having other more determinate acquired mental dispositions, e.g. the power to understand sentences in certain languages, the power to reproduce intelligently certain proofs in geometry, and so on. It is plain, then, that one means by the phrase 'my self' a *continuant*, with a history consisting of mental occurrents of various kinds, and possessed of various *causal* properties. If that is so, it is equally plain that it is not the kind of object which could conceivably be cognised in any one isolated momentary intuition. The fragments which one is introspecting or remembering at any moment must present them-selves to one *as* fragments. They must be filled out with thoughts or images of simultaneous states which one is not specially attending to, and of earlier states which one is not now remembering and perhaps could not now remember. And these must be thought of, however vaguely, as forming the history of a persistent *continuant* with characteristic active and passive *casual* properties. So far I entirely agree with Kant.

But it must be admitted that the differences between self-perception and perception of external objects are at least as great as the analogies. (a) The most fundamental difference is this. An external object is thought of as something which could in principle be perceived by any number of different persons. The sensations by which anyone perceives it are private to him, but what he perceives by means of them is a *public* object. On the other hand, a self is thought of as something which could in principle be perceived by only *one* person, viz. the one whose self it is. It is essentially a *private* object. (b) Suppose we take a phenomenalist view both of selves and of physical things. Then the characteristic interrelations of a number of actual and possible sense-data which entitle them all to count as *appearances of a certain physical thing* are of one kind. The characteristic interrelations of a number of actual and possible sense-data, images, feelings, etc. which entitle them all to count as *experiences of a certain self* are of an utterly different kind. Suppose, as Kant holds, that synthesis according to an innate plan is needed in both cases in order to generate perception of an object out of originally unorganised data. Then surely the innate plan, which the synthetic activity of the imagination follows, must be fundamentally different when it generates a perception of an external object and when it generates a perception of oneself. Kant never considered in detail what the principles of the synthesis would be in the latter case.

(4) Let us next consider awareness of a particular experience of one's own, either by simultaneous introspective attention or by subsequent memory. How far is this analogous to perceiving an external event, e.g. to seeing a flash of lightning or hearing the discharge of a gun? There are three points to notice about the latter. (a) The external event perceived is essentially *public*, though the sensation by which a particular person perceives it is private to him. (b) The sensation by which a person perceives an external event is a somewhat remote causal descendant of that external event. This becomes specially obvious in the case of hearing. For there may be a considerable time-interval between, e.g., the discharge of a gun and the occurrence of the auditory sensation by which a distant percipient hears that event. (c) When we reflect we find that we have to draw a *three-fold* distinction in regard to perception of external physical events. (i) As already said, we must distinguish between the external event itself, i.e. the *physical* flash or bang, and the sensation by which a particular person perceives it. The physical flash or bang occurs at a certain date and place and has a certain objective intensity. The sensations by which various individuals perceive it occur at various times, all of which are later than the objective date, and have various intensities. (ii) In addition to this we must distinguish between a perceived physical event and certain other events which scientists assert to be invariably associated with it but which are not perceptible by the senses. E.g. scientists assert that, whenever there is a perceptible flash at a place, there are certain correlated events going on in certain atoms and electrons there. In one sense we should say that these are imperceptible by us. In another sense we might say that, in perceiving the flash, we were perceiving them. Let us call these imperceptible events which scientists allege to be correlated with perceptible ones '*scientific* events'. Let us say that the correlated perceptible events are 'manifestations' of the scientific events. Then we might say that, in perceiving a manifestation of a scientific event, we are '*indirectly* perceiving' the scientific event.

(5) We can now ask ourselves how far all this is applicable to awareness

of a particular experience of one's own, either by simultaneous introspective attention or by subsequent memory.

(a) The first question is this: What is supposed to correspond to the sensation and what is supposed to correspond to the perceived external event? (i) In the case of *remembering* an experience there seems to be a fairly obvious answer. We might compare the memory-image, by which a past experience is remembered, to the auditory or visual sensation by which an external event is perceived. And the event remembered would correspond to the external event perceived. There is certainly this much analogy, though there are, no doubt, very important differences. One of them is this. Any experience is essentially *private*. It can be remembered only by the person whose experience it was. But perceptible external events are essentially *public*. (ii) In the case of simultaneous introspective awareness of a sensation or image or feeling, it is very difficult to see what is supposed to be analogous to the sensation and what to the perceived event in the case of ordinary sense-perception. Suppose, e.g., that I introspect a contemporary feeling of toothache or a contemporary visual sensation. Suppose we say that the experience of introspecting it is analogous to that of perceiving an external event, and that the introspected experience is analogous to a *perceived external event*, e.g. a physical flash or bang. Then what is supposed to be analogous to the visual or auditory *sensation* by which a person perceives an external event? Suppose, on the other hand, we say that the introspected experience, e.g. the feeling of toothache, is analogous to the visual or auditory *sensation* by which one perceives an external event, e.g. a distant flash or a bang. Then what is supposed to be analogous to the *external event* which a person perceives by means of a visual or an auditory sensation? It looks as if there were no room, in the case of simultaneous introspective awareness of an experience, for anything corresponding to the distinction between sensation and perceived external event in the case of ordinary sense-perception.

(b) The only way out of this difficulty that I can think of is the following. We might take the introspected experience, or the experience as introspected, to be analogous to the *sensation* in ordinary sense-perception. And we might say that, by means of it, a person *indirectly* perceives something in himself analogous to a *scientific* event. This would be some event or process in himself which is intrinsically non-introspectible but which manifests itself through the introspected experience or the experience as introspected. This would perhaps fit in with Kant's statement that the stimulus which acts on the inner sense of a person is the unconscious exercise of his own powers of synthesis and arrangement. We might compare this to the imperceptible processes in atoms and electrons which are alleged to be the common causal ancestor of the visual sensations by which various persons perceive a physical flash in an external thing.

(c) It seems to me that this analogy breaks down in several directions when one examines it in detail. Though scientific events in the physical world are held to be in principle imperceptible, they are held to be continuous in certain important respects with events which we can and do perceive with our senses. They are thought of in terms of space, time, and motion. And the determinate beliefs which scientists hold about them are derived by ordinary inductive and deductive reasoning from the observations which have been made on perceptible events and their correlations. None of this is true of the synthesising activities which Kant thinks manifest themselves to us in a remote and disguised form in our introspected experiences. These synthesising activities are held to be in themselves neither temporal nor spatial. Now it seems to me doubtful whether the phrase 'non-temporal activity' is intelligible at all. And, even if it is, I doubt whether one can attach any clear meaning to the statement that such an activity acts as a stimulus to the inner sense and thus manifests itself by the introspected or introspectible mental states which it evokes.

(6) On the whole, then, it seems to me that the attempt to treat empirical consciousness of oneself and one's states as analogous to sense-perception of external things and events is bound to be a failure. One wonders whether Kant had any better reason than the following for this part of his doctrine. (a) He started with the doctrine that *space* is an innate form of sensibility. For this he had quite plausible grounds in the apparent *a priori* certainty of geometry and its applicability to all objects of possible human sense-perception. (b) Next, he developed a similar doctrine about *time*. Here there is much less direct evidence for the theory. For there is no *a priori* and universally applicable science which can plausibly be held to stand to time in the sort of relation in which geometry stands to space. I suspect that he simply took for granted that any correct account of the nature of space *must* automatically apply to time also. This seems to me a very dangerous assumption; for the unlikenesses between time and space are at least as important as the likenesses. (c) Having decided that time, like space, is an innate form of sensibility, he was practically forced to assimilate empirical consciousness of oneself and one's states to sense-perception of external things and events. For oneself and one's experiences certainly present themselves to one on introspection as temporal.

(7) I think it may fairly be said that Kant made no serious attempt to work out this doctrine of self-consciousness in detail, and that he never seriously attempted to bring it and his doctrine of our knowledge of the external world into a single focus. It is plain that in most of what he says about knowledge of the external world he talks as if our sense-data and images were quite literally temporal in themselves, and as if our synthesising activities were temporal processes which rearrange them and generate appropriate images to fill in temporal gaps between them. Whether

the two parts of the doctrine could be fused into one consistent whole seems very doubtful.

(8) In different parts of the *Critique of Pure Reason* Kant makes statements about the relations of temporal and spatial inutition which might seem inconsistent with each other. Sometimes he seems to make temporal intuition prior to spatial, and sometimes the opposite. In the *Aesthetic*, e.g., he says that time is an *a priori* condition of *all* appearances, whilst space is an *a priori* condition only of a certain sub-class of them. The reason given is that 'all presentations, whether they have for their objects outer things or not, belong . . . as determinations of the mind to our inner state'. He sums this up by saying that time is 'the *immediate* condition of inner appearances, and thereby the *mediate* condition of outer appearances' (p. 77, A 34/B 50).

I think that the natural interpretation of this would be that we derive our temporal notions from inspecting and reflecting on our own experiences (including under that head our visual, tactual, and auditory sense-data). Then, on the basis of this, we ascribe them to the external things and events which we ostensibly perceive by means of our visual, tactual and auditory sensations.

In §24 of the *Transcendental Deduction* B Kant seems to go to the opposite extreme. He says there that we can present time to ourselves as an *object* only under the image of a line which we draw in the imagination. He says also that we can date our own experiences and assign various durations to them only by reference to changes which we perceive in certain *external* things, e.g. the apparent movements of the sun, the movement of the hands of a clock, and so on (p. 168. B 156).

I do not think that there is necessarily any inconsistency between the views expressed in these two passages. Kant might hold that we get our temporal notions in the first instance from inspecting and reflecting on our own experiences. But he might also hold that these notions are only vague in their *quantitative* aspect, and that the only way in which we can get a consistent objective system of dating and measuring the duration of events is by reference to certain perceptible *external* alterations. If this is what he meant, his view seems to be self-consistent and probably correct.

(9) I will end these comments by trying to give a synoptic view of Kant's critical theory of self-consciousness and the various factors which are involved in it. (a) We start with the *noumenal self*. This is known to us only as a something which synthesises data according to rules, in such a way as to produce the appearance of a self which persists through time and owns a number of experiences occurring at various dates and lasting for various periods. The noumenal self is timeless. A person is not acquainted with his noumenal self nor with any of its characteristic activities. All that he can know for certain is *that* there is something answering to the above descrip-

tion of his noumenal self. (b) Next we can take *pure apperception*. This appears to be the thought of oneself as something which can and does perform the synthetic activity which is characteristic of a noumenal self. (c) Next comes *sensibility*. This is the name for the sum total of *passive* powers which we find it necessary to ascribe to a noumenal self. It is subdivided into *external* and *internal* sense. *External sense* is those passive powers of a noumenal self which, when stimulated, give rise to such sense-data as form the basis of our ostensible perceptions of things or events located in physical space outside one's own body. Kant generally assumes that the appropriate stimulus for external sense comes in some way from *foreign* noumena. External sense imposes the *spatial* form upon the products of its stimulation. *Internal sense* is those passive powers of a noumenal self which are stimulated by its own synthesising activities. When stimulated it imposes the *temporal* form on the products of these synthesising activities. It thus imposes the temporal form upon the synth-esised products of the stimulation of the external sense. These synthesised products are called *presentations* or *percepts*. (d) The processes of synthesis are performed by a department of the noumenal self called the *productive imagination*, in accordance with certain concepts which are innate and belong to the *understanding*. The general name for these *a priori* concepts is *categories*; but the special determinate forms which they take in human beings, whose data are all presented under the form of *time*, are called *schemata*. (e) The product of these processes has two distinct but insepar-able aspects. (i) On the one hand, the presentations are so interconnected that one ostensibly perceives a world of *bodies* and events in bodies. This world is conceived as consisting of substances which neither come into being nor cease to be and which are subject in all their alterations to complete causal determination. (ii) On the other hand, this same type of interconnexion makes these same presentations appear as so many suc-cessive states of a single introspectible mental continuant, viz. one's *empir-ical self*. (f) There are, in addition, some contents of any empirical self which are *not* also presentations of external objects. Examples would be images, emotions, etc. But the history of an empirical self *could* not be composed *wholly* of such materials, whilst it might be composed wholly of presentations of external objects and presumably memories of such pres-entations. This is the least unplausible synopsis which I can give of Kant's theory as a whole.

2.2 Ontological part

The ontological part of Kant's doctrine of the human self may be divided into a *negative* and a *positive* side. The negative side is contained in the section of the *Transcendental Dialectic* called the *Paralogisms of Pure Reason*.

The positive side is contained in the *Critique of Practical Reason*. We will now take them in turn.

2.2.1 The negative side

Kant distinguished four paralogisms, or fallacious *a priori* arguments, about the human soul. They all start from the very abstract proposition which is expressed by the sentence 'I think'. The first draws the conclusion that I who think am a *substance*. The second draws the conclusion that that substance is *simple*. The third draws the conclusion that *one and the same* simple substance is the persistent owner of all my successive experiences. The fourth draws the conclusion that I can know the existence of *myself* with complete certainty, but that I am justified in regarding the existence of foreign objects only as more or less probable. These arguments and conclusions, together with certain further developments and applications of them, form the content of an alleged *a priori* science which Kant calls 'rational psychology'. He claims to show that no such science is possible.

In B Kant made great changes in his treatment of the paralogisms. He left out everything from p. 333 to p. 367 (A348–405) and he substituted a much shorter and more systematic version which occupies p. 368 to p. 383 (B406–32). The main differences are the following. (1) In B the fallacy in each case is held to consist in drawing a *synthetic* conclusion from an *analytic* premiss. This is rendered plausible by ambiguities in such terms as 'substance', 'simple', etc. (2) In B there is an important change in the fourth paralogism. As presented in A, it is practically identical with Descartes' doctrine of the relative degree of certainty of one's knowledge of one's own existence and of one's belief in the existences of foreign objects. This does not really fit very well into a supposed science of rational *psychology*. In B Kant replaced all this by the new section called *Refutation of Idealism*, which he added to his treatment of the *Postulates of Empirical Thought*. The fourth paralogism in B is concerned with the attempt to prove *a priori* that the substance which is the simple persistent owner of all my experiences cannot be my body or any part of it. This is of course also a proposition which Descartes claimed to prove. (3) In A Kant discusses at some length the questions of the pre-existence and the post-existence of a human soul and of its relation to the body which it animates during its earthly life (pp. 354–61, A384–96). In B this is discussed in a single paragraph (pp. 380–1, B427–8). (4) On the other hand, Kant added in B a section in refutation of an argument for the immortality of the soul which had been put forward by a German Jewish philosopher, Moses Mendelssohn, in a book called *Phädon*[1] (pp. 372–80, B413–27). I have already dealt with the A version of

---

[1] [*Phädon oder über die Unsterblichkeit der Seele* (Berlin and Stettin, 1776). Repr. in Moses Mendelssohn, *Gesammelte Schriften*, III, 1 (Berlin, 1932). Eng. trans. [by Charles Cullen] *Phaedon; or, The Death of Socrates* (London, 1789).]

the fourth paralogism in connexion with the *Refutation of Idealism*, so I shall say no more about it here. As regards the other paralogisms I shall take the A version and the B version together.

2.2.1.1 Self as substance

The arguments in the paralogisms begin with the kind of judgment which Kant holds that each of us would express by uttering the sentence 'I think'. Kant says that such a judgment 'contains the form of each and every judgment . . . and accompanies all the categories as their vehicle' (p. 332, A 348, and p. 368, B 406). On p. 329 he goes further and describes it as 'the vehicle of *all* concepts'. On p. 331 (A 346/B 404) he says that the word 'I' in the sentence 'I think' expresses 'a simple and in itself completely empty representation'. We cannot even say properly that it expresses a *concept*, but only that it expresses 'a bare consciousness which accompanies all concepts'. He then adds: 'Through this I or he or it . . which thinks, nothing further is represented than a transcendental subject of the thoughts, i.e. an *X*'.

The first question is what all this means. I suggest that Kant may have had in mind the following facts. (1) Any actual judgment must be made by a certain person on a certain occasion. It consists in his then and there ascribing a certain predicate to a certain subject, and in doing this he must be thinking of the predicate and either perceiving or thinking of the subject, and thinking of the predicate as characterising the subject. (2) We may divide statements for the present purpose into those which are and those which are not *explicitly autobiographical*. The former contain the word 'I' or some equivalent word or phrase as their grammatical subject, the latter do not. Examples of the former are 'I feel cold', 'I saw the vice-chancellor yesterday', 'I believe that Caesar conquered Gaul', and so on. Examples of the latter are 'It is raining', 'Metals expand when heated', and so on. (3) Even in the case of a non-autobiographical statement the fact that it is uttered is a sure sign of a state of affairs which could truly and properly be expressed by one or more autobiographical statements on the part of the person who utters it. Suppose a person utters the sentence 'Metals expand when heated', and suppose that he is not merely automatically making a series of intelligible sounds as a parrot or a gramophone might do. It does not matter for the present purpose whether what he says is true or whether he believes what he says. In any case one can be sure that he is *thinking* of metals as expanding when heated, and that in so doing he is *thinking* of metal and of expansion and of heat. We can therefore be sure that there exists a state of affairs which he *could* truly and appropriately express by making such *autobiographical* statements as 'I am thinking of metals as expanding when heated', 'I am thinking of metal', 'I am thinking of heat', and 'I am thinking of expansion'. (4) Suppose next that a person makes an *autobiographical* statement, e.g. 'I saw the vice-chancellor yesterday'. Then, subject to the same conditons as before, the fact that he utters this sentence is a sure sign of a state of affairs which could truly and properly be expressed by his making an autobiographical statement of the *second order*. He must be *thinking* of himself as having seen the vice-chancellor yesterday, and in so doing he must be *thinking* of *himself* and of his *experience of seeing*. (5) I suggest that this is the *positive* aspect of what Kant means by his remarks about 'I think'. The *negative* aspect certainly is that nothing whatever can be inferred as to the nature of that which thinks from such facts as these.

We can now come to the details of the fallacious arguments. I shall put these in my own way. With regard to every statement which a person can make, one or other of the following propositions is true. Either (1) it is explicitly autobiographical, like 'I saw the vice-chancellor yesterday'. Or (2), if it is not, the utterance of it indicates the existence of a state of affairs which, if it *were* expressed, would have to be expressed by explicitly autobiographical statements. Now in all explicitly autobiographical statements the word 'I' occurs as a *grammatical* subject and never as a *grammatical* predicate. We are therefore tempted to infer that that which thinks when a person makes a judgment of *any* kind, and which he refers to by the word 'I' when he makes an explicitly autobiographical statement, must be of such a nature that it *has* predicates but cannot *be* a predicate of anything. Now that is one well-known definition of 'substance'. So it is concluded that that which thinks and which a person refers to by the word 'I' is a substance.

To this Kant's answer is as follows. You can say that that which thinks is a substance in this sense of the word, if you like. But it will not follow that it is a substance in the sense of a *continuant*, i.e. a persistent identical something in which a person's various experiences are so many different occurrents. Now it is only in the *latter* sense of substance that it would be interesting to know that the ego is a substance. For it is only if it were a substance in the latter sense that we might have reason to think it existentially independent of the body and therefore possibly pre-existing and surviving it, and so on. In order to judge what is a continuant and what is merely a state of a continuant you need to have concrete *perceptual* experience of an appropriate kind. In point of fact Kant thinks that we have the appropriate kind of perceptual experience for this purpose only through *outer* sense, i.e. in our ostensible perceptions of bodies in space. It is true that we also have an *inner* sense. But what one perceives through that is only this, that, and the other *experience*. One does not perceive anything that one can regard as a continuant, comparable to a body, in which one's experiences can be regarded as states, comparable to the various shapes, sizes, positions, colours, etc. which one perceives succeeding each other in the same body.

So Kant's conclusion may be summed up as follows: From the premiss of the argument it is impossible to infer that that which thinks, and which a person refers to when he uses the word 'I' in autobiographical statements, is a substance in the sense of a *continuant*. In order to decide such a question *perceptual* experience of a certain particular kind is always needed. In ordinary sense-perception we have experiences of the required kind, viz. our ostensible perceptions of bodies in space. Introspection is indeed of the nature of perception, since it involves an inner *sense*. But it does not in fact supply data of the kind required for deciding that the ego is a continuant in which a person's various experiences are occurrents. So the question remains completely open.

2.2.1.2 Simplicity of the self

The argument which Kant criticises here may be put as follows. If a certain property or a certain action is ascribed to a *compound* substance, this must really mean that the property or the action is itself complex and that one factor in it belongs to one of the components, another to another of the components, and so on. Now let us consider any act of cognition, e.g. of judgment or of perception. No doubt this is in many cases complex. If, e.g., I perceive an extended whole, it might be argued that I must have perceptions of every one of a set of parts which together make up that whole. And it might be alleged that my perception of the whole is in some sense composed of my perceptions of these parts. Or, to take a less debatable case, suppose I understand a sentence. Then I certainly must perceive and understand each word in it, and it might be said that my understanding of the whole sentence is in some sense composed of my understandings of the several words. It might therefore be suggested that the self could be a *composite* substance, and that different parts of the object are perceived or understood by different parts of the self. To this the following answer is made by those who claim to prove the simplicity of the self. We know that, if the different members of a set of parts of an object O were each perceived by a different person, no one would be perceiving the whole object O. Again, if the different words of a sentence were each heard and understood by a different person, no one would be hearing or understanding the sentence. Hence, it is argued, we must reject the supposition that the self is a composite substance and that its cognitive acts are complexes composed of the acts of various parts of it. The *very same* substance which understands the whole sentence or perceives the whole object must understand all the separate words or perceive each member of a set of parts of the object. So the self must be a *simple* substance, in the sense that it is not a whole composed of other substances closely interrelated to each other.

Though Kant thinks this argument fallacious, he gives it high marks at any rate in A. He says that 'it is no mere sophistical play . . . but an inference which seems to withstand even the keenest scrutiny . . .' (p. 335, A351). There seem to be two attempts at refutation in the A version of the *second paralogism*. The first begins at the bottom of p. 335 and continues to the end of the second paragraph on p. 336 (A352–3). The second begins with the third paragraph on p. 336 and continues to the end of the first paragraph on p. 338 (A353–6).

The first refutation seems to consist merely in trying to show that our alleged knowledge of the simplicity of the self would not fit into any of the accepted epistemological pigeon-holes. (1) It is evidently held to be necessary. Therefore the evidence for it cannot be empirical. So we must suppose that it is known *a priori*. (2) If so, it must be supposed to be either analytic or synthetic. Now (a) it is certainly not *analytic*. For the concept of the unity of an act of thought (e.g. of the unity of the act of understanding a sentence) does not contain as an element the concept of being the act of a non-composite substance. But (b) according to Kant's principles it also cannot be *synthetically a priori*. For, according to him, it is impossible to see a necessary connexion between two concepts merely by reflecting on them and comparing them unless one is a factor in the analysis of the other. Hence Kant concludes that it is not a proposition which can be known in any way. This line of argument will convince only those who accept Kant's views about *a priori* knowledge.

The second refutation seems to come to the following. Persons who accept this argument pass unwittingly from the fact that one's idea of one's own ego is logically a simple *idea* to the conclusion that one's ego is a simple *substance*. 'But the simplicity of the representation of a subject is not *eo ipso* knowledge of the simplicity of the subject itself. . .' (p. 337, A355). The reason why one's idea of one's ego is logically simple is because it is so utterly abstract and empty. It is merely the thought of that which thinks my thoughts. 'It means a something in general (transcendental subject) the representation of which must no doubt be simple, if only for the reason that there is nothing determinate in it' (p. 337, A355). As regards this refutation I would say that, whilst some persons may have committed this fallacy, one would have preferred Kant to answer in detail the actual argument which he thinks so plausible. This I shall now attempt to do.

(1) The fundamental premiss of the argument is that any property or act of a compound substance must be a compound property or act composed of properties or acts each of which belongs to a different one of the component substances. This is certainly false. A chemical compound, such as chloroform, has properties, such as producing loss of consciousness,

boiling at 61°C etc., which are in no sense composed of the properties of its elements, carbon, hydrogen, and chlorine.

(2) The fact that, if each of the words of a sentence were heard and understood by a different person, no one would be hearing or understanding the sentence as a whole, is completely irrelevant for the purpose. At most it would show that, *if* a human ego is a compound substance, then it does not consist of a number of other egos interrelated in the sort of way in which the egos of different human individuals are interrelated. This leaves it quite possible that a human ego is a compound substance whose components are not egos. It even leaves it possible that it is a compound composed of egos interrelated in a very different way from that in which the egos associated with *different* human bodies are interrelated. So the argument is futile.

2.2.1.3 Personal identity

Kant treats the fallacious argument on this question in the *third paralogism*. I do not think that the syllogism with which he starts (p. 341, A 361) brings out the nature of the argument. It is certain that Kant thinks that the defect of the argument is that it starts from a premiss which is true but merely analytic and professes to reach a conclusion which is synthetic. There is also little doubt that the conclusion may be stated somewhat as follows. All the experiences which a person could at any time of his life have correctly described as *his* experiences are states of a single numerically identical entity, which is either timeless or persists at least from his birth to his death. And a person uses 'I' as a proper name for this numerically identical timeless or persistent entity. What is not so clear is the premiss, which is really analytic, from which this synthetic conclusion is mistakenly believed to follow. I suggest that it may be put in the obviously tautological form: Every one of *my* experiences, at whatever date it may have occurred, is an experience of one and the same self, whom I refer to at all times by the same word 'I'. I agree that nothing substantial can be inferred from this tautology.

Instead of considering in detail Kant's confused and confusing statements, it will be worth while to consider the facts which lie at the back of all this. In doing so I shall ignore certain facts which were not known or admitted at Kant's time, viz. those of multiple personality and of telepathy. If we ignore these, the following statements seem to be true or to be generally accepted.

There are certain sets of mental events which may be described as 'personal sets'. The following propositions are true of them. (1) Every event in a personal set has a certain one determinate characteristic, which we may express by the phrase 'being an experience of x' where 'x' is a personal name, like 'Smith' or 'Jones'. (2) Every mental event falls into *some* personal set. (3) No mental event falls into *more than one* personal set. (4) There is, or may be, a plurality of such sets, distinguished by the fact that all members of one have the determinate characteristic 'being an experience of *x*' and all the members of another have the different and incompatible determinate characteristic 'belonging to *y*'. (5) A personal set contains some mental events, viz. introspections and ostensible memories, which are or seem to be states of direct acquaintance with certain other members of that set. On these are founded the explicitly autobiographical judgments which are naturally expressed by such statements as 'I am feeling tired', 'I saw the vice-chancellor yesterday', etc. (6) No personal set contains any mental event which is or seems to be a state of direct acquaintance with any event in any other personal set. (7) There are many other relationships which hold between experiences belonging to the same personal set and do not hold between experiences belonging to different personal sets.

Now to say that Mr Smith's ego persists unchanged throughout all Mr Smith's successive experiences is in one sense a tautology and in another sense a synthetic but highly doubtful statement. It is a tautology in the following sense. There is certainly a single *characteristic*, viz. that which we describe by the phrase 'being an experience of Mr Smith', which is common and peculiar to all these successive experiences. Otherwise they would not be counted as forming a *personal* set at all, and still less as forming that particular personal set which is known as the mental history of *Mr Smith*. It is a synthetic but doubtful statement in the following sense. It may be taken to mean that there is at the back of that personal set which we call 'the mental history of Mr Smith' a certain timeless or persistent *particular*, for which Mr Smith would use the word 'I' as a proper name, and to which all the experiences in the set and no others stand in a common asymmetrical relationship.

Now there is no doubt that ordinary language does suggest this. It suggests that 'being an experience of Mr Smith' is a relational property. And it suggests that the identity of this property throughout a certain series of mental events consists in the fact that they all stand in the same asymmetrical relationship to a single timeless or persistent particular, of which 'Mr Smith' is the proper name. But although that is the kind of analysis which ordinary language suggests, it is by no means the only kind of analysis which is possible. E.g., the following alternative seems feasible. We might suggest that a personal set could be delimited by taking one particular mental event e, e.g. a certain twinge of toothache, or a small selection of mental events $e_1, e_2, \ldots, e_n$, e.g. a certain twinge of toothache, a certain visual sense-datum, a certain memory-image, and so on, as basic. We then define a particular personal set as all those mental events and only those which are either identical with or stand in certain relations R to the one or more mental events which we have taken as basic. Of course R would have to be such that, if x and y stand in the relation R or its converse to the basic events $e_1, e_2, \ldots, e_n$, then these stand in the relation R or its converse to each other. I.e. there is to be nothing special about $e_1, e_2, \ldots, e_n$ as compared with the other members of the set. Any of these might equally well have been taken as basic for delimiting the set. The following geometrical analogy may be helpful. Suppose we compare *points* with *mental events*, and the points on the circumference of a *certain circle* with a certain *personal set* of mental events. Then we can describe the circle by saying that all the points on it are equidistant from a *certain one point*, viz. its centre. This would correspond to the notion of a certain different *pure ego* associated with each different personal set of mental events. But we could equally describe the circle by taking any three points A, B, and C on its circumference as our basis, and then saying that it consists of these three points and of all other points X such that the angle AXB is either equal or supplementary to the angle ACB. All reference to the centre has now vanished. The points A, B, and C would correspond to the mental events $e_1, e_2, \ldots, e_n$ which are taken as basic in delimiting a certain personal set. And the relationship expressed by the statement that the angle AXB is either equal or supplementary to the angle ACB would correspond to the relation R used in delimiting the personal set by reference to these selected basic experiences.

2.2.1.4 Mind and body

Kant's main remarks on this topic are to be found in A under the heading *Consideration of Pure Psychology as a Whole* (pp. 352–61, A381–96). The most important points are the following.

(1) He begins by saying that there cannot by a pure *a priori* part of psychology as there is of physics. The *a priori* part of physics for Kant consists of the three Analogies of experience, the laws of pure kinematics, and perhaps Newton's three laws of motion. These, he thinks, can be proved by transcendental arguments or demonstrated, like the propositions of geometry, by appeal to our pure intuitions of space and time. Nothing of that kind is possible in psychology, which therefore must always remain a purely descriptive and classificatory science, like natural history.

The reason which Kant gives is that the empirical self is presented to us in time only and not in space. We can therefore intuit nothing permanent by introspection. I suspect that what Kant really means is that the pure category of substance can be schematised only as the notion of an object which fills the same region of space or a continuous series of adjacent

regions throughout a stretch of time. Now this schema does not apply to
the empirical self. But the unschematised category, or the category as
schematised only in time and not also in space, is too abstract for us to be
able to establish anything concrete about it *a priori*. I think it quite likely
that Kant came to hold a similar view about causation, viz. that it can be
schematised satisfactorily only as the notion of a relation between the
states of continuants in *space*. He did indeed hold that we can know *a priori*
that every alteration in the empirical self is completely determined by
some earlier alteration in accordance with some general rule. But he
thought that there was no possibility of establishing *a priori* fundamental
laws in psychology analogous to Newton's laws of motion in physics.

(2) Next he says that the only interest of the alleged science of pure
psychology is negative. It suffices to show that the *arguments* of materialists
are invalid, but it does not succeed in showing that a non-materialist view
of the self is true.

This seems to me to be an incorrect account of the facts and of Kant's
own procedure. If, as he rightly asserts, the alleged science of rational
psychology consists of nothing but plausible but fallacious arguments, it
cannot refute *anyone*. And what Kant in fact does is first to explode the
arguments by which rational psychology tries to prove its non-
materialistic conclusions, and then to explode the arguments by which
materialists try to prove their conclusions. Kant's answer to the materialists is as follows. They make the mistake (which is common to them and
most of their opponents) of treating bodies as things-in-themselves. If we
confine ourselves to bodies as *empirical objects*, then a body is a group of
suitably interconnected sense-data actual and possible. And nothing of the
nature of a sense-datum could conceivably exist except as an item in the
mental history of some person. So bodies depend on selves, rather than
selves on bodies. Suppose, on the other hand, we take 'bodies' to mean
those unknown things-in-themselves which are the ultimate source of the
sense-data of external sense. Then we cannot say whether there may not be
other selves or groups of selves. We simply know nothing about their
intrinsic nature.

(3) Kant deals in the same way with the problem of the connexion
between a person's mind and his body. Many philosophers have denied
that the two could interact, on the ground that the one is unextended and
not located in space whilst the other is extended and located. To this Kant
answers as follows. Are you using 'body' in the empirical or in the
metaphysical sense? In the former sense a person's body is nothing but a set
of suitably interconnected actual and possible sense-data of the external
sense. But all sense-data are essentially *mental* events; and so they are not
radically different in kind from volitions. Therefore the premiss of this
argument against interaction collapses. Suppose, on the other hand, that

you mean by a person's body the thing-in-itself which is the ultimate source of these sense-data which are the basis of his own and other men's perceptions of his body as an empirical object. Then, for all we know to the contrary, this may be the *very same* thing-in-itself which appears to him through internal sense and introspection based upon it as his empirical self. So the argument again collapses.

2.2.1.5 Immortality

Kant says, quite rightly I think, that the main reason why people have been interested in the supposed proofs that a man's soul is a simple substance, which persists unchanged at any rate from his birth to his death, is the following. They have thought that these conclusions would either show that the soul is naturally immortal or at any rate refute certain arguments for thinking it to be mortal. If, e.g., one's soul is a *simple* substance then it can be argued that it differs from one's body or from any finite part of one's body, since that is extended and therefore composite. In that case one can at least say that it will not *ipso facto* cease to exist when one's body is destroyed. Then, again, all the coming to be and the ceasing to exist which occurs in nature refers to *composite* substances. Generation of a new composite substance consists simply in a number of substances, which were formerly dispersed, coming into more intimate mutual relations and then remaining in them for a period. Destruction of an old composite substance is the reverse of that process. If the soul is a *simple* substance it cannot have been generated and it cannot be destroyed in *that* way.

For the reasons already given Kant does not admit that the premisses of these arguments can be established by philosophical reasoning. He does, however, state on p.360 (A393–4) what he thinks the pre-existence and the post-existence of a human soul would *mean* on his general principles. To say that Mr Jones's soul existed before the birth of his body would, he says, amount to saying that, before his soul began to perceive certain things-in-themselves as *bodies in space*, it already intuited the same things-in-themselves in some entirely different way, i.e. presumably *not* as extended objects in space. To say that Mr Jones's soul will survive the death of his body amounts to saying that it will go on intuiting in some non-spatial way the same things-in-themselves which it now perceives as bodies in space. Kant regards these speculations as *intelligible*, but says that there is no way of showing that such suggestions are *even possible* and equally no means of showing that they are *impossible*.

I cannot accept this account of what pre-existence and post-existence of the soul would mean on Kant's general principles. In order to answer this question one would need to do two things. (1) To state, in terms of the ordinary commonsense view of matter, what are the main facts at the back of the proposition that Mr Jones's soul now animates Mr Jones's body. (2) To interpret these facts in terms of the following features of Kant's theory. (a) That Mr Jones's body, as a phenomenal object, is a set of actual and possible sense-data of the outer senses, interconnected in accordance with rules of coexistence and sequence of a certain characteristic kind. (b) That Mr Jones's soul, as an introspectible object, is a set of actual and possible data of the inner sense, interconnected in accordance with rules of an equally characteristic but quite different kind. (c) That the ultimate source of all the data of both outer and inner sense are things-in-themselves, about whose intrinsic characteristics we know nothing positive, but about which we do know the negative fact that they are neither temporal nor spatial. Now, in terms of the ordinary commonsense view of matter, the main facts to be translated in terms of Kant's theory are the following. (1) That Mr Jones can perceive foreign bodies, and what is going on in his own body, only by means of certain specialised organs of his own body. (2) That he can perceive his own body *from within* by certain special sensory experiences, e.g. aches, tickles, etc.; that *he* can perceive no *other* body in *that* way; and that *no one else* can perceive *his* body in *that* way. (3) That the only changes in material things which he can *directly* initiate or inhibit by his volitions are changes in his own body. (4) That his thoughts, emotions, and character seem to be very closely dependent upon the structure and functioning of his brain and nervous system. *These* are the facts which need to be interpreted in terms of Kant's general theory of matter and mind, and it is obvious that the statements which I have quoted from p. 360 (A393–4) are utterly inadequate and largely irrelevant to them.

In B Kant added to his negative treatment of arguments for immortality by explicitly refuting an argument which had been put forward by Moses Mendelssohn in *Phädon*. The standard argument for the indestructibility of the soul had been from its simplicity. The only way in which a substance could cease to exist was by coming to pieces, and the soul had no pieces to come to. Kant had already dealt with this argument. But Mendelssohn took a different line. He admitted that, in order to show that a thing cannot cease to exist, it is not enough to show that it cannot disintegrate. But he argued that, if a *simple* substance ceased to exist, its cessation would have to be *sudden* and could not happen as the result of a continuous process. This, he thought, would involve an absurdity, owing to the continuity of time.

I think that what he had in mind might be put as follows. Suppose that a simple substance ceases to exist. Then up to and including a certain moment t it is true to say 'S exists now', and *after* t it is false to say it. Again, at and after a certain moment t' it is true to say 'S does not exist now', and *before* t' it is false to say it. Now either t and t' are the same moment or they are different moments. If they are the *same*, then at *that* moment *both* the propositions 'S exists now' and 'S does not exist now' would be *true*. This conflicts with the law of contradiction. Suppose, on the other hand, that *t* and *t'* are *different* moments. Then, since time is continuous, there must be moments between them, however near together they may be. But at any such intermediate moment *both* the propositions 'S exists now' and 'S does not exist now' would be *false*. For *t* was the last moment at which the former proposition is true and *t'* is the first moment at which the latter is true. But this conflicts with the law of excluded middle.

Kant's answer is that a simple substance must have *intensive* magnitude, though it could not have extensive magnitude. This intensive magnitude in the case of the soul would be degree of consciousness, i.e. the sort of magnitude which is present in a high degree when one is alert and attentive and in a low degree when one is drowsy. Now a soul might cease to exist through a continuous diminution to zero of its degree of consciousness. In that case it would, as Kant says, go out 'by elanguescence'.

Does this answer Mendelssohn's argument, as I have interpreted it? I think that it does, but that it needs to be further developed before this becomes obvious. It seems to me that the intermediate step needed is this. If Kant is right, there would be no moment which could be said to be the *last* moment at which a soul existed. For take any degree of consciousness, however low, and suppose that the soul *S* had that degree at a certain moment *t*. Then, since the series of degrees is continuous and the diminution takes place continuously, there must be a *later* moment *t'* at which the soul *S* had a *lower* degree of consciousness and therefore *still* existed. But, since time is continuous, that is quite consistent with there being a moment at and after which the soul *S* does *not* exist. Suppose a person begins to lose consciousness on his death-bed at a certain moment t_1 and dies at t_2. Then we could say, on Kant's view, that at every moment *after* t_1 and *before* t_2 his soul had *some* degree of consciousness and therefore existed, but that this degree of consciousness approached to zero as limit as the continuous series of moments approached t_2 as limit. *At* t_2 itself and at all later moments the degree of consciousness was actually zero, and so we could say that his soul was non-existent *at and after* t_2. On this view there would be no moment at which both the proposition 'His soul now exists' and 'His soul does not now exist' would be true. And there would be no intermediate moments at which those propositions would both be false. So the difficulty raised by Mendelssohn, as I understand it, is avoided.

2.2.2 The positive side: ethical argument for immortality

The positive side of Kant's doctrine of immortality is contained in the section of the *Critique of Practical Reason* entitled *Dialectic of Practical Reason* (pp. 202–46 in Abbott) and especially in sub-section IV (pp. 218–20).[1] I shall omit for the present the part of this section which deals with Kant's moral theology.

Kant had already thrown out hints in the *Critique of Pure Reason* that a valid argument for human immortality might be constructed if *ethical* facts were taken into account as premises. This is strongly indicated by the paragraph on pp. 379–80 (B424–5), which begins with the sentence 'Yet nothing is thereby lost as regards the right, nay the necessity, of postulating a future life in accordance with the principles of the practical employment of reason, which is closely bound up with its speculative employment.' There is, I think, no doubt that Kant personally believed in human immortality, though he held that all attempts to prove it by philosophical arguments from non-ethical premises are, and must from the nature of the case be, fallacious.

2.2.2.1 Virtue and happiness

Kant's argument in the *Dialectic of Practical Reason* begins with a discussion of the notion of the highest good (*summum bonum*). He points out that this is ambiguous. We must distinguish between the *supreme* good (*supremum bonum*) and the *complete* good (*bonum consummatum*). To say that X is the supreme good would mean that X is a necessary condition of every other good, whilst X itself is unconditionally good. X would not be good merely as a means to the realisation of some end Y which was itself good. And X would not be good merely in the sense of contributing to the value of a whole W, of which it was a part, without being good in isolation. Anything that was *supremely* good in Kant's sense would be *intrinsically* good in Moore's sense.[2] But the converse does not hold. Moore holds that there are probably a number of irreducibly different intrinsic goods, and therefore no supreme good in Kant's sense. But Kant held that there is one and only one thing which is good in itself and is a necessary condition of the goodness of all other good things. This is *virtue*, in the sense of an active and effective disposition to do what one judges to be right on every occasion where moral considerations enter, simply because it *is* right and not for any ulterior motive.

But Kant also held that virtue is not the *complete* good. A virtuous person deserves to be happy. Happiness has no *intrinsic* value. But the total state of affairs consisting of virtue *plus* the amount of happiness which that degree of virtue deserves is intrinsically better than that degree of virtue alone or combined with misery or with an undeservedly high or low amount of

---

[1] [*Kant's Critique of Practical Reason and Other Works on the Theory of Ethics*, trans. by T. K. Abbott (London, 1873), 6th ed. (London, 1909).]

[2] [G. E. Moore, *Principia Ethica* (Cambridge, 1903). Cf. also G. E. Moore, *Ethics* (London, 1912).]

happiness. This is not merely a selfish judgment based on the desire which everyone has for his own happiness. An impartial spectator, merely considering the case of other persons, recognises that, whilst undeserved happiness is worthless and unrequited virtue is valuable, virtue accompanied by the deserved amount of happiness is best of all. It will be seen, then, that Kant had anticipated Moore by accepting a particular case of the *principle of organic unities* in ethics.

So far Kant's position is certainly self-consistent and it seems to me to be by no means lacking in plausibility. He now proceeds as follows. We see, he says, that there is a necessary connexion between virtue and happiness. Now this connexion is synthetic and not analytic. For, on the one hand, happiness is not just consciousness of one's own virtue, as the Stoics maintained. And, on the other hand, virtue is not just the consistent pursuit of one's own greatest happiness, as the Epicureans maintained. The Stoic view is plainly contrary to the facts; the experiences of drinking good wine and of smelling the scent of a violet are pleasant, but are certainly not states of consciousness of one's own virtue. The Epicurean view would make virtue a mere means and one's own happiness the unconditional good; and this is plainly false on Kant's view. I agree with what Kant says here, but I think that it is confusing to put his doctrine in the form that the connexion between virtue and happiness is necessary and synthetic. What is necessary and synthetic is the connexion between being virtuous and *deserving* happiness. Once this is made plain the contentions of both the Stoics and the Epicureans are seen to be completely irrelevant, since neither of them introduces the notion of *desert* at all.

Now at the next stage of Kant's argument his unfortunate way of stating the case lands him in what seems to me to be a mare's nest. He says that, since the connexion between virtue and happiness is synthetic and necessary, it must be *causal*. He then proceeds to work in an antinomy. If the connexion be causal, there are two and only two alternatives. One is that the prospect of happiness is the ultimate motive of virtuous action. The other is that the virtuousness of an action must causally determine the occurrence of the appropriate amount of happiness. Now the first alternative is contrary to the notion of a virtuous action, since that is defined as one which is done from no other motive than the belief that it is right and respect for the moral law. The second alternative is contrary to fact. The consequences of an action follow from it in accordance with the laws of nature, and they are exactly the same no matter what the agent's *motive* may have been. But the question whether an act was virtuous or not depends entirely on whether it was or was not done from a certain motive. Kant concludes from this that, although the connexion between the two elements in the complete good must be causal, yet it cannot be a *direct* causal relation in either direction according to the laws of nature. This line of thought leads in an obvious way to Kant's moral theology, which I am ignoring for the present.

All this seems to me to be mere confusion. The only sense in which Kant has shown that virtue and happiness are necessarily connected is that to any degree of virtue there corresponds a certain amount of happiness which anyone who has that degree of virtue would *deserve* to enjoy. This is an *ethical* connexion; and it has absolutely nothing to do with causation, whether direct or indirect.

2.2.2.2 Virtue and moral perfection

We must now consider another aspect of the complete good. The notion of the complete good involves, not merely *virtue*, but *moral perfection*. A perfect or holy will would differ from a merely virtuous will as follows. A perfectly virtuous person would be one who, although in fact solicited by other motives beside the mere desire to do what is right as such, does in fact always act from that motive alone. These other motives would in some cases lead to the same action as that which the desire to do right as such would lead to. In other cases they would, if indulged, lead to a different kind of action. But the mere existence of these other solicitations is incompatible with holiness or moral perfection. 'Inclination is blind and slavish, whether it be of the good sort or not . . . The very feeling of compassion and tender sympathy . . . is annoying to right-thinking persons, brings their deliberate maxims into confusion, and makes them wish to be delivered from it and to be subject to law-giving reason alone' (p. 214). A holy or perfect will would be one that was altogether free from any other motive but the desire to do what is right as such. To such a will the moral law would not appear as imposing a constraint; and so the feeling of obligation, which is characteristic of a merely virtuous will, would be absent in it. The complete good is, then, a *holy* will enjoying the bliss which is appropriate to it.

2.2.2.3 The postulates of practical reason

The next stage in the argument is as follows. We are under a moral obligation to promote the complete good. But, if the complete good were in principle unattainable, we could not be under any such obligation. It is therefore a postulate of practical reason that the complete good is in principle attainable. Kant defines a postulate of pure practical reason as 'a theoretical proposition, not demonstrable as such, but which is the inseparable result of an unconditional *a priori* practical law' (p. 219). At the end of a long footnote (pp. 96–9) in the preface to the *Critique of Practical Reason* Kant sums up his position by saying that a postulate of pure practical reason has 'a rational necessity, which is subjective, but yet genuine and unconditional'. I think that the essential point may be stated as follows. A postulate of pure practical reason is a *factual* proposition which combines the two following characteristics. (1) There is no conclusive *factual* evidence for or against it. (2) Unless a person accepts it he finds himself in the practical dilemma of knowing himself to be under an *unconditional* obligation to strive to bring about a certain state of affairs and at the same time knowing that that state of affairs is in principle *unrealisable*.

The practical postulate connected with the unconditional obligation to promote the complete good divides into two. (a) Each of us must assume that he is capable of attaining moral perfection, i.e. of transforming his will into a *holy* will. (b) We must assume that there is some way in which virtue will be rewarded by the appropriate amount of happiness. The second postulate leads to Kant's moral theology, and we can ignore it for the present. The first leads to his ethical argument for immortality.

The argument runs as follows. It is certain that a person can always do anything which he is really under an obligation to do. This is involved in the very notion of obligation, and Kant has no doubt that we are under obligations. But it is equally certain that no one in this life could possibly free himself from the solicitation of non-moral impulses and desires, even though he need never succumb to them when they conflict with his duty. But each of us is under an unconditional obligation to strive to make himself *holy*, i.e. free from all non-moral impulses. Hence, if one's life were to end with the death of one's present body, one would be under an unconditional obligation to strive for something which one knows to be in principle incapable of attainment. In order to avoid this practical dilemma one must postulate the fulfilment of any conditions without which the end which one is required to aim at would be incapable of realisation. Plainly a minimal condition is that one should survive the death of one's present body. Now Kant assumes without question that complete holiness could not be reached by a finite being in any finite time. All that is possible to it is an endless progress towards holiness. Hence we must postulate an infinitely prolonged future existence.

We must remember, however, that time is not ultimately real according to Kant. He deals with this point in an important passage on p. 219. 'The infinite being, to whom the condition of time is nothing, sees in this to us endless succession a whole of accordance with the moral law; and the holiness which his command inexorably requires . . . is to be found in a single intellectual intuition of the whole existence of a rational being.' I think that what Kant must mean is this. One's self as it really is is not in time. Therefore what appears to oneself and to other men as one's mental history during and after this life cannot really consist of a series of experiences, each beginning at a certain date, going on for so long, ceasing, and being followed by another, without end. But this appearance, though delusive in its temporal aspects, is not completely misleading. Corresponding to the appearance of a *temporal* series of *temporal* states of one's *empirical* self, there is a *non-temporal* series of *non-temporal* states of one's *noumenal* self. We do not know what is the *real* serial relation that corresponds to the merely apparent relation of temporal sequence, but there must be some real non-temporal relation which does so. Now *sub specie temporis* the state of holiness appears to oneself and to others as a kind of limit, to which the endless temporal series of successive states of greater moral purity approaches indefinitely but never reaches. But the real non-temporal series of timeless states of one's noumenal self must have a property corresponding to this property of convergence to a limit which appears to belong to the apparently successive state of one's empirical self. Kant's suggestion comes to this. What appears to a person as a limiting state of holiness, to which he can only approximate indefinitely through endless time, *is* simply the whole timeless series of timeless states of his noumenal self which he misperceives as this endless temporal series of states of increasing moral purity.

2.2.2.4 Comments

I will now make some comments on this argument for human immortality.

(1) It is certainly not based on mere wishful thinking, i.e. on postulating something because we think that the world would be very good if it were true, or very bad if it were false. One fundamental premiss is that a person cannot be under an unconditional obligation to undertake an enterprise which is from the nature of the case incapable of achievement. Even the toughest of businessmen would presumably admit that there is no obligation to set out on a wild-goose chase. The other fundamental premiss is that each of us knows that he is under an unconditional obligation to strive after holiness, in Kant's sense of the word. This premiss may be true or false; but it is concerned not with our hopes or wishes, but with our alleged *duties*.

(2) As regards the logic of the argument, it is valid subject to one condition. It must be assumed that a person can *know* that he is under an unconditional obligation to strive after holiness without *needing to know already* that holiness is attainable. If he cannot know the former unless and until he knows the latter, the argument will be epistemologically circular. It would be like the argument 'All the Apostles were Jews and St Matthew was an Apostle, therefore St Matthew was a Jew'. There is no *formal* fallacy in this argument. But it is *epistemologically* circular, because no one could know that all the Apostles were Jews without having previously ascer-

tained, with regard to each of them separately (including St Matthew) that he was a Jew. Now I suspect that the argument is epistemologically circular. Unless one already assumed that holiness was in principle attainable, would one be prepared to admit any more than the premiss 'I am under an obligation to strive after holiness, *if and in so far as* it is in principle attainable'?

(3) How far is the command to strive after holiness, in Kant's sense, to be taken literally? There is certainly a saying in the New Testament: 'Be ye perfect, even as your Father in Heaven is perfect'; and Kant, as a Christian writing for Christians, might appeal to this. But surely even a Christian, in his saner moments, does not literally believe that any effort that he could make could ever render him morally perfect in the sense in which he believes God to be so. I should have thought that the command was only a rhetorical way of saying 'However seldom you may act on non-moral motives, and however little appeal they may make to you, you can always improve your moral character still further, and it is your duty to try to do so.' Why should not Kant have taken this as a merely regulative *practical* principle, just as he takes the antitheses of the two mathematical antinomies as embodying merely regulative theoretical principles? According to him the real function of the latter is to prevent us from ever resting content with the present spatio-temporal limits of our scientific knowledge. Why should not the real function of the former be to prevent us from ever resting content with our present level of moral achievement? If it is a mistake to treat the regulative principles of speculative reason as giving us information about the actual structure of nature, may it not equally be a mistake to treat this command of practical reason as giving us information about our actual future state?

(4) Can we accept Kant's suggestion that what appears to itself as a temporal being, gradually and endlessly progressing towards perfection as a limiting state, is seen by God as a timeless and perfect serial whole? Each of us appears to himself, not merely to be in time, but also to have various emotions, inclinations, and desires, which are independent of the desire to do what is right and which may conflict with it. According to Kant these would be absent in a person who was in a state of *holiness*. Now either there is or there is not something in a person's noumenal self corresponding to these non-moral emotions, desires, etc. which he seems to find in his empirical self. If there is *nothing* in his noumenal self corresponding to them, the appearance of them to him in his empirical self is a completely baseless and inexplicable delusion. So we may reject this alternative. Suppose, then, that there *is* something in his noumenal self corresponding to these non-moral emotions and desires. Then the noumenal self, even of a person who approaches *sub specie temporis* endlessly to a limiting state of holiness, would *not* be holy by Kant's definition.

To this I think that Kant's best answer would be on the following lines. We must distinguish between holiness as it appears to us here and now, and holiness as it is in itself and as God would see it. To us it appears as the property of a state of the self which is an ideal limit to an unending temporal sequence of states of increasing moral purity. And we think of it in negative terms, as a state in which all the impulses which now conflict with or allay the desire to do what is right as such would have been eradicated. But holiness, as it really is and as God sees it, is not a quality of any one state, ideal or actual. It is a pattern-quality, like a melody, which belongs to nothing less than the whole timeless series of timeless states which are the noumenal basis of the appearance of an empirical self's unending progress towards moral perfection in time.

3 Freedom and determinism

Kant dealt with the problem of freedom and determinism in the *Critique of Pure Reason* in the third antinomy (pp. 409–15, A 444–53/B 472–81) and the solution of it (pp. 461–79, A 528–59/B 556–87). The upshot of this may be said to be roughly that freedom is shown to be *possible* in a certain sense, notwithstanding the universal determination within the world of phenomena which has been proved in the second Analogy. In his ethical works, e.g. the *Critique of Practical Reason*, Kant claims to show that the fact of moral obligation compels us to hold that freedom in this sense is not merely possible but *actual*.

3.1 The third antinomy

The thesis asserts that causality in accordance with the laws of nature will not suffice to explain all phenomena. In order to explain them it is necessary to assume that there is another kind of causality, viz. that of *freedom*. The antithesis asserts that there is no freedom and that everything takes place solely in accordance with the laws of nature.

Before considering the arguments we must be clear as to what Kant means by his terms. He explains this on p. 464 (A 532–3/B 560–1). He says that there are only two kinds of causality which we can conceive, viz. causality *according to nature* and causality *arising from freedom*. The former is the necessitated sequence of one state upon an immediately preceding state in accordance with a general rule. The essential point about it is that one factor in the total cause of an event must itself be an event. So in causality according to nature the cause of an event must itself have a cause which contains an event as a factor, and so on backwards indefinitely. Causality arising from freedom means, Kant says, 'the power of beginning a state *spontaneously*', i.e. of initiating a change without the act of initiating being itself determined by any previous *event* in accordance with a rule. Obviously we seem *prima facie* to do this quite often. A person suddenly gets up from his chair because he has decided to do so; but his decision to do so does not seem *prima facie* to be necessitated by any immediately previous events, bodily or mental, in accordance with any general rule.

3.1.1 The argument

The argument for the *thesis* consists in a refutation of the antithesis. (1) Kant begins by pointing out that, if the occurrence of an event is explained by natural causation, there is always a feature in the explanation which itself requires to be explained in precisely the same way as the original event. For the cause will contain an event as an essential factor; this will need to be explained by reference to a law of nature and a previous state of affairs; this state of affairs will contain an event as an essential factor; and so on backwards in time without limit. (2) He then introduces the following premiss: 'But the law of nature is just this, that nothing takes place without a cause *sufficiently* determined *a priori*.' (3) He concludes from this that the proposition that there is no causality except in accordance with laws of nature is *self-contradictory*. There must be another kind of causality 'whereby a series of appearances, which proceeds in accordance with laws of nature', is initiated *spontaneously*, i.e. without any previous *event* determining the initiating in accordance with a law.

The alleged contradiction seems to me to rest on a verbal trick. After talking about '*laws* of nature', e.g. the law of gravitation, Kant suddenly begins to talk of '*the* law of nature'. He identifies this with the principle of sufficient reason. He takes this to mean that for every occurrence there must be an explanation of why just such an event happened just there and then, and that this explanation must be in terms which require no further explanation. Now it is perfectly true that explanations in terms of earlier events and the laws of nature do not answer to this condition. But there is no *contradiction* here. All that we can say is that, if the principle of sufficient reason, in the sense defined, is true, then there must be some *other* type of explanation of the occurrence of events beside referring them to earlier events and the laws of nature. But why should Kant expect us to accept the principle in this sense? It would presumably be a synthetic *a priori* proposition, and would therefore, on his view, need a transcendental proof. But he has nowhere attempted to provide one. Again, suppose we accepted the principle. Would an explanation in terms of *spontaneous* initiation satisfy it any better than one in terms of causation in accordance with laws of nature? It would of course have the negative advantage that the explanation would not refer back to an earlier *event*, which would need to be explained in the same way, and so on *ad infinitum*. But would not the occurrence of the act of initiating at the particular time and place at which it did occur be a typical instance of something unexplained and inexplicable? It seems to me, then, that the proof of the thesis is a complete failure.

We can now turn to the argument for the *antithesis*. This consists in a refutation of the thesis. The argument appears to come to the following. Suppose that an agent by a certain spontaneous act literally *initiates* a certain series of events. That act of initiating must be performed by the agent at a certain moment of its history. Yet to say that it is spontaneous implies that it has no causal connexion with any of the agent's previous states. The various acts of initiation performed by an agent would thus be completely unconnected with each other causally; one would simply say of them that they were all performed at various times by the same agent. Kant says that this would 'render all unity of experience impossible'. Later on he says: 'Nature and transcendental freedom differ as do conformity to law and lawlessness' (p. 411, A 447/B 475).

In the main I accept Kant's argument here. There are only two remarks that I would make. (1) It seems to me an exaggeration to say that the occurrence of completely spontaneous acts of initiation would render *all* unity of experience impossible. It is a matter of degree. If they were very frequent and very far-reaching in their consequences, this would be approximately true. If they were comparatively rare, and if the subsequent events in any series so initiated were all subject to ordinary causal laws, little harm would be done. (2) I do not know why Kant does not simply refer to his proof of the second Analogy. If that is valid, it would suffice automatically to refute the thesis.

There are two interesting points to be noticed in Kant's observations on this antinomy (pp. 412–15, A 448–53/B 476–81). (1) He admits that the utmost that the argument for the thesis would prove is that at least the series of events which constitute the history of the world *as a whole* must have been initiated by a *single* spontaneous *first act*. But he says that, once this is granted, then there is no reason to deny that particular series of events may be initiated from time to time *within* the history of the world by spontaneous acts of this, that, and another agent. (2) He admits that, if we confine ourselves to a single act of initiation at the beginning of world history, there need be no such incoherence in our experience as the argument for the antithesis alleges. And he softens down the extent of the consequent incoherence, even on the supposition that spontaneous acts of initiation occur within the history of the world. He says here that the criterion for distinguishing genuine experience from dreaming 'would *almost* entirely disappear', and that 'nature as an ordered system would be *hardly* thinkable'.

3.1.2 The solution

We can distinguish three parts in the solution of the third antinomy. (1) Kant's attempt to show that the *dynamical* antinomies, of which this is one, differ in character from the *mathematical* antinomies, i.e. the first and the second, and require and admit of a different kind of solution. (2) His solution of the general metaphysical problem which is raised by the dynamical antinomies. (3) Application of this solution to the special case of human volition. The second and third parts are a good deal mixed up with each other. The third forms a transition to his treatment of freedom in his ethical works. I will now take these three parts in turn.

3.1.2.1 Dynamical and mathematical antinomies

Kant's discussion of this distinction occurs on pp. 461–4 (A 523–33/ B 556–60). In the case of the first two antinomies, Kant says, the regress from term to term is *homogeneous*. It is, e.g., from one volume to a larger or a smaller volume, or from one duration to a longer or a shorter duration. But when we are dealing with *causal* series the terms need not be homogeneous, for a cause need not resemble its effect. So Kant suggests that in the dynamical antinomies *both* thesis and antithesis might be true when properly interpreted; whereas in the mathematical antinomies *neither* is true. The suggestion is that one and the same phenomenon may be subject at once to two utterly different kinds of causation, viz. *natural* causation, which connects it with other phenomenal events, and *non-natural* causation, which connects it with things-in-themselves. The antithesis might be true of phenomena in relation to other phenomena, whilst the thesis might be true of phenomena in relation to things-in-themselves.

I doubt whether the distinction between the two kinds of antinomy is really very fundamental. It seems to me that Kant could have given a solution of the third antinomy on the same lines as his solution of the first two. He could have said that the series of phenomenal conditions at any moment extends just as far as the earliest phenomenal condition which a person has at that moment perceived or remembered or inferred, and no further. It is at any moment of finite length, and that is the truth at the back of the thesis. It is also at every moment capable of being extended further, and that is the truth at the back of the antithesis. I think that there is little doubt that Kant took the other type of solution instead of this one because of his interest in ethics and in the question of freedom as applied to human volitions.

3.1.2.2 Solution of the general problem

Kant's solution of the general problem raised by the third antinomy may be summed up as follows. Nature, in the sense in which common sense and science are concerned with it, is a system of coherently interconnected phenomena. These phenomena are sensibilia or groups of interconnected sensibilia, and every sensibile is an actual sense-datum of one particular individual on one particular occasion. Their coherence consists in the fact that they are so interconnected that they could all enter into the experience of a single idealised self-conscious mind, i.e. a mind working on the same principles as a human mind, but without the special and contingent limitations of any particular human mind. Such coherence would be impossible unless every phenomenon were connected with certain immediately precedent phenomena in accordance with rules of necessitated sequence. This fact is all that is meant by natural causation. So we can and must say that there are no events in nature which are not caused by earlier events in accordance with natural laws.

On the other hand, phenomena from their very nature are incapable of existing in their own right, or of generating each other, or of *doing* anything whatever. We must therefore hold that nature, in the sense of the sum total of interconnected phenomena, stands in a relation of one-sided dependence on a world of things which are not phenomenal and are self-subsistent. About this noumenal world we know nothing positive except that it is the self-subsistent and active reality of which nature is the dependent and inert appearance. But we do know the negative fact that it is neither spatial nor temporal, since space and time are mere subjective forms which a percipient imposes on the data of outer and inner sense.

Since the noumenal world is *non-temporal*, the relation of one-sided dependence between nature and the noumenal world is not a relation between one event and an *earlier event*. Therefore we are not involved in the endless regress to which causal explanation *within* nature inevitably leads. When we refer a phenomenon to its noumenal conditions the first step takes us out of time, and we neither can nor need take any further step. Even if the noumenal condition of this phenomenon be in fact determined by other noumenal conditions, we can form no positive conception of what such determination within the noumenal world would be. But we do know the negative fact that it cannot involve temporal relations. Thus the thesis *can* be applied to the relation of a phenomenon to its noumenal conditions, whilst the antithesis *must* be applied to the relation of a phenomenon to its phenomenal conditions. The following comments may be made on this general solution.

(1) It may usefully be compared with Berkeley's discussion of causation

in the *Principles of Human Knowledge*. Berkeley takes very much the same view of the laws of nature as Kant does here. The main differences are these: (a) Berkeley regards them simply as *de facto* rules of concomitance and sequence among sensations, whilst Kant regards them as rules of *necessitated* sequence among phenomena. (b) Kant claims to have shown that, unless all phenomena were subject to such rules, there could be no ostensible perception of objects and no self-consciousness. Berkeley is content to say that life would be practically unlivable without such rules. On the metaphysical side Berkeley is much more definite than Kant. He asserts categorically that the only genuine causal agents are persons, and that the only genuine causes are volitions. He ascribes the occurrence of our sensations to the deliberate telepathic action of God on our minds. And he ascribes the particular laws of nature to particular rules which God *deliberately* follows, for our benefit, in generating sensations in us in a certain order.

(2) Can the relation of things-in-themselves to the inner and outer phenomena which are their appearances be properly described as a specific form of the general relationship of cause to effect? This seems to me very doubtful. It is part of the notion of cause and effect that they are *different* particular existents, even if they should be only different states of one and the same substance. But is a phenomenon a different particular existent from the thing-in-itself of which it is an appearance? Is it not simply that thing-in-itself *as it appears* to a certain person on a certain occasion? I suspect that in all this there is a confusion in Kant's mind between the following two propositions. (a) The *scientific* proposition that a remote cause of the sensations by which one perceives an empirical object is certain physical processes in that object, e.g. vibrations of its atoms. (b) The *metaphysical* proposition that empirical objects, including one's empirical self, are appearances to one, under the subjective forms of time and space, of things-in-themselves. The first proposition involves only *empirical* things and events and *natural* causation, and Kant should analyse it as best he can in phenomenalistic terms. The second seems not to involve causation at all. I suspect that Kant thinks that it does only because the first is hovering about at the back of his mind.

3.1.2.3 Application to human volition

Whether the general solution is valid or not, it is plainly not sufficient for Kant's purpose. It refers to a *general* relation of one-sided dependence in which the world of phenomena *as a whole* stands to the world of things-in-themselves *as a whole*. It gives no ground for holding that any one particular phenomenon in nature, e.g. a voluntary raising of one's hand, is freely initiated rather than any other, e.g. the fall of a leaf. Kant wanted to go into detail about particular events or types of event within nature, and the difficulties begin to accumulate as he does so.

3.1.2.3.1 'Intelligible' and 'empirical' characters of a thing

The first stage in this attempt to go into detail is the distinction which Kant draws between what he calls the 'intelligible' and the 'empirical' character of a thing. This is introduced on pp. 467–9 (A 538–42/B 566–70), and the general discussion of it goes on to the end of the first paragraph on p. 472 (A 546/B 574). At that point occurs the transition to the particular case of human volition.

Kant ascribes to every empirical substance what he calls an 'empirical character'. So far as I can see, this means simply the complex of all its causal properties, described in terms of the observable changes which it would produce or undergo in various circumstances which are themselves describable in observable terms. Thus, e.g., it is part of the empirical character of a bit of gold to be soluble in *aqua regia*, to have such-and-such a density, melting-point, and so on. Suppose that mathematical physicists were able to explain these causal properties in terms of the ultra-microscopic structure and processes in a bit of gold. Then the empirical character of a bit of gold would reduce to being composed of such-and-such particles, having such-and-such causal properties, and being arranged in such-and-such a pattern.

Now Kant assumes in this part of his work that each distinguishable empirical substance is the appearance of a different thing-in-itself. And he assumes that the empirical character of any empirical substance must be an appearance of a certain property of the thing-in-itself which appears as that empirical substance. He gives the name 'intelligible character' to that property of a thing-in-itself which manifests itself as the empirical character of the empirical substance. Let S be an empirical substance and Σ be the thing-in-itself which appears to us as S. Then Kant would describe the 'intelligible character of S' as that property of Σ which manifests itself as the empirical character of S. Since Σ is neither spatial nor temporal, no property of it can be so either. In fact we can think of the intelligible character of an empirical substance S only by a description; and the only description available to us is 'that character of the thing-in-itself Σ which manifests itself as the empirical character of S'.

Kant can now raise the following more specific question: Given an empirical substance S and an empirical event e in it, is it meaningful to suggest that this empirical event is both (1) completely determined by other empirical events going backwards indefinitely, and (2) freely or spontaneously originated?

His answer is as follows. The empirical substance S is an appearance of a certain thing-in-itself Σ. The empirical event e in S could be predicted with complete certainty from a sufficient knowledge of the empirical characters of S and of other empirical substances, of their spatio-temporal relations, and of the laws of nature. But the empirical character of S is itself the appearance of its intelligible character, i.e. of a certain property of Σ. Since Σ is non-temporal, there is no sense in suggesting that the intelligible character is itself determined by *previous events*. Therefore we may say that the intelligible character of S is the free or spontaneous cause of the event e. So the empirical event is, in one sense, produced spontaneously, and, in another sense, is a mere link in an endless chain of empirical events which cause and are caused by each other. The following comments may be made on this attempted solution.

(1) If it is valid at all, it will apply equally to *every* empirical event. There will be no ground for saying that certain of them, e.g. human voluntary movements, are caused freely, whilst others, e.g. the fall of a leaf, are not.

(2) It is open to all the objections which I made against the general solution, but it is also open to several additional objections. What right has Kant to assume that there is a different thing-in-itself corresponding to each different empirical substance? Elsewhere he has been quite sceptical about this. And he is right to be sceptical. In the first place, since the noumenal world is neither spatial nor temporal, it is not easy to conceive of its being differentiated into a plurality of things-in-themselves. And, secondly, even if it were, might not a group of empirical substances correspond to a single thing-in-itself, or conversely a single empirical substance correspond to a group of things-in-themselves?

(3) Even if we admit this one-to-one correspondence between empirical *substances* and things-in-themselves, the theory is inadequate to deal with the causation of this, that, and the other empirical *event*. We can easily see this in the following way. The *natural* causation of any empirical event always involves *two* sets of conditions. One is the permanent empirical characters of the interacting empirical substances, e.g. the masses and elasticities of two billiard-balls. The other is the immediately previous states of each substance and their immediately previous external relations, e.g. the coming into contact of the billiard-balls when moving with certain velocities in certain directions. Now the intelligible character is the noumenal counterpart of only *one* of these factors, viz. the empirical character. Kant has failed to see that he must also find something in the noumenal world to correspond to the variable states and external relations of empirical substances. Unless he can do this, he has left out an essential part of the noumenal conditions of any empirical event. He is trying to make the intelligible character do two incompatible things. It has to determine *both* the permanent empirical character *and* the variable empirical states and external relations of his interacting empirical substances.

It is not at all easy to see how this defect could be mended on Kant's view of the noumenal world. In a world of entities which are neither spatial nor temporal what could correspond to and manifest itself as the velocities of approach and the coming in contact of two billiard-balls?

3.1.2.3.2 'Practical' and 'transcendental' concepts of freedom

Kant now attempts to apply the distinction between empirical and intelligible character to human beings, considered as empirical substances, and in particular to human volitions. From the comments which I have just made it is plain that the omens are very unfavourable for such an undertaking.

Kant asserts that 'the practical concept of freedom is based on the transcendental idea of freedom' (p. 465, A 533/B 561). 'The denial of transcendental freedom must . . . involve the elimination of all practical freedom' (p. 465, A 534/B 562). We know what he means by the 'transcendental idea of freedom'; it is simply the notion of an agent initiating a series of events without the act of initiating being itself determined by any earlier event in accordance with a law of necessitated sequence. He explains what he means by 'the practical concept of freedom' on p. 465 (A 534/B 562). He defines it as 'the independence of the will from coercion by sensuous impulses'. Both the will of an animal and that of a man are *affected* by sensuous impulses, and each is therefore what Kant calls *arbitrium sensitivum*. The difference is this. The voluntary decisions of an animal are *entirely determined*, in accordance with psychological laws, by sensuous impulses. But that is not so in the case of a man. 'There is in man a power of self-determination, independently of any coercion through sensuous impulses.'

Now this by itself might mean only that in man there is a non-sensuous factor, which may co-operate or conflict with sensuous impulses, and that the decision in any case is determined jointly by these two kinds of factor. But Kant means much more than that. He holds that the non-sensuous factor is *sufficient* to determine human choice, *in the absence* of any sensuous impulses co-operating with it, and *against* any sensuous impulses, no matter how strong or how numerous, which may be conflicting with it. He holds that this is entailed by the fact that we can say of some voluntary actions which in fact happened that they *ought not* to have done so, and of some which did not happen that they *ought* to have done so. His statements are perfectly definite on this point. 'Practical freedom presupposes . . . a causality of our will . . . which independently of these natural causes and even contrary to their force and influence . . . can begin a series of events *entirely of itself*' (p. 465, A 534/B 562). The same point is made again when

Kant analyses the case of our attitude towards a man who has deliberately told a malicious lie. In so far as we blame him morally, we regard the non-sensuous cause of his action 'not . . . as only a co-operating agency, but as complete in itself, even when the sensuous impulses do not favour but are directly opposed to it' (p. 477, A555/B583).

3.1.2.3.3 Reason as practical

We can now raise the following question: What is this non-sensuous cause which is capable of completely determining a human voluntary decision no matter what other motives may be present? Kant says that it is *reason*, as distinct from both understanding and sensibility.

The theory of the peculiar kind of causality exercised by reason is developed from the middle of p. 472 to the end of p. 478 (A546–57/B574–85). We may begin with the following quotation. 'Reason . . . we distinguish in quite a peculiar way . . . from all empirical conditioned powers. For it views its objects exclusively in the light of ideas, and in accordance with them determines the understanding, which then proceeds to make an empirical use of its own equally pure concepts' (p. 472, A547/B575).

We must remember that when Kant talks of 'ideas of reason' he means very much what we mean by ideal concepts. According to him reason is the faculty which presents us with such concepts. These are of two kinds, viz. *speculative* and *moral* (or, as Kant calls them, *practical*). An example of the former would be the notion of the world as a complete self-explanatory system. In so far as reason is concerned with speculative ideals Kant calls it *pure*, and in so far as it is concerned with moral ideals he calls it *practical*. Now it is obvious that one of the motives which influences human conduct is the desire to do what is right as such, and in general the desire to act in accordance with moral principles or to live up to a moral ideal. This is an essential part of what Kant means when he ascribes *causality* to reason. So far he is plainly right. And he is pointing out a peculiar kind of causation, which is extremely unlike anything else that we can find in the world. It could exist only in rational beings, who are capable of contemplating and being moved by moral principles and ideals of conduct.

Now Kant holds that the desire to do what is right as such is not just one motive which may co-operate or conflict or take turns with others. It is in a unique position in certain respects. I think it will be best to take this in two stages, a negative and a positive. I would put the negative aspect of the case as follows.

Suppose a person is deliberating about alternative courses of action, each of which will take place if and only if he decides to initiate it. Suppose that this is a deliberation in which moral considerations enter. Then we should all be inclined to say that he *ought* to decide to initiate that alternative which he judges to be *morally right*. Now it seems obvious that a person cannot be under an obligation to do anything which is *causally impossible* or to avoid doing anything which is *causally inevitable*. It seems, therefore, to follow that it can never be causally impossible for a person to decide to initiate the alternative which he judges to be right, and that it can never be causally inevitable for him to decide to initiate any of the other alternatives. From this it seems to follow that it must be causally possible to decide to initiate the alternative which one judges to be right, no matter how numerous or how strong are the motives against doing this or in favour of deciding to initiate other alternatives. Suppose one looks back at a decision actually made by oneself or another person, and suppose that one has reason to think that he deliberately initiated an alternative which he believed at the time to be wrong. Then one has no hesitation in saying that he *ought not* to have decided as he did, and that he *ought* instead to have decided in a certain other way. This certainly seems to imply that the decision which he actually made was not causally inevitable, whatever may have been the motives for it; and that a certain alternative decision, which he did not make, was not causally impossible, whatever may have been the motives against it.

Up to this point I must confess that I can see no flaw in the argument. The premiss that a person *ought* to have initiated the alternative which he judged to be right, even when he in fact initiated a different alternative, seems to be significant and true. And it does seem to entail at least the negative conclusion that the actual initiation of the alternative which the agent judged to be wrong was *not* causally inevitable, and that the initiation of the one which he judged to be right would *not* have been causally impossible. It is when Kant tries to get beyond this negative conclusion to something positive that the difficulties begin.

The positive part of Kant's doctrine is to be found on pp. 472–9 (A 546–58/B 574–86). It starts by applying the distinction between the empirical and the intelligible character of an empirical substance to the human individual. A man, in so far as he is an object of sense-perception to his fellow men and of introspection to himself, is just one empirical substance among others. In this respect he has an empirical character, like any other empirical thing. Kant describes this as the character which 'we come to know through the powers and faculties which he reveals in his actions' (p. 472). This applies to a man as a rationally willing being just as much as it applies to him in his other capacities. We can talk of the empirical character of a man's will, in so far as we can gather, from his voluntary actions in various situations, his settled habits and rules of preference, i.e. what Kant calls 'the subjective principles of his will'. Kant asserts at the top of p. 474 that the empirical character of a man's will is *permanent*, though its effects appear in various forms under various circumstances. He asserts further that every action of a man, in so far as it is something *observable*, is determined in accordance with natural laws by his empirical character and other natural causes which co-operate with it. 'If we could exhaustively investigate all the appearances of men's wills, there would not be found a single human action which we could not predict with certainty and recognise as proceeding necessarily from its antecedent conditions' (p. 474, A 550/B 578).

So much for the empirical character; now for the intelligible character of a man. Kant opens his account of this with the following statement. 'Man . . . who knows all the rest of nature solely through the senses, knows himself also through pure apperception. Moreover, he knows himself thus in acts and inner determinations which he cannot regard as impressions of the senses. He is thus to himself . . . in respect of certain faculties, the action of which cannot be ascribed to the receptivity of sensibility, a purely intelligible object' (p. 472, A 547/B 575). Kant says that the two faculties in question are understanding and reason. What specially concerns us at present is the latter.

Kant makes the following assertions about reason in this connexion. (1) The concept of 'ought' and 'ought not' belongs to reason. The understanding is concerned only with what is or has been or will be. (2) The concept of 'ought to have done' or 'ought to exist' applies to conceived actions or states of affairs which may never be done and may never exist. It is indeed limited in application to actions or states of affairs which are *not inconsistent with* the facts and laws of nature, both physical and psychological. But the concept of 'ought' cannot be *derived from* the facts and laws of nature; it is peculiar to reason. Nor are the ultimate moral ideals and principles, which determine what ought and what ought not to be or to be done, *imposed upon* reason by anything in nature. The empirical nature of man and of his environment supplies only the occasions and the materials for reason to form concrete moral ideals and determinate moral rules in terms of its own ultimate ideals and principles. If, e.g., men were not liable to feel anger and jealousy, and were not capable of doing bodily harm to each other, there would be no point in the moral rule 'Thou shalt do no murder'. But these facts about the empirical nature of men furnish only the occasions and the materials for the rule. Its ultimate *moral* basis is some general rational principle such as 'It is wrong to do to others what you would not be willing that others should do to you'. In this sense reason is free or spontaneous in respect of the facts and laws of nature. (3) Reason is causally efficacious within nature. The mere fact that a person holds that a certain action would be right and that a certain other alternative would be wrong does sometimes cause him to initiate the former and to refrain from initiating the latter. Similarly the mere fact that a person holds that a certain possible state of affairs ought to exist and that a certain actual state of affairs ought not to exist does sometimes lead him to initiate and maintain action intended to realise the former and to abolish the latter. (4) So far it is quite easy to understand Kant's doctrine, whether one accepts it or not. We come now to a difficult but quite essential point. I will quote what he says: 'An action, in so far as it can be ascribed to a mode of thought as its cause, does not *follow* therefrom in accordance with empirical laws, i.e. it is not *preceded* by the conditions of pure reason but only by their effects in the field of the phenomena of inner sense. Pure reason, as a purely intelligible faculty, is not subject to the form of time . . . The causality of reason in its intelligible character does not, in producing an effect, *arise* or begin to be at a certain time . . . Reason . . . is a faculty *through* which the sensible condition of an empirical series of effects first begins . . . The condition which lies in reason is not sensible, and therefore does not begin to be' (p. 475, A 551–2/ B 579–80).

I will now make some comments on Kant's positive theory of pure reason as a timeless intelligible cause of empirical effects in time.

(1) It seems plain that here at least Kant takes a very different view of apperception from that which he takes in the *Paralogisms* and in *Transcendental Deduction* B. In the latter, e.g., he said that through apperception 'I am conscious of myself, *not* as I appear to myself, *nor* as I am in myself, but only *that* I am' (*Transcendental Deduction* B, §25). But now he evidently holds that reason and understanding are faculties which belong to a person as he is in himself, and that a person is directly aware of himself through apperception as possessing and exercising these faculties. Here Kant seems to be taking the Leibnizian view of apperception.

(2) It is important to be clear as to the meanings of the terms *intellectual, intelligible*, and *noumenal*, and the relations between the three. Kant speaks of reason as a purely *intelligible* faculty. He seems to think that this is the same as saying that it belongs to the noumenal self, or at any rate that the latter follows directly from the former. Now what everyone would admit is that reason is an *intellectual* faculty. But what is the connexion between this and its being an *intelligible* faculty, in Kant's technical sense? And what is the connexion between being an *intelligible* faculty, in this sense, and belonging to the self as *noumenon*? I will now try to clear this up. (a) We call reason and understanding *intellectual* powers in contrast with sensation, sense-perception, emotion, etc. I do not think that it would be easy to give a satisfactory definition of 'intellectual' in this sense. But plainly an important part of what we have in mind is the following. These cognitive powers are concerned with *abstract* entities, universals, numbers, ideal limits, etc. They are concerned with *logical* relations, such as entailment and exclusion, necessity, possibility, etc. Their connexion with sense-

perception is of the following kind. They are involved in making judgments and inferences about the particular existents which are presented to us in sense-perception. They are still more obviously involved in thinking of actual or possible particulars which are not present to the senses but are of such a kind that they could be perceived by the senses. (b) Kant calls an entity *intelligible*, if it is such that from the nature of the case it could not be perceived by the senses but could be cognised only by the intellect. (c) In the chapter on phenomena and noumena Kant distinguished between a positive and a negative sense of the word 'noumenon'. He said there that only the negative sense is of any use to us. But I suspect that he is here using it in the positive sense. If so, a noumenon may be defined as follows. It is an existent which either (i) can be cognised *only* by a kind of non-sensuous intuition; or (ii) though it can be perceived by the senses, can be known *as it is in itself* only by means of such non-sensuous intuition. (d) We can now consider the connexions between these three notions. (i) It is highly plausible to say that our *intellectual* powers and acts are of such a nature that they could not be cognised by sense-perception or anything in the least analogous to it. If we can cognise them at all, we can do so only *intellectually*. Thus our *intellectual* powers and acts are *intelligible* entities in Kant's technical sense. (ii) This covers two possibilities. (A) One is that we can cognise them only discursively and descriptively. We are not and cannot be *acquainted* with them, but we can think of them as the noumenal conditions of certain introspectible mental processes. I think that this is probably the alternative which Kant ought to have taken. It would be analogous to the doctrine of Ward in his *Psychological Principles*.[1] (B) The other alternative would be to hold that we *are* acquainted with our own intellectual powers and acts by a peculiar kind of *non-sensuous intuition*. This seems to be the view that Kant takes here; for 'apperception', as here described, seems to be just this. (iii) On either alternative these intellectual powers and acts would be *noumenal* entities. On alternative (A) they are so explicitly. On alternative (B) they are so in accordance with the definition of a noumenon in the positive sense.

(3) So far Kant's position seems to be self-consistent, if we grant that our intellectual powers and acts are of such a nature that we could not cognise them by anything remotely analogous to sense-perception. But now we come to the alleged timelessness of these powers and acts. Here I think there is a great deal of confusion.

(a) We must distinguish between reason as a *power or faculty* and particular *acts* of reason. It is a mere platitude to say of reason as a *faculty* that it does not occur at a particular date. The same would be true of any empirical causal property such as the elasticity of a ball. It would be quite in accordance with usage to say that the bouncing of a ball on a certain

[1] [J. Ward, *Psychological Principles* (Cambridge, 1918).]

particular occasion was caused by its elasticity. And it is true that its elasticity is a permanent property and not an event which happens immediately before the bouncing. The fact is that the complete cause of an event always involves two different kinds of factor, viz. dispositional and occurrent. It is very common, and usually quite harmless, in ordinary speech to talk sometimes of the dispositional factor alone, and sometimes of the occurrent factor alone, as 'the cause' of the event. Now suppose I say that Mr Jones's decision to tell the truth on a certain occasion when he was strongly tempted to tell a lie was determined by his reason. It seems to me that I am making the same kind of incomplete statement as I would be if I were to say that the bouncing of a ball on a certain occasion was determined by its elasticity.

(b) In this case there is a further ambiguity which does not exist in the case of physical events like the bouncing of a ball. Suppose that Mr Jones decides on a certain occasion not to make a certain witty but wounding remark which then occurred to him and which he was strongly tempted to make. It would be quite in accordance with usage to say that this decision was determined by the golden rule, i.e. by the principle that it is wrong to treat others in a way in which one would not like to be treated by others. Now this principle is a universal proposition or fact, and as such it is timeless. So one might be tempted to conclude that Mr Jones's decision on this occasion was determined by something timeless. But here again we are taking a convenient popular way of speaking and building upon it a conclusion which it cannot bear. What determined Mr Jones's decision on this occasion was not the golden rule considered as a universal proposition or fact *in vacuo*. It was his *acceptance* of the golden rule, i.e. the fact that he contemplated it, accepted it, applied it to the alternatives under consideration, saw that by making the witty but wounding remark he would be infringing it, and was moved thereby to avoid initiating this otherwise attractive alternative.

(4) Kant's doctrine, as stated in his own words, is this. 'The causality of reason in its intelligible character does not, in producing an effect, *arise* or begin at a certain time . . . The condition which lies in reason is not sensible, and therefore does not begin to be' (p. 475). What are we to say about this? (a) In so far as Kant was led to it by the confusions which I have pointed out, his *grounds* for it are invalid. But the question remains whether it is true or false. (b) I think that the most plausible interpretation which can be put upon it is this. One can be aware introspectively of the earlier process of deliberating and of the later process of having decided on a certain alternative and carrying it into effect. Possibly one can also be aware introspectively of the *transition* at a certain moment from the former to the latter state. But one cannot be aware introspectively of the *act of reason* which determines the change which takes place at this moment.

This is something in the noumenal world and is timeless. (c) If this is what Kant means, the fundamental difficulty is to conceive of something timeless determining a change which takes place at a particular time. (d) To this Kant might answer that nothing is *really* in time. The reality which appears as the earlier process of deliberating must in itself be timeless, and so too must be the reality which appears as the later process of having decided on a certain alternative and carrying it into effect. The whole introspectible sequence of events is the appearance in temporal form of some kind of *non-temporal* series within the noumenal world. I think that this would be the consistent answer for him to make. But, if so, it seems to me that it is inappropriate to talk of a noumenal act of reason as the *initiating cause* of a series of phenomenal events. The relation of a real non-temporal series to its partly delusive appearance as a temporal sequence of events is not a relation of causality. For here we have one and the same series, and the contrast is simply between that series as it is in itself and as it appears to a person who misperceives it under the form of time.

3.1.2.3.4 Reconciliation of freedom and determinism

We can now deal quite briefly with Kant's attempt to reconcile freedom and determinism in the case of human beings. It occupies pp. 475–9 (A 551–8/B 579–86). It appears to come to this. Any action of a man is completely determined, as an event in time, in accordance with natural laws, by his empirical character, his past experiences, and his present circumstances. But his empirical character is itself determined by his intelligible character. So we must also say that every action of a man is determined by his intelligible character, i.e. by something which is not in time and therefore is not itself determined by any previous event. Kant seems to *identify* the intelligible character of a man with his reason. And he seems to think that this guarantees that in every case the man could have decided to initiate the alternative which he believed to be right. This, Kant holds, is true even when he in fact acted against his conscience. It is true though all his actions could be completely predicted from a sufficient knowledge of his empirical character and history and circumstances and the laws of human psychology. 'Reason, irrespective of all empirical conditions of the act, is completely free, and [if a man deliberately tells a lie] the lie is entirely due to *its* default' (p. 477). Kant says that the only question that can be asked is: 'Why did the noumenal self, which in fact determined the phenomenon of a deliberate lie, not instead determine the phenomenon of a truthful answer?' His comment is as follows. 'To this question no answer is possible. For a different intelligible character would have given a different empirical character . . . To explain why in the given circumstances the intelligible character should give just these appearances

and this empirical character transcends . . . all . . . rights of questioning'
(p. 478).

Now it seems to me that, if we think this out, it comes to the following.
To say that a person X *could have* chosen the right alternative A on an
occasion when he in fact chose a wrong alternative A' comes to this. X's
intelligible character *in fact* appears to himself and to others under the guise
of an empirical character E' and a mental history H', from which, in
accordance with the laws of psychology, it could have been predicted with
certainty that he would choose alternative A'. But the very same intelligible character *could have* appeared to X himself and to others under the
guise of a different empirical character E and a different mental history H,
from which, in accordance with the laws of psychology, it could have been
predicted with certainty that he would choose alternative A.

But in what sense are we using 'could have' here? So far as I can see, only
in the *purely negative* sense that it would not be inconsistent with the facts
and laws of nature that the same intelligible character should have
appeared under the guise of E instead of under the guise of E'. That is true.
For the facts and laws of nature concern phenomena and their mutual
relations, and not noumena and their relation to the phenomena which are
their appearances. But surely those who say that a person always could
have chosen what he believed to be the right alternative, even when he in
fact chose a different alternative, must be using 'could have' in some more
positive sense than this. The fundamental difficulty is to get any clear idea
of this positive sense of 'could have'.

Two other remarks seem worth making. (1) Kant has no right to *identify*
a person's noumenal character with his rational nature, even if he has
proved that reason belongs to a person as he is in himself. For, as
phenomena, we are not purely rational. Our characters as noumena must
surely contain something corresponding to the sensitive, emotional, and
passional aspects of our empirical characters. (2) If we accept Kant's
solution would not merely instinctive and impulsive actions be free in
precisely the same sense as deliberate actions? Even of the most impulsive
action it would be true to say that it is determined by the empirical
character; that this in turn is determined by the noumenal character; and
that the very same noumenal character 'could have' manifested itself as a
different empirical character, which would have determined a different
impulsive action on the same occasion.

In conclusion it is worth while to note that Kant says explicitly that he
does not pretend to have proved here the *reality* or even the *possibility* of
human freedom (p. 479, A 558/B 586). The first statement is obviously
true. For all that has been said here the notions of 'ought' and 'ought not'
might be purely delusive. So he has certainly not proved the *reality* of
freedom. The second statement needs a little explanation. He does claim to

have shown that freedom is not logically incompatible with the general conception of nature, including man, as a system of phenomena in which every event is determined by earlier events in accordance with natural laws. What he presumably means is that he has not shown that freedom is compatible with the *particular* facts and laws of nature.

3.2 Freedom in Kant's ethical works

Kant discusses the notion of freedom very fully in connexion with ethics both in the *Fundamental Principles of the Metaphysic of Morals* (section III, p. 65 to end of p. 84)[1] and in the *Critique of Practical Reason*. There is no substantial difference between the two, but some points are brought out more clearly in the latter.

3.2.1 Freedom and the moral law

(1) If by 'will' we mean the power of making a rational choice between alternatives, and by 'free' we mean not determined by foreign causes, then the proposition that the will is free is *analytic*. Kant calls this the 'negative sense of freedom'. I think that the essential point is that it is part of the notion of rational choice that one deliberates and decides in view of the relations of the various alternatives to some *general principle* which goes beyond the present case. If so, he is plainly right.

(2) The negative sense of freedom implies freedom in the positive sense of being determined by laws which reason *imposes upon itself*. 'What else can freedom of the will be but autonomy, i.e. the property of the will to be a law to itself?' (Pp. 65–6.) I think that the essential point here might be put as follows. The positive peculiarity of rational choice is that one of the factors involved in the complete cause of a rational decision is the thought of some general principle of conduct or some ideal scheme of life, by reference to which the various alternatives under consideration are appraised. And this general principle or ideal scheme must be one which the agent himself freely accepts as his own, though it may of course have been thought out and presented to him by others. I accept the conclusion, when so interpreted. But I think that Kant tends to ignore or minimise the fact that other factors enter into the complete cause of a rational decision or into its causal ancestors. The various alternatives must be presented to the agent's attention, and this generally depends on circumstances which are foreign to his will. And the moral principles and ideals, which he accepts and in view of which he now decides, were originally presented to him and inculcated into him by parents, teachers, companions, and so on.

[1] [Broad's references are to Abbott's translation (op. cit.). A more recent translation is *The Moral Law or Kant's Groundwork of the Metaphysic of Morals,* trans. by H. J. Paton (London, n.d.).]

(3) Kant says that it follows from the fact that the will is autonomous in rational decisions that it acts 'on no other maxim than that which can also have as its object itself as a universal law' (p. 66 top). I think that the meaning of this obscure statement is roughly the following. Any *ultimate* principle of conduct on which a free agent acts in making a rational decision must be one which he could consistently will that *everyone* should act upon in *all* circumstances in which it is *relevant*. Now it is an essential part of Kant's ethical theory that the fundamental moral law is to act only on such principles as these. So he concludes: 'A free will and a will subject to moral laws is one and the same' (p. 66). I will now make some comments on this.

(a) In order to be fair to Kant we must distinguish between *ultimate* and *subordinate* principles of action. What I take Kant to mean is that it would be irrational to act on different *ultimate* principles in dealing with oneself or others or in dealing with different persons or classes of person. It may, e.g., be rational to act in certain respects on different principles towards civilised men and primitive savages. But, if so, this must be because the differences in their tastes, capacities, and circumstances require these different subordinate principles in order to carry out an ultimate principle which applies to all men alike. A plausible instance of such an ultimate principle would be the maxim to produce as much happiness and as little unhappiness on the whole as possible, though Kant would *not* accept this as ultimate. Then, again, I think we must introduce the phrase 'all circumstances which are *relevant*'. Some principles which have been claimed as ultimate are relevant to *all* men in *all* circumstances, e.g. the principle of maximising happiness or the golden rule. But others are relevant only in certain circumstances. E.g. the maxim to keep one's promises is relevant only to persons who have made promises and only under the circumstances when they are due for fulfilment.

(b) I agree with Kant in thinking that the notion of *rational* choice involves the notion of acting on no ultimate principles which will not pass this test. But it seems to me that this follows from the *rationality* of the decision and not from its freedom alone. It seems to me that the mere freedom of the choice entails only that it is made on some principle or other which the agent has freely accepted as his own. An examiner who made it his maxim to give first classes in the Tripos to candidates with red hair and green eyes would be acting on a freely accepted principle and therefore acting *freely*. But he would not commonly be held to be acting *rationally*.

(4) Kant actually draws a stronger conclusion than that which I have so far ascribed to him. He seems to hold that, if a decision is to be free and rational, the ultimate principle on which it is made must be not only *acceptable to* reason but also *deducible from* the mere concept of a rational

being. This, e.g., suffices to exclude the principle of maximising general happiness. For it is no part of the concept of a rational being to have sensations and feelings at all, and therefore the notion of happiness introduces something foreign to reason. It is obviously conceivable that there might be rational beings without the capacity for sensations, just as there are rational beings who do not like chocolate. So the maxim 'Make men happy!' can at best be a subordinate principle like 'Give children chocolates!'

Kant admits that nothing can be deduced from the concept of a rational being except the second-order principle that all its first-order ultimate principles of conduct would be such that he would be prepared to act upon them and see them acted upon by everyone in every relevant situation. Actual morality presupposes the existence of a whole lot of first-order principles, which cannot be deduced from the concept of a rational being. But these can and must be tested for rationality by reference to the second-order principle, which can be deduced from the concept of a rational being.

Now what Kant calls the moral law just is this second-order principle. With these definitions, I think we may agree with Kant that any purely rational being, if it could be said to act and to make choices at all, would necessarily decide and act in all cases in accordance with the moral law. But it is well to notice how little this comes to. We do not know whether a purely rational being could act at all. We have no idea what its first-order principles of action would be, if it could act. And the second-order principle, which Kant identifies with the moral law, is a purely negative test for the rationality of first-order principles of action which must be supplied from elsewhere.

(5) I think that the whole position up to this point can be summarised clearly if we draw a distinction between 'being determined *in accordance with* a principle' and 'being determined *by* a principle'. Every action of every agent is determined *in accordance with* some principle. E.g. a stone falls in accordance with the law of gravitation. But only the deliberate choices of a free conscious agent are *determined by* a principle. The law of gravitation is not a cause-factor which determines the fall of a stone; it is merely a formula in accordance with which stones and other bodies fall. But suppose I am a utilitarian and I decide on a certain course of action because I believe that it will produce more happiness on the whole than any other alternative open to me. Then my choice is determined *by* the principle of maximising general happiness. The fact that I accept that principle is a cause-factor in determining my choice.

Now rational decisions are not merely determined, in this sense, *by* principles. They are also, like all events, determined *in accordance with* principles. The principle in accordance with which all purely rational decisions are determined is the second-order principle which Kant identifies with the moral law. This is the law that the ultimate principles by which the decisions of a free rational agent are determined are such that he would be prepared to act on them and see them acted upon by others in all relevant circumstances. Thus the moral law, in Kant's sense, stands to the first-order principles of rational choice in much the same relation as the principle of relativity stands to particular physical laws.

3.2.2 Freedom and determinism

We come now to the following question: How can we pass from the analytic conditional proposition 'If I were a purely rational being, all my decisions *would necessarily* be in accordance with the moral law' to the synthetic categorical proposition 'Although I am not a purely rational being, but also a sensitive and emotional one, all my decisions *ought* to be and therefore *could* be in accordance with the moral law'?

(1) Kant first draws his usual distinction between the intelligible or noumenal self and the sensible or phenomenal self. His statements on this point are to be found on pp. 70 and 71. His doctrine here seems to be exactly the same as that in the solution of the third antinomy in the *Critique of Pure Reason*. It comes to this. We are active in so far as we use our understanding and our reason. What acts must be a self-subsistent entity and not a mere appearance of something to someone. Each of us has direct awareness of himself as a reasoning and understanding being. Kant does not use the word 'apperception' here, but he evidently means to assert that each of us has a kind of non-sensuous immediate knowledge of himself as he really is. It should be added that Kant here draws the following important distinction between understanding and reason. Both are activities of our real self with which we are non-sensuously acquainted. But understanding is more closely connected with sensibility than is reason. Understanding 'cannot produce by its activity any other conceptions but those which merely serve to bring the intuitions of sense under rules . . .' But reason '. . . exhibits its most important function in distinguishing the world of sense from that of understanding, and thereby presenting the limits of the understanding itself' (p. 71, §2).

(2) Kant then argues as follows. A man, *as he really is*, is a purely rational being, and the decisions of a purely rational being would necessarily be in accord with the moral law. The notion of *ought* applies to a man only as a being who is both rational and sensitive. His phenomenal self and all its apparent sensations, emotions, and actions are merely appearances in temporal guise of his noumenal self, which is purely rational, and of its real actions. Therefore it can be said of him as a phenomenon that all his actions *ought* to accord with the moral law. The following quotation is perfectly

explicit: 'What one morally *ought* is what one *necessarily would* as a member of the intelligible world. It is conceived by oneself as an *ought* only because one also considers oneself as a member of the world of sense' (p. 75 top). This theory seems to me to be quite futile for the following reasons.

(a) According to the theory, as I really am I am a purely rational being. As such any choice that I make must be in accordance with the moral law. Suppose now that, as a phenomenon, I perform a phenomenal action, such as telling a deliberate lie, which is not in accord with the moral law. This phenomenal action, like everything else in my phenomenal self, must be an appearance to me and others of *something* in my real self. But, since my real self cannot make a morally wrong decision, there are only two alternatives possible. Either the wrong phenomenal action is the appearance of a *right* noumenal decision, or it is the appearance of something in my noumenal self which is *not an act of choice at all*. On the first alternative it is difficult to see why a right noumenal decision should be represented in the phenomenal self by a wrong phenomenal action. And it is impossible to see how the agent could justly blame himself or be blamed by others for it. Surely an appearance of what is in fact right can be only apparently wrong. The same difficulty arises on the second alternative. An appearance of what is not really an act of choice is only apparently a deliberate action, and it is therefore only apparently susceptible of moral praise or blame. The difficulty may be summed up as follows. If the theory were true, it would be impossible for a person to perform an action which is really wrong. For his *noumenal* self necessarily acts in accordance with the moral law if it does act; and his *phenomenal* self, like all phenomena, does not really *act* at all. What are called its actions are merely certain timeless noumenal processes, as they appear to him and to others under the subjective form of time.

(b) The fundamental fallacy of Kant's doctrine is to identify the noumenal or real self with something which is purely rational. This identification must be false, and it does not follow from Kant's premisses. Granted that sensations, images, emotions, desires, etc. are only phenomena, they do exist. And, on Kant's view, they are products of the actions of foreign things-in-themselves on one's own noumenal self, and of the reactions of certain activities of one's noumenal self upon itself. Therefore it cannot be the whole truth about a noumenal self to say that it has the active powers of reason and understanding. It must also be true of it that it has certain *passive or receptive* powers; though it cannot be aware of these directly, but only through the phenomena which they in part determine. It is therefore quite certain that no noumenal self which appears to itself as a phenomenon, or to which anything else appears as a phenomenon, can be a purley rational active being. The fallacy which Kant makes is this. He passes from the premiss that the only characteristics of a noumenal self of which it can be directly and non-sensuously aware are its active powers of understanding and reason, to the conclusion that it has no other characteristics but these active powers. The transition is invalid and the conclusion is false.

(c) Once this is admitted, Kant's attempt to reconcile freedom and determinism is seen to break down completely. The hypothetical proposition 'If we were purely rational beings, our decisions would necessarily accord with the moral law, as defined by Kant', remains true. But it is without application. For even as noumena we are not purely rational beings. So it does not enable us to see why we are under a moral obligation to behave as such beings would necessarily behave, nor to see in what sense it is always possible for us to do so. We may sum up this criticism as follows. On the false view that the noumenal self is purely rational it is impossible to see how we can perform really wrong actions at all. On the true view that the noumenal self is not purely rational it is possible to see that we could perform really wrong actions. But the attempted explanation of why we *could* always have avoided doing them, and why we are under a *moral obligation* to avoid doing them, breaks down.

(3) In the *Critique of Practical Reason* Kant makes the following important points. To be free is a necessary condition of being subject to the moral law. But epistemologically our *knowledge* that we are subject to the moral law is prior to our *knowledge* that we are free in our decisions. We are not directly aware that we are free. But we are directly aware of the moral law and of our obligation to act in accordance with it. From this we can infer that we must be free in our decisions. As Kant puts it, freedom is the *ratio essendi* of the obligation to conform to the moral law, but the moral law is the *ratio cognoscendi* of freedom (pp. 116–19). This is a consistent position, and it removes all appearance of a logical circle (p. 88n).

(4) Another point which Kant makes in the *Critique of Practical Reason* (pp. 136–7) is this. The moral law cannot be 'deduced', i.e. justified, as the categories can be by transcendental arguments. But it needs no justification. It is a *datum*, though it is in the peculiar position that it is presented to us *a priori* by reason and not empirically by the senses (pp. 120, 136–7). On the other hand, the concept of freedom, which was left as a mere logical possibility in the *Critique of Pure Reason*, is shown to have actual application by means of our knowledge of the moral law and of our duty to conform to it. Moreover, it is this which enables us to pass from a merely negative conception of freedom to a positive conception of it. The merely negative conception is absence of determination by *earlier events* in accordance with a *law of nature*. The positive conception is determination by a principle which the agent freely accepts as one to be acted upon by *all* men in *all* circumstances in which it is relevant. It should be noted that even the negative sense of freedom is not the same as *in*determinism. Kant

never accepted this. He says explicitly that the notion of a will whose decisions are not subject to law of any kind is a mere chimaera (p. 65).

(5) On pp. 139–47 Kant discusses elaborately the question whether he is justified in ascribing causality to the noumenal self after saying in the *Critique of Pure Reason* that the categories have no meaning or application outside the range of possible sense-perception. I think that the essence of his answer might be put as follows. We must remember the distinction between the *pure category* of ground and consequent and the corresponding *schema* of cause and effect. The pure category is intelligible in itself and apart from the reference to time which is involved in its schema. It is therefore not meaningless nonsense to apply it to noumena, if we have any positive ground for doing so. And the facts of moral obligation make it necessary to do so. But this does not extend our knowledge of noumena in any other respect. For, although the pure category is not unintelligible, it remains unimaginable. Since noumena are neither spatial nor temporal we can form no concrete idea of their causal relations. We cannot, e.g., imagine anything in the noumenal world which could be compared with interaction by impact or by attractive or repulsive forces in the world of phenomena.

4 God

Kant deals with theology in each of the three *Critiques* and also in a work called *Religion within the Bounds of Mere Reason*.[1] The division is roughly as follows. In the *Critique of Pure Reason* he deals with the three main traditional arguments for the existence of God. He concludes that they are all invalid. But they are not merely contingent mistakes; they arise naturally in the course of human thought, like the antinomies. In the *Critique of Practical Reason* he tries to show that the existence of God is a postulate which must be granted unless the demands of the moral law are to be self-stultifying. In the latter part of the *Critique of Judgment* he is concerned with the notion of teleology, and particularly with the apparent teleology displayed in living organisms. He there considers how far this must be accepted as a fact, and in what sense if any it requires us to admit the existence of a wise and benevolent author of nature.

4.1 Theology in the Critique of Pure Reason

The main treatment here is in book II, chapter 3 of the *Transcendental Dialectic*, which is entitled *The Ideal of Pure Reason*. But it should be noted that really the thesis of the fourth antinomy is essentially the same as what

[1] [*Religion within the Limits of Reason Alone,* trans. by T. M. Green and H. H. Hudson, 2nd ed. (La Salle, Illinois, 1960).]

Kant later calls the *cosmological argument* for the existence of God. Each claims to prove from the existence of contingent beings, such as oneself, that there is a being whose existence is necessary and on whom the existence of contingent beings depends. Kant asserts that there is a fundamental difference, but I am quite sure that there is not.

4.1.1 The transcendental ideal

By an 'ideal', in his special technical sense, Kant means the concept of an individual existent regarded as being an actual instance of an idea of reason. An idea of reason could not possibly be exemplified by any *perceptible* object; but we can *conceive*, or talk as if we conceived, of individual objects answering to ideas.

Now Kant holds that we have a conception of the totality of all positive predicates. A complete account of any finite thing would consist in saying that it had such-and-such of these and lacked the rest. Now the conception of a conjunction of all the positive predicates that there are would be just an *idea* of reason. But we go further. We have the concept of an *individual existent* possessing all the positive predicates that there are. This is the concept of the *ens realissimum* or *most perfect being*. This is what Kant calls the *transcendental ideal*.

Kant appears to hold that this concept is natural to any rational mind, and that it is useful. But we are not content just to entertain it as a concept. We think that the *ens realissimum* actually exists and is the source of the existence of all other things. This seems plausible because all the positive qualities possessed by any finite existent are a selection from those possessed by the *ens realissimum*.

4.1.2 The three speculative arguments

The *ens realissimum* is what is meant by 'God' in the philosophical sense of the word. Kant distinguishes arguments for the existence of God into *speculative* and *practical*. The former make no use of ethical premisses, whilst the latter do use an ethical premiss. The speculative arguments may be classified as follows. We can begin by dividing them into (1) those which do *not*, and (2) those which *do*, use an existential premiss. The only instance of class (1) is the *ontological argument*. We can then subdivide class (2) as follows. (2a) Those in which the existential premiss is extremely abstract, e.g. 'Something contingent (e.g. myself) exists'. (2b) Those in which the existential premiss is fairly definite and takes the form 'Nature exists and has such-and-such peculiar features'. The argument from an indefinite existential premiss is called by Kant the *cosmological argument*. It is often called the argument for a *first cause*. The argument from the definite existential premiss is called by Kant the *physico-theological argument*. It is commonly called the *argument from design*.

4.1.2.1 Interrelations of the three arguments

The order in which these arguments present themselves to the human mind is first the physico-theological, then the cosmological, and finally the ontological. Any plain man can understand the argument from design and will be a good deal impressed by it. The argument for a first cause is a little more abstract. But it occurs to most reflective persons, and it goes back at least as far as Plato in the western world. The ontological argument is extremely abstract and sophisticated. No plain man would ever think of it. It was first invented by St Anselm, and it has never won general acceptance even among experts.

Now Kant thinks that the logical order is exactly the opposite of the psychological order. The argument from design needs to be supplemented by the argument for a first cause, and this in turn needs to be supplemented by the ontological argument. We must now ask why he held this.

For this purpose we can start with the argument from design. Kant points out that this by itself could not do more than render probable the existence of an *architect* of nature who works with pre-existing material having its own laws and properties. If the argument from design is to get beyond this, it must assume that the *existence* of matter, as well as its *arrangement*, is contingent. It must then be argued that this entails the existence of a necessarily existent being on whom the existence and properties of matter depend. But this is the cosmological argument. So at best the argument from design cannot prove or render probable the existence of a supreme being, in the sense in which theology and religion understand that phrase, except by appealing tacitly or openly to the cosmological argument. There is one comment which I would make on this. Even if one accepted both the argument from design and the cosmological argument, there is no reason why one should *identify* the architect, proved by the former, with the first cause, proved by the latter. Surely matter might have been created by one being and arranged by another. Plato in the *Timaeus* does in fact distinguish between God and the demiurge.

We come now to the relation between the cosmological and the ontological arguments. Kant here indulges in a curious exercise in formal logic. He argues that anyone who wishes to pass from the conclusion of the cosmological argument to the conclusion that there is an entity possessing all positive predicates will have to add the premiss 'Any entity whose existence is intrinsically necessary is one which has all positive predicates'. Now this is the *converse* of the proposition which the ontological argument asserts. Kant then argues that, since from the nature of the case there could not be *more* than one entity possessing all positive predicates, it is legitimate to employ single conversion here, although it would not be valid in general for an affirmative universal proposition. The upshot of the discussion is this. Suppose that a person who accepts the cosmological argument wants to prove by means of it that there must be an entity possessing all positive predicates, i.e. an *ens realissimum*. Then he will have to accept an additional premiss which is, in view of the essential uniqueness of an *ens realissimum*, logically equivalent to the conclusion of the ontological argument. I think that Kant's argument here is formally correct. It rests on the following formal principle: 'If every S is P and there is at least one S and at most one P, then every P is S'. This principle is formally valid.

It seems to me that a more important relation between the two arguments is the following. If the cosmological argument is valid, it proves the existence of at least one entity whose existence is intrinsically necessary. Now to say of a thing that its existence is intrinsically necessary is to say that its nature is such that it would be *logically impossible* for there not to be a thing of this nature. But that is precisely what the ontological argument asserts about the property of having all positive predicates. For it argues that there could not fail to be an entity having this property, since it would be self-contradictory to suppose that the property does not include the predicate of existence.

4.1.2.2 The ontological argument

We can now consider Kant's special objections to each of the three arguments. We will begin, as he does, with the ontological argument. The following are the most important criticisms that he makes.

(1) Are we thinking of anything definite when we talk of a being whose existence is intrinsically necessary? Analogies from necessary propositions in mathematics are quite irrelevant. Any such proposition when fully stated is found to be *conditional* and to state that *if* a certain antecedent be admitted *then* a certain consequent necessarily follows. E.g. *if* there were anything answering to the definition of a plane triangle *then* it would necessarily follow that the sum of its angles is equal to two right angles. In such cases there would be no inconsistency in doubting or denying *both* the antecedent *and* the consequent. Now the question with which we are here concerned is quite different. It comes to this: Is it intelligible to assert that there are certain definitions or descriptions of possible existents, such that it would be self-contradictory to suppose that there is nothing answering to them? It is quite irrelevant to produce examples of conditional pro-

positions, where it would be self-contradictory to deny the consequent after having accepted the antecedent.

(2) Kant points out that all existential propositions are *synthetic*, and therefore it can never be *self-contradictory* to deny such a proposition. They are in fact always of the form 'There is something answering to such-and-such a definition or description'. Now it is obvious that this asserts something which goes beyond the contents of the definition or description.

(3) Very closely connected with this is the fact that existence is not a predicate, in the sense in which red or square is. This is disguised by language. The *sentence* 'Smith exists' is of the same *grammatical* form as the *sentence* 'Smith snores'. But the *propositions* which they express require quite different kinds of logical analysis. 'Smith exists' cannot express a proposition about the individual Smith, or it would be a tautology. 'Apollo does not exist' cannot express a proposition about the individual Apollo. For there is no such individual, and, if there were, the proposition would be false.

(4) Lastly, Kant points out that we have no means of knowing whether the notion of a being possessed of all positive qualities to the highest degree is the notion of even a *possible* existent. We know indeed that it involves no *formal* contradiction, for this can arise only between q and not-q and not between two positive qualities q_1 and q_2. But we also know that some positive qualities are incompatible, e.g. being red all over and green all over at the same time. It is true that these are two *determinates* under a single determinable, viz. colour. But it is not even certain that all supreme *determinable* characteristics are compatible with each other. Extension and consciousness, e.g., are supreme determinables and are both positive. But many eminent philosophers, e.g. Descartes and McTaggart, have held that they are obviously incompatible with each other.

It seems to me that Kant's objections to the ontological argument are quite conclusive. It should be noticed that some of them are objections, not merely to the *argument*, but also to the *conclusion*. For one of them is an objection to the very notion of a being whose existence is intrinsically necessary, and another of them is a doubt about the validity of the very notion of *ens realissimum*.

4.1.2.3 The cosmological argument

This argument starts with the premiss that something exists whose existence is contingent, e.g. any finite individual. Indeed the existence of everything in nature is contingent. It is then argued that anything whose existence is contingent must derive its existence from something else, and that in the end it must derive its existence from something whose existence is intrinsically necessary. Kant's main criticisms are as follows.

(1) The principle of universal causation, on which the argument is based, is valid only within the world of possible sense-perception. Outside this it cannot be proved and Kant says that it has no clear meaning. Yet it is used here to carry us from the world of nature to a non-natural first cause of nature.

(2) At the top of p. 528 (A635/B663) Kant uses a rather different argument. He says that the law of causation properly refers, not to the existence of things, but to the occurrence of changes in things. When we reason about the causation of *events* in nature we are using our reason properly. When we reason about the causation of the *existence of things* in nature we are using our reason speculatively and improperly.

It seems to me that Kant's objections are fundamentally sound even if we reject his view about the law of causation being only a principle of possible experience. The essential point may be put as follows. We are certainly using the word 'causation' ambiguously when we talk (1) of the causal connexion of one event with another event in nature, and (2) of a relation of one-sided dependence between nature as a whole and something which is other than nature. We know fairly well what we mean by the first, and we do not know what we mean by the second. Now it is logically invalid to argue that, because the first kind of causation involves an endless series of conditions which are themselves conditioned, we must assume the existence of something outside nature, on which nature as a whole depends in the second sense.

4.1.2.4 The physico-theological argument

Kant, like Hume, treats the argument from purposiveness within nature to the existence of a designer of nature with considerable respect. If it is content to state its conclusion in terms of probability and does not pretend to prove the existence of a single supreme being whose existence is intrinsically necessary and who created the world, it has some force. But if it goes beyond this it is invalid. That is practically the same conclusion as Hume reached in the *Dialogues concerning Natural Religion*. Kant's treatment of this whole question is much fuller and more profound in the *Critique of Judgment*, and so we will defer it for the present.

4.1.3 Explanation of the illusion in these arguments

The fundamental difficulty in all these arguments is this. We seem to be faced with two principles, each of which appeals to us as rational beings, but which seem to contradict each other. The first is that, if anything exists, then *something* must exist in its own right. It cannot be that *everything* that exists derives its existence from something else. This is the principle at the back of the cosmological argument and the thesis of the fourth antinomy. The second is that it is impossible that the existence of anything should be a necessary consequence of its mere nature or definition. This is the principle which is fatal both to the ontological argument and to the conclusion of the cosmological argument.

Now Kant says that the only way out of the dilemma is to suppose that neither of these two principles concerns *things*, but that both are merely methodological rules for the guidance of reason. The positive principle might be put in the form of the following maxim: 'In all your researches try to explain everything that you can be deduction from the minimum number of ultimate facts and ultimate laws. Never be contented with a plurality of isolated brute facts, but try to make natural science as nearly a deductive system as you can.' The negative principle might be put in the form of the following warning: 'Remember, nevertheless, that this ideal is in principle quite unattainable. No empirical thing exists of intrinsic necessity and no empirical law is intrinsically necessary. If a necessarily existent being were possible at all, it would be something quite outside nature and quite inconceivable to us. And, if nature depended on this being for its existence, this relation of dependence would be something quite different from the causal dependence of one event in nature upon earlier events, which is all that we can understand.' Kant expresses this doctrine by saying that the two principles are *regulative* and not *constitutive*.

Particular phenomena can be explained only in terms of other phenomena and laws of natural causation. An appeal to the supposed necessarily existent being, on whom all nature depends, explains no particular fact in nature. On the other hand, we can get our knowledge of phenomena into a more and more purely deductive form. We ought to try to do this, although the ideal of a completely deductive natural science, with a single self-evident law and a single necessarily existent material, is a complete chimaera if taken literally. Though speculative theology can *prove* nothing, it can *disprove* all theories which regard nature as a self-explanatory system which exists of intrinsic necessity. We can see that the kind of knowledge which natural science could give us, even when carried to the highest conceivable pitch of perfection, could not completely satisfy our intellects, as they are satisfied in pure mathematics. For it would always contain brute facts and laws which are not intrinsically necessary. But we can also see that we can have nothing better to put in its place.

The only comment that I will make is this. In order to avoid the contradiction it is not necessary that *both* principles should be merely regulative. One might be merely regulative and the other constitutive. Now it seems to me that Kant's view ought to be that the negative principle, viz. that it is impossible that the existence of anything should be a necessary consequence of its mere nature or definition, is a law about things and not *merely* a rule for the guidance of reason. It may nevertheless be also the foundation for such a rule. On the other hand, Kant must certainly hold that the positive principle, i.e. the one on which the cosmological argument rests, is valid *only* when interpreted regulatively.

4.2 Theology in the Critique of Practical Reason

In the first *Critique* Kant says definitely that, if there can be any proof of the existence of God, it must use *ethical* and not merely factual premises. In the second *Critique* he tries to give such a proof. The argument may be put as follows.

We recognise that the *complete* good consists not merely of moral perfection (which is the *supreme* good), but of this accompanied by the appropriate amount of happiness. Now it is evident that the complete good *ought* to exist. Since it ought to exist, it must be *possible*, and therefore anything which is an essential condition of its possibility must be *actual*. Now its possibility is certainly not guaranteed by the ordinary facts and laws of nature. In the world of phenomena there is nothing to ensure that a virtuous person will enjoy the appropriate amount of happiness, even if we suppose that he survives the death of his present body. The only guarantee of the possibility of this is the supposition that the noumena which appear as our own bodies and as external things are completely under the control of a noumenal being who arranges them so that the virtuous shall eventually receive the amount of happiness which they deserve. We are thus entitled to postulate a being on whom nature depends. Since this being arranges that virtue shall be rewarded it is not merely powerful but *good*. And such a being is what most men understand by God.

I have already criticised the corresponding ethical argument for immortality. This ethical argument for the existence of God seems to me to be very much weaker. We must distinguish the statements 'You ought to do so-and-so' and 'Such-and-such a state of affairs ought to be'. The first implies that you *could* do so-and-so, i.e. that the action is not merely logically possible, but also physically and psychologically possible for you to do. But the second does not imply that the existence of such-and-such a state of affairs is physically possible. It seems to me to come to no more than the following hypothetical proposition. '*If* this state of affairs were physically possible, *then* anyone who had the power to bring it into existence would have a *prima facie* duty to do so.' Now I agree that what Kant calls the 'complete good' is a state of affairs which ought to be. But this does not imply that it is causally possible either here and now or in the super-sensible world. It implies only that, *if* there were a being who could bring it about, *then* he ought to do so. We have no right to pass from this conditional proposition to the categorical proposition that there *is* a being who can and will bring it about.

4.3 Theology in the Critique of Judgment

The *Critique of Judgment*[1] is concerned with two subjects which Kant holds to be closely connected, viz. aesthetics and teleology. We shall not be concerned here with the former, nor with Kant's reasons for thinking that it is closely connected with the latter. But we must consider the views on teleology, because they are important in themselves and because they underlie the theological doctrines of the third *Critique*.

4.3.1 'Determinant' and 'reflective' judgments

We will begin with an important distinction which Kant draws between what he calls *determinant* and *reflective* judgments. We may put this as follows.

All judgment consists in subsuming a particular case under a general principle, or a narrower principle under a wider one. Now two alternatives are possible. (1) The general principle may be already given and established. The judgment which subsumes particular cases or narrower principles under it is then called *determinant*. (2) The judgment may interpret the special cases or the narrower principles in accordance with a principle which is not independently given and established.

These distinctions are not very clear in the abstract, but Kant's meaning comes out fairly clearly in his examples. There are certain concepts, e.g. cause, substance, etc., which are native to the understanding. And there are certain general principles, involving these concepts, which Kant thinks can be proved transcendentally, e.g. the law of universal causation within the world of phenomena. A determinant judgment is one which uses these concepts and principles and interprets particular cases and laws in terms of them. But, as Kant points out, these give us only the skeleton of any possible system of nature. The actual system of nature contains innumerable singular facts and particular causal laws, and none of these can be established by transcendental arguments. Now we try to establish the particular laws of nature inductively from observations on the singular facts of nature. And then we try to connect all these particular empirical laws into a single deductive system.

In doing this we use certain principles of a peculiar kind. They are not empirical. It would be circular, e.g., to pretend to base the principles of induction on induction. On the other hand, they are neither self-evident

[1] [Broad's references are to *Kant's Kritik of Judgment*, trans. by J. H. Bernard (London, 1892); 2nd ed. *Kant's Critique of Judgement* (London, 1914).]

nor transcendentally *a priori*. If they were, they would apply equally to every possible system of nature, whilst the principles in question are concerned with features which may be peculiar to the actual system of nature. They are what I should call *postulates*, as distinct from *a priori* principles and inductive generalisations. Kant gives examples of them: 'There are no jumps in nature' (principle of *continuity*); 'The great variety of empirical laws is not ultimate. They are deducible from a comparatively few fundamental laws' (principle of *limited variety*); 'The ultimate laws of nature are expressible in simple mathematical functions'. And so on. Now *reflective judgments* are those which make use of postulates such as these.

Kant thinks that all these postulates come under the following supreme postulate: 'The particular laws of nature must be regarded as if they formed such a system as they would form if they were laws of a single understanding'. According to Kant the *a priori* principles of natural science, such as the principles of causation and of the permanence of substance, actually *are* the laws according to which any possible non-intuitive understanding must synthesise its sense-given materials, if experience of self and of objects is to be possible. The supreme postulate is that the particular laws of nature, e.g. the law of gravitation, are of the same kind, though it is impossible to prove this.

If this is interpreted fairly charitably, I think we can accept it. The postulates which we make about nature are propositions which we might expect to be true if nature were the product of an intelligent being whose mind worked on the same general principles as our minds do. To put it in another way, they all come under the general postulate that nature is so constructed in its details that we shall be able to discover and to systematise its special laws better and better the more we try. There is no kind of *a priori* necessity about this. Every event might be causally determined, and yet we might have been unable to discover a single causal law, unless other conditions had been fulfilled which seem to be quite contingent. The mathematical form of the laws might have been too complicated for us to grasp. Or there might have been a vast number of totally disconnected laws. Or the laws and properties of matter might have been such that it would be impossible to isolate any one set of phenomena even approximately from other phenomena in the neighbourhood or even in the remoter parts of space.

4.3.2 Purposiveness

This brings us to Kant's discussion of the notion of *purposiveness* in nature. He distinguishes *formal or subjective* purposiveness, and *real or objective* purposiveness. He then subdivides the latter into (1) *formal* and (2) *material*. Finally he divides material objective purposiveness into (2a) *relative* and

(2b) *inner*. We will now consider these in turn. It will be noticed that Kant uses the word 'formal' both as the name of one of his two primary divisions and as the name of one subdivision of real or objective purposiveness. This is obviously inconvenient. I shall therefore use the names *subjective* and *objective*, and discard the names *formal* and *real*, in referring to the two primary divisions.

4.3.2.1 Subjective purposiveness

By '*subjective* purposiveness' Kant means an adaptation of nature to our cognitive faculties, which is, so far as we can see, quite contingent. It is thus closely bound up with the postulates which are used as principles in reflective judgment. The proposition that nature has subjective purposiveness is non-empirical, in the sense that it cannot legitimately be established by induction. On the other hand, it is not *a priori*, since it is neither intuitively nor demonstratively certain and is incapable of transcendental proof. Kant points out that subjective purposiveness, in this sense, must be distinguished from *practical* purposiveness, i.e. the utility of nature to supply our practical needs. We can, however, think of subjective purposiveness by analogy with practical purposiveness, i.e. we can say that nature seems as if it had been constructed by a being who wanted it to be intelligible to us if we took enough trouble to understand it. Kant holds, correctly I think, that we feel a certain kind of intellectual pleasure whenever we discover subjective purposiveness in nature. The mere fact that nature is found to obey the general principles of pure understanding gives us no particular pleasure, because nature and consciousness of self and objects would be utterly impossible unless this were so. But whenever we discover unity in complexity and law in apparent disorder, we do have a feeling of intellectual satisfaction. Nature has answered to a postulate which *we* cannot help making, but which we know that *it* need not have fulfilled. We welcome this as a kind of uncovenanted mercy.

4.3.2.2 Objective purposiveness

By '*objective* purposiveness' Kant means the adaptation of the parts of an object to the object as a whole and the adaptation of objects to their environment, as distinct from the adaptation of nature to our cognitive faculties.

He now subdivides this into 'formal' and 'material'. By '*formal* objective purposiveness' he means the fact that a very simple geometrical figure, e.g. a circle, may have an enormous number of unsuspected properties and may furnish the key to solve a number of different geometrical problems. He holds that it is somewhat misleading to talk of 'purposiveness' in such cases. Strictly speaking, we use the word only when we find an adaptation, or a unity in complexity, which seems *contingent* to the subject-matter. We then cannot help regarding this as imposed on the materials from outside. Now in the case of the so-called formal objective purposiveness this contingency is lacking. The properties do all follow necessarily from the concept of the figure when constructed in the *a priori* intuitum of space.

Kant therefore concentrates on *material* objective purposiveness. This he subdivides into 'relative' and 'inner'. I think it will be better to substitute 'extrinsic' for 'relative' and 'intrinsic' for 'inner' here. Whenever we say that a thing is 'purposive' we imply that we regard it *as if* it were in part at least due to the design of some intelligent being. Now a thing might be designed simply as an *end*. In that case the functions of its parts would be to keep it existing and performing its characteristic activities and perhaps to produce other things like itself. When the purposiveness which we ascribe to a thing is of this kind we call it *intrinsic*. But a thing might be designed simply as a means by which things of the first kind can exist and flourish. When the purposiveness which we ascribe to a thing is only of this kind we call it *extrinsic*. Now we cannot properly call anything an '*extrinsic* purpose of nature' unless we admit that some things are '*intrinsic* purposes of nature'. The mere fact that many things are useful or essential for the existence and welfare of certain other things does not suffice to justify us in making teleological judgments unless we hold that these other things are themselves *intrinsic* purposes of nature.

4.3.2.3 'Natural purposes' and 'purposes of nature'

Kant describes an object as an *intrinsic natural purpose* if it fulfils all the following conditions. (1) In order to account for the forms and the relative positions of its parts we have to refer to the whole and to consider the function of each part in maintaining the whole. (2) The parts must produce and maintain each other by their mutual actions. (It should be noticed that an artificial machine answers to the first condition but not to the second.) (3) The object must have the power to take up foreign material and transform it so that it serves to build up and maintain the whole. (4) Although the object itself may eventually break down, it has the power to produce other objects which are intrinsic natural purposes like itself.

Kant holds that living organisms are the only known examples of intrinsic natural purposes. The four conditions are no doubt suggested by the study of living organisms. Kant says that we know of nothing else strictly analogous to living organisms. To compare them with artificial machines is inadequate. For machines do not take up foreign matter and organise it so as to replace the wastage of their parts, and they do not produce other machines like themselves. It is equally futile to attempt to explain the peculiarities of organisms by assuming a kind of immaterial directive agent, or so-called 'vegetable' or 'animal' soul or 'entelechy'. Either these entelechies are *sui generis*, in which case they throw no light on the problem. Or they are conceived to be analogous to our minds. But our minds seem to depend for their functioning on the pre-existing organisation of our bodies. They certainly do not appear to have anything to do with the processes which keep our bodies going and build them up. If our minds do control the organic processes of our bodies, their action is quite unconscious, and we know neither *that* they do it nor *how* they do it. So nothing is gained by supposing the entelechies to be like our minds.

Now organisms are only a small part of nature. Can we say that nature *as a whole* is purposive? Kant here draws a distinction between a 'purpose of nature' and a 'natural purpose'. We can see that any organism is a natural purpose by merely studying its internal organisation and seeing how the parts mutually determine each other and maintain the whole by their interaction. But when we ask whether a thing is a *purpose of nature* we have to consider its relations to other things in nature. The question comes to this: 'Can we and must we regard this thing as an *end*, to which the rest of nature is a means?'

So long as we confine ourselves to the study of nature, and of man as a mere part of nature, we cannot find anything which obviously must be regarded in this way. As one animal species among others, men are subject to precisely the same conditions as other living beings. There is no sign that everything else is made for man *as an animal organism*. If we are to conceive anything as an ultimate purpose of nature, we must regard it as having *intrinsic value*. Now, on Kant's view, nothing has intrinsic value except a rational being who deliberately does what he believes to be right for its own sake.

If, then, it can be said that there is a final purpose of creation, it must be the existence and activity of such beings. Now nature, in the sense of the material world, is a part of creation. Again, men are rational beings who are also parts of nature, in so far as they have animal organisms and sensations and impulses which they share with animals. When we consider man, not merely as one animal among others, but as the only animal which is also rational and capable of guiding his actions by the moral law, we can say that man is the ultimate purpose of nature on earth.

We can then raise the following question: If we regard man as the ultimate purpose of nature, and the rest of nature as a means designed for the benefit of man, what precise benefit must we suppose that nature is designed to supply to man? Kant says that *prima facie* there are two alternative answers. (1) That nature is designed to provide man with *happiness*, or (2) that it is designed to provide him with a means of exercising and cultivating his *faculties*. The first alternative he rejects. It is plainly false that nature takes any special care of human happiness. Even if it did, the impulses which men share with animals prevent them from enjoying any permanent happiness and often make them more inimical to each other's welfare than nature itself. We must therefore look for something which nature does for *us* and for no other creatures, and which prepares us for what is *beyond* nature and can be done only by ourselves as free agents. Now nature cannot *make* us virtuous. But it can and does provide us with opportunities for acquiring technical and intellectual skill and for controlling and organising our impulses. This happens in the course of our struggles with nature. In these we learn to understand ourselves and our fellow men and external things, to discipline ourselves, and to transform external nature in accordance with our wills. Now this is the necessary condition without which we cannot become free moral agents.

Kant's view may be summarised as follows. If we consider the whole world of finite things, including ourselves, animals, plants, and inorganic matter, we can find nothing in it valuable for its own sake except rational beings freely obeying a self-imposed moral law. Suppose now that we think of the whole world as the deliberate product of an intelligent being. Then the only ultimate purpose which we can reasonably ascribe to him is the production, maintenance, and development of free rational beings. Everything else in nature will be subservient to that end. Now men are rational beings, but they are also animals and to that extent parts of nature. The ultimate purpose of nature on earth must be to serve as a training-ground in which men learn by trial and error to act more and more as rational beings and less and less as irrational animals. Unregenerate human nature is by no means adapted to great or lasting happiness, and there is nothing in external nature to suggest that it is specially adapted to make men *happy*. But when it most fails to make us happy it may best succeed in training us to be virtuous.

4.3.3 The status of teleological judgments

The next point to be considered is the nature and uses of teleological judgments. Here Kant draws an important distinction between the *fact* of teleology in nature and the alleged theological explanation of it in terms of *design* by an intelligent author of nature. It is vitally important not to mix up the two.

4.3.3.1 The use of teleological concepts in natural science

It is a plain fact that there are certain things in nature, viz. living organisms, which are intrinsically teleological. Moreover there is a practical maxim of teleology which all biologists do in fact use whatever their theoretical opinions may be. It may be put in the form 'Assume that everything in an organism tends directly or indirectly to maintain it or to enable it to reproduce itself and maintain its species.' This maxim, Kant says, is in one sense derived from experience. Unless we had met with living organisms and had studied them we should not have formed the notion of intrinsically teleological objects. But although the maxim is *suggested* by particular empirical facts, it goes beyond them. It says that the appearance of teleology, which stares us in the face when organisms are viewed superficially, will continue to be verified in the minutest detail as they are investigated more and more carefully. Not only do biologists in fact act on this assumption. It has again and again been verified, and discoveries have been made by means of it which would not otherwise have been made.

So far, the teleological judgment has a perfectly legitimate place in natural science. But the doctrine that organisms actually have been intentionally designed and produced by an intelligent author of nature has no place in natural science, whether it be true or false. Such a hypothesis provides no explanation for any particular fact in nature. Scientific explanation must be wholly in terms of phenomena and laws of natural causation, for this is the only kind of causation that we really understand. Kant says that it is perfectly certain that we shall never be able to give a completely satisfactory account of any living organism in terms of mechanics, physics, chemistry, and the other inorganic sciences. It is not clear to me how he thought he could prove this. But, however that may be, he is sure that we can always go on explaining more and more facts about organisms in terms of mechanism and the inorganic sciences. And in any case, he holds, no other alternative kind of explanation is really available to us.

4.3.3.2 The intrinsic nature of teleological judgments

We now pass to the following question: What is the intrinsic nature of a teleological judgment about a natural object, apart from all reference to theology? When we say of an organism that it is a 'natural purpose' or is 'intrinsically teleological' are we saying something which *every* rational being would have to say of it, on pain of being mistaken? Or are we only saying something about the attitude which specifically *human* minds inevitably take towards it? Kant discusses this in the form of an antinomy.

The two sides of the antinomy are the following propositions. (1) All production of material things is possible according to merely mechanical laws. (2) Some material things, viz. organisms, cannot be produced according to merely mechanical laws. Now, if these are taken as determinant judgments which are simply about the objects themselves, they are flatly contradictory. But they need not conflict if they are taken as merely regulative judgments, which state the attitudes to be taken up or the postulates to be made in investigating nature. The first principle then comes to this: 'No other principle of explanation is open to human minds except to analyse complex wholes into parts which interact mechanically with each other. So we must always try to carry this analysis as far as we can.' The second principle would come to this: 'Nevertheless there are some material things, viz. organisms, which human minds cannot completely explain in mechanical terms, and which no human mind can help regarding as if they were the products of design.'

When the two propositions are put in this way there is no necessary conflict between them. It is perfectly possible that the noumenal world, which is the ground of all natural phenomena, may be subject to a single principle which appears both as mechanism and as teleology. We cannot see how this can be, but we also cannot see that it is impossible. According to Kant all philosophical systems which try to give a dogmatic decision for or against teleology in nature inevitably come to grief, and this shows that the question is wrongly put. If put as a question about nature itself, it is unanswerable. If put as a question about how specifically *human* minds inevitably regard certain aspects of nature, it raises no difficulty.

After discussing and rejecting various dogmatic answers, positive and negative, to the question of teleology within nature, Kant comes to the following conclusion. We have a right to say this much and this much only: 'Specifically *human* minds are so constituted that they cannot help regarding living organisms *as if* they were the products of an intelligent being who designed them and put his designs into practice as we do.' We are *not* entitled to say 'Living organisms *are in fact* products of the designs of such an intelligent being.' The latter would be a determinant judgment, true for *all* rational beings or false for *all* rational beings. The former is merely a maxim for the use of *specifically human* rational beings; it is a reflective judgment.

Kant distinguishes here between the application of teleological notions to living organisms and their application to nature as a whole. In dealing with living organisms the teleological judgment is absolutely inevitable to every human being, no matter what his scientific or philosophical theories may be. But we are not in the same way compelled to regard nature as a whole as a teleological system. For nature is not presented to one as a whole, as an organism is. We can only say that the purposiveness of certain parts of nature, viz. organisms, suggests to us that nature as a whole may be purposive, and that it is worth while to investigate even inorganic nature on the supposition that it is purposively adapted to the production and maintenance of life.

4.3.3.3 The notion of 'intuitive understanding'

Teleological judgments are inevitable to all *human* beings, but we cannot say whether they are or are not inevitable to all *rational* beings. Kant proceeds to illustrate this distinction by reference to the notion of what he calls an 'intuitive understanding'. If we are to hold that certain principles or certain types of judgment depend on peculiarities of the *human* understanding but may not apply to every conceivable understanding, we must think of understanding as a genus and human understanding as one species under it. Now Kant says that the peculiarity of *human* understanding is that it is discursive and not intuitive. He thinks that we can conceive of an understanding which was not merely discursive but intuitive. And he thinks that teleological judgments may be bound up with the discursiveness which characterises the human understanding.

(1) The distinction between a discursive and an intuitive understanding has already been mentioned by Kant in several places in the *Critique of Pure Reason*. (a) The first occurrence is in some remarks in the *Transcendental Aesthetic* added in B (p. 90, B 72), where he is contrasting human cognition with divine cognition. He says there that divine cognition must consist entirely of *intuition* and not of thought; but this intuition must be *intellectual* and not sensuous, whilst the intuition of all *human* beings, and probably of all *finite* beings, is sensuous and not intellectual. The point is that all awareness of existent objects by us takes place by means of sensations, and sensations are effects produced in us by things which exist independently of us. God, on the other hand, is supposed to be purely active, and everything else is supposed to depend on him for its existence. Kant goes even further. He says that the intellectual intuition of an object would itself generate and maintain the object. I think that this can best be understood by analogy with our own voluntarily produced visual images. We can think of all that God perceives as being created and maintained by him in perceiving it, as our voluntarily produced images seem to be created and maintained by ourselves in calling them up and holding them before our minds.

(b) The second main occurrence of the notion of an intuitive understanding in the first *Critique* is in §§16, 17, and 21 of *Transcendental Deduction* B. Here Kant makes the following assertions. (i) A mind which created all its own manifold of data, as we seem to create our voluntarily produced images, 'would not require for the unity of consciousness a special act of synthesis of the manifold' (p. 157, B 138–9). (ii) The categories would have no meaning for an intuitive understanding. For they are essentially *a priori* principles, in accordance with which an intelligent being synthesises data which it *passively receives* from elsewhere, thus generating at the same time consciousness of itself and of a world of external objects independent of itself (p. 161, B 145–6). (iii) In §17 Kant says that we can form no positive conception of an understanding which is intuitive. We cannot even form a positive conception of an understanding which should receive its data under other forms of sensibility than the spatial and the temporal (p. 157, B 139). In §21 he says that, nevertheless, these peculiarities of the human understanding are quite contingent. 'This peculiarity of our understanding, that it can produce *a priori* unity of apperception solely by means of categories, and only by such and so many categories, is as little capable of explanation as why . . . space and time are the only forms of our possible intuition' (p. 161, B 145–6).

(2) Nothing that Kant says in the *Critique of Pure Reason* about the notion of an intuitive understanding has any obvious connexion with the problem of teleological judgments. But in the *Critique of Judgment* he seems to be working with a different contrast between 'intuitive' and 'discursive'. Here he ascribes to a discursive understanding what appear to me to be *two* logically independent limitations. But it is not clear that he regards them as different, or, if so, as logically independent. (a) 'Our understanding has . . . this peculiarity . . . that in cognition by it the particular is not determined by the universal. But at the same time this particular . . . must accord with the universal by means of concepts and laws . . . This accordance under such circumstances must be very contingent and without definite principle . . .' (pp. 321–2). This might mean many things; but the following would be true and important.

(i) The human understanding is concerned primarily with *generalities*, viz. with universals and general laws. The only way in which it can cognise a particular thing or event is by thinking of it as the only instance of a certain description. Now, however complicated you make the description, it is always possible that there might be innumerable different particulars answering to it. A description can be made unique only by introducing a reference to some particular existent which is known by *acquaintance* and not merely by description. And the only ways in which a human being can be acquainted with any particular is by sense-perception or introspection. To say that a person had an *intuitive* understanding in this respect would come to the following. It would mean that he could become acquainted at will with this or that particular existent, as it is in itself, by merely turning his attention to it. He would not be limited to cognising it merely through certain *effects* which it produces in him by acting upon him.

(ii) If Kant is right, the human understanding can know *a priori* that every empirical event happens in *some* empirical substance and is fully determined by earlier empirical events in accordance with *some* general rule. But it cannot tell *a priori* what kinds of substances there are in nature or what are the actual laws of nature. It seems to be just a contingent fact that there are such-and-such chemical elements, that the genus *animal* includes the species *lion* and not the species *unicorn* and so on. It seems to be just a contingent fact that metals expand when heated, that ice floats on water, and so on. Now we can conceive as an intellectual ideal that the actual laws of nature should be severally necessary and should be necessarily interconnected in a single intelligible system. We may *postulate* this as a methodological principle, but we certainly cannot *see for ourselves* that it is realised in nature. In this respect an *intuitive* understanding would be one for which every fact and law of nature was obviously necessary and obviously fitted into its place in a single intelligible system. Perhaps this would be conceivable only in the case of a mind which *created* all the details of nature in accordance with a single scheme. For an understanding which was intuitive in this sense there would be no need for the methodological postulate which *we* have to make, viz. that nature as a whole should be regarded *as if* it were the product of a single intelligent designer.

(b) The second peculiarity which Kant ascribes to a discursive understanding in the *Critique of Judgment* is to be found on p. 323. 'According to the constitution of our understanding a real whole . . . is regarded only as the effect of the concurrent motive powers of the parts.' The alternative possibility is stated on p. 322. 'We can however think of an understanding which, being, not like ours, discursive, but intuitive, proceeds from the *synthetical-universal* (i.e. the intuition of a whole as such) to the particular, i.e. from the whole to the parts.'

(3) Before considering what this means I will make the following comment. It seems to me clear from the second quotation and from the whole context in which it occurs that Kant held the following view. He either *identified* the property of cognising a particular only through universals with the property of cognising a whole through its parts, or at any rate held that there is some very close logical connexion between the two properties.

This seems to me to be a mistake. The confusion is visible when he talks of a whole as a *synthetical-universal* and its parts as *particulars*. A human body is just as much a particular as a human hand which is one of its organs. Conversely the *concept* of a human hand is as much a universal as the *concept* of the human body of which it is an organ. It seems to me therefore that Kant is here mentioning a difference between a discursive and an intuitive understanding which is other than and independent of the distinctions which we have already considered. This new distinction is highly relevant to the question of apparently teleological objects, viz. living organisms, *within* nature. The former distinction has no particular relevance to this, but it is relevant to the notion of *nature as a whole* being a teleological system, in the sense of answering to all our demands as intelligent beings.

(4) If we ignore this confusion, it is easy to state clearly what Kant had in mind here. The only way in which a human mind can conceive the generation of a systematic whole W is by thinking of certain substances S_1, $S_2, \ldots, S_n$, which already existed in certain less intimate relations to each other, coming together into a certain more intimate relation R to each other. And the only way in which it can explain the characteristic properties of a whole W is by inferring them from the properties which its parts would have and the laws which they would obey *outside* this whole, together with the characteristic relations in which they stand *within* this whole. This is certainly how we think of the generation of the properties of any artificial machine, e.g. a watch. And it is also the way in which we think of the generation and the properties of many natural objects, e.g. a crystal.

Now this way of conceiving the generation and the properties of a systematic whole does not seem to fit the case of a living organism at all well. *Prima facie* it develops spontaneously from a very simple homogeneous object. It does this by taking in foreign materials; transforming them into tissues, fluids, etc. of various kinds; and differentiating itself into various organs. These are so composed and so arranged that each contributes in a characteristic way to maintain the whole, and is in turn maintained by the co-operation of all the rest. The only way in which we can think of the development of an organism is by saying that it proceeds *as if* it were guided by an idea of what the whole is to be and to do. And the only way in which we can think of the functioning of the parts of a developed organism is to say that they function *as if* they were intended to maintain and reproduce the whole. But, if you try to take this literally, it breaks down hopelessly. The only ideas and intentions which we can conceive are the ideas and intentions of *definite persons*. And the only way known to us in which a person can carry out an intention is by initiating appropriate movements in *his own body* and thus modifying foreign things. But *who* is it whose ideas and intentions guide the development and the functioning of an organism? And would he not need already to have an *organism of his own*, in which he could initiate appropriate movements, in order to carry out his ideas and intentions?

(5) It remains to consider how an *intuitive* understanding might be supposed to deal with this kind of situation. Suppose that there were a certain description of a whole W which did not *explicitly contain* descriptions of its various parts or of their mutual relations. Suppose that one could infer from this description that anything answering to it would necessarily be composed of such-and-such parts standing in such-and-such relations to each other. E.g. suppose that there were a description of a human organism which did not explicitly contain descriptions of heart, liver, hands, etc. Suppose that one could infer from this description

that anything answering to it would necessarily be composed of a heart, a liver, two hands, etc. interrelated in certain ways and performing certain functions. Then anyone who could conceive this description and could see what it entailed might be said to proceed from a certain concept of the whole to the concepts of its parts.

I think that Kant may be suggesting that in the case of an organism there may be such a description, and that an intuitive understanding might be able to conceive it and to see in detail all that it entailed. If so, an intuitive understanding would have no need to say that the development of an organism and the functioning of its parts go on *as if* they were guided by an idea of what the whole is to be and of how it is to be maintained and reproduced. But no human being can conceive such a description of an organism. When a discursive understanding meets with things which answer to a description of this kind, which it cannot possibly grasp, its only resort is to say that they look *as if* they were products of design, and *as if* every organ and process in them were designed to secure their main-tenance and reproduction.

(6) Now a material system, such as a living organism, is after all only a phenomenal object. But it is the appearance of a certain thing-in-itself, which we can know only through its appearances. The suggestion is that a thing-in-itself which appears as a living organism may be a whole of this peculiar kind, which only an intuitive understanding could have an ade-quate idea of. But the phenomenal manifestations of such a thing-in-itself have to be dealt with on the only principles available to a discursive understanding. As an empirical thing it has to be thought of as the result of the coming together of pre-existing substances, which have the same properties and obey the same laws inside it as outside it. Yet the peculiarity of such a thing-in-itself shows itself in the corresponding phenomenon. For the phenomenon is of such a kind that the discursive understanding cannot help regarding it as if its origin, development, and functioning were guided by design. If that is so, internal teleology is simply the interpretation which a *discursive* understanding has to put on any natural phenomenon which is the appearance of a thing-in-itself of that peculiar kind which only an *intuitive* understanding could adequately conceive.

(7) Kant tries to illustrate and support this theory by other instances of principles which depend on the peculiarities of the *human* understanding and would not apply to an intuitive understanding.

(a) He suggests that the distinction which we draw between the actual and the possible would not exist for an intuitive understanding. He also suggests that the principle, which is valid for us, that no concept can ever guarantee the existence of an instance of it, would not hold for an intuitive understanding. Here he is thinking of a discursive understanding as one which is essentially confined to general concepts and propositions. It can cognise a particular existent only by thinking of it as the sole instance of a certain description which is itself wholly in terms of universal qualities and relations. He is thinking of an intuitive understanding here as being directly acquainted with things-in-themselves and with nothing else. It does not have sensations and get to know about things-in-themselves only in a roundabout way through the effects which they produce in it. Anything that it knows it knows by acquaintance and not by mere description. Such a mind, he says, would not distinguish the actual from the possible or regard the former as a small department within the latter. This distinction, and the correlated principle that the existence of a thing never follows of necessity from its nature or definition, would not occur to an intuitive understanding, though it holds for all discursive understandings.

This may be compared with an observation which St Thomas makes on the ontological argument.[1] He rejects the argument. But of course he does hold that God is a being whose existence follows of necessity from his nature. His objection to the argument is that no *human being* could have such a concept of God's nature that God's existence would follow necessarily from *that* concept. God's existence does follow from the completely adequate concept which *God* has of his own nature. And it might follow even from the concept which some superior created being, viz. an angel, might have of God's nature.

(b) Kant's other parallel is the distinction between 'is' and 'ought'. This, he thinks, holds only for a being who has sensibility as well as understanding and reason. In a world of purely rational beings every action would necessarily be in accordance with the moral law. The distinction between 'is' and 'ought' arises for us because we are beings who can act on impulse and on maxims which we could not consistently will that everyone should act upon in similar circumstances. We always *can* act in accordance with the moral law; but there are motives in us which oppose such action though they cannot prevent it unless we choose to give way to them. Hence the moral law appears to us in the form of commands and obligations.

4.3.3.4 Teleology and mechanism in science

Let us admit (1) that we cannot help regarding organisms as if they were products of design, and (2) that we cannot understand the origin and behaviour of any whole except in terms of the laws and properties of pre-existing parts and of their coming together in certain intimate relationships. We are then bound to use both the teleological and the mechanical principles in the biological sciences. How then are they related to each other in scientific procedure?

[1] [*Summa theologica*, Ia, q.2, art. 1. *Summa contra gentiles*, 1, 11.]

Kant's answer is as follows. We must distinguish between what he calls *'explanation'* and *'exposition'*. A thing is *explained* only when we can account for its origin and its characteristic behaviour in terms of principles which we clearly understand. Now we can quite well admit that the appearance of mechanism and the appearance of teleology in the same natural phenomenon may spring from a common ground in the thing-in-itself of which that phenomenon is an appearance. But we cannot *explain* anything by this suggestion, because our intellects are not capable of grasping that feature in a thing-in-itself which is the common ground of the appearance of teleology and of mechanism in a natural phenomenon. We can only *point to* this possible common super-sensible ground, and there we must leave the matter. This is *exposition*, as opposed to explanation.

Suppose, then, we confine ourselves to phenomena. Then, if we think of living things as designed, we must in one sense subordinate mechanism to teleology. We must think of the mechanism of nature as thè means by which the design is carried out. Mechanism does not involve design, but design does involve mechanism. For design presupposes the existence of materials with definite properties and subject to definite laws. It can be carried out only by selecting appropriate materials and bringing them together in such combinations that their own laws and properties will automatically produce the desired result.

So Kant's position comes to this. In things-in-themselves there is a common ground for the appearance of mechanism and for the appearance of design in living organisms. But this is neither mechanism nor design, and our intellects are incapable of grasping and formulating it. In those natural phenomena which we cannot help regarding as products of design we must regard the internal mechanism as the means by which the design is carried out. The principle of mechanism provides the only *explanation* of vital phenomena which we can understand, but we know that it can never provide a completely satisfactory explanation. The principle of teleology provides us with no explanation, in the strict sense. But it is indispensable as a guiding principle, leading us always to look for the use of every organ and every vital process in the life of the individual organism or the species. It thus leads to discoveries, though it explains nothing.

4.3.4 Application to theology
4.3.4.1 Natural theology

At the end of the *Critique of Judgment* Kant restates his position about theology. The elaborate discussion of purposiveness in nature does not lead him to alter the unfavourable view which he took about the argument from design in the *Critique of Pure Reason*. However far we may pursue the argument from the inner teleology of organisms and the adaptation of the rest of nature to them we cannot reach on these lines the notion of any ultimate purpose of creation. For that requires the notion of something which has *intrinsic* value, and no natural product has intrinsic value. Hence the utmost that could be reached in this way would be the concept of an intelligent and powerful *architect of nature*. We could not, however, establish the existence even of such a being. We are justified only in saying that, as persons whose minds work discursively, we cannot help regarding *organic* nature, at any rate, as if it were the product of such a being. We can see that this inability to conceive organic nature in any other way may well be due to the special limitations of the human intellect, and may not prove that nature actually was produced by such a being. So the argument from design will not establish the existence even of an architect of nature, and, even if it could, it would not justify us in ascribing *moral perfection* to him. From premises about purely physical and biological facts one cannot legitimately derive a conclusion which involves moral predicates. To prove the existence of God, in the sense in which religion understands that word, we must start with *ethical* premises. So Kant comes back to the conclusion drawn in the *Critique of Practical Reason*. The only possible theology is moral theology. So-called 'natural theology' is not theology at all; it is at most a preparation for moral theology.

4.3.4.2 Moral theology

Nothing has intrinsic value except rational beings, and any value which the rest of nature may have it gets through its relations to rational beings. Now Kant maintains that the mere contemplation of the rest of nature by rational beings would have no value, and so nature would derive no value from being the object of such contemplation. Again, mere happiness has no intrinsic value, and therefore nature can derive no value from being a means to providing rational beings with pleasant sensations. The one point which makes a rational being intrinsically valuable is that it is capable of acting from pure respect for the moral law. Thus, if creation has any final end, this can only be the production and maintenance of moral beings. If we are to use the argument from design to establish the existence of a morally perfect being we shall have to start by showing that the world cannot but be regarded as designed for the production and maintenance of moral agents.

So far the moral argument is merely a modification and supplementation of the old physico-theological argument. But Kant insists that this is not the whole truth about it. Even if there were no traces of design in the material world, we could still use certain ethical facts about human nature as the basis of a moral argument.

In the first place, Kant points to certain facts on the borderline of psychology and ethics which he did not stress in the *Critique of Practical Reason*. (1) When surrounded by beautiful scenery, which we peacefully enjoy, we feel a need to be *grateful* for this privilege to some being or other. (2) When we overcome temptation with an effort, and when we deliberately make a sacrifice in order to do our duty, we tend to regard such action as done in obedience to the commands of a moral being who is our rightful sovereign. (3) When we succumb to temptation without others knowing that we have done so we tend to interpret our self-reproach as expressing the judgment of a supreme moral being to whom we are accountable. Here we have three moral sentiments, viz. impersonal gratitude, feeling of rightful obedience, and feeling of deserved humiliation; and we have a natural tendency to postulate a supreme moral being as the appropriate object of these sentiments.

Now I think that Kant's view about such facts may be stated as follows. If one were to perform externally right acts merely because one believed in the existence of a powerful and omniscient being, who knows all our secret thoughts and will punish us if we disobey his orders, this would have no moral value whatever. But that is not necessarily the way in which religious beliefs and feelings act. Gratitude towards any being for benefits which we believe him to have bestowed on us is a morally good disposition. So too is the pleasure that we take in obeying the rightful commands of a morally good sovereign, and the pain that we feel in knowing that we have disobeyed them. These are feelings which we can have quite apart from all consideration of the consequences which such actions will bring upon ourselves. Such beliefs and feelings strengthen us to perform our duties, and they widen and deepen morality without in any way substituting an unworthy motive for pure respect for the moral law. All these other feelings presuppose respect for the moral law as such. Now the supposition of a supreme moral being, who knows all our intentions and is pleased when we do right and grieved when we do wrong, is not theoretically impossible. It answers to certain needs which we feel as moral beings, and it strengthens us to act rightly in difficult circumstances. It is thus in the same position as those postulates which natural scientists make as methodological principles, e.g. that the laws of nature are expressible in simple mathematical formulae, that there are only a few kinds of ultimate substances and only a few ultimate laws, and so on. We can say of both the practical and the theoretical postulates that they are not impossible intrinsically; that they can be neither proved nor disproved; and that the results of acting as if they were true are better, in the respective spheres of scientific research and of moral conduct, than the results of acting as if they were false.

Lastly, Kant reverts to the argument which he had already used in the

Critique of Practical Reason. He now puts the case as follows (*Critique of Judgment*, pt II, app. §§87 and 88, pp. 377–92). The obligation to act in accordance with the moral law is ultimate. It does not depend, as utilitarians mistakenly believe, on such action being conducive to a certain end which is intrinsically good. But, on the other hand, the moral law does impose on each of us an obligation to strive to bring about a certain state of affairs. This is a state in which every rational being should be completely virtuous, and should enjoy as much happiness as his degree of virtue deserves.

Now, according to Kant, one and only one part of this ideal, at which we all ought to aim, is certainly attainable by the efforts of any one individual. It is within his power to progress indefinitely in *virtue* so long as he lives. But whether other persons will be virtuous, and whether either he or they will enjoy happiness proportional to their virtue, depends largely on circumstances outside his voluntary control. Indeed the latter depends largely on conditions outside the voluntary control of all finite beings, whether severally or collectively. We have no independent reason for believing that these conditions are fulfilled.

Now the obligation to strive after this ideal is unconditional. It does not depend on knowing independently that it can be realised. It is open to us either to postulate that the necessary conditions for its realisation are fulfilled in spite of appearances to the contrary, or simply to take the appearances at their face value and to make no such postulate. On the latter alternative there will be a conflict in one's moral life. For the moral law will command us to strive to bring about a state of affairs which is to all appearances incapable of realisation. It will be difficult in practice to keep one's respect for the moral law if it commands one to embark on what one believes to be a wild-goose chase. Suppose, on the other hand, that we make the postulate that the necessary conditions are somehow fulfilled. This postulate is not intrinsically impossible, and it can no more be *dis*proved than it can be proved. We must conduct our lives on *some* hypothesis or other. Now the results of acting on *this* hypothesis are likely to be better than those of acting as if it were known to be false. We may state the postulate in the form that, if we do our part to the best of our ability, the remaining conditions which are out of our power will be fulfilled for us. If we postulate this, we must postulate whatever seems to us to be necessary for its fulfilment. As human beings we can conceive this necessary condition only in one way. We must think of ourselves and others as immortal, and we must think of ourselves and external nature as created and controlled by an all-powerful wise and good being who arranges nature in such a way that in the long run happiness is adjusted to virtue.

I think that this account of the moral argument is better than that in the *Critique of Practical Reason* in two respects.

(1) It divides the postulate into two layers. (a) That somehow or other the world is so constituted that, if we do our best to fulfil that part of the moral ideal which lies in our power, the remaining conditions will be fulfilled for us. (b) The particular interpretation which human beings are obliged to put on these conditions. The first may be compared to the maxim that every part of an organism subserves the welfare of the individual or the species. The second may be compared to the fact that human beings can conceive this supposed fact about organisms only in terms of design, though this may well be due only to a limitation in the human intellect.

(2) Closely connected with this is the greater caution of the conclusion. (a) We cannot say even that the postulate that the moral ideal can be fulfilled is certainly true. All that we can say is that it is not intrinsically impossible; that it cannot be disproved; and that, in order to fulfil the obligations which certainly are binding upon us, it is better to act on the assumption that it is true. The relation in which this postulate stands to morality is analogous to the relation in which the postulate that the ultimate laws of nature are few and simple stands to scientific practice in general. It is also analogous to the relation in which the postulate that everything in an organism is useful to it stands to biology. (b) Even if the postulate be accepted we are not justified in saying 'Men *are* immortal' or 'There *is* a supreme being who created and governs the universe in such a way that virtue in the long run receives its appropriate reward in happiness'. We can say only: 'The human mind is so constituted that it can conceive no other way in which this postulate can be satisfied'. The analogy to design in biology holds here too. Design in biology may well be only the way in which certain facts about things-in-themselves appear to human beings whose intellects cannot grasp these facts as they are. Similarly the propositions of moral theology may be only the way in which human minds have to represent to themselves certain facts about the noumenal world as a whole which they cannot conceive as they are.

INDEX OF PROPER NAMES